HOW TO CLIMB™ SERIES

Training for Climbing

The Definitive Guide to Improving Your Performance

Third Edition

Eric J. Hörst

Foreword by Phil Watts

FALCON GUIDES

GUILFORD, CONNECTICUT
HELENA, MONTANA

FALCONGUIDES®

An imprint of Rowman & Littlefield
Falcon, FalconGuides, and Chockstone are registered trademarks and Make Adventure Your Story is a trademark of Rowman & Littlefield.
Distributed by NATIONAL BOOK NETWORK

All interior photos: Eric J. Hörst unless otherwise credited
Exercise photos depicting the author: Jonathan and Cameron Hörst

Cover photo: German phenom, Alex Megos, on the third ascent of Lucid Dreaming (V15), Bishop, CA. Alex is trained by Patrick Matros and Dicki Korb, authors of the popular book, *Gimme Kraft.* KEN ETZEL

Illustrations: Judy Newhouse unless otherwise credited

Portions of this book are based on information from *Flash Training* by Eric J. Hörst, previously published by FalconGuides and Chockstone Press.

British Library Cataloguing-in-Publication Information available

The Library of Congress has cataloged a previous edition as follows:
Hörst, Eric J.
Training for climbing : the definitive guide to improving your performance / Eric Horst.—2nd ed.
p. cm. — (A Falcon guide)
ISBN: 978-0-7627-4692-7
1. Rock climbing—Training. I. Title.
GV 200.2.H685 2008
796.522'3—dc22

ISBN 978-1-4930-1761-4 (paperback)
ISBN 978-1-4930-1762-1 (e-book)

∞™ The paper used in this publication meets the minimum requirements of American National Standard for Information Sciences—Permanence of Paper for Printed Library Materials, ANSI/NISO Z39.48-1992.

Praise for the second edition of *Training for Climbing*

"Covering everything from mental exercises to injury prevention to nutrition to goal-specific workouts, *Training for Climbing* is a must-read for climbers of any ability who are looking to take their performance to the next level." –*Climbing* Magazine

"Eric Hörst has taken complex scientific training concepts and integrated these with contemporary research on climbing to produce a very readable and useful training guide. This book will lead the climber to new heights of performance." —Phillip B. Watts, PhD, exercise physiologist and climbing researcher, Northern Michigan University

"Hörst is uniquely positioned to bring current methods in sports psychology and exercise science to the world of climbing, and he has hit the mark in superb style! If you are passionate about climbing and getting better, *Training for Climbing* will become your dog-eared companion!" —Richard K. Fleming, PhD, assistant professor of psychology, University of Massachusetts Medical School

Reader Reviews from Around the World

"I would like to thank you for writing *Training for Climbing*! It has been incredibly helpful and inspiring, and has helped me improve quickly. I've recommended it to everyone on my climbing team!" —Sarah (New Hampshire)

"Thanks for writing *Training for Climbing*; it's an amazing book!" —Alex (Spain)

"Hello Eric, thank you for all the time and energy spent researching and writing. I purchased *Training for Climbing* when it first came out and within a year I was climbing 2 grades harder. We call it the 'clible.'" —Cody (Utah)

"Having never climbed, at age 26 I dove into climbing and thanks to *Training for Climbing* I lost 15 pounds and got myself to 5.10s in just four months. I sincerely appreciate the specific attention you give to mental training and what I like to call 'enlightened climbing.' Your writing is beautifully clear." —Paul (Michigan)

"*Training for Climbing* is a great book—it is testament to a sport filled with nuance. I love learning as much as I can about every aspect of this sport, and your books make me want to get out there and climb!" —Chris (UK)

"Let me say that I am a HUGE fan of your writing. Your books *Training for Climbing*, *Conditioning for Climbers*, and *How to Climb 5.12* have changed my life and approach to training for the better!" —John (Massachusetts)

"Hey Eric, just to say thanks for your book *Training for Climbing*. I have read it more than once and every time I find some new valuable info for improving my climbing." —Felipe (Guatemala)

"I'm a huge fan of your climbing training products, books, and training programs. If only I had found them sooner!!" —Jake (Virginia)

"I have been reading your recent book *Training for Climbing* (twice, cover to cover) and I'm now on my way to rescheduling my training with a much more nuanced focus than before. Thank you for the enlightenment and inspiration!" —Sigurd (California)

"I want to tell you that *Training for Climbing* is clearly the best and most comprehensive book on climbing training methodology I have ever read. In particular, the chapters on mental training and skills/strategy training have inspired me and given me extremely valuable insights for my future workouts. Thanks for such a great work!" —Guido (Switzerland)

"I have just read your book *Training for Climbing*, and I think it is great!" —Sven (Croatia)

"Eric, just wanted to say thanks for writing *Training for Climbing*. Since I started reading it and training, I have improved tremendously. I am having a great time doing the strength-training exercises and just enjoying the process of climbing with a different mentality." —Carlos (California)

"Thank you, Mr. Hörst, for helping me achieve my first 5.12a just a few days ago!" —Hiroyasu (Japan)

"Hi Eric, I've just finished reading *Training for Climbing*—great work! Over the last fourteen years I have studied climbing, and to date your book is by far the most accessible to average climbers." —Paul (Australia)

"I read a quote from your training book and consequently bought it. This book has changed my whole attitude in climbing and life due to your mental training chapter. Just wanted to say thank you!" —Scott (Pennsylvania)

"Thanks for your great books, Eric. I have read them all—they are the best!" —Ofer (Israel)

"What a great book! Your HIT workout definitely gave me much more strength. Thank you very much for your great work, Eric!" —Andre (California)

"Hi Eric, I read your book *Training for Climbing*. I think it is the best book in the field." —Roberto (Ecuador)

Bohica (5.13b), Red River Gorge, Kentucky

To two of the strongest, most innovative and humble men ever to pull down on rock: the "Master of Rock" John Gill and the late, great Wolfgang Güllich.

Nina Williams crimping up Baboon Platoon (V8), Rocklands, South Africa.
BRUCE WILSON

Contents

Foreword

Elite athletes and coaches are well aware of the importance of sport-specific physiological, technical, and mental training for optimizing progress toward high-level performance. Even those of us who are more than a bit distant from elite-level performance can still realize improvement and an enhanced experience from the application of known training principles. Sifting the truth from the full array of information available these days can be difficult. Fortunately, there are a few writers who present contemporary evidence-based concepts in a manner that is easily understood and applied. Eric Hörst is one of these writers.

I have been in communication with Eric since the first edition of *Training for Climbing*. We have discussed the science of climbing via phone, e-mail, and over Miguel's pizza at the Red River Gorge. I am impressed by Eric's consumption and digestion of both rock climbing–specific research and sports science research in general. He has a keen ability to bring the science into application. As a bonus, Eric has insights only a practitioner can have through his more than three decades as a veteran high-end climber and coach.

Effective and optimal physical training is more than the old adages of "break a sweat a couple of days per week" or "no pain, no gain." As an exercise science researcher and educator, I stress the importance of understanding the physiological performance model for a specific activity. With rock climbing, this model includes basic components such as muscular strength and endurance, rate of force development, aerobic and anaerobic power, anatomical range of motion, and energy economy. Specific workout designs for developing each component differ. A climber is challenged by the process of deciding which workout designs to use, how much to do, and how to best recover. When movement techniques and mental aspects, along with proper nutrition, are added into the mix, the task can be overwhelming. In *Training for Climbing*, Eric has provided workable details in an organized and logical manner and in a way that enables the climber to customize training to his or her specific needs.

I have been in the academic and research areas of exercise science for over forty years and have seen concepts develop and evolve, come and go, and come again. I began in exercise physiology at a time when lactic acid was considered a problematic end product of anaerobic metabolism . . . a "bad" thing to avoid at all costs. Now we appreciate lactate as a dynamic component of high power production that may also serve as an energy source away from the specific site of its production . . . a "good" thing. I also grew up in a time when protein intake was only a concern for "strength" athletes such as football players and weight lifters. Now we know protein intake per body mass unit can be higher in "endurance" athletes during periods of high-volume exercise. The exercise physiology text I used during my master's-level graduate studies was 200 pages and around half a kilogram in weight. The text I currently use with my undergraduate students is over 800 pages and weighs three kilograms! The sheer volume of available information presents a challenge. This new edition of *Training for Climbing* eases the information overload and presents a solid foundation upon which to explore.

Whether you aspire to stand upon the podium at competitions, bump your peak level a grade or two, or squeeze more moves out of limited vacation time on the rock, there are words for you here. By all means read *Training for Climbing*, work out a plan that is a good fit for you and your goals, then get on the rock for the joy of it.

—Phil Watts, PhD, FACSM
Professor of Exercise Physiology
Northern Michigan University

Acknowledgments

Writing a book is an Everest-like undertaking. It is a team effort that can take years to plan and execute, but getting to the summit still takes an immense individual effort and an indomitably singular focus.

Having completed this climb (more than a few times!), I reflect on all that has brought me to this point—the thousands of wonderful days I've spent on the rock, the countless climbers from around the world I've had the pleasure to meet, and the dozens of partners I am grateful to have shared a rope with—and my recent climbing adventures with my badass sons. Learning to climb is a long, continuous process with no end, and I thank all the people who have influenced me from my days as a wide-eyed teenage rock jock to a fifty-something veteran climber. Specifically, I must thank directly a few key players who inspired me as a climber and coach: John Gill, the late Wolfgang Güllich, Lynn Hill, John Long, Jim McCarthy, Pat Ament, Richard Goldstone, Mark Robinson, the late and legendary Todd Skinner, and Tony Yaniro—all of you, knowingly or unknowingly, have inspired me and contributed to this book in some way.

Though I continue to train and climb with a passion similar to my younger days as a national-class climber, I enjoy more every year the role of climbing coach and researcher. I am humbled by all the letters and e-mails I've received from climbers in more than fifty countries who have read my books, magazine articles, and Internet posts. I appreciate all the feedback, the suggestions, and, most of all, the success stories of those who have benefited from my work. Writing climbing books is certainly not a lucrative endeavor, but knowing that I've helped thousands of people from around the world climb better is priceless.

Creating this third edition of *Training for Climbing* turned out to be another massive undertaking. It's been an eight-year journey since the last edition, and during this time I've read hundreds of research papers and integrated the key findings into my training programs and this book. And lucky for me (and you), I have a dream team of great climbing minds to discuss new concepts and training applications—many thanks to my PhD'd and coaching friends Simon Fryer, Phil Watts, Eva Lopez, Rick Fleming, Richard Schmidt, Jim Sullivan, Natasha Barnes, Steve Bechtel, Dicki Korb, and Patrick Matros. Thanks for sharing your unique insights!

I'd like to extend a sincere thank you to John Burbidge, Julie Marsh, and everyone at FalconGuides and Globe Pequot who helped bring this book to fruition. I am also very appreciative of all the climbing companies that support me and my many projects, including Nicros, La Sportiva, Maxim Ropes, DMM/Excalibur, Organic Climbing, and Kühl. I am most grateful for the input and participation of Kris Hampton, Hannes Huch, Anna Davey, Chadd Gray, Jessica and Geoff Britten, Alex Megos, Crystal Norman, Jessica Rohm, and the gyms Earth Treks, Vertical Endeavors, Philly Rock Gym, and Spooky Nook. Mega kudos to Claudia Zeigler, Savannah Cummins, Matty Hong, Chris Noble, Kyle Duba, Thomas Ballenberger, Phil Bard, Gerd Heidorn, Andrew Chao, Theron Kirkman, and Bruce Wilson, whose photography is featured throughout the book. Heartfelt thank yous to my parents, Bob and Ethel, my sons, Cameron and Jonathan, and my wife, Lisa, for joining me in my training and climbing and for teaching me so much—I love you each more than you can imagine.

Finally, I am sincerely thankful for my original climbing partner and real-life hero, Jeff Batzer. Despite losing five fingers and half a leg, you still possess—and show by example—the power of climbing. Jeff, you are a true inspiration—thanks, man.

Introduction

A man's reach should exceed his grasp or what's a heaven for?

—Robert Browning

Training for Climbing is a unique synthesis of more than three decades of studying, researching, imagining, and experimenting with new ways to increase climbing performance. Building on the foundation laid out in the first two editions of *Training for Climbing*, this massively revised and expanded third edition of *TFC* establishes a new benchmark for cutting-edge, comprehensive, and evidence-based expert instruction on the subject of elevating climbing performance.

Training for Climbing presents a success strategy based on leading-edge sports science and the latest climbing research that's amplified by powerful practice and training techniques used by Olympic athletes (but unknown to many climbers). If you commit to dovetailing your physical training with regular use of the potent mental-training techniques described herein, you will become a far better climber regardless of your present ability. By faithfully applying just 50 percent of the methods contained in this text, you will surely grow to outperform the mass of climbers. And if you integrate most of the material into your training, climbing, and daily life, you may very well progress to a level beyond your current comprehension!

Training for Climbing is as much about developing new ways of thinking as it is about engaging in new ways of training. A common thread that weaves throughout this book is that you must train smarter to climb harder; intelligence in climbing is not measured by IQ, but instead by the quality of your thoughts and actions. The thoughts you carry and the things you do (or don't do) are ultimately what separate you from the mass of climbers. Whether you flash or fall, become superstrong or get injured, or feel happy or frustrated, springs forth from subtle differences in the ways you think, feel, and act compared with other climbers. Therefore, the primary goal of this book is to help guide you to more deliberate and effective ways of thinking and acting—both training and non-training actions—in your pursuit of peak climbing performance.

Since climbing is all about an intimate dance between you and the rock, it's vital to recognize that your climbing performance evolves from the inside out, and that you only slip and fall when you blow a move. Goethe wrote, "Nature understands no jesting; she is always true, always serious, always severe; she is always right, and the errors and faults are always those of man. The man incapable of appreciating her, she despises; and only to the apt, the pure, and the true, does she resign herself and reveal her secrets." From this perspective it becomes obvious that we must always look inside ourselves to determine the cause of our struggles. Looking outward for the reason or to place blame is a loser's game.

This book begins with a logical progression of self-analysis, goal setting, mental training, and technique training before you ever lift a weight. Chapters 1 through 4 are focused on helping you learn, most quickly, the vital mental and technical skills that separate the best of climbers from the rest of climbers. After a brief review of the history of training for climbing, you'll get started on the road to better climbing by taking a self-evaluation test that will reveal your true strengths and weaknesses on the rock. Armed with this diagnosis, you can effectively address your limiting constraints, whatever they might be. If they are technical or mental in nature, then there's lots of gold to be mined from the pages of chapters 3 and 4.

Chapters 5 through 10 present the most in-depth look at strength training for climbing ever published. As an intensely practical person with a background in math and science, I have always felt it important to delve into the theory and application of cutting-edge sports science—after all, knowledge is power. Accordingly, chapter 5 provides a 200-level understanding of the exercise physiology of training for climbing. Read slowly and carefully, and you'll discover many training secrets and nuances that, if applied steadfastly, will make your training more effective than likely anyone else you know. Chapters 6 and 7 are brand new to this edition of *TFC*, and they present essential stabilizer, core, and posterior chain training that will make a huge difference in your climbing and help reduce injury risk as you move into the higher grades. Chapters 8 and 9 provide dozens of climbing-specific exercises for increased strength, power, and endurance in the important finger flexor and pulling muscles. Then, in chapter 10 you'll learn how to craft a high-quality training program and integrate it with the rest of your everyday activities.

Performing in the vertical extreme requires strength, power, and endurance; vast technical skills; and the ability to focus and manage fear in potentially dangerous situations. In aggregate, these factors make climbing one of the most complex sporting activities on this third rock from the sun.

The concluding chapters 11 through 13 cover the often overlooked subjects of performance nutrition, recovery, and proper treatment and prevention of common climbing injuries. Becoming a complete climber requires that you embrace these subjects with the same fervor as you execute your training program or plot your next climb. Throughout the text I have cited select research in case you'd like to peruse the nitty-gritty details—these references and other useful information can be found in the back of the book.

To glean the greatest benefit from *Training for Climbing*, I encourage you to employ active reading techniques such as highlighting key passages, putting a star next to the most meaningful strategies, and taking notes for later review. Consider lifting some of the most powerful phrases and posting them in places where you'll see them throughout the day. Review your highlighted passages and notes every few weeks, and reread the entire book in six months to a year. Not only will this reinforce your understanding and mastery of the concepts, but you also will gain new insight and distinctions as you become a different person at each read-through.

As you cast off on your training-for-climbing journey, I want to wish you much strength and power, as well as many grand, transcending days as you climb through this world of wonder. Though we may never meet, we are connected through our shared passion for climbing. I welcome your feedback, and I look forward to hearing from you after some grand success that undoubtedly awaits you. Here's wishing you many safe and wonderful days on the rock!

—Eric J. Hörst
www.Training4Climbing.com

Adam Ondra on the first ascent of Move (5.15b/c), Flatanger, Norway.
CLAUDIA ZEIGLER

CHAPTER ONE

An Overview of Training for Climbing

It's the journey, experience, and self-discovery in climbing that hold the greatest value. But climbing hard routes is a heck of a lot of fun, too!

Many words can describe the wonderful activity of rock climbing—elegant, powerful, rewarding, and, sometimes, frustrating. While there may be nothing more natural and intuitive than climbing (just watch how children climb around on everything in sight!), rock climbing is indeed a complex activity with demands unique from those of living and playing in the everyday, horizontal world.

Performing in the vertical plane requires physical capabilities such as strength, power, flexibility, and endurance. It also demands the development of technical skills such as balance and economic movement while gripping and stepping in an infinite variety of ways, positions, and angles. Most important, the inherent stress of climbing away from the safety of the ground requires acute control of your thoughts, focus, anxiety, and fears. In aggregate, the above factors dovetail into what may be one of the more complex sporting activities on this third rock from the sun.

The goal of this book is to explore all the topics relevant to increasing the effectiveness of your training and the quality of your climbing. As a climber of forty years (who's been fortunate enough to meet and climb with many brilliant individuals), I feel the journey should begin with a primer on the history of training for rock climbing. Clearly, the advancements we make today are possible only because we are standing on the shoulders of the giants who preceded us. Next we'll explore the interesting subject of genetics and the possible genetic limitations to climbing performance. This will lead us into an overview of training for climbing and the things you should consider in your quest for the biggest gains in performance in the shortest possible time.

Training for Climbing: A Brief History

Compared with many other sports, the science of performance rock climbing is still quite young. Well over a hundred years of literature exists on technical aspects of the golf swing, and Olympic sports have been the subject of performance analysis for centuries. Far removed from the mainstream of organized sports, and an almost countercultural pursuit just a generation ago, rock climbing was completely off the map in the emergence of sports sciences. What little information did exist on the technical aspects of climbing was mainly passed on by word of mouth in the form of tips on technique and equipment.

Nevertheless, some climbers used basic gymnastics, weight training, elementary bouldering, and buildering to either emulate actual climbing moves or gain the strength to perform at higher levels of the sport. Oscar Eckenstein, a Brit of Teutonic heritage and possibly the first documented boulderer, climbed ropes in the gym, did one-arm pull-ups, and pushed himself on small rocks during

John Gill's amazing one-arm front lever. JOHN GILL COLLECTION

the 1890s; George Leigh Mallory was a high-bar enthusiast and one of the first to do giant swings; E. A. Baker in *Moors, Caves, and Crags* (1903) tells of a colleague who "ascends the outside of an iron staircase on his fingers . . . and crosses in a sitting posture the tie-bars of a lofty roof"; Claude E. Benson in *British Mountaineering* (1909) talks of being "blessed with a basement staircase of stone . . . I am to be found hanging by my fingertips to the outside thereof." And a gymnastic exercise of the nineteenth century involved climbing the underside of an oblique ladder using arms only—a precursor of the Bachar Ladder and campus training.

Given the extreme and run-out technical climbs being done on the Elbe River sandstone near Dresden a century ago—the hardest of which are now recognized as being near 5.10 difficulty—it is reasonable to conclude that early German free climbers placed a high value on style and difficulty. It is hard to conceive of such sustained routes being climbed without some specific regime to build forearm and upper-body strength, although working routes on toprope may have been their primary method of training.

The strongest climbers of the early and mid-1900s included Oliver Perry-Smith, Albert Ellingwood, Joe and Paul Stettner, Fritz Wiessner, Jack Durrance, Hans Kraus, John Salathe, and Harold Goodro, as well as some of the early Yosemite masters such as Warren Harding, Dave Rearick, Bob Kamps, and Royal Robbins. All were natural athletes or had competed in other athletic activities prior to becoming climbers. More important, they all possessed a great sense of adventure and daring—a hallmark trait of all great climbers of this era. Mike Sherrick, Robbins's companion on the first ascent of the Northwest Face of Half Dome, was an excellent gymnast who often backflipped to the ground after finishing a boulder problem, much to the chagrin of his tamer companions. Yet training as a rock climbing discipline built on vision, specificity, and intention was the innovation of a young man from Alabama who began climbing in the early 1950s.

Now one of the undisputed legends of American climbing, John Gill is the first person known to engage in highly regimented training for climbing. Unlike the others of his day who pushed themselves on vertical crags and long rock routes in the mountains, Gill—although an alpinist and rock climber—spent more of his time on short, overhanging faces on low boulders at the base of mountains or in river valleys. Bagging summits and climbing big walls had less aesthetic appeal for Gill; he instead sought the kinesthetics of dynamic movement up overhanging rock and adroitly built a novel training program to suit.

For more than fifteen years beginning in the mid-1950s, Gill trained on a gym rope, the still rings, and with weighted, fingertip pull-ups, one-arm and one-finger pull-ups, and one-arm front levers, in preparation for his powerful bouldering ascents throughout the Midwest, Southeast, and Rocky Mountains. In the early years Gill's gymnastic moves and the extremely muscular problems they produced—even his use of gymnasts' chalk—were viewed by most climbers with bemusement, if not bewilderment. Today his legacy as an innovator, visionary, and, in fact, the father of both modern bouldering and training for climbing is the foundation that has allowed route ratings to move into 5.13 and beyond. Gill's technical ability was years ahead of everyone else, as illustrated by his very bold 1961 free-solo first ascent of The Thimble in South Dakota's Black Hills, an overhanging 30-foot inspiration now rated V4 (5.12a), and his improbable center problem (incredibly, grade V9 by modern standards!) up the Red Cross Boulder in the Tetons two years before The Thimble. Unrecognized and underappreciated at the time, Gill in establishing these standards was an early prototype of today's top-end rock gymnasts, characterized like them by precise footwork, intense focus, and awesome power.

By the mid-1960s a number of other climbers, most with a background in gymnastics, also began training specific to climbing. Pat Ament, a young gymnast from Colorado, was an early training enthusiast and went on to become a leading climber and prolific developer of hard boulder problems. In 1967 Ament and Gill began a long friendship, and these two powerful boulderers undoubtedly inspired countless climbers throughout the Front Range and beyond.

At about the same time, famed 'Gunks hardman Richard Goldstone met Gill during a summer trip out west and was enormously impressed with Gill's one-arm pull-ups, front levers, and stiff boulder problems. Goldstone went back to the University of Chicago with an enthusiasm for training and adapted the use of surgical tubing (long utilized by gymnasts to build enough strength to do an Iron Cross) as a training aid for portions of his workouts. A few years later Goldstone returned east and became a significant presence during the rapid expansion of difficult free climbing at the Shawangunks. Goldstone discovered that Dick Williams (another former gymnast) was already training for climbing and incorporating dynamic movements in his campaign to free climb the many steep aid routes at the 'Gunks. Other Uberfall icons of the era such as Hans Kraus, Bonnie Prudden, Jim McCarthy, and John Stannard also had great interest and long personal histories in physical fitness. Kraus went on to form the President's Council on Physical Fitness, while Bonnie Prudden became a nationally recognized fitness expert and the first female athlete to appear on the cover of *Sports Illustrated*.

Meanwhile, it seemed California climbers were increasingly toying with one form or another of climbing training. Dave Rearick and Mike Sherrick were specifically oriented toward gymnastics and could do presses into handstands and other gym stunts; Layton Kor was lifting weights regularly for his many outstanding ascents around Colorado and

German climbing icon Wolfgang Güllich demonstrating his one-arm power in Yosemite's Camp 4, circa 1980. GERD HEIDORN

in Yosemite. Remarkably, three of the top Yosemite free climbers of the day—Royal Robbins, Chuck Pratt, and Frank Sacherer—did very little training other than the usual regimen of pull-ups and push-ups. Jim Bridwell and Barry Bates followed in the spirit of their master-predecessors, training hard at such things as pull-ups on tree limbs in the Valley. Bates quickly developed the ability to do a one-finger pull-up with his middle finger on a sling hanging from a tree. The main thrust of their training, however, was simply to climb several days per week.

Bridwell, Bates, and others in the Camp 4 crowd were also likely influenced, directly or otherwise, by visiting climbers such as Goldstone and Ament. Rich Goldstone is believed to have installed the first pull-up bar in Camp 4, while Ament brought the toughest bouldering discipline of the time to the Valley with his first ascents of 1968. Pat Ament also brought the slack chain to Yosemite, challenging climbers to develop refined balance and focus. The revered tradition of chain and rope walking in Yosemite began with the 40 feet of slack links that Ament strung between two Camp 4 trees. Bridwell and others went on to develop and deploy an array of training stations around Camp 4 so impressive that Warren Harding, the Yosemite Generation's sharpest wit, soon dubbed the area the "Olympic Training Village." Harding himself preferred to build stamina for his epic multiday big-wall adventures by running to the top of Half Dome and back, a 17-mile round trip with nearly 1 mile of elevation change (and also, by his own admission, by refraining from hard liquor in the weeks before an ascent). In the years that followed, Camp 4 workout rigs introduced countless climbers from around the world to the basic elements of the future science of training for climbing.

Still, sports scientists in academia and the European mountain heartland had yet to view climbing as a subject worthy of serious and sustained study. Though ascents of the world's highest mountains were long a source of national pride in Europe, there were no Olympic medals (nor commercial sponsorships) to be won around which to build a culture of sport-specific training and achievement aimed at visible rewards. Climbing remained a rarefied pursuit, and research—where it pertained to climbing at all—was narrowly focused on the effects of long exposure to low-oxygen atmosphere. Still, the steadily growing popularity of climbing throughout the 1970s eventually gave birth to the first European studies relating to the physiological stresses and injuries associated with rock climbing.

In 1977 Pat Ament's *Master of Rock* was published. This biography of John Gill, though not focused specifically on training, served to document Gill's strength-training techniques and introduce them to a wider audience; the book quickly became not just an American classic but a kind of sacred writ for a new generation of climbers interested in pushing the absolute technical limits. *Master of Rock* opened a new door of consciousness, so to speak, of what it would take to be the best—not only in terms of physical ability but also in the broader context of performance—Gill being the epitome of performance excellence in virtually all his pursuits.

From the mid-1970s through the 1980s, the worldwide growth of technical rock climbing and the first climbing competitions produced an unprecedented exchange of ideas and innovations among European, Russian and Caucasian, and American

One of the first climbers to train with weighted pull-ups, John Bachar could pull up with nearly 140 pounds hanging from his waist! Here he trains with a "light" 50 pounds circa 1985.
PHIL BARD

climbers. In Yosemite's Camp 4; Boulder, Colorado; and the Shawangunks of New York, small groups trained and free climbed with increasing fervor, as energetic newcomers such as John Bachar, Jim Collins, Christian Griffith, Lynn Hill, Jim Holloway, John Long, Ron Kauk, Todd Skinner, Alan Watts, Tony Yaniro, and others arrived on the scene. Similarly, small groups of energetic climbers began to train in England, France, Italy, and Germany. The boulders of Fontainebleau and the ubiquitous limestone crags of the region became the proving grounds

The author (circa 1986) on his version of the "death board," a training tool used by a handful of climbers in the pre-climbing-gym era.
HÖRST COLLECTION

for the first "sport climbers" in the early 1980s. The hard-training European climbers of the early sport-climbing era were Brits Ron Fawcett, Jerry Moffat, and Ben Moon; French icons Jibé Tribout, Antoine LeMénestral, and Patrick Edlinger; Italians Roberto Bossi and Heinz Mariacher; and the powerful Germans Kurt Albert and Wolfgang Güllich.

In the United States no technique or aesthetic had a bigger impact on the rapid development of extreme free climbing than the import of sport-climbing tactics from Europe. Rappel-bolted routes eliminated the psychological stress and risks associated with marginal protection, and through liberal use of hangdogging, the practitioner could safely work extreme sequences and thus bring Gill-level difficulty (5.13 moves) to roped climbing. At about this time, articles on physical performance and training began to appear in American climbing magazines; academic studies, too, began to proliferate, although initially focused on the subject of injuries specific to rock climbers. Strength-training techniques remained relatively unsophisticated, although a few key innovations such as the Bachar Ladder and fingerboard jacked generic finger and pull-power training up to a higher level of intensity and specificity.

In Europe's sport-climbing culture, indoor walls had already taken hold, but it was not until 1987 that the first commercial climbing gym opened in the United States. Around the same time at the Campus Center—a weight-lifting facility at the University of Nürnberg—a strong German climber named Wolfgang Güllich developed a sport-specific form of reactive training known today simply as "campus training." Between 1985 and 1991 Güllich went on to establish the world's hardest free climbs and wrote a breakthrough training book, *Sportklettern Heute* (1986), and campus training quickly became a staple of elite climbers around the world. Toward the end of the century, as at its beginning, German climbers led the way to new levels of technical difficulty and athletic achievement.

The 1990s saw climbing go mainstream with televised competitions and dozens of well-sponsored full-time climbers in training year-round. The first two books on training for climbing by American authors were published in 1993 and 1994—Dale Goddard and Udo Neumann's *Performance Rock Climbing* and *Flash Training* by this author—and articles on training became regular features of *Climbing* and *Rock and Ice* magazines. But the proliferation of indoor walls was the real wild card that allowed the average climber to practice more frequently and climb harder than ever before. All the above-mentioned factors, along with improved equipment, made what was once the maximum grade, 5.10, quickly achievable by the masses; and remarkably 5.14 has become attainable by a handful of youngsters not even old enough to drive!

Beginning the new millennium, climbing is as popular as ever, as evidenced by outdoor crags now crowded with "weekend warriors" and the increasing number of semi-professional climbers training for World Cup competitions. A rapidly expanding knowledge base—professional climbing coaches, peer-review climbing research, and myriad online and print media on instruction and training—is now guiding recreational climbers into the lofty grades, once the domain of only a small group of professionals.

Top coaches such as Patxi Usobiaga, Patrick Matros, Dicki Korb, and Robyn Erbesfeld, among many others, are now leveraging new training technologies and the latest climbing research (as revealed throughout this book) to train current rock stars like Adam Ondra and Alex Megos. As a result these leading-edge climbers, along with veterans like Chris Sharma, Tommy Caldwell, and Daniel Woods, have recently advanced the cutting edge of climbing to V16 boulders, 5.15c/9b+ sport climbs, and, incredibly, 5.14d/9a Grade VII on the granite big walls of Yosemite.

As detailed in the previous pages, the rich century-plus history of training for climbing has delivered us to the exciting present era of evidence-based, technology-guided exercise programming. So while past generations trained largely in accordance with myth, anecdote, and trial and error, those entering the sport today have more credible information and more effective tools to leverage in training for the vertical extreme. (*Training for Climbing* is just one of several good texts now available, and I encourage you to explore some of the books on my Suggested Reading list at the end of this book.) Many of today's up-and-coming climbers will quickly succeed at the once lofty grades of 5.12/7b and 5.13/8a, while a subset possessing uncommon disciple and engaging in well-designed, long-term training programs have a good chance of reaching the 5.14a/8b+ benchmark . . . and for the genetically blessed, perhaps even 5.15d!

No one has climbed more 5.15a and harder routes than Adam Ondra, shown here training at home. CLAUDIA ZEIGLER

Genetics and Climbing Performance

Excuses are like parents—everybody has them. Ironically, your parents, or more precisely the genetic material you inherited from them, might be the best excuse why you or I may never climb 5.15. Still, your genetic makeup, which substantially determines your height, flexibility, and natural strength, among other things, is a poor excuse for not being able to climb 5.10 or even 5.12. Yes, some specific 5.12 climb might require a long reach or high step that you will never be capable of making, but numerous research studies confirm my belief that the mass of climbers have the potential to succeed at the lofty grade of 5.12, regardless of genetics.

The Role of Genetics in Sports Performance

All other things being equal, genes seem to determine the differences in performance among individuals. In a sport as complex as climbing, however, you could argue that "all other things are never equal"—making the role of genetics in climbing performance hard to pin down. But let's try!

The role of genetics in what we become has been a favorite subject of scientists over the years—it's the old "nature-versus-nurture" debate. Certainly genetics would seem to play an underlying role in our natural mental climate and personality. However, it's in the physical realm of strength and motor skill that genetics appear to play the largest role (or at least this is where genetics seem most observable and measurable for scientists). Interestingly, a review of the research on the role of genetics on performance reveals an extremely complex subject with contradictory theories and findings among academics. One study (Ericsson 1993) suggested that hours of deliberate practice are the most important factor in determining performance, while another (Fox 1996) found that genes are responsible for half the variations in performance among individuals.

In the real, nonacademic world, it seems that neither of these studies is unequivocally correct. It appears that genetics play the greatest role in sports where the raw physical demands far outweigh the mental or technical requirements. For example, excelling at the 100-meter dash requires extreme explosive power but only basic mental and technical skill. Conversely, golf requires mastery of a wide range of technical skills and a well-cultivated mental calm, but the physical demands are much less noteworthy. Therefore, while genetics clearly play a major role in determining who makes it to the Olympics in the 100-meter dash, they should have much less influence in determining who plays in this year's PGA Championship.

Summing up: Hours of deliberate practice are a requisite for performing at a high level in complex (technical and mental) sports, whereas ideal genetics are a prerequisite for achieving greatness

Figure 1.1 Relative Demands of Various Sports

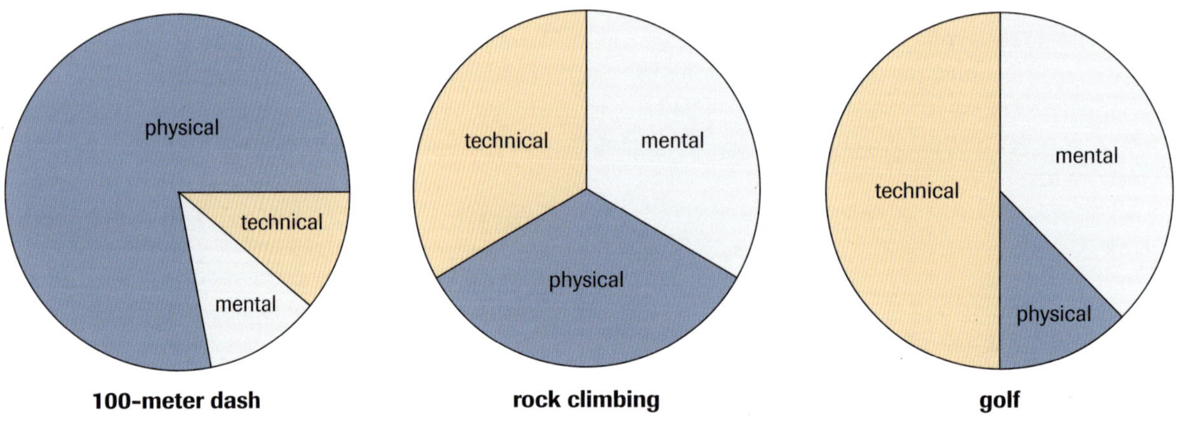

in the most physical pursuits, such as running and weight lifting. Rock climbing is unique among sports, however, in that it requires a near-equal balance of mental, technical, and physical prowess (see figure 1.1). So you can argue that genetics do play a significant, though not primary, role in determining your level of performance in this sport.

Genetic Factors Relating to Climbing Performance

So just what genetic factors might be helping or hurting you? I bet they are different and more subtle than you think. Height and weight seem to be what most climbers consider their blessing or curse, but it's likely a number of less obvious attributes that help make possible the incredible achievements of climber icons like Chris Sharma, Adam Ondra, and the Nicole, Huber, and LeMénestral brothers.

While the aforementioned climbers exhibit a variety of body shapes and sizes, they all possess unusually high maximum grip strength, upper-body power, and/or local (forearm) endurance—beyond that which can be acquired by the average climber training "perfectly" for many years. The genetic gifts enabling these feats probably relate to hard-to-observe factors such as tendon insertions (where they originate from and insert into the bones of the hands and arms), lever length (length of bones), muscle fiber type, and hormone profiles.

With regard to tendon insertions, a slight shift in the location compared with normal provides additional leverage that gives a few lucky folks more grip strength (off the couch!) than others could achieve through years of training. Similarly, your innate ratio of fast-twitch to slow-twitch muscle fiber determines whether your natural aptitude tends toward high endurance, high strength, or neither. Finally, we each have unique hormone profiles (testosterone, cortisol, and so forth) that vary with age and sex, and this plays an underlying role in our response to training and ability to recover (Bloomfield 1994). Because of this, some people can climb hard three days in a row or respond more dramatically to training, while most of us need far more rest in order to perform well, and our training adaptations are more gradual.

If you still aren't convinced that genetics play a role in determining who will be the very best climbers, consider the three pairs of brothers mentioned earlier. Frederic and François Nicole, Alex and Thomas Huber, and Marc and Antoine LeMénestral have all climbed at the fringe of maximum difficulty. This is not coincidence, but instead a screaming message that genetic makeup is a factor in climbing performance.

Your Genetic Potential as a Climber

If you're beginning to sense that you might lack some or all of the above genetic gifts, don't be depressed! As I stated earlier, odds are that you're "normal enough" to climb 5.12 and, if you climb a lot and train just right, deep into the 5.13 grade as well. Because of the large role that mental and technical skill plays in climbing performance, you can push very high up the grade scale by maximizing your capabilities in these areas. The bell curve (see figure 1.2) shows that most of the population falls

Figure 1.2 Genetic Potential

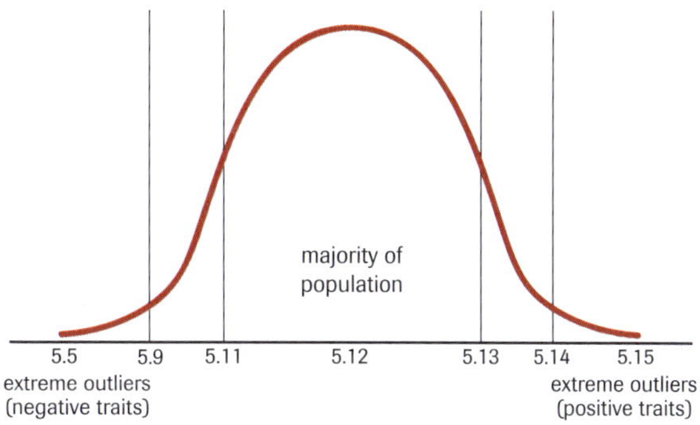

Adam Ondra and Daniel Woods would fall into the far right portion of the curve, whereas actors John Goodman and Verne Troyer would be far left.

in the middle of the bell, in the area representing near-average genetic characteristics. A much smaller number of folks—call them outliers (say, one in ten)—have somewhat better or worse genetics than average. Then there are the extreme outliers (say, 1 in 1,000 or more) who have the potential to be brilliant if they discover their gift and apply themselves completely.

The fact that most of us fall somewhere in the middle of the bell curve can be uplifting or depressing, depending on your perspective. If you dream of climbing 5.15 or V15, the chart shows that even if you do everything right and dedicate your entire life to it, the odds are low that you have the genetic potential to make this dream a reality. But if you currently climb 5.10 or V3 (or whatever), you should be psyched that 5.12—and likely even 5.13—is within your reach!

A few recent studies support this idea. One study (Barss 1997) divided a group of twenty-four recreational climbers into two groups based on climbing ability. With the exception of a straight-armed hang endurance test, there was no statistical difference in the performance of a wide variety of general and sport-specific tests between the "less skilled" group (those climbing 5.7 to 5.10a) and the "more skilled" group (those climbing 5.10b to 5.11b). Therefore, at the intermediate levels (5.7 to 5.11b), there's a poor correlation between fitness and climbing ability. The stronger climbers were not necessarily the better climbers, so mental and technical differences account for the difference in ability.

Another, more complex study (Mermier 2000) looked at a larger group of forty-four male and female climbers with a wider range of abilities (5.6 to 5.13c). The results showed that the variance in climbing performance relates primarily to trainable variables, and that anthropometric variables (height, weight, arm and leg length, arm span, percent of body fat, and the like) are not a statistically significant factor. So this study also supports my sense that by optimizing technical and mental skills (the trainable variables), the average climber should be able to progress to a high level of climbing, possibly even as high as 5.13c. Note that no 5.14 climbers were included in the study, so we don't know if inclusion of these world-class individuals would have yielded similar results (I suspect not).

In fact, a third, very similar study (Watts 1993) looked only at world-class climbers (those competing in the semifinals at a World Cup event). It found that these elite individuals exhibited a higher grip-strength-to-body-mass ratio, had a lower percentage of body fat, and were of a slightly smaller stature when compared with other athletic groups. This study supports the idea that those world-class 5.14+/V15 climbers are born, not made, in that they are extreme outliers with just the right build to be able to climb at the highest levels of difficulty.

Great Genetics Don't Guarantee You'll Be a Great Climber

Still, the premise that climbing requires equal mastery of mental, technical, and physical abilities means that good genes aren't enough to make you a rock star. Just as genetically average individuals can progress to climbing 5.12 or 5.13 by perfecting their technical and mental skill sets, genetic freaks who can crush bricks in their hands may forever remain "average" climbers due to poor technique or lack of mental skills.

Consider figure 1.3, which depicts the genetic potential (solid line) and real-life ability (dashed line) of a climber with average genetic makeup versus the brick-crushing genetic freak. Through dedicated, intelligent training of all the elements under her control, the average climber has pushed her ability almost the whole way out to her genetic potential. The superstrong genetic freak, on the other hand, with his poor technique and mental control, is an underachiever when you compare his real-life performance with his genetic potential. Comparatively, the genetically average climber pushed the dashed line out farther and is thus the real master of rock!

Figure 1.3 Genetic Potential

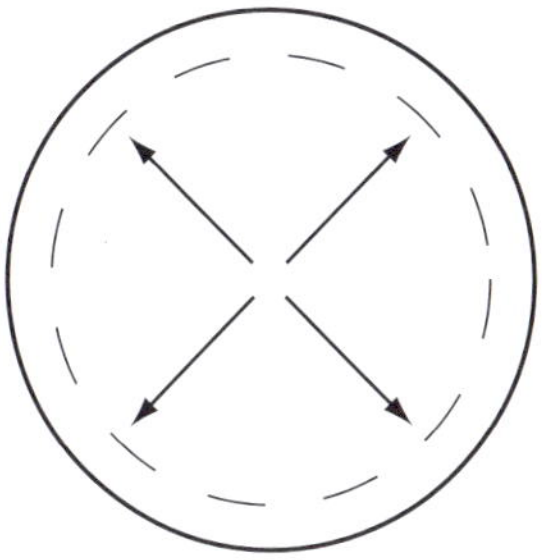

average climber performing optimally

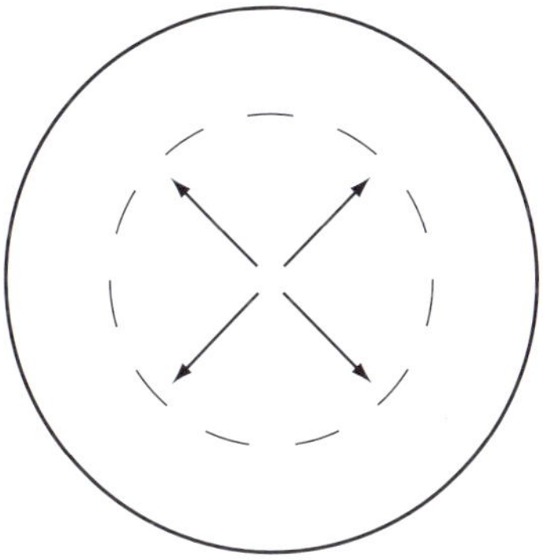

gifted climber performing poorly

Genetic potential (solid line) versus real-life ability (dashed line). Who's the peak performer?

Next time you go to the gym or crag, observe all the men and women, of all ages, shapes, and sizes, who are climbing 5.11, 5.12, and even 5.13. The vast majority of these folks are of average genetic makeup (located near the middle of the bell curve in figure 1.2), but through dedication and hard work on all aspects of the climbing game, they have succeeded at pushing their dashed line out toward the edge of their genetic limitations.

Limits to Climbing Performance

The top climbing grade exploded upward from 5.12d in the mid-1970s to 5.14b by the end of the 1980s. The primary reasons for this marked improvement are equipment (better shoes, stickier shoe rubber, easy-to-place active camming devices, and bolt-protected routes), better training (indoor walls, fingerboards, and so on), and more effective practice methods (hangdogging). In 1991 Wolfgang Güllich upped the ante with his ascent of Action Directe (5.14d/9a) in Germany. Incredibly, this route went unrepeated for five years and has since seen only about one ascent per year, despite being the world's most famous sport climb.

Now, more than twenty-five years after the first ascent of Action Directe, the benchmark of maximum difficulty has been stretched to 5.15c and V16—but the advancement has been relatively

Wolfgang Güllich on his breakthrough route Action Directe, the world's first 5.14d.
THOMAS BALLENBERGER

Melissa Le Neve training on the one-of-a-kind system wall at the Bloc Out gym in Fontainebleau, France.
CLAUDIA ZEIGLER

slow, especially in bouldering, which most directly tracks the absolute maximum climbing level. After Güllich's first ascent of Action Directe, it took a full decade until the first consensus 5.15a/9b, Realization, was established by Chris Sharma in 2001. Seven more years passed before Sharma completed his long-term project, Jumbo Love, widely considered the world's first 5.15b/9b+. However, only a comparatively short four years was needed for Adam Ondra to establish 5.15c/9c with his mega roof route, Change, at Flatanger, Norway.

Given the length of time required to consolidate the 5.15 grade—and even more remarkable, the slow push into the realm of V16 by top boulderers—we have to wonder if we are approaching human limitations to free climbing. While we can never rule out another breakthrough in technology (equipment), it's highly unlikely that we will see another grade explosion as occurred during the 1980s. Instead, slow increases will occur over the time frame of decades.

For a glimpse of what we might expect, let's look at several "mature" Olympic events. Over the last half century, improvements per decade have been approximately as follows: sprinting—1 percent, distance running—1.5 percent, jumping—3 percent, pole vaulting—5 percent, swimming—5 percent, skiing—10 percent (Seiler 2000). Improved equipment surely contributed to the higher values for pole vaulting (fiberglass poles), swimming ("frictionless" speed suits), and skiing (ski technology seems to be constantly improving). Unfortunately, performance-enhancing drugs are also a very real factor in the improvements in many Olympic events.

Assuming no technological breakthroughs and no drugs (though I'm sure there are some), a good bet would be that the top climbing level would increase by just a few percent per decade. I believe these gains will result from the identification of more extreme outliers as participation in climbing increases, and from better matching of appropriate training on a more individual basis. The recent breakthrough ascents of a small crop of Generation Z superstar climbers—Adam Ondra, Alex Megos, Ashima Shiraishi—are a result of the intersection of talent identification, high-quality coaching, and a near single-minded focus. Ondra has now established three 5.15c/9c routes; Alex Megos, at age nineteen, achieved the world's first 5.14d/9a onsight and soon thereafter dispatched Action Directe and Biography in just a few tries; and at the age of thirteen, Ashima Shiraishi achieved her first V14 boulder and completed the first 5.15a redpoint ascent by a woman!

While 5.15d may soon become a reality, it could be that our current method of rating routes is on the verge of breaking down—the difference between 5.15b and 5.15c (or V15 and V16) may be purely a function of anatomical variation in the context of a single move or sequence. This argues for an entirely different system of assessing difficulty at the top levels, such as a scale that counts the number of climbers able to do a given move or problem. Interestingly, this is the essence of John Gill's B-scale for grading bouldering problems, developed back in the late 1950s.

Training for Climbing

As discussed earlier, there are many trainable variables to work on as part of your training for climbing program. In chapter 2 you will perform a self-assessment test to determine which of these trainable variables is most holding you back. The best training program (for you) will concentrate on the areas that can produce the greatest gain in performance output for a given training input. Of course, the goal is to train most effectively, not maximally.

A Definition of Training for Climbing

I define training for climbing as any practice, exercise, or discipline that increases absolute climbing performance. Clearly, this represents a broad spectrum of subjects—hence the wide range of topics covered in this book.

Through this paradigm you should recognize that training includes a wide range of activities and practices such as bouldering (to learn problem solving and develop power); climbing on a home wall or at a climbing gym (to improve technique and strength); on-sighting, hangdogging, or for that matter any climbing (to enhance your mental and physical skill sets); and traveling to experience many different types of climbing (to gain experience and a broad range of technical skills). Training also includes efforts made in ancillary areas such as stretching and antagonist-muscle training (for flexibility and injury prevention), eating properly (to enhance recovery and maintain optimal body composition), visualization and targeted thinking (to maximize mind programming and disconnect from bad habits), resting sufficiently and listening to your body (to optimize training results and avoid injury), and evaluating yourself regularly (to determine your current strengths and weaknesses). Finally, of course, training includes proper execution of various general and climbing-specific exercises (to work toward your physical genetic potential).

For the sake of discriminating among these many types of training throughout the rest of the book, let's define several training subtypes—mental training, skill practice, fitness and strength training, and training support activities—as shown in figure 1.4.

Mental training involves any thought control, discipline, or mind-programming activity that will directly or indirectly impact your climbing in a

Figure 1.4 Subtypes of Training

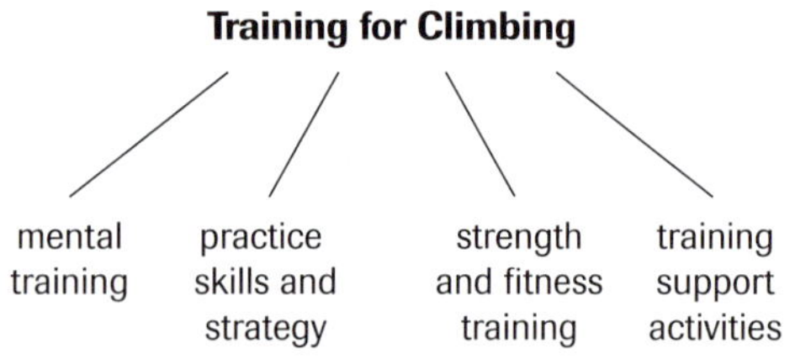

positive way. The best climbers train mentally every day—this is one activity in which you can never overtrain—by targeting their thoughts only on things that can, in some way, influence their climbing and by deleting thoughts and habits that might hold them back. Unfortunately, many individuals possess mental muscle that's in an advanced stage of atrophy from underuse. Visualization is just one of the many mental exercises that can improve your climbing. Chapter 3 lays out an array of mental-training methods and on-the-rock strategies that will have a combined effect similar to unloading a heavy weight from your back (which you've unknowingly been hauling up routes). Are you ready to spread your Mental Wings?

Skill practice relates to time spent learning and refining actual sport skills and strategies outside of a performance setting. Just as baseball, basketball, and football players spend many hours practicing their skills outside of competition, climbers must practice by climbing a lot with the sole intention of improving climbing skill (and not worrying about an outcome such as a flash, redpoint, or on-sight ascent). It's my sense that many climbers' training programs are devoid of this vital subtype of training. We'll take an in-depth look at the subject of effective skill practice in chapter 4.

Fitness and strength training covers a wide range of activities that are performed with the primary intent of improving physiological capabilities. This includes general conditioning activities such as running, stretching, and light free-weight training as well as the more important climbing-specific activities such as fingerboard, campus, and hypergravity training. Many other activities can fall under this heading, as long as they somehow help improve your climbing performance or prevent injury. It's surprising, however, how many things done in the name of training for climbing actually have a negative effect on climbing performance. Get ready to sort things out as we take a cutting-edge look at physical training for climbing in chapters 5 through 9. Then, in chapter

10 you will be guided on developing an effective and time-efficient personalized training program.

Finally, training support activities comprise a variety of crucial, yet often overlooked (or ignored), issues outside of your actual physical practice and training for climbing. Athletes in many other sports have known the vital role that rest, nutrition, and recovery acceleration techniques play in their ultimate level of performance. Serious climbers looking to press out their ability level toward their genetic limit must act on these issues with utmost discipline. Chapters 11 and 12 cover these important topics—applying the material may be the key to succeeding on your own "personal Action Directe"!

The Relationship Between Skill and Fitness

While the various subtypes of training for climbing will be discussed separately, they clearly affect one another. This is especially true when it comes to skill practice and fitness and strength training, so let's dig a little deeper.

For a beginning climber in the earliest stages of learning, a low level of fitness can slow the learning of climbing skill. A certain level of strength is necessary in order to practice enough (i.e., climb) to develop the basic skills of movement, hand- and footwork, and body positioning. Conversely, too much strength enables a beginner to get by on easy to moderate routes despite inefficient movement, poor footwork, and improper body position. Obviously, this will also slow (or prevent) the development of good technique—unless, that is, the strong person makes good technique the primary goal, instead of just getting up the route no matter what.

The problem is further aggravated by the fact that people tend to develop their talents disproportionately. Strong people are most likely into strength training, flexible people probably stretch regularly, and skillful people undoubtedly climb a lot. Sure, the drudgery of working on weak points isn't fun, and at times it can be discouraging. But if you really

Figure 1.5 Relative Gains

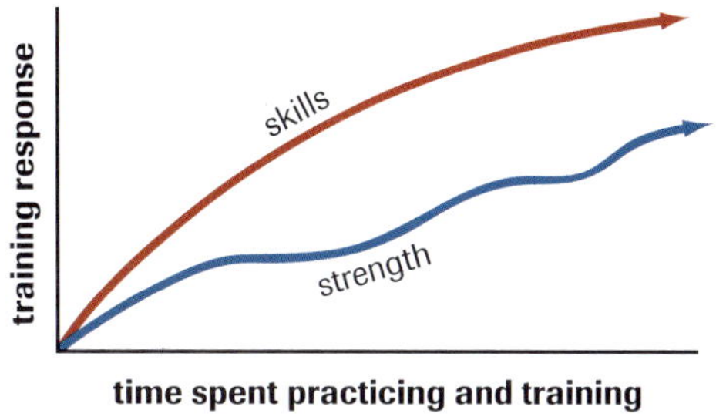

Relative gains from skill practice and strength training.

want to climb harder, you must train smarter. That means knowing where to best invest your time to get the most output for your training input. For the majority of climbers, the best investment is on further development of climbing skills and strategy (see figure 1.5).

Elite climbers may have less to gain from practicing familiar forms of climbing. These expert climbers are way out on the learning curve near their ultimate skill potential, so maximum strength (and the mind) become the crucial factor in performance. Hence, we commonly see magazine articles about these rock stars that describe seemingly lethal or disastrously stressful strength-training regimes that would surely send the ordinary climber into a state of overtraining, the doctor's office, or a self-defeating over-reliance on strength training as the key to improvement.

Focused strength training is of greater importance for all climbers after a layoff, whether due to injury, winter, or some other reason (see figure 1.6). The rapid loss of fitness that occurs when training or climbing ceases for a period of weeks or months is best counteracted by several weeks of dedicated physical training (fortunately, you largely maintain climbing skill once the motor programs are well established). While this short-term training focus helps in regaining your old form, the long-term and

Figure 1.6 Performance Losses

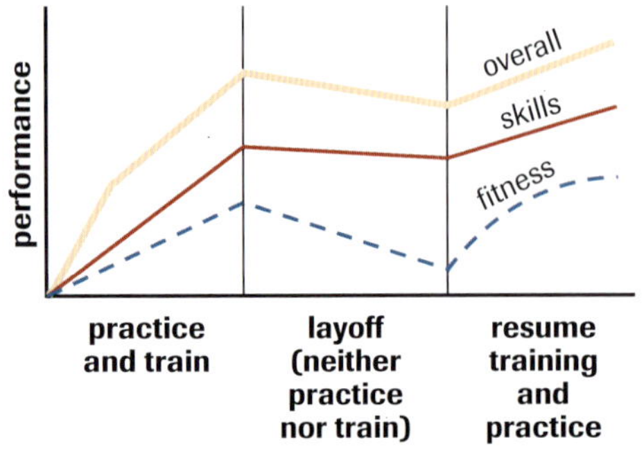

Performance losses (gains) during (and after) a layoff.

most significant improvements in climbing ability will still result from effective skill practice until late in your career. Only at the lofty grades of 5.12 and above does climbing-specific strength become a major limiting factor.

Specific Adaptation to Imposed Demands (SAID)

Serious climbers would be wise to train and climb in accordance with the cornerstone principles of the field of exercise science. For example, knowledge of the SAID Principle (specific adaptation to imposed demands) can be leveraged to maximize the effectiveness of your training for a specific climbing goal or dream climb.

The SAID Principle explains that a certain exercise or type of training produces adaptations specific to the activity performed and only in the muscles (and energy systems) that are stressed by the activity. For instance, running produces favorable adaptations in the leg muscles and the cardiovascular system. But the muscles and systems not stressed show no adaptation, so even heroic amounts of running will produce no favorable changes in, say, the arms. Of course, the adaptations that result from running do transfer somewhat to other activities that depend on the same body parts and systems (such as mountain biking or hiking). **Bottom line:** The SAID Principle demands that effective training for climbing must target your body in ways very similar to climbing (body position, muscles used, energy systems trained, and so forth).

Similarly, your body adapts in a specific fashion to the specific demands you place on it while climbing. If you boulder a lot, you will adapt to the specific skill and strength demands of bouldering. If you climb mostly one-pitch sport routes, you adapt to the unique demands of zipping up, say, 30 meters of rock before muscular failure. If you favor multipitch routes or big walls, your body will adapt in accordance to the demands of these longer climbs. Or, if your outings are alpine in nature, your physiological response will be specific to the very unique demands of climbing in the mountains.

The vitally important distinction here is that while all these activities fall under the headline of "climbing," they each have unique demands that produce very specific physical adaptations. Therefore, the training effect from regular bouldering will do very little to enhance your physical ability for alpine climbing. Figure 1.7 shows that the specific demands of sport climbing are much closer to those of bouldering. Consequently, the adaptations incurred from frequent bouldering will largely carry over to sport climbing (especially short sport climbs) and vice versa.

Due to the SAID Principle, your practice and training on the rocks should be spent mostly on the type of climbing in which you wish to excel. It's no

Figure 1.7 Continuum of Specific Adaptations for Various Subdisciplines of Climbing

mistake that the best boulderers in the world rarely tie in to a rope. Likewise, the best alpine climbers spend little time working thirty-meter sport routes. Targeting your training on the specific demands of your preferred form of climbing is the essence of the SAID Principle.

In the end you must make a philosophical choice whether you want to specialize—and therefore excel—in one or two of the climbing subdisciplines, or become a moderately successful all-around climber. Certainly there is merit and reward in both approaches.

Summary of Training for Climbing

1. Training for climbing is any practice, exercise, or discipline that increases absolute climbing performance.
2. Mental training begins by increasing your commitment to all things climbing (while reducing time, energy, and thought invested in lower-value activities and hobbies) and continues with the development of uncommon self-awareness and superior thought control and risk management skills.
3. Skill practice is paramount, since climbing skills and tactics are distinctly unique from those of other sports. Only going climbing will make you a more skilled climber.
4. Fitness training comprises both general and sport-specific exercises and activities. Novice climbers should engage in a period of general conditioning before advancing to the more stressful climbing-specific exercises.
5. Training support activities are essential for all serious climbers, including scheduled rest days, proper nutrition, and use of techniques to accelerate recovery.
6. Ultimately, the most effective training-for-climbing program will target limiting constraints in highly climbing-specific ways (in accordance with the SAID Principle).

Paige Claassen climbing Ganesh (5.14a) Badami, India.

JON GLASSBERG OF LOUDER THAN 11 (WWW.LT11.COM)

CHAPTER TWO

Self-Assessment and Goal Setting

Search vigilantly for the true, but often underlying, causes of failure on the rock—that's the ultimate secret to optimizing your training and taking your climbing to the next level.

The first step to improving your situation—in anything—can be expressed simply as "Know thyself." You cannot progress beyond your current state with the same thoughts and actions that brought you here. Therefore, only through constant self-evaluation will you unlock the secrets to incremental improvement. For instance, you must actively distinguish what works from what does not work, as well be able to recognize what you need to learn versus what must be unlearned. Often the key elements are not obvious or clear, but you must accept that life is subtle; only through improving on the little things will you succeed in the big things.

In climbing, the process of improvement begins with getting to know your patterns at the crags, in the gym, and in your everyday life. You must become aware of your climbing-related strengths and weaknesses in each area of the performance triad—technical, mental, and physical—and learn to leverage your strengths and improve upon the weaknesses. Toward this end, your prime directive must be to train intelligently—that is, to engage in training activities that best address your weaknesses, while not getting drawn into the trap of training as others do.

Of course, a clear understanding of your mega goals in this sport is equally important to achieving success. Only with a clear goal in mind can you take consistent actions that keep you on route, as well as have the sense to recognize when you have wandered off route. Finally, at the very deepest level, you must closely examine your level of commitment to climbing—are you willing to make the sacrifices necessary for reaching your mega goals? This chapter will guide you through the fundamental steps of self-assessment and goal setting that, in turn, will initiate your ascent to becoming a better, more successful climber (no matter your gauge of measuring success).

Self-Assessment: The Breakfast of Champions

Identifying personal weaknesses often requires a paradigm shift—a dramatic change in the way we see things—because it's human nature to think about and practice the things at which we excel. Too many climbers (myself included) have wasted precious years practicing and training the things at which they already shine, while the ball-and-chain of their weaknesses holds them back. For instance, many climbers think "more strength" is the panacea to their climbing woes; but as shown in figure 1.1, it's just one piece of the climbing performance puzzle. It requires an awakening for most climbers to recognize the thoughts and life patterns that are really holding them back, and that their time and energy could be invested more productively elsewhere.

Introspection and curiosity are key attributes you must foster because, at least at the first superficial glance, your real-life experiences with failure on a climb will almost always appear to result from a lack of strength. But what about all the underlying causes that may have led to premature fatigue—poor footwork, bad body positioning, overgripping of holds, climbing too slowly, scattered focus, a missed rest, unreasonable fears, or a lack of energy due to poor diet or dehydration? As you can see, the other two-thirds of the climbing performance puzzle (technical and mental) determine how effectively you use the physical strength and energy reserves you possess. Consequently, it's my belief that the average climber wastes 50 percent (or more!) of his strength and energy due to flawed technique, inefficient movement, and poor mental control. This is analogous to having a thirty-miles-per-gallon car that only gets fifteen miles per gallon as the result of a horrible tune-up and a heavy foot. Therefore, the average climber can obtain a huge windfall of relative strength gains—and dramatically improve performance—by training up technique, quality of movement, and mental control.

The moral of the story, then, is that the best training program for climbing must include lots of climbing and constant self-evaluation. Spending three or four days a week on the rock (or an artificial wall) deliberately practicing skills and refining your climber's mind-set is far more beneficial than spending those days strength training in the gym. This is not to say that you can simply climb a lot and ignore all the other facets of performance. The best climbers clearly focus on putting the complete puzzle together, and this undoubtedly includes a targeted strength-training program. Still, if you can do ten fingertip pull-ups, you are probably strong enough to climb most 5.12a routes! So search vigilantly for the true, but often underlying, causes of your failure on routes. That's the ultimate secret to optimizing your training program and establishing new personal bests on the rock.

Objective Evaluation

The best way to identify your weaknesses is to ask yourself a series of detailed questions. To identify physical and technical weaknesses, ask yourself targeted questions like: *Do I fail on a route because I'm too weak or do I overgrip and hang out too long in the midst of hard moves? Does my footwork deteriorate in the moves prior to where I fall? Do I climb too slowly through crux moves and consequently come up short on routes? Do I lack the flexibility to step onto a crucial hold or do I miss a better, easier foot placement? Am I really too short for this move or have I failed to find the body position that makes it possible for someone my height?*

Some questions for identifying mental errors are: *Do I fail to see the sequence or do I fail to try something new when the obvious doesn't work? Do I try too hard or give up too easily? Am I controlling my internal self-talk or is the critic within doing a hatchet job on me? Do I monitor and control my body tension or does my perceived pressure of the situation run the show? Do I sabotage myself before leaving the ground by doubting my ability and pondering past failures?*

In addition to investigating yourself, consider enlisting a coach to provide an even more objective view of your performance or, at the least, have a friend shoot some video of you on the rock. These detached perspectives are especially useful in identifying obvious flaws in technique, tactics, and your overall economy of effort. For example, feet skidding or popping off footholds signals lack of attention to footwork, while constant stretching for holds seemingly just out of reach is a sign you're missing critical intermediate holds or using less effective body positions. In more general terms, evaluate whether your movement looks relaxed and fluid or appears tight, mechanical, and hesitant. These outside perspectives can be a real eye-opener, and you'll probably be surprised at what you find. Still, some fundamental mistakes and weaknesses are so subtle that they are not easily observed by others or by viewing yourself on video. This is where a detailed self-assessment test comes in handy.

Taking the Self-Assessment Test

A good self-assessment test takes the white light of your climbing performance and, like a prism, disassembles it into the rainbow of colors representing specific skills. The results will reveal your true (not perceived) strengths and weaknesses—and possibly even an unknown Achilles' heel that must be addressed if you are to ever reach your potential (or break through a long-term plateau). With this knowledge, you can create the most effective training program for you!

In taking the assessment that follows, it's important to read each question once and then immediately answer it based on your recent experiences on the rock. Don't read anything into the questions; nor should you try to figure out their focus and shade your answers in any way. Instead of working in the book, consider making a photocopy of the test pages in order to maintain an unmarked self-assessment test with which to work (or copy again) in the future. Of course, it would be ideal to date your test and file it for future reference. Comparing successive self-assessments is a powerful way to track your long-term improvement in each area of the performance triad.

Exercise: Self-Assessment Test

Answer each question by circling the number that best characterizes your performance. To obtain the most accurate results, it's essential that you score each question according to your most recent experiences on the rock. Pause for a moment and review recent climbs to determine the correct answer for each question. Do not overanalyze the questions, however, or try to read between the lines—you will have a chance to ponder the meaning of your answers when you tally the final results.

0 = almost always

1 = often

2 = about half the time

3 = occasionally

4 = seldom

5 = never

1. My footwork (use of feet) deteriorates during the hardest part of a climb.

0 1 2 3 4 5

2. My forearms balloon and my grip begins to fail even on routes that are easy for me.

0 1 2 3 4 5

3. On hard sequences, I have difficulty stepping onto critical footholds.

0 1 2 3 4 5

4. I get anxious and tight as I head into crux sequences.

0 1 2 3 4 5

5. My biceps (upper arms) pump out before my forearms.

0 1 2 3 4 5

6. I have difficulty hanging on small, necessary-to-use holds.

0 1 2 3 4 5

7. I blow sequences I have wired and know by heart.

0 1 2 3 4 5

8. I stall at the start of crux sequences. I end up having to hang on the rope and rest before I can give it a good, solid try.

0 1 2 3 4 5

9. I climb three or four days in a row.

0 1 2 3 4 5

10. I get sewing-machine leg ("Elvis leg").

0 1 2 3 4 5

11. I pump out on overhanging climbs no matter how big the holds.

0 1 2 3 4 5

12. I get out of breath when I climb.

0 1 2 3 4 5

13. I make excuses for why I might fail on a route before I even begin to climb.

0 1 2 3 4 5

14. I miss hidden holds on routes.

0 1 2 3 4 5

15. I have difficulty hanging on to sloping holds, pockets, and/or pinches.

0 1 2 3 4 5

16. I grab quickdraws, the rope, or other gear instead of risking a fall trying a hard move of which I am unsure.

0 1 2 3 4 5

17. On a typical climb, I feel like much of my body weight is hanging on my arms.

0 1 2 3 4 5

18. I get very sore the day after climbing at the crags.

0 1 2 3 4 5

19. I have difficulty visualizing myself successfully climbing the route before I leave the ground.

0 1 2 3 4 5

20. I cannot reach key holds on difficult routes.

0 1 2 3 4 5

21. On overhanging routes and roofs, I have difficulty keeping my feet from cutting loose and swinging out.

0 1 2 3 4 5

22. While climbing, I get distracted by activity on the ground and/or I think about whether the belayer is paying attention.

0 1 2 3 4 5

23. I have difficulty reading sequences.

0 1 2 3 4 5

24. I get a flash pump on the first climb of the day.

0 1 2 3 4 5

25. I have more difficulty climbing when people are watching.

0 1 2 3 4 5

26. My feet unexpectedly pop off footholds.

0 1 2 3 4 5

27. I experience elbow or shoulder pain when I train or climb on a regular basis.

0 1 2 3 4 5

28. When lead climbing a safe route, I have difficulty pushing myself to the complete limit.

0 1 2 3 4 5

29. I have difficulty finding mid-route rest positions and shakeouts.

0 1 2 3 4 5

30. My first attempt on a hard route is usually better than my second or third attempts of the day.

0 1 2 3 4 5

Table 2.1 Score Yourself

Mental	Technique and Tactics	Physical
1.	2.	3.
4.	5.	6.
7.	8.	9.
10.	11.	12.
13.	14.	15.
16.	17.	18.
19.	20.	21.
22.	23.	24.
25.	26.	27.
28.	29.	30.
(Total)	(Total)	(Total)

Looking at Your Test Results

Record the scores from each question in table 2.1, and then add up each column to obtain a final score for each area of the performance triad. Compare your mental, technical, and physical scores to gain a sense of which area is your strong or weak aspect of the performance triad. If all three areas are within five points of one another, congratulate yourself for being a climber of balanced abilities. It is more common, however, to discover that one aspect of performance is much lower-scoring than the other two. This area is your major weakness, and the most effective training program for you is one that targets this area for improvement.

Next, review each question of the self-assessment test and mark a star next to those on which you scored a 3 or less. Each of these low-scoring questions identifies a specific element of your climbing performance that is holding you back. List on a separate piece of paper or in your training log a brief description of each problem revealed. Sort and group them according to the aspects of the performance triad. As you read through the remainder of the book, keep this list of problem areas nearby, and make notes of the exercises and strategies presented that address these weaknesses. Creating such a written "mind map" that displays both the problem areas and the action-oriented solutions will keep these highly powerful keys to better climbing in the forefront of your attention. Only with this awareness will your training remain on track and effective in the weeks and months to come.

As you move into the goal-setting exercises later in this chapter, refer back to the self-assessment test or your summary mind map. Focus your short- and medium-term training goals on the most dramatic weaknesses identified (the five or six lowest-scoring items). As you recognize improvement in these areas, shift your training focus onto other lower-scoring areas of the self-assessment or retake the entire test and develop a new training strategy based on the new results. For additional training tips that address each question of the self-assessment, see appendix C.

The Cycle of Improvement

Your completed self-assessment is your "boarding pass" to the Cycle of Improvement. This process cycle has three stages: Set goals, take action, and make course corrections (see figure 2.1).

A successful trip around the cycle gives birth to a new level of climbing performance—the Cycle of Improvement, in fact, becomes a Spiral of Improvement! Occasionally, reassessments are needed to update your goals relative to the "new you" and whatever new issues are now responsible for holding you back from further improvement. These new goals give birth to new actions and even more spectacular results.

Figure 2.1 Cycle of Improvement

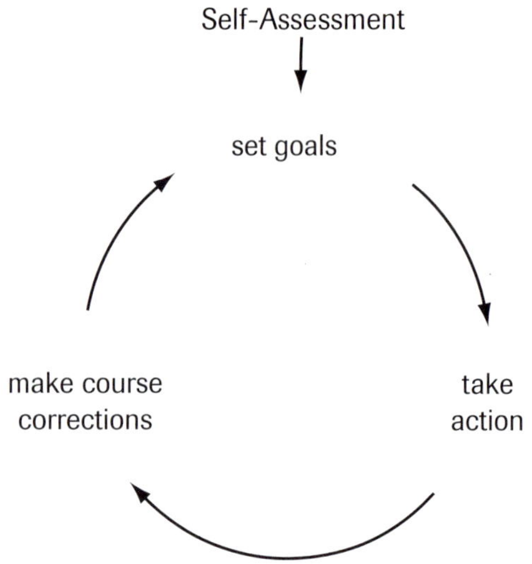

Use this three-step process to elevate your performance to the next level.

Depending on your desires, commitment, and skill level, one trip around the cycle may take anywhere from a couple of months to a year. Signs that you are ready for a reassessment and a new cycle include a plateau in performance, training that feels flat, or a drop in motivation. If you experience more than one of these signs, take a week or two off, then retake the self-assessment test and start a new cycle.

Remember that there is a big difference between employing the Cycle of Improvement and just going climbing year-round. The latter approach is unfocused and will yield slow results and frequent plateaus in performance. Conversely, a deliberate effort in all three stages—setting new goals, taking intelligent action, and making appropriate course corrections—keeps the spiral going upward toward your ultimate genetic potential.

Goal Setting

Defining specific goals enables you to perform a gap analysis of what actions you must take to bridge the gap (or possibly chasm) between where you are now and what you want to become or achieve. Effective goal setting begins with a pen or pencil and a calendar, training log, or climbing notebook. If you don't write down your goals, chances are they will remain intangible hopes and dreams that never materialize.

It's best to set goals in three time frames: short-term (daily), medium-term (weekly or monthly), and long-term (yearly or "career") goals. Write down the goals in precise terms and with realistic deadlines. And since pictures are even more motivating than words on paper, it's crucial to create a mental picture (representing the goal) that you can recall in your mind's eye on demand. The more precise and focused your picture and written goal, the easier it will be for you to zero in on the target and take actions that will someday lead you to realize the goal.

Next, create a mission statement that summarizes the purpose of each goal-setting time frame, such as "Short term, I will strive for the most effective ninety-minute workout possible" or "Medium term, I am committed to climbing my first 5.12 (V6, or whatever) by the end of the summer." Now share these goals with your climbing partner, a close friend, or significant other—someone who will hold you accountable and help motivate you to stay on mission.

Finally, write down what one or two (or more) things you will give up in order to reach your short-, medium-, and long-term goals. This vital step is missing from most conventional goal-setting exercises, and it may be the number one reason why so many people fail to achieve their big goals in life. It's a fact that you cannot add something new and achieve the ideal outcome without sacrificing something else in its place. Ponder this powerful idea. It may explain why some of your past or present goals remain elusive.

SHORT-TERM GOALS

Short-term goals define your daily game plan. They help focus your thoughts and actions so that you are not swayed by what others are doing and don't waste precious time on less important activities (TV, partying, surfing the Net, excessive socializing). The more hectic your life, the more crucial it is that you spend a few minutes before bed or first thing in the morning doing some short-term goal setting. Folks with less difficult daily schedules may only need to set short-term goals relating to the workout du jour. Begin by writing down the primary mission of the workout, then list the specific exercises, sets, and reps as well as the approximate amount of time you will dedicate to each part of the workout (see "An Example of Short-Term Goal Setting" below). Don't forget to list what you will give up (relative to previous days or your peers) in order to fulfill these short-term commitments.

MEDIUM-TERM GOALS

Medium-term goals give shape and direction to your schedule over the course of weeks and months. This planning is best done on a calendar so you can effectively dovetail your workouts and climbing trips with your other nonclimbing activities. Try to roughly plan things out a few months in advance (see the "Setting Medium-Term Goals" exercise below).

First, block in the big events such as climbing trips, competitions, work and family obligations, and the like. Next, write in your proposed workout and climbing schedule, with special attention to maintaining enough rest days in the game plan. With the most important items now in place, you can fill in the many little, less important things in life where time allows (or this can be done on an ad hoc basis). Remember to sum up your medium-term goals with one overriding primary goal, as well as listing the activities you will forfeit in order to attain this lofty goal.

LONG-TERM GOALS

Long-term goal setting is a fun and invaluable activity in which you condense onto paper the numerous "dream" or "I wish" goals floating around in your mind. If there is to be any chance of them ever becoming reality, it's vital that they be liberated from the dreamland of your mind and put down in black and white (see the "Setting Long-Term Goals" exercise below). A magical force begins to act in your life when you write down these mega goals—your subconscious mind will go to work day and night on achieving them, and your conscious mind will suddenly find them more believable (and achievable).

An Example of Short-Term Goal Setting

Today's Mission:

Focus on improving my footwork and conserving energy by practicing skills and techniques.

What I will give up to achieve this goal:

The usual bouldering games and competitions at the gym.
For today, I'll stay off all routes that are beyond my on-site ability.
I won't rush home to watch TV.

What I will do:

1. Warm up with fifteen minutes of light bouldering, gentle stretching, and two sets of pull-ups.
2. Perform ten to fifteen minutes of the traverse-training drill with focus on light grip, precise footwork, and smooth movement.
3. Toprope several climbs within one number grade of my limit with the focus on practicing technique, not performance outcome (whether or not I fall). My practice goals are to concentrate on careful positioning and use of each foothold; to climb as briskly, smoothly, and decisively as possible between rests; to accurately read sequences before leaving the ground and while at each rest position; and to remain positive, relaxed, and centered during each climb.
4. Perform three sets of six repetitions of the One-Arm Lunging exercise.
5. Perform three sets of weighted pull-ups with ten pounds.
6. Perform a minimum of ten minutes of wrist, rotator cuff, and scapular stabilizer training.
7. Cool down with five to ten minutes of stretching.
8. Eat a good meal within one to two hours after the workout.
9. Get seven to eight hours of sleep.

Exercise: Setting Medium-Term Goals

Your medium-term goals can include both climbing and nonclimbing items; we'll focus on the climbing-related goals here. Write down your top training goals (mental, physical, and technical) for the next three months, as well as a few climbing goals such as to-do routes or new areas to visit. Distill these goals into a single primary goal for the period, and remember to list a few things you will freely give up in order to reach these goals.

Exercise: Setting Long-Term Goals

Go somewhere quiet, allow yourself to relax for a few minutes, and then ponder what long-term mega goals would really energize you and make for an exceptional journey. I call these mega goals because they are the few events that you most want to achieve in your life given your current perspective. For example, you might have an ultimate grade of climbing you'd like to achieve, or possibly a specific dream climb to send or mountain to summit. Think about where you'd go if time and money were not an issue—put it down on paper and the odds increase a thousandfold that you will someday be pulling down there! By all means write down a few of your nonclimbing mega goals as well, but keep the total list down to between six and eight items.

As in setting your short- and medium-term goals, it's absolutely critical that you write down a couple of major things that you will completely give up in order to reach these mega goals. Consider the activities, possessions, and people that drain your time, focus, and energy.

Taking Action and Making Course Corrections

The Cycle of Improvement will spiral you upward in ability as long as the actions taken provide movement toward your goals. Sadly, taking consistent, disciplined action in the direction of worthy goals is very difficult for some people. The results of their misdirected actions always seem to leave them in an all-too-familiar situation. The phrase *same shit, different day* is born of this affliction.

If any of this sounds familiar (in climbing or life), it's important to begin taking notice of just who is directing the actions you take on a daily basis. In many cases you'll discover that outside forces are calling the shots for you—that is, you are taking the actions someone else wants you to make, not those congruent with your goals. This is what the multibillion-dollar advertising industry is all about. Large companies spend millions with the sole intent of directing your actions in their favor (to make them money and drain your wallet). So while you might have a very worthy goal of, say, "getting out of debt" or "saving for a house," advertisers cleverly divert your actions in their favor. Unless you are acutely aware of what's going on (and the power they wield over you), you will veer off your course and onto theirs—and maybe never reach your goals.

This may sound negative, but the same thing often happens when you're training at the gym or climbing at the crag. Instead of doing the precise exercises and drills you need to improve your weaknesses, you end up climbing down the blind alley of someone else's agenda. Consider how many climbing days you've spent working on someone else's dream project (one that is either over your head or just not what you had planned) when you would have gained more by getting on a different type of climb. Or ponder how often you've gone to the gym and ended up socializing and just climbing mindlessly with no goal or direction. Sure, these kinds of evenings can be relaxing and fun once in a while, but on a regular basis they will not make you a better climber.

The win–win solution is to find a partner equally motivated to taking actions that will produce the fastest possible gains in ability. With this person you can evenly split the climbing time, so that you each can work effectively toward your goals. Unfortunately, in many partnerships one person makes all the calls and gets most of the benefits of the time spent training or climbing.

In summary, strive for hour-to-hour, day-to-day awareness of the "whats" and "whys" of the actions you are taking. By formulating short-term goals, as discussed earlier, you can best maintain your focus on the things you need to do to improve short term and advance toward your meaningful medium- and long-term goals. Finally, foster an acute awareness of the results you are getting from your actions. Peak performers are those who most rapidly recognize when they are off course and respond with a reassessment of the situation and an appropriate course correction toward the desired goal.

If it's beginning to sound like becoming a better climber is a very mental thing, you are right! So let's dive into chapter 3, "Mental Training."

Tips for Achieving Your Goals

1. Know yourself. Live your passion. What worthy goals will drive you to excellence?
2. Regularly assess your strengths and weaknesses. What's holding you back in terms of action (or inaction) and self-defeating thoughts and habits?
3. Take the self-assessment in this chapter at least once per year, and consider getting the objective evaluation of a climbing coach.
4. Regularly evaluate the effectiveness of your actions—are you obtaining the intended results? If not, make course corrections that will yield more effective actions.
5. Don't be afraid to step away from the crowd and pursue your own mega goals. Ally with like-minded individuals, and avoid people with bad attitudes and unproductive behavior.
6. Set mega goals that will inspire and energize you from sunrise to sunset and, ultimately, make your life an amazing journey.

B. J. Tilden killing the Big Bad Wolf (5.14a), Wolf Point, Wyoming. KYLE DUBA

CHAPTER THREE

Mental Training

We climb with our mind—our hands and feet are merely an extension of our thoughts and will.

The quickest way to enhance your performance in almost anything is to improve the quality of your thinking. This is definitely true in climbing, whether you're working a highball boulder problem, sport route, multipitch traditional line, or alpine route. All performance operates from the inside out—your beliefs, focus, fears, confidence, preparation, and problem-solving abilities form the foundation from which you will either succeed or fail.

Great performances begin with bulletproof confidence, singular focus, positive emotions, and a tough yet agile mind-set. Conversely, setbacks and failures often result from the worry, doubts, tension, and uncertainties that are born from a poorly harnessed mind running wild with fearful thoughts. It's my belief that whether you (or I) will succeed or fail on a climb is often predetermined in your subconscious (and perhaps even conscious) mind before you ever step off the ground.

While off-season strength training and year-round technique training are paramount for progressing into the higher grades, during the climbing season your biggest breakthroughs will come from toning and flexing your mental muscle. Toward this end, this chapter details two dozen powerful mental strategies and skills that will help elevate your performance and enjoyment.

Practice these skills with the same dedication and resolve as you would a new strength-training program, and you'll be pleasantly surprised with the results. Obtain the greatest payoff by applying these skills every day, not just when you feel like it. For some, an almost instant breakthrough will follow on the rock, while others will need to persist and let these mental skills build to a critical value before they will produce a noticeable impact on climbing. (This depends upon the current degree of tone or atrophy of your mental muscle.)

Recognize that all these mental-training skills are interlaced and can produce a powerful synergy when all are put in practice. In aggregate they may produce an effect similar to unloading a ten-pound weight (or more!) from your back that you have unknowingly been hauling up climbs. I call this using your Mental Wings.

Mental Wings for Improving Performance

The late, great Wolfgang Güllich was fond of saying that "the brain is the most important muscle for climbing." What makes this statement even more provocative is the fact that Güllich was one of the strongest people to ever pull down on stone. From the mid-1980s until his death in a car accident in 1992, he opened up several new grades of maximum difficulty by leveraging the synergy of his physical and mental fortitude. I support Wolfie's sentiment not only because the mind is one-third of the climbing performance triad (see figure 1.1) but also due to the fact that poor mental control can instantly sabotage your physical and technical abilities.

Below are ten strategies that you can start using today in all aspects of your life. Apply them faithfully with the knowledge that most truly successful men and women in this sport possess these skills.

1. Separate your self-image from your performance.

If you are reading this book, then climbing surely plays a major role in your life. However, if your self-image is tied too strongly or singularly to this role, it leads to an obsessive need to perform perfectly every time you touch the rock. The result is intense pressure, anxiety, and fear of failure—all of which will make performing your best difficult, if not impossible.

The fact is, you will perform best in a process-oriented frame of mind, where the outcome is accepted as unknown and allowed to unfold without anticipation. Detaching your self-image from your climbing performance is the first step to escaping an outcome-oriented mind-set. Strive to focus only on things immediate to the act of climbing—your warm-up, mental rehearsal, gear selection; when climbing, focus only on the move and sequence at hand, never projecting ahead. Accept the feedback the route gives you without frustration or judgment, and liberate yourself to try new things, take chances, and—most important—fall. Such process orientation and self-image detachment will reduce pressure and anxiety; paradoxically, you'll climb better by not needing to!

2. Surround yourself with positive people.

There is an aura of influence that surrounds each of us, and its effects are based on our personality and attitude toward life and its events. Your thoughts and actions will affect the thoughts and actions of those around you, and vice versa. As I see it, there are three options—either climb alone, climb with upbeat and positive people, or climb with cynical and negative people. But why would you ever want to climb with the negative, excuse-making complainers of the climbing world? Their negative aura will adversely impact your climbing and enjoyment whether you recognize it or not. The bottom line: Vow to either climb with positive individuals or climb solo. Both approaches can be hugely rewarding.

3. Stretch your comfort zone.

To improve in anything, your goals must exceed your current grasp and you must be willing to push beyond your comfort zone in your reach. In performing on the vertical plane, this means climbing onward despite mental and physical discomfort; it means challenging your fears head-on by doing what you fear; and it means attempting what looks impossible to you based on past experience. Through this process you will stretch your abilities to a new level, redefine your belief system, and reshape your personal vision of what is possible.

4. Anticipate and proactively manage your risk.

Climbing is an activity with obvious inherent risks, and the desire to climb harder often requires taking on even more. This can come in the form of obvious physical danger such as a potentially injurious fall, or as less tangible mental risk like opening yourself up to failure, criticism, and embarrassment. It's interesting to note that for some climbers, the physical danger can feel more tolerable than the mental. As an example, consider a climber who foolishly continues upward on a horrendously dangerous route he's not prepared for because of the fear of being dissed (by those standing safely on the ground!) should he back off.

Make it your MO to carefully assess all the possible risks before starting up every climb. Determine ways that you can reduce the risk of the climb (such as rigging a belay differently than usual or getting an extra spotter or crash pad), and anticipate how you will respond to new emerging risks as you climb (for instance, discovering there are no protection placements higher up the route). As for the

Chelsea Rude is focused and in the zone on Dolce Vita (5.13c), Ceuse, France. MATTY HONG

mental risks you might face (like the fear of failure), see the first mental strategy on separating your self-image from your performance.

5. Fortify your confidence.

Your degree of self-confidence is primarily based on your self-image and the thoughts you possess minute by minute and day by day. For example, pondering past failures, allowing free rein to demeaning self-talk, or dwelling on the chance of falling will deflate self-confidence and sow the seeds of failure.

Conversely, peak performers consciously narrow their thoughts and focus onto things that will fortify and build confidence. You, too, can do this as you prepare for an ascent, by taking a mental inventory of past successes, reviewing and believing in your skills and strengths, and acknowledging your preparation and investment in training. Do all this and you will grow more energized and confident as you engage the rock, and most likely climb your very best.

6. Use visualization to foster a peak performance zone.

"The zone" is that state where everything comes together for a perfect ascent that seems almost effortless and automatic. The trick is being able to create this state on demand, despite stressful conditions such as the heat of competition or before a hard redpoint attempt. Here's how.

First, use visualization to reenact the positive feelings of a good performance in a past similar situation. Create about a sixty-second mental movie of this past event using all your senses. Make the pictures crisp and bright, and let the emotion and feeling of the success take over your body. With the positive, confident emotions of this past event now internalized for use in the present, you can begin mental rehearsal of the upcoming climb. Begin by visualizing yourself climbing the route from a detached on-TV perspective—it's in this mode of visualization that you'll develop a sequence and strategy for the ascent. Next, close your eyes and climb the route in your mind's eye—feel the moves play out successfully to create a mental blueprint for action (you'll find more detailed instruction on visualization later in this chapter). Now open your eyes and take on the route for real, one move at a time.

7. Use preclimb rituals to create an ideal performance state.

The things you think and do in the minutes and moments before you climb form the foundation onto which your performance is built. A shaky foundation generally leads to a shaky performance; a solid foundation usually gives birth to a solid performance. The nature of your foundation (sand or stone?) is influenced by the quality of your preclimb rituals. These are things you do to best prepare for the ascent, including scoping the route, visualizing the sequence, preparing your gear, warming up, and even your way of putting on your shoes. Everything down to tiny details, such as breathing rate, posture, and final thoughts, should be programmed into the rituals that lead up to the moment you step onto the rock.

Develop your rituals based on past experience. What things did you think or do before some of your best ascents in the past? What did you eat or drink, how did you warm up, and how long did you rest between climbs? Awareness of all the things (little and big) that led up to your best performances is key to being able to reproduce similar results in the future. Once your rituals become tried and true, stick to them!

8. Control stress and tension before they control you.

This strategy is central to climbing your best, because tension kills performance. Period. Tension is often a physical manifestation of mental stress, although it can also develop in overstressed muscles or as the result of an inadequate warm-up. Either way, the outcome is the same—poor motor control (inefficient movement), unproductive emotions, and quite often failure. Here are two ways to control tension and stress on the fly. First, direct your thinking away from pressure-producing thoughts and focus only on the process of climbing. Engage the route completely and stay in the moment. Second, use rest positions to break from the process of climbing and direct your thoughts inward for a tension check. Use the six-step ANSWER Sequence (see page 43) to clear tension and return to center in less than one minute—perfect for use at every mid-route rest position.

9. Engage in positive self-talk.

Inside our heads, each of us has a "critic" voice and a "doer" voice that gab throughout our waking hours. While the critic voice can be useful in a few situations (such as evaluating weaknesses or performance errors), it's the doer voice that compels action, keeps us positive, and, in fact, helps us perform effectively. Controlling this internal self-talk is fundamental to controlling our attitude and climbing our best.

Which voice—the critic or the doer—rules your mind? Hopefully you'll conclude that the doer's voice rules your mental roost about 95 percent of the time (or more). If not, you can surely improve your performance by eliminating any self-destructive internal dialogue. The first step is to sever your ties to negative, critical people: Their verbal and nonverbal communication will absolutely pollute your thoughts and attitude.

Next, strive to heighten your awareness of your self-talk—the goal is to think about what you are thinking about!—and allow the doer voice to run the talk show. When you notice the critic voice speaking up, determine if it is useful (for instance, to help with risk management) or just trash talk. Take the critic's non-useful comments and invert them into positive statements. For example, change *This route looks impossible* to *This route looks challenging*; replace *I feel nervous* with *I feel energized*; convert *I'll probably fall* into *I think I can do this, but if I fall it's okay because I'll get it next time.* Direct such positive self-talk on every climb and throughout every day and you will marshal psychic energy that enhances your performance in all you do.

10. Love climbing, no matter what.

A common trait of successful people is resilience to criticism and bad results, and an unwavering belief that success will come with time and effort. Developing such a mind-set takes a disciplined effort to constantly spin negative feedback into some kind of a positive—real winners never dwell on the setbacks or accept defeat.

Remember, climbing is about the journey, not the summit. Vow to love the process of climbing and all it entails, whether it is a perfect send or a painful struggle. Sure, a perfect ascent is immensely gratifying; however, it's on the arduous journey that you actually become a better climber and grow as a person. The bottom line: Love climbing unconditionally and you will always have a great day on the rocks!

Controlling Your Emotions

Your emotions have a direct effect on your body and mind. What you are feeling exerts an influence over the quality of your actions and your ways of thinking (see figure 3.1). Consider how nervousness before a climb can derail your concentration as well as trigger preclimb jitters throughout your body. We can then conclude that emotional control is essential for optimal performance.

Figure 3.1 How Emotions Run the Show

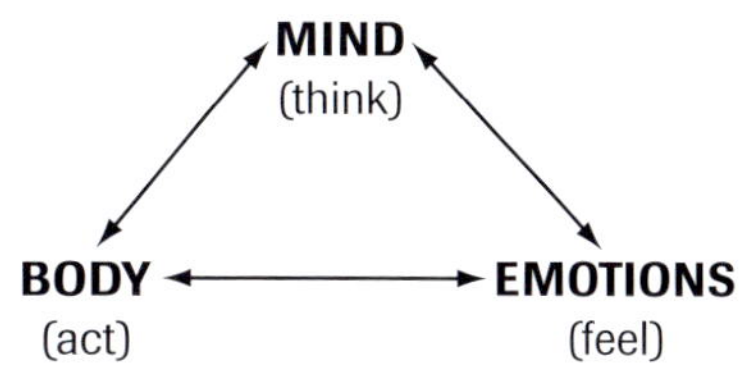

What you feel exerts an influence over how you think and what you do. Likewise, ways of thinking and acting affect how you feel.

Observe great climbers such as Chris Sharma and Alex Megos at work and you will notice either positive, productive emotions or no emotion at all. Even when they fall, you sense little anger or angst—only love of the process of climbing, which occasionally includes falling. Now consider how your thoughts and emotions evolve when the going gets tough—do you sometimes become negative, fearful, or even self-defeating? If so, then your physical performance will absolutely suffer given the intimate mind-emotion-body relationship shown in figure 3.1.

The following storyline illustrates how negative emotions can sabotage performance.

1. The climber leaves the ground and moves cautiously through the initial moves. He looks apprehensive, as if he's trying not to make any mistakes.
2. As he enters more difficult moves, his breathing becomes shallow and irregular.
3. Negative emotional energy rises, resulting in increased muscular tension and mental stress.
4. This building stress disrupts his coordination, balance, and footwork. Movements become

tight, mechanical, and inefficient. He begins to overgrip holds.

5. He begins to hold back on hard moves, afraid to fully commit, and hangs out too long on marginal rests.
6. The fight-or-flight syndrome is triggered, adding some adrenaline to the mix. This burst of energy may help the climber thrash through a few more moves; more commonly, however, the jolt causes him to grab the rope or a quickdraw and retreat from the route.
7. The death grip sets in and muscles flame out.
8. He falls and lets loose a few expletives.
9. Hanging on the rope, he engages in critical thinking that further raises the tide of negative emotions.

Does any part of this story sound familiar? If so, I have some good news. You can learn to rein in your emotions and thus open up a whole new level of climbing performance and enjoyment. If you have good emotional control already, I bet you can still improve your climbing by modulating your arousal level. Let's explore this murky subject of emotions and discuss how you can make some immediate positive changes.

Evaluating Your Emotional State

In evaluating your emotional state, the goal is to become aware of the "sign" of your emotions—positive or negative—and the magnitude of your arousal, high or low. Obviously, positive emotions have different effects on the mind and body than negative emotions. Similarly, the intensity of these emotions (the arousal level) plays a role in how you think and feel. To better understand this relationship, consider the Energy–Emotion Matrix (see figure 3.2).

The Energy–Emotion Matrix has four quadrants: high energy, positive emotion (upper right); low energy, positive emotion (lower right); high energy, negative emotion (upper left); and low energy, negative emotion (lower left). The matrix

Figure 3.2 The Energy–Emotion Matrix

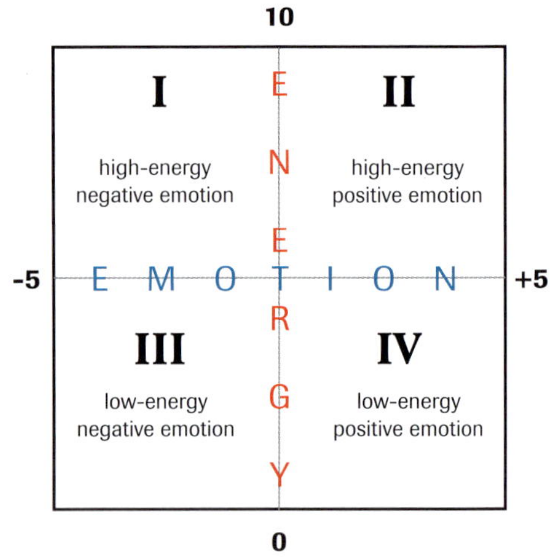

What quadrant of the matrix are you most often in?

represents a continuum of emotion and energy across these four quadrants. Therefore, you can evaluate your present location in the matrix by grading your current energy level on a scale from 0 to 10 (low to high) and scoring your current emotional state on a scale from –5 (extremely negative) to +5 (extremely positive). Knowing where you are in the matrix and having the ability to change this location if it's not optimal in the current situation is fundamental to becoming a peak performer in any endeavor.

Obviously, your energy level and emotions fluctuate throughout the day and over the course of a climb, so your place in the matrix changes hour by hour and, maybe, minute to minute in extreme situations. I believe it's valuable to study your place in the matrix in everyday, nonclimbing situations, since your most common daily state will heavily determine your disposition when climbing (it's unlikely you can be a negative person at home and work, then become completely positive when you go climbing). Use the blank energy–emotion time line contained in appendix B to plot your changing energy–emotional state throughout the day, as shown in figure 3.3. Begin upon waking in the morning, and score your state every thirty minutes, or when some event causes your emotion or energy to change in an instant.

After evaluating your energy–emotional state for a few days, see if you can identify any patterns. What time(s) of the day is your energy high or low? What events seem to trigger you becoming more positive or negative? Recognizing these patterns (and effects) empowers you to make modifications,

Figure 3.3 Sample Chart of Energy–Emotion Levels

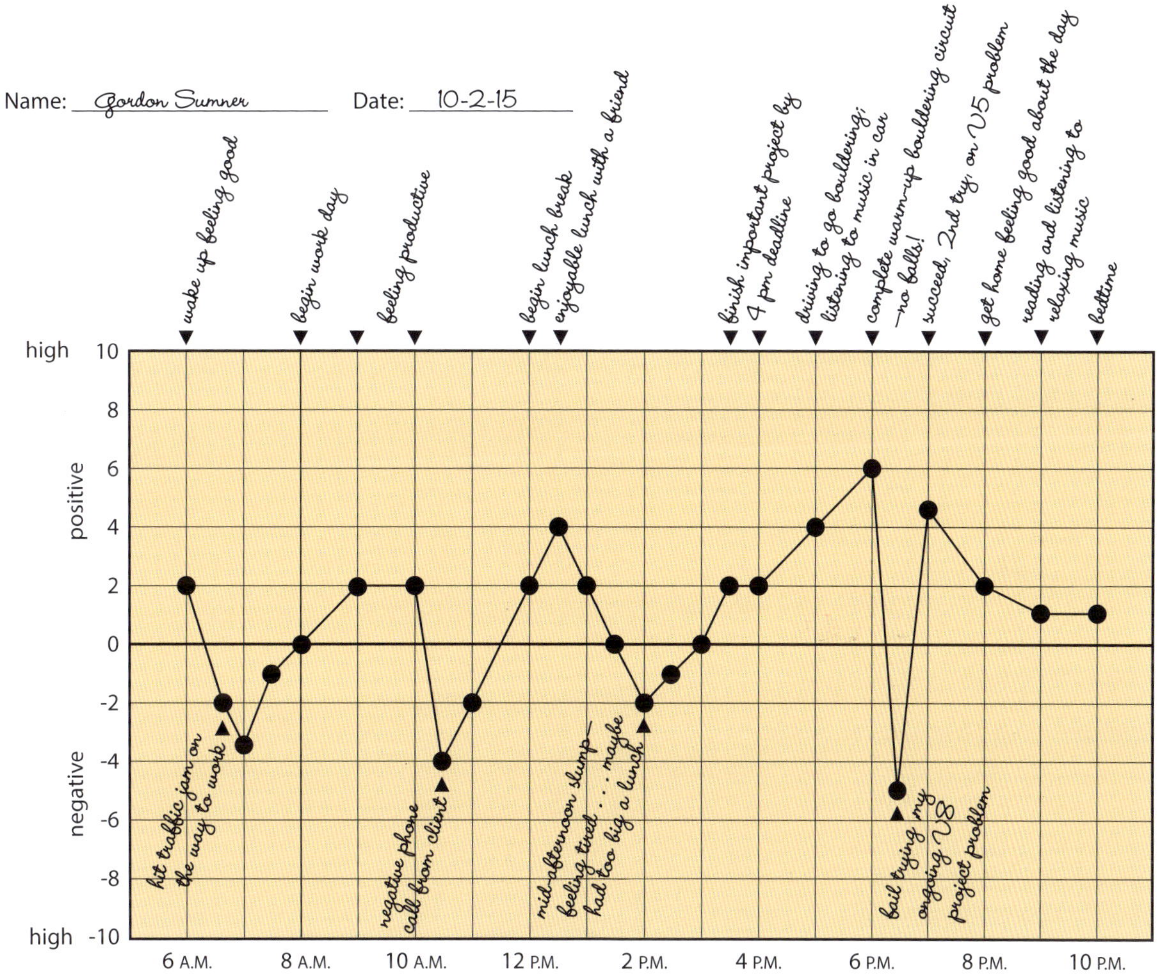

Sample chart of energy–emotion levels throughout the day, including notes of triggers or events that effected an energy–emotion change.

such as striving to avoid negative triggers. Likewise, you may be able to see what charges up your energy level (and when) and what type of things make it tank. If you can't avoid negative triggers, it's vital that you know how to turn your state around. Below we'll discuss ways to modify your emotional state.

It's also beneficial to track how your state changes over the course of a day at the crags, and especially during an attempt of a hard boulder problem or route. While you certainly can't write down your score while on a route, you can mentally score yourself by simply asking, What quadrant am I in?

Before you can change your state, you must first determine the optimal state for the present moment. Of course, beginning in a positive emotional state is always ideal, but the optimal magnitude of your arousal (energy level) will vary depending on the type of task you are involved in. For instance, a low-positive (Quadrant IV) state is ideal for taking a test or meeting with your boss, while a high-positive (Quadrant II) is best for working out at the gym or playing a high-intensity sport. In climbing, it's almost always best to be in the low-energy, positive-emotion quadrant—creative thinking, learning, and fine motor skills all demand a relaxed, positive state. The exception would be when psyching up for a vicious boulder problem or a short, powerful sport route. In these cases, a high-energy, positive state is ideal.

Changing Your Emotional State

You can rapidly change your emotional state by leveraging the known relationships among the mind, emotions, and body (see figure 3.1). Just as your emotions exert an influence over your mind and body, you can use your mind and body to influence your emotions. In negative people the process tends to be reactive and runs itself, whereas happy, productive people are skilled at using their mind and body to produce positive emotions. So if you make it habit to carry your body in a positive way (good posture, head up, smiling) and think in a positive way (grateful for what you have, reliving only good memories, focusing on future goals), you will feel positive and, in fact, be a generally happy and successful person. This is one of the most powerful distinctions in this book—live it!

You should now have a good sense of the things you can do to shift into a more positive state. Physiologically, you can take on a more extended posture and crack a smile, you can jump up and down or do anything physical, you can pump your fist in the air and exclaim "Yeah!" All these physical things will effect a rapid change in your emotions—try it now! Mentally, you can replay great events or climbs from the past, think about all you've accomplished in your life, ponder your good health or your fortune to have been born in a first-world country (where you can actually engage in a luxury activity like climbing), or visualize the medium- and long-term goals that excite you.

Tips for Optimizing Your Emotions

1. Regularly tune into your thoughts and self-talk. Evaluate what you are hearing. What quadrant are you in?
2. Supplant negative thinking with positive, productive thoughts. Direct solution-oriented thinking and dwell on your goals.
3. Use your body to change your state. Roll your shoulders back, take a few deep belly breaths, crack a big smile and laugh.
4. Leverage your emotional resources by reviewing past successes. In your mind's eye, vividly relive past great climbs and other amazing life events—feel the positive emotions charge you up in the present moment.

Hopefully you now recognize that either your emotions are controlling you or you are in control of your emotions. Happy people and peak performers (in sports and life) are those who are able to control their emotions and adjust their arousal level on demand. In our frantic society, and when participating in a potentially high-stress sport such as climbing, these emotion-modulating skills are invaluable. Strive to monitor your position in the matrix throughout the day and optimize your state when needed, and you'll discover a new quality of climbing and living!

Dealing with Fear

As I stated in *How to Climb 5.12*, "the 'no fear' mentality is for buffoons, beer-guzzling frat boys, and couch potatoes." In climbing, *reasonable fears* keep you alive long enough to realize your potential and to send a long lifetime's worth of stellar routes. For example, fear of taking a groundfall compels you to seek good protection on the lead and to drag a rope in the first place.

It's *unreasonable fears* that derail performance. Things such as fear of falling on a well-protected route, fear of physical discomfort, fear of failure, and fear of embarrassment must all be eliminated if you are to climb your best. There are also preclimb fears such as I might be too tall, or too short, or too weak to do the climb, which—left unchecked—give birth to reality.

Finally, there are subconscious, preprogrammed fears that are the root of many of the "dumb things" that seem to just happen. Have you ever fallen after the crux when the route is in the bag? Or have you slipped off a large hold or botched a wired sequence even though you felt in control? It may be that such mistakes are the result of unchallenged inner fears, not lack of ability. The key is to deal with your fears head-on, and not to run from them. Use the following exercise to identify and analyze your common fears. As the fears reveal themselves, use logic and reason to specifically counter each. If no logical counter is evident, however, the fear may be reasonable and worth heeding.

IDENTIFY AND ANALYZE YOUR COMMON CLIMBING FEARS

Start by writing down recurrent fears that regularly hurt your performance. If you can't think of any on the spot, go for a climb and pay special attention to every preclimb thought and while-you-climb concern. List your fears down the left column, and then write an assessment of each fear in the space to the right. Use logic and reason to counter each fear. Your fraudulent fears should be easy to counter. If you identify a fear that is real and useful (for saving your neck), however, then you want to write down what action you can take to mitigate the fear.

Dealing with fear is an ongoing process since our fears are always changing. Review each poor

Fear:	***Assessment:***

performance and identify what fear(s) may have contributed to your difficulties. To help you with this analysis, here's a primer on four basic climbing fears: fear of falling, fear of pain, fear of failure, and fear of embarrassment.

Fear of Falling

Fear of falling is inherent to climbing. Interestingly enough, it's not really falling that we fear but not knowing what the fall will be like. This explains why your first fall on a route is the scariest, while subsequent falls are often much less stressful. Beginners probably need some hands-on proof that falls can be safe. The best way for a would-be leader to gain trust in the system is by taking some intentional falls. Find a steep climb with bomber protection, use a good rope (and double-check your knot and buckle) and belayer, and then take a few practice falls. Start off with two-foot falls and build up to about twelve-footers (with the gear just below your feet). A more experienced climber fearful of falling on an upcoming on-sight climb can counter the fear during the preclimb warm-up. The tactic here is to mentally replay some past inconsequential falls and to believe fully that falls on this climb will be no different (if that is indeed the case—some falls are obviously deadly, and only a fool would ignore that possibility).

Fear of Pain

When pushing your limits, fear of pain can become a critical weakness. It causes you to give up long before your body has reached its physical limitations. The pain of climbing a continuously strenuous route is akin to that of running a mile at full speed—it freaking hurts! Fortunately, the pain is brief, and perseverance pays big dividends. Decide to push yourself a bit further into the discomfort zone each time you're on a hard route. Soon your pain threshold will be redefined, as will your limits on the rock. Ultimately, you'll advance into the realm of an elite climber when you become comfortable with being uncomfortable.

Fear of Failure

This deep-seated fear is often instilled during childhood when almost every action is classified by our family, teachers, and friends as either a success or a failure. We've all had childhood situations where the fear of failure was so gripping that we became immobilized and time seemed to stop. Fortunately, adults generally don't react quite this intensely, but it's still common for us to imagine all the bad things that could possibly go wrong. Once triggered, these negative thoughts can snowball and, more often than not, bring meaningful action to a halt and, in the worst case, become a self-fulfilling prophecy.

In climbing, fear of failure causes you to hold back. As your attack on a route becomes less aggressive than required, you'll find yourself second-guessing sequences in the midst of doing them, your breathing will become shallow, and you'll begin to overgrip the rock. You may even fall prey to paralysis by analysis.

Eliminate fear of failure in one of three ways. First, focus on what is *probable* instead of what is *possible*. Sure, it's human nature to always consider the worst-case scenario, but this almost never comes to pass. Counter these thoughts by considering what is probable and realistic based on past experiences.

The second way to nix this fear is to focus all your attention on the process of climbing, instead of pondering the possible outcomes. Concentrate on the things immediate to your performance—precise foot placements, relaxing your grip, moving quickly onto the next rest position, and so on. Your limited supply of energy is too valuable to waste worrying about how high you will climb or the eventual results. As William Levinson points out in his book *The Way of Strategy*, "To succeed, we must not care if we fail."

Along this same line, you must adopt the attitude that *It's okay to fall* (assuming a safe fall) and that *Falling won't bother me. I'll just get back up and give it another go.* By willingly accepting this fate (if it should even happen), you totally dissolve the fear of failure that handcuffs so many climbers. Therefore, by being okay with falling, it's less likely you will. This simple idea is one of the most powerful in this book.

Fear of Embarrassment

Finally, there is fear of embarrassment and being dissed. Get over this now or you'll never fully enjoy climbing, or reach your potential. Realize that occasional bad-performance days are inevitable. Instead of trying to avoid them, simply accept that they happen, analyze why they happened, then bury them. With this attitude you will be free to try chancy moves and risk an occasional mistake. In the long run you'll often look like a hero, but never like a zero. Surely this is better than embracing the critics and accepting mediocrity all the time.

Tips for Managing Fear

1. Analyze your fears to determine if they are real or imagined. Take action to mitigate the risk(s) associated with your legitimate fears.
2. Overcome imagined fears with reason—know that these phantom fears are bogus. Redirect your thinking in productive ways, and resolve to dismiss all other illusionary fears that might surface.
3. Focus on the process of climbing, and detach from the possible outcomes. Let the climb unfold one move at a time.
4. Predetermine that you will accept failure should it happen. Recognize that you are not defined by your successes or failures; however, you are defined by the way you react to success and failure.
5. For a more in-depth study of fear—and many more powerful strategies for overcoming fear—check out my book *Maximum Climbing: Mental Training for Peak Performance and Optimal Experience.*

Don't forget, your friends know how good a climber you are, and they won't think any worse of you because of a poor performance. Anyone else critical of you really doesn't matter. Work on improving your self-confidence, and don't let the criticisms of others invade your thoughts.

In the end, embrace the attitude that there are no failures, only results. The results might not be ideal, but they do in fact contain important clues for improvement—do not overlook these guideposts for future success! The bottom line: By challenging your fears and doubling your exposure to fearful situations, you will double your rate of improvement and learn to excel in the most difficult and stressful situations.

Relaxation Training and Centering

More than ever before, there are a multitude of things in our lives that can result in high levels of stress. Our jobs, relationships, possessions, even driving to the crag can trigger a stress response such as muscular tension or negative thoughts. Interestingly, it's not the events or things in our lives that actually cause the stress, but instead our reaction to them. Knowing this, you are empowered to control your reactions to everything you experience and, in turn, regulate the total amount of stress in your life.

Recognizing that an event or situation is causing you to become stressed is the first step toward controlling its effects. Foster an acute awareness of your tension levels by regularly asking yourself things like *How do I feel?* or *Are there any growing pockets of muscular tension?* Make such tension checks a regular part of your day. For instance, do a quick check of your tension and stress levels every hour, and especially before any type of event that requires an optimal physiological state (a big meeting or hard climb). Keep an eye out for telltale signs of building tension such as a clenched jaw, overgripping a pencil or the steering wheel, or tightness and burning in the muscles of your neck, shoulders, or back.

On the rock, tension reveals itself in overgripping of holds, nervously muscling through a crux move, or a general lack of fluid motion. Again, your goal is to recognize and tone down the tension when it begins; otherwise it will rapidly snowball and sabotage your performance. This, in fact, is a common cause of blowing a sequence you thought you had wired, or falling off a route that should be well within your ability. By killing your economy of movement, building tension and stress may very well kill your performance. And it's probably been happening for so long that you don't even recognize its negative effects on your climbing.

The antidote to tension is, of course, relaxation. Following are two highly effective relaxation strategies as well as a great on-the-rock centering sequence that I call the ANSWER. Experiment with all three, and try to incorporate their use throughout your daily activities. In a short time you will become a master of stress and find yourself feeling much more relaxed—and also climbing harder, thanks to an increase in apparent strength (a result of reduced tension in the antagonist muscles and elimination of overgripping).

Progressive Relaxation

In the early 1940s American physician Edmund Jacobson developed a technique known as progressive relaxation, because he felt that by fully relaxing the muscles, you would in turn relax the mind (Garfield 1984). He found that relaxation could be best learned by deliberately tensing and relaxing specific muscle groups (see the "Progressive Relaxation Sequence" exercise that follows). This process results in a sharpened awareness of tension levels in the different parts of your body, and the ability to release the tension on demand. In time, you will be able to discern even small increases in muscular tension and act to immediately eliminate the tension before there's any degradation in performance.

PROGRESSIVE RELAXATION SEQUENCE

Perform the following procedure at least once a day. I find it most useful during a midday break, as part of a long rest period at the crag, or the last thing before falling asleep. Initially, the process will take about fifteen minutes. With practice, you'll be able to move quickly through the sequence and reach a state of complete relaxation in less than five minutes. Concentrate on flexing only the muscle(s) specified in each step. This is an invaluable skill you will find very handy when using the differential relaxation and ANSWER Sequences that are discussed later.

1. Go to a quiet location and sit or lie in a comfortable position.
2. Close your eyes and take five deep belly breaths. Inhale slowly through your nose to a slow, silent count to five, and then gradually exhale through your mouth to a slow, silent eight-count.
3. Keeping your eyes closed and maintaining slow, relaxed breathing, tense the muscles in your right lower leg for five seconds. Feel the tension in your right foot and calf muscles, then let go and relax the muscles completely. Compare the difference in sensation between the tense and relaxed states. Repeat this process with the left lower leg. With both of your lower legs now relaxed, think, My feet and lower legs feel warm and light. You should now feel your lower legs enter a deep state of relaxation.
4. Next, perform the same sequence in the muscles of the upper leg (one leg at a time). Tense the muscles in your upper leg for five seconds, then relax them. After doing this with both legs, finish up by thinking, My upper legs feel warm and light. Feel all tension dissolve as your upper legs drop into deep relaxation.
5. Repeat this process in your hands and lower arms. Begin by tensing the muscles below your right elbow by making a tight fist for five

seconds, then relax these muscles completely. Repeat this with the left hand and forearm, and conclude with the thought, My hands and forearms feel warm and light.

6. Repeat this procedure on the muscles in the upper arm.
7. Next, shift the focus to the many muscles of the torso (including the chest, abdominal, back, and shoulder areas). Repeat the process exactly.
8. Conclude with the muscles of the face and neck.
9. You should now be in a deep state of relaxation (possibly you will have fallen asleep by now). Mentally scan yourself from head to toe for any isolated pockets of remaining tension—if you discover any, visualize the tension escaping the muscle like air from a balloon.
10. At this point you can open your eyes and return to work or climbing with a renewed sense of calm and focus. Or you can leverage this relaxed state by performing some mind programming—visualization of the process of reaching some goal or the act of climbing some project route.

Using Differential Relaxation to Enhance Performance

Differential relaxation is used in active situations where you wish to relax any muscle(s) not needed for the task at hand. I find this skill especially useful in regaining an optimal state while hanging out and chalking at rest positions on the rock. I scan for unnecessary muscular contractions or pockets of tension and, with a few deep belly breaths, visualize the tension draining from the muscle like air escaping from a balloon. Try this next time you go climbing.

Many climbers shortchange themselves and reduce their apparent strength because of undue tension in muscles not needed for upward motion or stability. Unwanted contraction of the antagonist muscles or over-contraction of the prime movers interferes with even the simplest movements and wastes a tremendous amount of energy. Observe how climbers who try too hard or get gripped on a route become extremely rigid and mechanical, maybe even while moving through an easy sequence. Instead of using their muscles optimally, they're pitting one muscle against another, resulting in stress, fatigue, and premature failure. Conversely, the best climbers actively control undue tension (it's a mainly unconscious process in top climbers), move with grace and fluidity, and maximize economy of motion and energy use. As masters of differential relaxation, they can move smooth and fast like a Porsche but still get the high "miles-per-gallon" of a Honda.

Skill in differential relaxation comes with increased sensitivity to various degrees of relaxation and tension—something you will learn quickly through daily use. Practice by releasing tension in unused muscles while in the midst of common everyday activities like driving your car, sitting at your desk, working around home, or even lying down for a quick nap. Scan your body for pockets of tension or any contracting muscles that aren't critical for the task at hand. For me, it's typically tension in the shoulders, a clenched jaw (if I'm concentrating intensely), or unnecessary fidgeting by my feet.

On the rock, strive for acute awareness of rising tension so you can nip it in the bud before it results in a drop-off in performance. It's my practice to perform these "quality assurance checks" at all rest positions. Sometimes I recognize things like general tightness in my shoulders, unnecessary tension in my legs, or a little more contraction of my arm and forearm muscles than is needed to stick the grip or body position. Differential relaxation allows me to correct these problems almost instantly—although I find centering and the ANSWER Sequence to be beneficial in these situations as well.

THE ANSWER SEQUENCE

Perform the ANSWER Sequence before and during each climb and in everyday situations where you need to control tension, anxiety, and focus. Initially this six-step procedure will take a few minutes to perform. With practice you'll be able to go through the sequence in about ten seconds—perfect for use at marginal rest positions where getting centered could make the difference between success and failure.

A—AWARENESS OF RISING TENSION, ANXIETY, OR NEGATIVE THOUGHTS.

Acute awareness of unfavorable mental and physical changes is fundamental to optimal performance. It takes a conscious effort to turn your thoughts away from the outer world toward your inner world. Peak performers habitually make these tension checks every few minutes, so they can nix any negative changes before they snowball out of control. Make this your goal.

N—NORMALIZE BREATHING.

In climbing, your breathing should be deep, relaxed, and regular. Unfortunately, many climbers breathe unevenly during hard sequences, thus creating tension and degrading performance. Your goal is to foster deep, even breathing throughout the climb. The exception is "holding your breath" (Valsalva Maneuver) to create core tension during a hard move—a frequent requisite in doing hard boulder problems or sport climbs.

S—SCAN FOR SPECIFIC AREAS OF MUSCULAR TENSION.

In this step you perform a tension check. Scan all your muscles in a quick sweep to locate pockets of tightness. Commonly tight areas are the forearms (are you overgripping?), shoulders, upper back, chest, abdominals, and calves. The best way to relax a specific muscle is to consciously contract that muscle for a few seconds, then relax it and visualize the tension draining from it like air from a balloon (the differential relaxation technique).

W—WAVE OF RELAXATION.

Upon completing the tension check above, take a single deep breath and feel a wave of relaxation wash from your head to your toes.

E—ERASE THOUGHTS OF PAST EVENTS (AND POSSIBLE FUTURE OUTCOMES) AND FOCUS ON THE PRESENT.

This step involves freeing your mind from the ball-and-chain of undesirable past events. There is no benefit to pondering the last failed attempt or the heinous sequence you just barely fought through. Let go of the past and do not ponder the future—thoughts of the past and future are enemies of excellence in the present. Refocus on and engage the present moment.

R—RESET POSTURE AND FLASH A SMILE.

It's amazing how much positive energy you can generate simply by resetting your posture and flashing a smile. This final step of the ANSWER Sequence will leave you in a peak performance state and ready to climb into the zone. Trust your skills, have fun, and let the outcome take care of itself.

Getting Centered

Centering is a simple, effective means of maintaining (or regaining) complete control of your mind and body as you head up a difficult climb or into competition. When you're centered, you feel balanced, relaxed, and confident. Conversely, being out of center is characterized by feelings of imbalance, tension, awkward movement, and sometimes even growing stress and anxiety. And since it takes just one botched move, one piece of gear to pop out, or one burst of adrenaline to knock you way out of center, it's essential that you are aware of this dynamic and able to respond quickly with countermeasures.

The ANSWER Sequence is a powerful means for returning yourself to center in just a few seconds. The sequence involves deliberately redirecting

Tips for Controlling Tension and Anxiety

- Practice progressive and differential relaxation to develop the ability to relax individual muscles on demand.
- Strive for constant awareness of growing tension and anxiety. Take a tension check at each rest on a climb and intermittently throughout the day.
- Target relaxation in antagonist muscles—this will improve your climbing economy and enhance flow and fluidity of movement.
- While you climb, employ the ANSWER Sequence at each rest position to regain your center and optimal performance state.

your thoughts inward for a moment (usually at a rest on a climb) to modulate your breathing, level of muscle tension, posture, and mental attitude. Make its use as regular and automatic as chalking up, and you'll find yourself climbing more efficiently and consistently.

Visualization Training

Let's start off with an example of visualization. Sit back, relax, and vividly imagine the following scene as if it were a movie playing out before your eyes.

> You are attempting to redpoint a route you have worked on before. You have just successfully climbed to the rest position that precedes the route's crux sequence. You are relaxed, calm, and confident as you shake out and rechalk. You feel a cool breeze blow across your body, and it seems to enhance the light, centered feeling you already possess. You gently grip the starting hold of the sequence, a sharp, positive fingertip edge. With steady breathing, you flash a smile and continue climbing.
>
> You match hands and pull the fingertip edge to your chest. You then high-step your right foot onto a tiny, crescent-shaped flake. You've hit it just right—it feels bomber. You rock over that glued right foot, spot, and then grab a matchbook side-pull edge with your right hand. You flag your left leg across and below your high right foot to shift your center of mass over the right foot. You then extend off the right foot with a smooth, steady motion. Your left hand reaches up to snag a two-finger pocket—it feels solid. You move your left foot up to a high smear on a small dish hold and, with relaxed breathing, take aim on the final lunge. Then, with your mind locked on to the next hold, you throw the lunge and easily latch on to the mini bucket hold that's been so elusive. You clip the anchors and feel the rush of having ticked this personal best route.

This sequence exemplifies a fundamental and important exercise used by all the world's top athletes. Although similar to the mental rehearsals performed by some climbers, visualization goes beyond the simple task of reviewing route sequences. As in the above example, visualization involves making and playing a detailed mental movie, one with touch, sound, color, and all the kinesthetic feel of doing the moves. These mental movies enhance your climbing by helping to hardwire sequences (moves, body positions, and "feel"), increasing memory, and fortifying confidence. For this reason, use of visualization is as important to your success as your use of climbing shoes and a chalk bag. Don't leave the ground without doing it!

Many studies have shown that the brain is not always capable of distinguishing between something that actually happened and something that was vividly imagined (Kubistant 1986). (Déjà vu is such an experience—you can't always recall if the clear mental image that just surfaced is an actual memory or simply something you've thought about or dreamed.) Therefore, repeated visualization can trick the mind into thinking you've been there and done that before. Think of these mental movies as a blueprint for future actions—with this perspective, you should understand why visualization must be as detailed and accurate as possible. Any bad coding (wrong moves) or fuzzy detail (uncertain sequences) may lead to a botched sequence or fall when you climb the route for real.

Types of Visualization

There are two primary modes of visualization: disassociated and associated. Disassociated visualization provides an "on-TV" perspective, where you see yourself climbing from an observer's point of view. This mode of visualization is best for reviewing some past poor performance that you hope to improve upon. As a detached observer, you can replay the movie and objectively view the mistakes or falls without reliving the possibly unhappy emotions of the situation.

Associated visualization provides a "through-your-own-eyes" perspective and thus triggers small neurological reactions as if you were doing the climb, as well as the feel and emotion of the movie you are playing. This makes associated visualization ideal for preprogramming some future ascent. As discussed above, repeated playing of a highly detailed, positive mental movie helps trick the subconscious mind into thinking you've done the climb before. Just make sure you are using the associated, not disassociated, perspective when visualizing some future event.

DISASSOCIATED VISUALIZATION

If you are new to the practice of visualization, I suggest you begin with a simple, nonclimbing example. Go to a quiet location, sit or lie down comfortably, and relax. Using an observer's point of view (disassociated), play a mental movie of the following scene as it might appear in your apartment or home.

> Visualize yourself sitting on the couch and watching TV. Note the clothes you are wearing in the scene. See yourself get up from the couch, walk over to the refrigerator, and open it. See yourself reaching in and grabbing a can of soda, then watch yourself close the fridge. See yourself opening the can as you begin to walk back toward the couch. Note the way you are walking and observe the exact instant that you see yourself open the can. Now watch yourself sit back down on the couch and take a sip of the soda.

In this disassociated example you watched the scene play out before your eyes, but you did not feel or sense, in any way, what it was like to go get the soda and drink it. Reserve this perspective for reviewing negative events from the past, climbing or nonclimbing, and for route finding, imagining possible sequences, and risk management. Gather the basic information you need to improve your performance or do the climb, and then engage in associated visualization to preprogram the actual moves for a successful future event.

ASSOCIATED VISUALIZATION

Now let's reshoot the mental movie of the at-home scene from the associated point of view. This time you will live the scene through your own eyes. Feel the action play out in your imagination just as if you were acting out the scene for real. Again, sit back, relax, and picture this scene playing out in real-life detail.

> As you sit on the couch, you laugh at the opening skit of a rerun episode of The Office. You decide to go get a soda from the fridge, so you get up and begin walking toward the kitchen. Look around the room at the various pieces of furniture (or pictures on the wall) you pass on your way to the fridge. Enter the kitchen and feel your arm tug the refrigerator door open. Feel the cool air rush out and chill your face. As you reach into the fridge for the soda, notice the colors and design of the can, then sense the cold, damp feel of the can in your hand. Now feel your arm slam the door shut and hear the sound it makes in closing. Conclude the scene by tasting the soda as you gulp it down—what flavors do you taste?

This example reveals the explicit detail you should try to build into your associated visualization. Granted, it will take some practice to develop Steven Spielberg–like detail into your mental movies, but that's the goal. Commit to making a short "film" for all your project routes, and don't hesitate to reshoot or edit the mental movie as you gain new information or beta for the route. Quality mind programming will improve the quality of your real-life performances. Guaranteed!

Uses of Visualization

I hope you now recognize that visualization is an immensely powerful tool that can be used to enhance performance in all aspects of your life. I'm sure you use simple visualization every day, maybe without even knowing it. For example, when you think about the best way to drive across town, I'm sure you see the key turns or landmarks along the way in your mind's eye beforehand. Visualization is also used "effectively" by people who worry a lot—part of their worry ritual is wild visualization of some future event that may or may not happen to them (or some loved one). This type of negative visualization is most painful and depressing when done from an associated perspective. Such negative visualization is pathological, since you are putting yourself through the pain of some future event that may never happen.

Some climbers become consumed in the same types of negative moviemaking of future events. For instance, if you visualize yourself failing on a route or in competition, you not only preprogram this possible outcome but also destroy your self-confidence in the process. To avoid this, it's vital that you visualize only positive events and ideal outcomes when you project into the future in the associated state. Switch to the disassociated mode if you need to visualize things (from a risk management perspective) that might go wrong—say, on an on-sight lead. See from the on-TV view the possible falls you could take and what risks might be involved in the ascent. Described below are several settings where you can use visualization to improve your safety and mind-set (among other things), as well as the chances of the ideal outcome coming true.

PREPROGRAMMING A REDPOINT ASCENT

Since you've been on the route before, you could begin with disassociated visualization of your last attempt. See yourself climbing the route and note what things need to be corrected or refined for the next attempt. Now use the associated perspective to create a movie, as seen through your own eyes, of the perfect ascent you plan to make. Imagine all the important aspects of doing the route, including the crux moves, gear placements or clips, rest positions, and such. Create the feel of doing the moves as well as the feeling of being relaxed and centered as you move into the crux. Make the movie positive and perfect in every way, and always conclude with the feeling of reaching the top.

PREPARING FOR AN ON-SIGHT ASCENT

Visualization is invaluable when applied to a climb you've never been on before. Since you have no firsthand experience, it will be very hard to create an accurate movie from the associated perspective. Therefore, you'll want to spend most of your time visualizing from a disassociated perspective.

After studying the climb from below, create images or a movie of yourself climbing the route from the on-TV perspective. See yourself dropping in gear at the obvious placements as well as hanging out at what appear to be good rest positions. As described above, you will want to visualize any hazards unique to this climb—where a lead fall might be dangerous, what you can do to minimize the risk, and so forth. Also, if you can see enough detail from the ground, consider creating two movies of possible sequences through the crux. This way, if you get up there and find that one will obviously not work, you can call up the second movie and continue climbing without delay.

You might finish up your visualization by moving into the associated state and trying to imagine what you might feel and see as you climb the sequence you came up with from the disassociated perspective. This is not always possible but would be beneficial.

PREPARING FOR COMPETITION

In competition climbing, good visualization skills might mean the difference between winning and finishing in the middle of the pack. Depending on the competition format, you will want to employ the redpoint and on-sight visualization strategies discussed above. Since many events allow only a brief preview period, you will only be able to create a "rough-cut" movie, including the basic route path, location of the obvious rests, and whatever you can glean about the moves or sequence. Even if you can't decipher a sequence (or if you didn't get a route preview), you can still take a mental picture of the wall and project yourself climbing with grace and confidence to the top. Most important, strive to eliminate any self-defeating images that might cross your mind in the hours and minutes leading up to your ascent of the wall.

"CLIMBING" INJURED OR TIRED

If you climb for enough years, you will at some point likely find yourself laid up due to some type of injury. Whether you are out for a few weeks due to a finger injury or out for the season with a more serious problem, you can still keep climbing in your mind's eye! While this may not sound like much fun, it is an effective way to maintain your knowledge of a sequence on your project route. Vivid, associated visualization has been shown to cause low-level neuromuscular activity that helps enhance motor learning (Feltz 1983) and maintain the feel of performing the skill.

You can also use this effect to your advantage next time you pump out while working a route. Instead of thrashing around on the climb for the umpteenth time (and risking injury), call it a day and spend the time pumping a few more "mental laps" on the route. This will help solidify your knowledge of the sequence without the extra physical strain and risk of injury.

Tips for Enhancing Performance with Visualization

- Use disassociated visualization (observer's perspective) for route finding, imagining possible sequences, risk management, and to review failed attempts.
- Use associated visualization to mentally climb the route (climber's perspective). Feel the ascent evolve, including all physical movements and thought processes. The goal is to mentally practice—virtual experience!—all aspects of doing the climb.
- Make associated visualization as bright and detailed as possible. Avoid any negative visualization.
- To get the best results, engage in visualization in a quiet area. Relax and don't rush through it—your goal is to visualize the complete ascent from bottom to top with no interruptions.

Creating Laserlike Focus

The ability to narrow and maintain focus is a crucial sports skill, especially in an activity like climbing where elements of danger exert a constant pull diverting the focus from the move at hand. Widely used, but often misunderstood in the context of a climber's lexicon, focus is a laserlike concentration of mental energy aimed at the most important task at any particular instant. Since every movement in climbing possesses a different most-important task, it's vital to be able to redirect your focus, in an instant, to the finger or foot placement most critical at that moment.

Think of focus as a narrowing of your concentration, much like a zoom lens on a camera. At any given moment you must zoom in on the single task most critical to your performance—toeing down on a small pocket, pulling on a manky finger jam, or shifting your center of mass to just the right balance point. Think about anything else and you may fail at this critical task and fall.

The most difficult part of focusing is learning to zoom in and out quickly from a pinpoint focus to a more wide-angle perspective. For example, a quarterback starts a pass play with a broad focus (when in search for an open receiver), but he instantly zooms in on a single player as he delivers the pass. In climbing, you have to do much the same thing—use a broad focus when hanging out looking for the next hold, then zoom in tight as you reach toward the hold and latch on to it. Similarly, you must zoom in tight when high-stepping on a dime edge, locking off and making a long reach, or floating a deadpoint. If you focus on anything else—your gear, your belayer, your pain, or spectators on the ground—you may as well add a ten-pound weight to your back. Poor focus makes hard moves harder, maybe even impossible.

Practicing Focus

Detailed below is a practice drill for developing focus and a preclimbing strategy for gathering focus in preparation to climb. The Singular Focus Drill is best used when you are climbing on toprope and well below your maximum grade. The Pinpointing Your Focus for a Climb exercise can be used before attempting any climb, though it's especially effective when preparing to start up a difficult route.

SINGULAR FOCUS DRILL

The best time to work on your focus is when climbing a route a couple of grades below your maximum ability. Whether you're at a gym or the crag, on toprope or lead, attempt to climb a whole route by focusing solely on one aspect of movement.

For instance, try to do a route with your complete focus on just hand placements. Find the best way to grab each hold, use the minimum amount of grip strength necessary to hang on, and feel how your purchase changes as you pull on the hold. Place as little focus as is safely possible on other areas such as your feet, balance, belayer, and the like. For now, let these areas take care of themselves—allow your intuitive sense to determine where your feet go and how your balance should shift.

Chances are you'll find this exercise quite difficult. Your thoughts will naturally wander to other tasks or even be directed to distractions on the ground. If this occurs, simply redirect your focus to the predetermined task—in this case the handholds. It is this process of becoming aware of your lost focus and returning it to the critical task that you are after. Sharpened awareness of lost focus is tantamount to gaining control of focus.

Repeat this exercise regularly but change the focus (onto, say, foot placements or weight shifts) each time. Work on increasing the length of time you can maintain a singular focus—this helps build mental endurance. As you become more skilled, convert this singular focus drill into a dynamic focus drill where your focus constantly shifts to the most critical task at any moment. The goal is to be able to shift your focus quickly among the various tasks involved in doing a route, like the flickering beams of a laser light show.

With practice, the process of directing and redirecting focus will become largely subconscious. On the rare occasions when your focus does wander away from the task of climbing, your well-trained mind will instantly recognize this loss and redirect the focus onto the climb. In this way, becoming constantly engaged and automatic on the climb helps in achieving the highly desired flow state.

Enemies of Concentration

The ability to maintain concentration and focus is a principal factor that separates the best from the rest. Peak performers are less likely to be distracted by irrelevant stimuli or to succumb to worry and outcome-oriented thoughts—they exude confidence and possess a remarkable ability to maintain focus and stay on mission despite distractions, criticism, setbacks, fatigue, or current struggles. So in your quest to improve concentration—and enhance performance—it's helpful to understand the enemies of concentration and the common targets of misplaced focus. Following are six common concentration killers and tips for avoiding them.

1. **Focusing on mechanics of well-learned skills.** Skills and climbing moves that you possess high competence in (autonomous learning stage) should be turned over to the preconscious mind. Focusing on execution of well-learned movements often results in mechanical, lower-efficiency movement and diverts concentration from other task-relevant targets. Therefore, on all but the most cruxy or tricky moves, you're best to focus on properly engaging the foot- and handholds (and the move sequence) and allow the mechanics of climbing to take care of themselves.
2. **Dwelling on internal feelings and sensations of fatigue.** While you must monitor internal conditions by occasionally turning your focus inward, dwelling on such internal feelings will rob external focus and inhibit performance. A common trait of hardman (and -woman) climbers is the ability to dissociate from the fatigue and pain of an exhausting workout or climb. It's a fact that in focusing on the strain and deepening fatigue during a hard climb, you magnify these feelings and open the door to powerful stopping thoughts. Dissociating from such non-injury-producing "good pain" and dismissing phantom stopping thoughts empowers you to transcend previous limitations and achieve the uncommon.
3. **Entertaining nonproductive self-talk.** Vocal and subvocal self-talk is an inherent and almost ever-present feature of our conscious mind; however, the nature and quality of this self-talk is not always in our favor. Negative self-talk is a powerful concentration and performance killer because it directs attention inward to fretful or fearful thoughts. Therefore, it's essential that you direct positive, productive self-talk that helps maintain focus, aids execution, and sustains motivation. Strive to direct positive self-talk in all you do, and it will become a powerful ally in your toughest times.
4. **Focusing on the past.** The essence of effective concentration in sport is being fully engaged in the action of the moment. If you look into the rearview mirror and engage in thoughts of past failures or other irrelevant events, it will quickly diminish or derail your performance. So in engaging the vertical extreme, it's essential that you remain in the present and reflect on past experiences only as is briefly necessary in strategic planning and managing risk.
5. **Focusing on the future.** Projecting into the future and pondering a possible performance outcome will thwart task-relevant concentration and impede your performance. Worse yet, in entertaining future-oriented thoughts of failure, you generate pressure and anxiety that makes this unwanted outcome more likely! Controlling concentration and climbing your best therefore demands that you detach from outcome-oriented thinking and engage the moment completely.
6. **Visual and auditory distractions.** We live in an era of ubiquitous distractions, rampant ADD (attention deficit disorder), and almost unlimited

potential for electronic and social engagement. Possessing a quiet, in-the-moment mental state can be exceedingly difficult to attain and maintain if you allow all this interference to reach your brain. The first step to developing better concentrative skills, then, is to endeavor to systematically eliminate distractions in all aspects of your life. In climbing, strive to eliminate possible distractions before you engage the route, and aspire to become a master at blocking out distracting people and sounds as you climb. As a final note, I want to stress that your mental state can benefit greatly by eliminating some of the things that hinder concentration in your nonclimbing hours. What electronics can you turn off (or discard), and what other actions could you take to reduce non-task-relevant stimuli and other distractions? The payoff is the gift of improved mental clarity, concentration, and self-awareness.

Kyle O'Meara focused on sticking the crux of Unbirthday (V6) at the Stone Garden, Uinta Mountains, UT.
SAVANNAH CUMMINS

PINPOINTING YOUR FOCUS FOR A CLIMB

This exercise will gather your focus into a single "beam" and quiet your mind as you get ready to cast off up a climb. Perform it after you've gone through your preclimb ritual and been put on belay.

Stand at the base of the climb, assume an extended posture (shoulders back), close your eyes, and place the fingertips of your dominant hand against the rock face. Your fingertips should be touching the wall lightly (not gripping a hold), and your hand and arm should be completely relaxed. Now take three deep belly breaths, inhaling through your nose to a count of five and exhaling through your mouth to a count of ten. Let a wave of relaxation wash across your body, and then narrow your focus to the tips of your fingers touching the rock. Concentrate singly on the sensation of your fingertips touching the rock—you should begin to feel the thermal energy moving from your fingers to the rock (on rare occasions when the rock is hotter than your body, you will feel thermal energy conducting into your fingertips). Maintain a relaxed, singular focus on the energy exchange between your fingertips and the rock for anywhere from thirty seconds to a minute or two. If your focus ever wanders, simply redirect it to your fingertips. Soon your mind will become completely still: All your attention is pinpointed on the tips of your fingers. On reaching this state, open your eyes and begin climbing.

Using Preclimb Rituals to Create Focus

Preclimb rituals are a powerful way to narrow your focus in the hours and minutes leading up to an ascent. Like a pilot's preflight checklist, a climber's preclimb ritual should consist of every single activity, big or small, that is necessary to ensure a safe, successful journey. For example, my typical preclimb ritual begins with scoping the route to determine the best path and, hopefully, figure out the key moves and rest positions. Next, I perform a few minutes (or more) of mental rehearsal and visualization as I try to feel the moves and preprogram in the sequence. Upon gaining a sense of comfort and knowledge about the route, I put on my shoes and tie in to the rope. I complete my preclimb ritual by taking a few slow, deep breaths, straightening my posture, and cracking a smile in anticipation of the great fun that awaits me. This entire ritual typically takes between five and fifteen minutes (depending on the difficulty and length of the climb), and it leaves me in an ideal state to make my best effort.

Develop your own unique rituals based on what makes you feel most prepared and psyched for a route. Think back to some of your best past performances to gain some clues as to what to include. What did you think and do in preparing for that climb? What did you eat or drink, how did you warm up, and how long did you rest between

Tips for Creating Focus

1. Train focus by using the Singular Focus Drill (page 49) while lead climbing in the gym or toproping outside.
2. Develop a detailed preclimb ritual that includes warming up, scoping the route, analyzing risk, visualizing the ascent, preparing your gear, putting on your shoes, and tying in to the rope. Use this same ritual before every climb and you will consistently create a high level of focus.
3. Use the Pinpointing Your Focus for a Climb exercise (on this page) as your final task before beginning up the route.
4. Strive for process-oriented thought and avoid dwelling on past outcomes or what's ahead. Stay in the moment.
5. If you discover that your focus is scattered, simply acknowledge this and redirect your attention to the move or action at hand. Consider using the Pinpointing Your Focus exercise again.

climbs? Awareness of all the factors—little and big—that lead up to your best performances is a key to being able to reproduce similar results in the future.

Experiment with different rituals and analyze what seems to work best. An effective preclimb ritual doesn't need to be extravagant or long. In fact, a short, concise ritual that quickly gets you prepared and focused to climb is best. Upon developing a ritual that works, stick with it!

Mental Wings Strategies to Enhance Problem Solving and Learning

I conclude this chapter with six mental strategies to enhance your skills at problem solving and learning of a difficult sequence or complex route. Being able to quickly decipher perplexing cruxes while conserving mental and physical energy is a master skill. Learn to utilize these skills effectively and you'll be on your way to becoming a grand master at flashing.

I should add that if you find this chapter on mental training to be enlightening and exciting, due to the huge potential this subject holds for breakthroughs in climbing performance, then do check out my book *Maximum Climbing: Mental Training for Peak Performance and Optimal Experience.* This text presents what I believe you will find to be a fascinating, in-depth study of the many facets of mental training, including dozens of powerful mind-training techniques and climbing strategies. Learn more at www.MaximumClimbing.com.

1. Focus on problem solving, not performance.

One thing I love about working a hard boulder problem or project route is the challenge of studying a complex problem and gradually seeing a beautiful, unique sequence take form. Just like piecing together a puzzle when you were a kid, you can best solve a rock puzzle by remaining focused on the task and having fun regardless of how the long the puzzle takes to complete.

For instance, when working a boulder problem or crux sequence, ponder the beauty of the rock puzzle and feel the joy of being engaged in this challenging process. This disposition will shift you out of the must-not-fail mind-set of frustration and help turn your focus away from the problem and onto finding a solution. Remember, the brain naturally magnifies whatever you focus on. Obviously you want to magnify the possible solution, not the problem, so always be solution oriented.

2. Relax and remain positive.

Both problem solving and motor learning occur most rapidly in a stress- and anxiety-free state. Therefore, controlling tension through deep breathing, positive visualization, and remaining process oriented is crucial for accelerating these processes.

It's also fundamental that you eliminate thoughts of needing to flash the route or having to redpoint the climb this attempt—these are both positions that work against you. By entertaining such needs, you create stress and anxiety that may prevent the very thing you desire. Instead, acknowledge that falling is part of the learning process, and accept each fall as providing a clue for success—so don't ignore it! Predetermine that you will accept a fall (and find the clue) if it happens, and believe completely that success will come with creativity, effort, and patience. In doing so, you create the optimal state for learning and succeeding most quickly.

3. Chunk down the route.

Chunking down a long, hard route into a series of short problems makes the climb less overwhelming and easier to learn. Furthermore, these short problems or chunks can each be viewed as a short-term goal to be reached or accomplished. So, while you may fail for several days on the project as a whole, you will experience short-term success as you solve each of the individual chunks. This sense of success helps keep you energized, positive, and on track to eventually succeed on the route.

When working through the individual chunks, avoid becoming obsessed on any one of them. Beating yourself up on, say, the second chunk of a six-chunk route is self-defeating: Even if you eventually solve this chunk, you'll be too mentally and physically wasted to put in meaningful work on the others. Therefore, it's best to move on to working the next chunk upon the onset of frustration or any judgmental self-talk such as I can't do this or I'll never figure this out. If allowed to burrow into your subconscious, such judgments form the basis for reality. You are much better off solving the rest of the route before returning to the problem section.

Long-term achievement of a formidable goal (where short-term failures are inevitable) demands mental agility as well as the ability to trick yourself into persevering in the face of adversity. Breaking a climb into a series of more manageable chunks and setting yourself up for several small wins is a most effective strategy.

4. Engage both sides of the brain.

You may be familiar with the fact that the brain has two hemispheres—the left hemisphere, which presides over logical, practical, language, mathematical, and related matters, and the right hemisphere, which dominates in creative, artistic, intuitive, situational, and imaginary matters. The majority of people are "left-brained," and even if you aren't, intense situations with lots of information—like climbing—tend to bring the left brain into command. The result is that many climbers leave their right brain on the ground and therefore handicap their problem-solving ability, big time! I can think of countless times I've fallen on routes because I was thinking in a linear fashion and with blinders on that prevented me from finding a key hold, sequence, or rest. (Cut me a break, I'm a scientist, not an artist!)

The right brain is best accessed when you are in a relaxed state (another reason some climbers have a tough time freeing it up). Thus, bringing it into play requires that you resist the Type A behavior of rushing up to a route and quickly going for the send, and instead get comfortable at the base of the climb, warm up slowly, and make a relaxed study of the climb before tying in to the rope. Some severely left-brained people will need to force themselves to think out of the box. Seeing the big picture and imagining all the possible approaches and sequences on a climb is a habit you may need to foster through your own initiative. Your goal should be a balanced approach to problem solving in which you can think logically and practically as well as intuitively and creatively. Being able to create (on demand) and leverage this state is one of the hallmarks of brilliant climbers such as Lynn Hill and Chris Sharma, who can perform at an exceedingly high level in a wide range of styles and settings.

5. Employ multisensory learning.

Everything we learn comes through one of our five senses, and the more senses we use in learning, the faster and easier it becomes. Climbers tend to use primarily the sense of vision before they leave the ground, and feel once they begin to climb. While the senses of smell and taste can't contribute to performance in this sport, the auditory sense can also be a powerful learning tool (Knudson 1997), particularly when faced with a tricky boulder problem or when working to memorize a difficult sequence. Climbers who give names to key holds and moves and then create verbal beta are using this trick. Remembering an obscure sequence of tiny holds by feel or vision can be enhanced with descriptive verbal beta like high-step to the credit card edge, then deadpoint to the potato chip flake. It may sound funny, but it works.

Multisensory learning is a sign of the intelligent climber, so begin to talk yourself through sequences in addition to visualizing and feeling the moves. By talking the talk, you make it easier to climb the climb!

6. Try something ridiculous.

The biggest block to learning is judgment. Self-talk like *Others use this sequence, so that must be the best way*, or discounting a novel or improbable sequence that flashes into your mind without trying it first, is a form of self-sabotage. It's vital that you don't limit yourself this way—your brain doesn't know what you can or cannot do until you tell it. Don't prejudge sequences or your capabilities!

The best problem solvers are both creative and uninhibited. They never hesitate to try a novel solution that's entirely different from the known sequence. You can foster these skills by ignoring the obvious solution—the one that's not currently working for you—and attempting a few completely different, even ridiculous sequences.

Regardless of how improbable a given technique looks—heel hook, undercling, high step, knee bar—don't pass judgment on it until you make a few attempts with that technique. Try a variety of body positions, foot flags, and lunges, and don't ignore less positive holds like Gastons, side pulls, and pinches. Eliminate the seemingly must-use hold—or at least try using it with the opposite hand. Search for unchalked holds that might unlock the sequence, and keep a constant watch for footholds that are off the main line of the route—a single missed foothold or high step can make the difference between "impossible" and "possible."

A common thread running through this chapter is that the mental and technical aspects of climbing are intimately connected. Ahead in chapter 4 you will find an in-depth study of motor learning and performance (how you acquire skill), as well as a primer on the fundamental climbing techniques and several powerful strategies for developing superior technique. Let's climb onward.

Problem-Solving Tips and Success Strategies

1. Focus on problem solving, not performance. View each climb as a puzzle that you will enjoy and learn from, no matter what the outcome.
2. Relax and remain confident. Use the ANSWER Sequence to maintain a relaxed state, and direct positive, productive self-talk to fortify confidence and sustain effective action in the face of difficult climbing.
3. Chunk down the route into manageable sections. Work the most difficult chunks first, then begin linking the sections from the top down.
4. Engage both sides of the brain. Which side is more dominant for you? Strive to bring both creative, intuitive (right brain) and analytical, practical (left brain) power to work for you.
5. Employ multisensory learning by seeing, feeling, and talking yourself through tough sequences.
6. When all else fails, try something ridiculous! Seemingly impossible cruxes often require a trick move or non-intuitive sequence, so experiment with a variety of moves and techniques, no matter how improbable or inappropriate they seem to be.

Steph Davis cruising up Hidden Treasure (5.13), Moab, Utah. CHRIS NOBLE

CHAPTER FOUR

Training Technique and Skill

Despite the unattainable goal of perfection, it's in striving for perfection that you depart on a trajectory toward true mastery.

Moving over stone is the essence of climbing, and therefore no subject can be more central to improving your climbing than this chapter on training skill and developing technique. Despite this, the subject of strength training tends to get all the attention and hype in conversations among climbers, and getting stronger is the most popular topic of magazine articles about climbing performance. In this book mental training and improving skill and strategy come before the subject of strength training because I feel most climbers can benefit greatly from focused training in these areas. If you want to put yourself on the fast track to the higher grades, strive to understand and apply the information contained in this chapter as much as or more than any other chapter in the book. This *will* make you a better climber.

Ironically, the majority of climbers spend little, if any, time on dedicated practice of the vast spectrum of techniques inherent to our sport. With little coaching or guidance available, most climbers unknowingly service their lust for ticking routes by constantly climbing for performance. Of course, becoming proficient (or excellent) at any sport requires focused practice of new skills and work on weaknesses that need improvement. Still, some climbers just don't want to spend time practicing on routes below their maximum grade; others avoid routes that might highlight their weaknesses. Can you imagine a baseball player who never took batting or fielding practice outside of the competition of a nine-inning game, or a quarterback who never threw a pass except on game day?

In this chapter you will learn the three stages of motor learning involved in acquiring a new climbing skill or move, as well as how the brain creates motor programs to execute specific skilled movements and generates "software" that can approximate solutions, on the fly, to unknown moves. This is powerful information if you understand it, because it will empower you to practice more effectively than the mass of climbers, rapidly develop superior technique, and grow to become a true master of rock.

Next I present a primer on the fundamental techniques of efficient climbing movement. Beginning climbers would be wise to read the unabridged coverage of climbing technique presented in my book *Learning to Climb Indoors*. Intermediate and advanced climbers can likewise benefit by reviewing—and, if needed, shoring up their use of—the key techniques detailed in this chapter.

The action portion of this chapter is a series of practice drills that you can use year-round whether you climb indoors or out. Regardless of your tenure in the sport, significant gains in your climbing technique and overall ability will result from a commitment to regularly employing some of these drills in your routine. Apply these drills to accelerate learning (or to unlearn bad habits of movement) of the fundamental techniques outlined in this chapter.

An Overview of Motor Learning and Effective Skill Practice

The importance of motor learning theory to the subject of training for climbing became apparent to me in the early 1990s as a result of conversations with Dr. Mark Robinson and thanks to ongoing input from my wife, Lisa. As an LPGA golf pro (and climber) with an education in the field of kinesiology, Lisa occasionally discussed the methods used by elite golfers to learn very difficult skills (for me, impossible!). At about the same time, Mark Robinson (former 'Gunks hardman and now an orthopedic surgeon in California) turned me on to an excellent text on the subject, *Motor Learning and Performance* by Dr. Richard Schmidt (1991, 2004). Robinson then penned a breakthrough piece on the application of motor learning and performance to climbing for my first climbing book, *Flash Training* (1994). Subsequently I've studied the subject in depth, and I've even had the good fortune to engage Dr. Schmidt (the founder of schema theory) and discuss motor learning and performance (MLP) and its application to climbing. The result is a much-expanded section on MLP in this edition, along with numerous powerful practice strategies to hone your skills and technique.

Types of Skills and Transference of Skill

Skill is defined as the capability to bring about an end result with maximum certainty and minimum time and energy. Climbing skills possess motor and cognitive components. Another important distinction is that between *discrete* and *serial* skills. A discrete climbing skill is a single movement with a definite beginning and end—a mantle, lunge, high step, down pull, lieback, deadpoint, and the like. String many discrete skills together, however, and you now have a more complex skilled action called a serial skill. Like a gymnast performing a routine, a climber must successfully execute specific moves, but also possess the skill to link all the moves into a complete ascent. This explains why, in preparation for a redpoint ascent, you can't just practice the individual moves—it's equally important to practice connecting the moves, since this is a new skill in and of itself.

Also relevant to the process of learning and application of motor skills is the matter of skill transference, which relates to how practice of a skill in one activity carries over to enhance performance of another, different activity. Research and anecdotal evidence both confirm that transference is either small or completely absent, even between seemingly similar activities. The complexity, coordination, and integration of skilled movement are so specific that they derive very little help from other skilled movements. Therefore, practice at crack climbing will improve crack climbing skill but not face climbing ability. Furthermore, engaging in any type of "cross-training" activity will also fail to improve climbing skill. Kicking a Hacky Sack, snowboarding, slacklining, or what have you is a waste of time for the purpose of improving climbing skill (although these activities may develop cognitive attributes, such as focus, that may translate to climbing).

Sources of Sensory Information

Inherent to skilled performance is the need to receive and understand sensory information from the environment and your body. In climbing, the amount of information to process moment by moment is remarkably vast. Most obvious is the data collected through our senses regarding the climb and the surrounding environment. More subtle, but exceedingly important, is the wealth of information provided by our body relating to balance, muscle function, and quality of movement, among other things. Let's examine more closely the two sources of sensory information.

EXTEROCEPTION

Sensory information from outside the body is called exteroception. Of the five traditional senses, vision is the primary source of exteroception for physical activities such as climbing. Not only does vision provide the data needed to discover holds and unlock sequences, but it also offers a wealth of less conscious input on the spatial and temporal aspects of our movements.

Less obvious, but still valuable, is exteroception via touch and hearing. Whether you are aware of it or not, your sense of touch provides essential data on rock texture and quality of contact with the hands and feet. Every moment that you are on a climb, either your conscious or preconscious mind monitors this tactile input, enabling you to make subtle adjustments of grip and foot position. The auditory sense provides other novel environmental data, such as warning of approaching rockfall and confirming that a carabiner gate has closed (hearing that important *snap* of the gate), among other things.

PROPRIOCEPTION

Proprioception is your internal sense of body position and movement in space (also called kinesthesis). No matter what you do physically, proprioception provides the brain with a high bandwidth of sensory data from the nerves in all of your muscles, tendons, and joints, as well as from the vestibular apparatus of your inner ear (which allows you to sense orientation with regard to gravity). This vast amount of sensory feedback from the limbs and inner ear is processed unconsciously in doing simple tasks such as walking, cranking pull-ups, or dancing up an easy climb that requires little thought. More complex tasks, however, require conscious attention to proprioception—and it's the awareness and diligent use of this information that separate master climbers from the mass of climbers.

Awareness of specific aspects of proprioception, or what I call *proprioceptive cues*, varies on a continuum from extremely coarse and general on one end to exquisitely subtle and well defined on the other. Beginning climbers initially possess a coarse, limited sense of internal feeling as they climb. For example, they may sense the basic quality of a foot placement, whether they are in balance, and, most obvious, how pumped they are getting! This most basic proprioception is important, but it represents just a tiny fraction of the broad bandwidth of proprioceptive cues that an elite climber can perceive and leverage.

With increasing experience (hundreds of hours of climbing) and a determination to grow your awareness of proprioceptive cues, you will come to recognize a steady stream of valuable movement cues from your body's internal sense organs. When practicing a new skill or working a move on a hard boulder problem or project climb, it is highly instructive to ask yourself, *How does it feel when I do it the right way (most efficiently) compared with when I do it the wrong way?* Making this distinction empowers you to detect flawed execution and make corrective adjustments on the fly. This subtle but immensely important skill is one of a handful of master skills that you must develop if you want to pursue your ultimate potential in climbing.

Becoming an intermediate or advanced climber, then, will correlate to your deepening sense of proprioception in a wide variety of climbing situations. Each type of rock, cliff angle, type of climbing, body position, and family of moves provides unique proprioceptive feedback that you must learn to interpret in order to move with fluidity and high efficiency. Much of this proprioception (and the resultant physical adjustments) occurs preconsciously when you are climbing submaximal sequences. Crux movements and many novel moves, however, demand full attention to proprioception, thus leaving little remaining cognitive focus for other purposes. Many falls off crux moves that you have rehearsed and seemingly wired—or off easier moves when on-sighting—are the result of poor attention to proprioceptive cues.

The bottom line: The more subtle the level of proprioception that you can perceive, the better you will be able to climb given your current skill level and physical abilities. Serious climbers, therefore, are serious about developing their awareness and use of proprioceptive cues.

Three Stages of Motor Learning

Motor learning is the process by which we acquire physical skills. Regardless of the skill—walking, driving, climbing—learning occurs in three identifiable and overlapping stages: the cognitive, motor, and autonomous stages.

COGNITIVE STAGE

The cognitive stage of learning involves a lot of thinking (hence the name) about technique and moves, along with repeated trial-and-error attempts to execute novel moves. This first stage of learning is more visual than feel-oriented, so it helps to be shown a move and then verbally guided through execution. Early attempts are clumsy, inefficient, and jerky, expending energy and strength in wasteful ways. This is the normal modus operandi during your first few weeks or months as a climber, as well as when you are more experienced and make the first few attempts at a new type of climbing (crack, slab, pocketed face, etc.) or on a route that's especially hard for you.

In preparing for a climb, you tend to examine the route from the ground in an effort to figure out the moves and rest positions, and then you attempt the climb via toprope or, perhaps, leading bolt-to-bolt. The results of such early attempts typically are rough and imperfect. With continued practice, however, the quality of performance improves as you learn the feel of the moves via sharpened proprioception and knowledge of the climb.

Given the many and complex types of climbing, it may take weeks or months to advance through the cognitive stage when learning a new climbing skill set (e.g., crack climbing). Two keys to effective learning are letting go of judgments relating to poor performance (view errors as clues for improvement), and not rushing or overwhelming yourself by trying many different types of climbing during initial sessions. Most important, strive to develop good technique by repeating moves (and entire routes for that matter) until you can climb them smoothly and efficiently. Remember, success by way of thrashing up a climb is really a failure when it comes to learning—it wires bad habits of movement into the brain, thus developing bad technique rather than good technique!

It's during this first stage of learning that a climbing coach is most valuable. Not only can the coach demonstrate new skills and proper ways of movement, but she can also provide verbal cues to guide proper posture, body positioning, tactics, and problem solving. The coach's feedback should be positive and highly specific, yet not overwhelming in volume—the focus should be on correcting major flaws, not tweaking minor technical details. Finally, it's only in this stage of learning that the coach (or others) should provide significant beta, or sequence instruction. A beginner generally lacks the experience to see some of the necessary holds and to read complex sequences, so providing beta is actually a good way of growing experience and creativity in sequencing.

MOTOR STAGE

The motor, or associative, stage is less a product of self-conscious effort and thought than one of automatic increases in the efficiency and organization of the activity by the nervous system and brain as a response to continued practice. The brain wires new neural associations as a result of regular practice of a class of skills and multiple attempts at a specific movement. The climber exhibits more fluid, confident, and economical movement. Energy expenditure decreases, and the natural momentum of the body and limbs is used to advantage. This marked increase in economy of movement is the hallmark of the motor stage of learning.

When working a climb, this stage is represented by the attempts at redpoint when the moves and clips are known, and the goals are to develop efficiency and conserve power and endurance for the cruxes. The underlying factors involved in this stage differ from those that lead to early success. Here they involve improving proprioception, the accuracy of limb movement, the speed of detection and correction of minor errors, and the sensitivity of the performance to anxiety, doubt, and so on. These things are obviously less available to conscious awareness or control and are thus acquired only through dedicated practice and the chase of perfection.

In this stage the goal of action becomes more refined and demanding. The moves must be done efficiently with strength to spare, not eked out in desperation. Early, crude success should not be accepted as "good enough," since this will not lead to the best ultimate development of technique and efficiency. Having demanding goals has been shown experimentally to produce both better performance and faster gains. The goal should be to perfect movement and dominate at a certain grade, not just get by at it.

Coaching input during this stage should be far less than during the cognitive stage. The climber must be allowed to self-diagnose errors and make a first attempt at correction. In many cases the coach may want to save feedback until after the climb—then, in a relaxed setting, talk through specific errors and techniques to practice in the future. Two important keys to rapid learning during the motor stage are broadening the skill set through exposure to new types of moves and climbs, and extensive use of proprioceptive cues to increase awareness and feel of technically correct movement. The climber should be encouraged to talk through (and even write down) what he feels when performing specific moves, although the coach may need to draw out this information by asking, "How does the move feel when you do it correctly versus when you do it poorly?"

AUTONOMOUS STAGE

The final stage of learning is called the autonomous stage. At this point many climbing moves are automatic and require very little conscious attention, because movement has reached a stable and polished form. You can often do other things while in this state: For instance, you can carry on a conversation while driving a car, or you can decipher and send a moderate route in perfect form, on-sight. This apparent ease of execution is one aspect of the flow state, or "zone," so often touted by elite athletes. In climbing, it is reached only through dedicated, disciplined, long-term practice.

Veteran climbers with many years or decades of experience exemplify autonomous performance when they fluidly on-sight the majority of nonmaximal climbs they touch. The average climber with just a few years' experience may have this level of automatic, efficient movement on a well-rehearsed redpoint ascent or when on-sight climbing well below maximum ability. Given the complexity of climbing, it usually takes more than ten years to reach a consistent autonomous stage of mastery. Still, such elite climbers always have room for learning and refining skills, and the very best embrace a lifelong, ever-learning mind-set to exploring their potential.

As the name implies, climbers in this performance stage need little input from a coach—the fundamentals are well known, and the climber is capable of self-correcting errors and self-directing practices and training. Coaching input here should focus on questioning the climber about how he feels, with the goal of enhancing his awareness of lingering (often very subtle) technical and mental constraints on performance, and helping develop an effective long-term training strategy.

Motor Programs and How We Perform Novel Moves

Despite being as intuitive and natural as walking or running, climbing can be a remarkably complex and demanding activity. Consider that the climbing gyms and crags of the world offer a playing field of infinite variation and demand for skilled performance. Compound this with the potential for adrenaline-releasing risk and the perplexing challenge of ascending a gigantic wall, and it becomes apparent that climbing is indeed a most complex sporting activity.

The goal of this section, then, is to provide a primer on the theory of skilled performance that empowers you to learn and develop climbing skills most effectively and rapidly. While the mass of climbers stumble through the maze of trial-and-error learning, your knowledge of how the brain wires motor programs and executes novel moves is a lever that opens the door to techniques for accelerating technical improvement (described in the next section).

MOTOR PROGRAMS

Discrete climbing skills are directed by motor programs wired into long-term memory. These motor programs, which define and shape movement, become more stable, elaborate, and long lasting as you progress through the three stages of motor learning described earlier. With consistent, quality practice, the programs become highly precise and largely unconscious, thus freeing attention for other matters such as finding the next handhold or remembering the sequence. Conversely, climbing skills that you rarely practice (or avoid) will be represented by less detailed, unstable motor programs that may lead to poor execution and require high attentional demands.

A highly skilled climber can often look at a section of rock, see the moves, and know what skills he will need to employ. For example, he might view a short boulder problem and see a lieback move that leads to a backstep move, followed by a two-foot deadpoint move to a good hold. In ascending the boulder problem, motor programs for "lieback," "backstep," and "deadpoint" yield a sort of movement script directing essential details of movement, like the muscles to be used and in what order, the force and duration of each contraction, and such. Still, the motor programs will not specify every aspect of movement, and so the climber will make many tiny reflexive, preconscious, or conscious proprioceptive adjustments that modify the commands of the movement script.

A less skilled climber may be challenged in many ways by the same boulder problem. First, she may lack the experience and cognitive skills to "see" the necessary moves. Furthermore, she may possess less refined motor programs for the lieback, backstep, and deadpoint skills that are necessary to ascend the sequence. Chances are she will need numerous attempts to feel out the moves and gather proprioceptive feedback on body position, the muscles to be used, and the force of contraction, among other things. Repeated blocked practice attempts may eventually lead to a successful ascent of the boulder problem.

PERFORMING NOVEL SKILLS

The hallmark of an expert climber is the ability to on-sight climb at a high level on a wide variety of terrain and rock types. But how does this climber execute novel moves with a high rate of success? After all, our playing field has infinite variability—so even a well-traveled professional climber will fail to experience every possible move and body position. Understanding how novel movements are generated will empower you to practice more effectively so that you can become a master at on-sight climbing through moves you've never before experienced!

Let's use the boulder problem example above, which concluded with a deadpoint to a good hold exactly 24 inches away. Given the infinite variability of climbing moves and rock surface, it is unlikely that the climber will have previously performed a deadpoint move, from a backstep position, to a hold exactly 24 inches away. However, if the climber has thrown deadpoint moves from several different distances (say, from 15, 21, 28, and 30 inches away) and from different body positions and rock angles, he will likely be able to execute the novel move on-sight. This is because all the different deadpoint moves call the same "deadpoint" motor program into use, and this motor program is scaled to fit the novel situation according to a learned set of rules, called a *schema*.

A schema is a set of rules, developed and applied unconsciously by the central nervous system, that enables you to adjust a motor program for different environmental conditions (hold location, rock angle, friction properties, and such) by changing parameters of muscle force, body position, and speed of movement (see figure 4.1). Becoming a proficient on-sight climber, therefore, isn't just a matter of learning all the different classes of skills (jamming, side pulling, down pulling, lunging, flagging, etc.), but it also demands that you practice these skills in a wide range of configurations and settings. Such variable practice (more on this in a bit) refines the existing schema-rule for each generalized motor program, thus allowing more accurate estimation of the necessary parameters for execution of a skill in a novel situation.

Figure 4.1 Developing Schemas

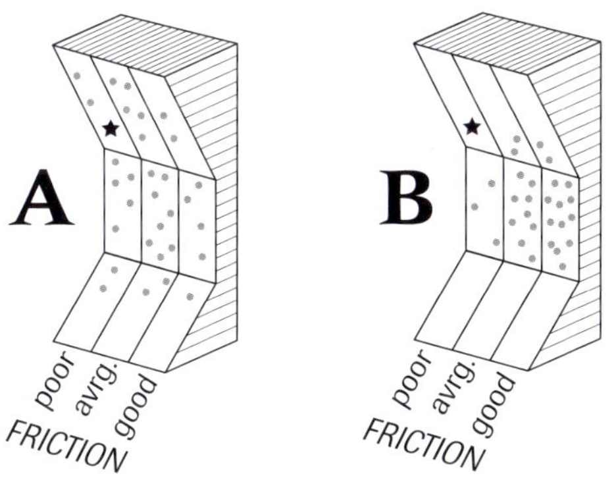

Climber A has practiced a specific skill over a wide range of conditions (dots) and thus possesses a more refined schema-rule. She will be able to closely approximate the novel move (star)—and possibly on-sight it!
Climber B has practiced the skill primarily on vertical rock with good frictional properties. Therefore, he is likely to struggle in executing the novel move (star) on slick, overhanging rock.

The practical application of schema theory should now be obvious: Upon learning a new climbing skill, say finger jamming, you'll want to practice finger jamming in cracks of different sizes, on different wall angles, and on rock with different frictional properties. Doing so will expand your use of the finger-jamming schema-rule to effectively ascend finger cracks at almost any crag on the planet. The same goes for other climbing skills—strive to expand their use to a variety of rock types and terrain, and you will be on your way to becoming a master of rock!

Conversely, if you climb at only a few cliffs and favor a specific type of climbing, you will develop fewer motor programs and less refined schema-rules for each. These motor programs, no matter how well learned, will work only for similar situations—and they may not apply particularly well at the outer limits of difficulty at these crags. Worse yet, when you travel to new areas, your limited skills and schema-rules will leave you climbing at a much lower grade or flailing on routes of the grade you're accustomed to sending at your home area.

The Importance of Feedback in Developing Expert-Level Skill

In wrapping up our study of motor learning, I must stress the importance of growing your awareness of feedback in all your climbing endeavors. No matter the task, you must consciously compare the ongoing feedback with the desired goal to determine the nature and amount of error. You are then empowered to amend your actions in a way that improves efficacy and moves you closer to your goal.

The desired goal in learning to climb should be to expand your skill set, improve quality of movement, and practice in ways that will accelerate your journey toward becoming an advanced climber steeped in autonomous-level performance. Making the most of both extrinsic and intrinsic feedback will hasten progress up the learning curve. Let's examine these two critical types of feedback.

EXTRINSIC FEEDBACK

Extrinsic feedback is information provided by some outside source, such as a belayer, coach, or videotape, that augments your internal sensory feedback. Extrinsic feedback is an inherent part of cognitive-stage learning, in which a beginner receives extensive verbal instruction to guide learning of new skills and proper movement. As you progress to intermediate-level ability (the motor stage), it's important to accept—and ask for—a lesser amount of extrinsic feedback. Growing your abilities demands that you learn to utilize the high bandwidth of internal feedback (more on this in a bit) in place of extrinsic feedback in self-analyzing and self-correcting movement error. Advanced climbers need very little extrinsic feedback in daily climbing and training activities, although the objective feedback of a coach is valuable in the case of a performance slump or long-term plateau in improvement.

A most common form of extrinsic feedback is *beta*—highly specific instruction on the proper sequence for a given climb. Beta is extremely helpful in developing hold recognition and sequencing skills during the formative stage of learning. As you progress beyond the cognitive performance stage, however, continued use of beta will handicap the development of problem-solving skills and other advanced cognitive abilities. What's more, long-term reliance on beta will lead to a false sense of ability, in that your climbing performance will degrade significantly when beta is not available. The bottom line: Beyond your first few months as a climber, make it a practice to shut off beta from your partner (or others); the exception is those rare cases when beta is essential for safety or speed.

INTRINSIC FEEDBACK

Intrinsic feedback is sensory information via your five senses and proprioception gleaned from your muscles, tendons, joints, and the vestibular apparatus of the inner ear. The most obvious intrinsic feedback is what you visually observe as the gross results of your efforts: falling off a move, seeing that a hold is not what you expected it to be, or discovering that a sequence you visualized won't work. Most climbers, regardless of ability, have good awareness of such basic intrinsic feedback.

It's the subtler intrinsic feedback of "feel" (proprioception) that beginners—and many non-beginners as well—lack awareness of. It's understandable, of course, for a novice to lack the subtle senses of touch, body position, and levels of muscular tension, for example, due to the aggregate overwhelm of fearful thoughts, technical struggles, and getting pumped! As your quality of movement improves (the motor stage) and you gain greater control over fear and excessive muscular tension, the subtler proprioceptive cues begin to reveal themselves. Still, you need to direct your attention inward to fully harvest the proprioceptive cues and come to understand and leverage them completely. Growing your awareness and use of proprioceptive cues is a mental skill that you need to develop through disciplined effort.

As described earlier in this chapter, it's a beneficial practice method to talk through and write down proprioceptive cues that you discover for specific types of moves and crux sequences of project routes—this process will foster uncommon sensory awareness, accelerate motor learning, and put you on the fast track to the higher grades. For many advanced climbers, use of proprioceptive cues will become largely preconscious; the exception may be in stressful, effortful moments when movement quality suffers and you need to proactively modulate tension and consciously utilize proprioceptive cues to maintain high-quality movement.

Rate of Improvement and Your Ultimate Skill Level

According to the Law of Practice, performance improves rapidly from its baseline level when the activity is first practiced and continues to improve in gradually decreasing amounts as ability approaches some ultimate (personal) skill level (see figure 4.2). In learning a simple task, like driving a car, it only takes a few weeks to become fairly skilled. Beyond this, all the thousands of hours you spend driving over the rest of your life will yield only a small amount of improvement.

The learning curve for complex activities, like golf or climbing, also rises rapidly as a result of the initial practice sessions. Because of the high complexity and wide range of skills inherent to these sports, however, you can continue to improve for many years, even decades. In fact, golf would seem to be the more technically difficult sport of the two, since several gifted climbers have reached world-class status in less than five years, while the best golfer ever, Tiger Woods, took fifteen years to ascend to that level—and that was unusually fast!

Figure 4.2 Rate of Skill Acquisition

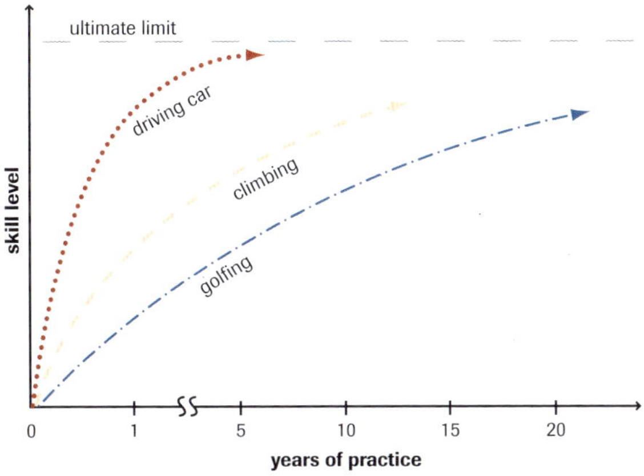

Performance improves rapidly from its baseline level when the activity is first practiced and continues to improve at a slower rate as ability approaches some ultimate personal skill level.

As discussed in chapter 1, you can maximize your rate of improvement in a specific style of climbing by focusing your practice and training in that one area. It's increasingly common to observe climbers who quickly progress to a high level of ability in one type of climbing—say, gymnastic bouldering or overhanging crimpfest routes. Since both of these endeavors require only a small subset of total climbing skills, it's possible to focus your practice on developing the small set of motor programs necessary to excel. The trade-off is that your limited motor programs will be a handicap when attempting routes outside your area of specialization—these climbs will feel hard for the grade, perhaps even "impossible."

The bottom line: Becoming a proficient, all-around climber is a long-term proposition. The most intelligent approach to training for climbing would be to emphasize learning skills over getting wickedly strong during your first few years in the sport. Developing refined schema-rules for the many different climbing skills will take many years of climbing at a wide range of areas and rock types. So while you may become a highly skilled specialist climber in just a few years, you can continue to expand the depth and breadth of your skills even after twenty or thirty years (I know that I still am!).

Practice Strategies to Accelerate Learning of Skills and Enhance Schema-Rules

If you want to maximize improvement, then you need to know how to practice optimally. Acquiring a new skill requires a progression through the three stages of motor learning before you will be able to use the new skill efficiently and intuitively. Depending on the difficulty of the skill, this process may be slow, awkward, and frustrating. Therefore, discipline and an intense belief that you will become excellent in the skill (with effort) are fundamental to the process. You must not try to get around having to learn it by relying on your strengths in other areas.

Unfortunately, many climbers do exactly this when they lunge, swing, or scum wildly through a sequence that could be done more efficiently by learning a new move, technique, or body position. Another example plays out when a competent gym or face climber first attempts to learn crack climbing. The common tendency is to avoid the awkward—and possibly painful—jams and paw up the face on either side of the crack. In this case the climber will rapidly fatigue and likely exclaim that the route felt way harder than its grade (which of course it did, since the climber wasn't using the proper technique for ascending the route).

The moral of the story is that you must convince yourself that no matter how hard a new move feels at first, it will become easier to execute—and perhaps even intuitive—as the result of intelligent practice. Toward this end, keep in mind that you will become most competent at a skill by practicing it on as many different rock varieties, angles, and settings as possible.

Another important principle states that learning new skills is difficult in states of fatigue, stress, fear, and urgency, whereas a fresh, relaxed, and confident approach yields rapid acquisition of new skills. Consequently, it's best to practice new skills early in your training sessions and to employ liberal hangdogging for blocked practice of crux moves. Interestingly, you can solidify skills you already possess by practicing them in a fatigued state! If all this motor learning theory is beginning to overwhelm you, worry not—following are five powerful practice strategies that distill and apply this information to produce optimal skill-learning results.

MODELING ADVANCED CLIMBERS

Modeling is a powerful technique for learning basic skills and climbing strategy. It's best used in a climbing gym where you can observe the movements, positions, techniques, and tactics of a more advanced climber, and then immediately give them a try on your own. Make a mental picture of what you want to attempt, and use that vision as a starting point. Experiment, modify, and make the move your own. In practicing the new move, progress through the following four practice strategies: blocked practice, variable practice, fatigued practice, and random skill practice (described below).

You can also model what you observe at the crags. In addition to actual moves, take special note of the tactics and strategy used by high-end climbers. For example, how do they work crux sequences? Where do they find rests? At what pace do they climb? How do they go about equipping routes? Again, it's best to first experiment with your observations in the gym before testing them outdoors.

Although modeling technical skills is a powerful weapon for your arsenal, copying an elite climber's strength and power training program is usually a big mistake. Remember that elite climbers have spent years conditioning their muscles and tendons to withstand extreme levels of stress. To train as they do without this long-term preparation could be disastrous.

BLOCKED PRACTICE

Blocked practice—identical repetitions of a specific move—is the most popular method of practicing a hard climbing move because it produces rapid learning of the skill in that specific situation. In learning the undercling move, for example, you would repeat the same undercling move over and over in order to refine your body position and the application of force needed to optimally perform the move.

Upon development of "feel" and early success at a new skill, however, a radical change is needed. Further blocked practice will have little value and may even result in a false sense of confidence and poor use of the skill in novel settings. Returning to our example, suppose you only practiced the one basic undercling move you first learned at the gym. Despite your expertise at that specific undercling move, you will struggle and likely fail on undercling moves on different wall angles and on the infinite playing field of outdoor climbing. The same phenomenon is seen in other sports, like a golfer who hits great wedge shots from the perfect lie of a practice range mat (blocked practice), yet on the golf course is unable to hit a solid shot from the novel lies of the fairway and rough. These examples show that beyond the first few successful trials of a new skill, blocked practice is for blockheads! Upon achieving initial success at a new skill, you must graduate to variable and random practice.

VARIABLE PRACTICE

As explained above, learning a new skill in a specific way is just the first step in the learning process. The ultimate goal is instant and proficient use of the skill in any new situation you come upon. The tried and proven way to do this is with variable practice.

Suppose you've just learned the drop-knee move on a vertical indoor wall with large, positive holds. To incorporate variable practice, you would now change the "route" conditions slightly and attempt the same drop-knee move again. After a few reps in this new setting, you'd again modify the route by changing the hold spacing and wall angle to further expand use of the skill—then continue this progression to the point that you could perform the drop-knee move in a variety of random settings. Such variable practice will refine schema-rules to direct effective execution of the drop-knee motor program over a wide range of conditions (angle, hold size, rock type, and frictional properties) that you may encounter in the future.

FATIGUED SKILL PRACTICE

Earlier I mentioned that you can increase your command of a skill by practicing it while in a fatigued state. In fact, beyond the initial successful trials of a skill, practice should be performed with variable conditions and levels of fatigue and never again "blocked." This may increase your rate of failure at doing certain moves—but remember, performance isn't your goal, practice is! The benefits of this practice, no matter how poor it feels, will become evident in the future. Besides, this concept actually makes good sense. If you want the ability to stick a deadpoint in the midst of a dicey lead climb while pumped, you'd better log some deadpoints in various states of fatigue during practice.

Here's the best approach. Use the first thirty minutes of your workout (while fresh) to train new skills, then move on to chalking up some mileage on a variety of routes. After an hour or so, or when you're moderately fatigued, attempt several reps of recently acquired moves and sequences. As fatigue increases, finish up with some reps of sequences or boulder problems you have more completely mastered.

In the context of a two-hour climbing gym workout, this rule emphasizes the benefit of squeezing in a greater volume of climbing "practice" ascents over doing just a few "performance" ascents with extensive rest in between. The long rests and performance climbing may make you look better, but the greater volume of practice will make you climb better!

RANDOM SKILL PRACTICE

The ability to on-sight a sequence of novel moves on "foreign" rock is the ultimate goal of your skill practice time. Toward this end, the best workout approach is a randomized free-for-all of skill types. This highly effective method is widely used in other sports and should not be overlooked by climbers as optimal training for the unknown.

There are two approaches to random training of climbing skills. First, on an indoor wall, attempt to link a sequence of very different bouldering moves. Contrive an unusual sequence of moves that will call a wide range of skills into use, and make several attempts at sending it. Alternatively, team up with your most deranged friend for a round of the Stick Game (described later in this chapter). Take turns pointing (with a broomstick or laser pointer) each

Tips for Rapid Learning of Skills and Developing Good Technique

1. Engage in regular climbing "practice." That is, go climbing with the intention of learning new skills and improving quality of movement, with little regard for absolute difficulty. Climb on as many different types of rock, wall angles, and areas as possible to build diverse skills and true climbing expertise.
2. Practice new skills and techniques early in the session while you are physically and mentally fresh.
3. Use blocked practice to accelerate learning during the initial trials of a new move, skill, or sequence. After two or three successful repetitions, cease blocked practice in favor of variable and randomized practice.
4. Employ variable practice to expand command of newly acquired skills over a wide range of conditions (angle, hold size, rock type, and so forth). Vary the "route" conditions more than you expect would be the case in a real-life climbing situation.
5. Practice known skills while in varying states of fatigue to increase your mastery of them and to build long-term retention.
6. Use random practice—climb a random series of moves back-to-back—to enhance proficiency of serial skill performance. Another random practice strategy is to climb several very different routes back-to-back to mandate recall of many different motor programs.
7. Model the techniques and tactics of advanced climbers. Stretch your imagination for climbing movement and strategy by observing and mimicking the techniques and tactics of top climbers.
8. Aspire to dominate at a climbing grade, and not just get by. Focus practice on routes at or just below your maximum difficulty, and resist the urge to constantly work routes beyond your ability level.
9. When working a route, resolve to find the best way to do a move or sequence, and resist the urge to just thrash up the route and deem that acceptable. As a practice method, climb a route several times to identify and learn the most effective and efficient moves and tactics.
10. Maintain a long-term perspective toward learning to climb. No matter how fast you improve or how hard you climb, realize that you can still improve technique and learn new skills—even after ten, twenty, or more years!

other through an unusual sequence of widely varied skills and movements. Don't get too wrapped up in performance outcomes—if you link a random series of moves, then you are a winner in terms of developing superior climbing skill.

Another powerful method of random skill training is to climb a series of widely differing routes in rapid succession. A commercial gym with many different wall angles, a few cracks, and a roof or two is ideal. Team with a partner and toprope ten to fifteen routes of different character over the course of an hour or so. The first route may be a vertical face, the next a slab, the third a finger crack, the fourth an overhanging pumpfest, the fifth a hand crack, the sixth a roof route, and so on. This rapid recall of a wide range of motor and cognitive skills is like taking skill-fortifying steroids!

Fundamental Techniques

The essence of climbing is a dance up the wall using the four points of contact as your dance steps. Since each climb possesses a novel configuration of hand- and footholds, your challenge is to unlock the perfect sequence of moves and leverage your points of contact into this dynamic dance.

In executing any physical skill—whether it's shooting a basketball or simply running—there are fundamental techniques that represent optimal use of body position, leverage, and physical energy. While the specific techniques may be hard to observe with an untrained eye, just about any novice can spot an athlete steeped in the fundamentals: Her movements are smooth, crisp, and confident, and her demeanor reveals a poise and ease of execution, despite inherent difficulties of the situation. The bottom line: Fundamentally sound movement affords perfect economy and looks easy.

Unfortunately, becoming a highly skilled, proficient climber rarely just happens—it results from a conscious decision to develop superior technique via disciplined long-term practice. Make it your goal to learn to climb every move and every route in the optimal way, and not to be satisfied to succeed with sloppy, inefficient movement. Excellence in climbing comes only to those with knowledge of the fundamentals and a desire to make them habit. To help you on this journey, this section provides a primer on twelve fundamental techniques that you must practice to the point of mastery. As you read through each section, ponder your current level of competency in each fundamental technique and make it an urgent part of your training-for-climbing program to improve these weak areas. For a more tangible record of your technical ability, score your command of each fundamental technique using the checklist assessment in table 4.1.

Table 4.1 Score Your Technical Ability

Evaluate yourself in each area and check the box that best represents your current ability.

Technique	Excellent	Good	So-So	Poor
Precise, quiet foot placements that carry your weight				
Handholds gripped lightly; arms in a secondary role				
Use of the Left–Right Rule for stable movement				
Economy of movement (rhythm, pace, poise)				
Use of rest positions				
Use of non-downpull and nonpositive handholds (side pulls, underclings, slopers)				
Use of flagging to aid stability and prevent barndooring				
Hand–foot matching and mantling				
Twist lock, backstep, and efficient movement on overhanging terrain				
Use of creative footwork (heel and toe hooks, and knee locks)				
Dynamic moves (deadpoints and lunges)				
Jam crack climbing				

Precise Foot Placements That Carry Your Weight

Given that your legs are stronger than your arms, the first fundamental of climbing is that the legs should do the majority of the work. The exceptions to this rule are severely overhanging routes, which demand greater use of the arms (more on this in a bit). The process of effectively using your feet begins with spotting the footholds and positioning your feet on the best part of each hold. Directing your foot placement demands attention to detail beyond that given to hand placements. Whereas handholds are easy to inspect, the greater eye-to-foot distance commonly leads to less-than-ideal foot placements. Furthermore, your feet don't provide the same degree of feel as the hands, making the quality of each foot placement more difficult to assess. For these reasons, developing good footwork is an attribute that you must make happen via constant foot focus and practice.

The other aspect of sound footwork is proper alignment of your center of mass directly over a foothold. Balance, stability, and application of force are optimized when your center of mass is

1. Keep your center of mass over your feet so they carry most of your weight. This requires a hips-out position when climbing slabs.

2. On vertical rock, it's essential to keep your hips in near the rock to position your center of mass over your feet.

positioned directly over your feet, forming a line perpendicular to level ground. On a less-than-vertical wall or slab, this requires a hip position out from the wall and over the foothold. On a near-vertical climbing surface, you simply need to keep your body position straight and over your feet as much as possible. When the climbing wall overhangs, it becomes impossible to position your weight over your feet, so a new fundamental skill takes over (see "Twist Lock and Backstep" later in this chapter).

Grip Handholds Lightly and Let Arms Play a Secondary Role

In a sport where anxiety and fear often rule, it's understandable that many climbers hang on with their hands for dear life. This tendency manifests itself with overgripping of the handholds and unnecessary muscling of moves with the arms. The end result is rapid fatigue, pumped forearms, and an eventual need to hang on the rope in order to rest and recover.

You can avoid this outcome by practicing—and making habitual—the fundamentals of proper hand and arm use. These critical skills include gripping each handhold with the minimum force required, using the arms mainly for balance and not as a primary source of locomotion, and pushing with the feet in unison with modest arm pull.

Begin by making each hand contact a conscious process. Whereas many climbers just grab a hold with little thought and continue with the process of climbing, you must make each hand placement a thoughtful act. First, consider where the best place is to grab the hold. It's not always on the top of the hold, and it often relates to the location of your last foot placement. As you grab the hold, focus on using a light touch that yields soft forearms. Sure, certain holds will demand that you bear down hard on them, but many don't. Your goal must be to try to use each hold with a light touch, and then increase the gripping force only as much as is required for the move at hand. This process of minimally gripping each handhold takes but a split second, yet it's a master skill that separates the best from the rest. Commit to targeted practice of this important skill (use the drills detailed on page 83, and in time it will actually become an unconscious act as you cruise up hard routes with high efficiency!

Beyond gripping the rock, you need to decide just how much you need to pull down on a given handhold. As discussed earlier, it is imperative that you push with your feet and let the leg muscles carry the load. In climbing a slab or near-vertical wall, think of your arms as points of contact that simply prevent you from falling backward off the wall. In climbing a ladder, for example, your legs do all the work while the arms mainly provide balance. While rock climbing is far more complex, hold this model in your mind as the ultimate goal—the arms maintain balance while the legs drive movement.

Still, there will be occasions in which your arms will need to briefly carry much of your weight. In these situations it's imperative that you pull quickly through the strenuous move in order to get back onto good footholds that can carry your weight. A final tip for strenuous situations is to maintain straight arms as much as possible—this way, much your weight is supported by the skeletal system of your upper body and not by your muscles.

The Left–Right Rule for Stable Movement

The magic of efficient climbing movement comes from the synergistic interaction of the arms and legs and a constant transfer of force and torque through your body. To this end, the Left–Right Rule states that maximum stability and ease of movement comes from the pairing of a left hand and right foot (or a left foot and right hand) in harmonious action. Let's again use climbing a ladder as our model. Ascending a ladder with opposing hand–foot combinations (say, the left hand pulling and right foot pushing at the same time) is so intuitive that it's almost impossible to climb a ladder any other way.

Suppose you tried to climb a ladder with non-opposing hand–foot combinations, such as a right hand and right foot working together; you'd immediately begin to barndoor or rotate sideways off the ladder. Thus, the Left–Right Rule is fundamental for balanced, stable movement.

While you don't need to even consider the Left–Right Rule in ascending a ladder, formulating movement up a climbing wall is much more complex: The position and shape of the hand- and footholds wreak havoc with your intuitive sense of movement. Thus, in seeking to reposition your hands and feet on the wall, it's helpful to ponder which holds will provide the best opportunity for a left–right combination. Easy climbs will often provide a pulling right hand that can combine with a pushing left foot (or vice versa). More difficult climbs tend to be more devious because the holds are smaller, farther apart, or displaced off to the side of the route line. Advanced climbers will often be able to intuit the best way to proceed; however, beginners must be willing to try difficult sequences multiple ways to discover and learn the best solution.

Move with High Economy

The technical paramount is to climb with high economy. Make these two words—*high economy*—your mantra every time you touch the rock.

High economy means discovering the way to do each move, and an entire route for that matter, with minimal energy expenditure. If you have a cat, you can observe highly economical movement firsthand. Most of the time a cat moves in a slow, smooth, deliberate way; however, sometimes a situation demands a powerful, dynamic leap to maintain perfect economy. Catlike movement should be your technical model for efficient climbing: smooth, quiet, leg-driven movements, but with an unhesitating shift to an arm-pulling, dynamic movement when it is required to most efficiently execute a difficult move. Here are five attributes of economical movement that you should aspire to acquire.

QUIET FEET

Quiet foot movements are one of the hallmarks of a climber with great technique. Conversely, feet that regularly pop off footholds or skid on the wall surface are typical of an individual possessing lackluster footwork and poor economy. For many climbers, noisy footwork is just the way they climb—it's a habit that developed over a long period of time, as well as a flaw in their technique that will prevent them from ever reaching their true potential. Your goal, of course, is to learn to climb with good foot technique even in the toughest times. This means concentrating on each foot placement, keeping your foot steady and firm to the hold, and standing up on the foot with confidence as you proceed smoothly to the next hand- or foothold.

RHYTHM AND MOMENTUM

Like any dance, climbing should have a natural rhythm that utilizes momentum and inertia. Climbing in a ladderlike motion yields the rhythm step, reach, step, reach. However, a better rhythm for effective movement is often step, step, reach, reach, since it allow the legs to direct and drive the movement. There are obviously many other rhythms, such as step, reach, step, step, reach, reach and step, step, reach, step, reach, reach. Consider that every unique sequence possesses a best rhythm of movement, and you'll eventually learn to intuit this on the fly. As a beginner climber, however, it takes a conscious effort to avoid leading with the hands in a strenuous and inefficient reach, reach, step, step rhythm. Strive to tap into the rhythm of each route, and climb accordingly.

Similarly, you want to utilize momentum in a way that helps propel successive moves. This is especially important on difficult climbs with large spacing between holds. Think of how you would move hand-over-hand across monkey bars at a playground, each movement blending with the next in a perfect continuity of motion. This style of smooth, continuous motion is critical when climbing through crux sequences. Interestingly, many folks do just the opposite, engaging the crux sequence with measure and caution. In doing so, they not only lose upward movement but also have the inertia of stillness to overcome. Hopefully you can avoid this tendency by consciously directing a steady rhythm that maintains forward momentum through the most difficult parts of a climb.

SMOOTH MOVES AND RELAXED BODY

Smooth, fluid movement is another sign of high economy. A climber appears to flow up a route when only the muscles necessary for stability and upward motion are contracting and all other opposing, or antagonist, muscles remain relatively passive.

Unfortunately, many climbers wrought with anxiety, fear, or the need to perform find themselves contracting most all their muscles from head to toe in an attempt to hang on or fight through a crux. Such tension in the antagonist muscles forces the prime movers to work harder than needed and leads to inefficient movements and rapid energy expenditure. You can spot climbers suffering from this affliction by their stiff, rigid, and forced movements, which will likely soon have them hanging on the rope in frustration. And if they somehow succeed in fighting up the route, it will be at the expense of a great amount of energy and further ingraining of bad habits of technique.

The key to smooth, efficient movement is to maintain a high level of relaxation throughout the climb. You can best achieve this with a two-pronged approach. First, think about contracting only the muscles necessary for engaging the rock, maintaining stability, and directing movement; usually these will be the muscles of your forearms, shoulders, core, thighs, and calves. Next, switch your focus to the antagonist muscles and scan for unnecessary tension that might be developing in your upper arms, hips and legs, neck, and face. While taking deep, slow breaths, visualize this tension escaping like air from a balloon—such mental imagery really helps the process. Now return your focus to executing the next climbing movement, but continue alternating your focus back and forth between directing movement and directing relaxation.

PACE

Pace is another aspect of climbing economy that becomes increasingly important as a route gains in steepness and difficulty. While an easy climb with large holds allows you to ascend at a leisurely pace, a crux sequence or overhanging terrain will demand that you kick into high gear and surmount the difficulty in short order. When climbing near your limit, it must be your intention to move as briskly as possible without any drop-off in technique (skidding feet, botching sequences, and such). Reduce the pace at the first sign that your technique is suffering. It helps to identify obvious rest positions ahead of time, and then make it a goal to move from one to the next as fast as possible. Ultimately, knowing just the right pace on a given route is a sense you will develop with experience. Practice climbing at different speeds and on different types of routes, and you'll quickly foster the subtle skill of proper pace.

STEADY BREATHING

Breathing is the essence of life. Steady breathing is essential to sustain the life in your climbing. Conversely, restricted breathing is akin to tightening your muscles, constraining your thinking, and fostering failure.

Obviously, a steady flow of oxygen to the muscles is important for energy production and recovery, and it's the slow, deep, steady belly breaths that best get the job done. Many climbers, however, have a tendency to shift into shallow, rapid breathing as fatigue and mental anxiety grow. Worse yet, some climbers unknowingly hold their breath at times of high stress. These are two tendencies that you must be aware of and proactively counteract if you are to climb your best.

Before every climb, take a moment to close your eyes and take several slow, deep breaths. Feel your belly expand outward as you slowly inhale, and then allow the air to escape sparingly through pursed lips in a slow ten-second count (count in your mind). Visualize a wave of relaxation washing across your body—this sets the stage for optimal performance. As you commence climbing, strive to maintain the same slow, steady breathing that you initiated on the ground. This is, of course, often difficult since a dicey sequence or strenuous move can trigger irregular breathing patterns. Consequently, it is critical that you use every rest position as an opportunity to reset your breathing cycle with a few slow, deep belly breaths. Such proactive breath control is like topping off your gas tank—do it frequently, and you'll rarely hit empty.

Optimize Use of Rest Positions

Finding efficient rest positions is as important as finding the best way to do a crux sequence. If you miss a good rest stance, you miss an opportunity to physically recover as well as mentally "read" and prepare for the next section of the climb. Consequently, locating rest positions on a climb should be viewed with the same sense of importance as locating all the key holds.

This process begins with on-ground visualization of the route (see chapter 3) in an attempt to estimate the location and body position of rest stops. Upon reaching a rest stop, assume a body position that will allow the most fatigued muscles to rest (usually the forearms, biceps, and calves). An optimal rest position would consist of your feet in the rest-step position, legs straight, and hips over the legs or in a position midway between the feet (should they be on holds more than shoulder width apart). If the climb is less than vertical, your upper body can relax completely, and in some cases you might even be able to assume a no-hands rest position. Such a casual stance places no time limits on how long you can remain parked there—although this luxury is rare on more difficult routes.

Rest positions on vertical to overhanging climbs make complete weighting of the feet more difficult and often impossible. While you still want to place as much weight as possible on the footholds, a significant amount of weight will remain on your arms. In this case it's absolutely vital that you hang with straight arms, so that the bones are providing the support, not the muscles of the upper arm. It is also advantageous if you can obtain a heel hook or knee bar from which you can hang a high percentage of body weight. Still, your forearm muscles will need to contract in order to maintain a grip on the handhold. The best strategy, then, is to attain a stable stance and shake out alternate arms every five to ten seconds. This way, both arms take turns resting. At some point, however, hanging out at the rest begins to cost more energy than you can recover. It's at this time that you need to begin climbing toward the next rest spot.

A big part of becoming a fundamentally sound climber is learning to gain brief rests in the midst of even the most difficult routes. Practice and unbridled creativity are the only two requisites for solving difficult sequences and finding vital rest positions. Remember that the best climbers are not always the strongest; their prowess instead comes from uncommon mastery of climbing economy and effective resting.

Clever Use of Opposing Forces

You have already learned the importance of the Left–Right Rule for enabling stable movement. On easy climbs this left-right combination is usually a pulling right hand along with a pushing left foot (or vice versa). More difficult climbs tend to be more devious, however, so you'll need to consider all the other possible arm positions—side pull, Gaston, and undercling—and figure out how to match one of these with an opposing foot placement. Detailed below are a few of the most common left–right combinations called into use on difficult climbs. You should practice each of these on the bouldering wall in order to develop its unique motor skills. Vary your hand and foot placements as much as possible to acquire a broad range of use for each hand–foot combination.

SIDE-PULL ARM AND OUTSIDE EDGE OF OPPOSITE FOOT

Side-pulling arms are a staple move on almost every moderate to advanced climb, but it's your foothold selection that often determines the effectiveness of this move. In most cases it's best to use the outside edge of the opposing foot, not the inside edge. Doing this may feel awkward at first, but you'll find a natural sense of stability once you learn to appropriately set your hips over the outside-edging foot. The key is to concentrate on rotating your hips so that the hip opposite the pulling hand is turned into the wall—that is, your face and chest will rotate toward the side pulling hand. This very stable position will allow you to step up your free (non-opposing) leg and quite possibly your free (non-opposing) hand as well. Occasionally a move will dictate that a side-pulling hand must be combined with use of the inside edge of the opposing foot. While this, too, is a fairly stable body position, it provides less reach upward with the free hand. Therefore, anytime you are struggling to reach a handhold, try using the outside edge of your shoe and a hip turn to maximize reach.

Pairing a side-pulling hand with the outside edge of the opposite foot (and a hip turn) provides great stability and reach.

GASTON AND INSIDE EDGE OF OPPOSITE FOOT

The Gaston (aka reverse side pull) is the most unnatural and weak arm position, yet it's a fairly common move needed to unlock many crux sequences. Use of the Gaston is best opposed by the inside edge of the opposite foot. Combining a Gaston with an outside-edging foot is strenuous but doable if absolutely needed. Practice this move in a variety of ways to gain comfort and strength in its use. As with all these advanced moves, the bouldering area is the ideal proving ground to experiment with and learn the skills.

UNDERCLING AND INSIDE OR OUTSIDE EDGE OF OPPOSITE FOOT

Frequently overlooked by less-experienced climbers, undercling hand positions are often essential for unlocking difficult sequences on steep terrain. What's more, an underclinging hand helps maximize your reach with the free hand, and it positions your arm and body in a naturally strong position.

The undercling move can save the day on a reachy move lacking a positive down-pull hold. Use a hip turn and the outside edge of your opposite foot to maximize reach, stability, and power. BRUCE WILSON

Typically you will undercling a hold somewhere near your torso while you press with an opposing foot. This foot can edge with either the inside, outside, or toe portion of the shoe, although use of the outside edge is best for maximizing your reach. Remember that in edging with the outside of your foot, it's best to turn the hip opposite the pulling hand to the wall. In extreme situations you may even need to use a foot smear to oppose the underclinging hand. This is a very powerful but important move that you should train on a bouldering or System Wall.

SIDE-PULLING LEFT AND RIGHT HANDS

Use of opposing handholds is a key move for unlocking a sequence that lacks any usable down-pull or undercling handholds. Most common are two opposing side pulls that you'll draw inward to create tension through your arms, shoulders, and upper body. While you will be unable to create much upward movement, this opposition will allow you to upgrade one or both feet. Ideally, you'll want to upgrade the foot that opposes the better of the two side pulls, so that it sets up a stable left–right combination. This will enable you to release the other side-pulling hand so as to upgrade it to the next hold. Another possibility is opposing Gaston holds. Though strenuous, you may occasionally need to grab two Gastons at or just above head height and pull outward in order to support your weight while upgrading a foot position. This is a most advanced move that requires a high level of base strength. A word of caution, however: Using a Gaston hold on an overhanging wall places great force on the shoulder joint and in rare cases can cause injury. Proceed carefully.

Use Foot Flagging to Enhance Stability

Flagging is the alternative technique for maintaining stability when a left–right hand–foot combination

Unstable moves and a tendency to barndoor can often be overcome by a flagging foot, which shifts your center of mass closer to the weight-bearing foot.

is not possible. Suppose you are attempting to use a right hand and right foot combination to propel upward movement. Upon releasing your left hand to make a reach upward, you will immediately begin to barndoor (see the photo on this page). This sideways rotation is hard to fight and often results in a fall. However, a simple flagging of the free leg (in this case the left) significantly improves stability and balance by shifting your center of mass more directly over the supporting (right) foot and under the supporting (right) hand.

Let's take a look at the two methods of flagging; which one you use depends on whether your supporting leg is edging with the inside or outside edge of the shoe. For example, consider a move in which you are edging on the inside of your right foot and pulling with your right hand. In order to avoid barndooring, you would flag the left leg across the right leg. However, if your supporting leg is edging with the outside edge of the shoe, it's best to flag the free (left) leg out left along the wall surface in an effort to find a balance point. If you're lucky, you'll find a foothold or wall feature on which to splay the flagging foot. Practice using these flagging techniques on a vertical wall, and then expand their use onto overhanging terrain.

Mantling and Hand–Foot Matching

The mantle move is often called upon to overcome a long reach between holds. Depending on the size of the hold to be mantled, you may be able to press your entire palm onto the hold or, possibly, just your fingertips. The left–right combination of pushing and pulling hands provides great stability, so you will be able to upgrade one or, possibly, both feet. In many cases you will match a foot (the same side as the mantling hand) on the same hold that you are mantling; it is then often possible to shift your center of mass over that foot and stand up.

Severe climbs frequently demand that you adroitly match your foot onto a tiny crimp or finger pocket hold. Quick, precise execution is essential to maintain forward momentum as you progress through such tenuous sequences.

Twist Lock and Backstep on Steep Terrain

The twist lock and backstep are the bread-and-butter moves of a steep-wall connoisseur. As a climbing wall tilts back past vertical, it becomes increasingly difficult to place a high percentage of weight on your legs. Consequently, a greater portion of body weight must be supported by the arms—which, of course, possess less absolute strength than the legs. Use of the twist lock and backstep together helps draw your body in toward the surface of the overhanging wall. This changes the force vector on the

Use of Twist Lock

1. Without the twist lock, the climber's neutral, straight-on body position places the center of mass way out from the wall. This makes for strenuous, inefficient movement.

2. The twist lock with its hallmark hip turn draws the center of mass in closer to the wall, thus placing more body weight onto the feet, increasing reach and enhancing grip on handholds (thanks to the changing force vector of the arm pull).

handholds, making them feel more positive and secure. More important, this drawing-in of the body places more weight onto the footholds. However, proper execution of these moves requires practice and a significant amount of strength through the core muscles of the torso. (See chapter 7 to learn exercises for strengthening these core muscles.)

The twist lock is typically used to ease the upgrading of a hand on an overhanging section of wall. For example, consider the situation in which your left hand is on a good hold and you'd like to reach up high with the right hand. While you could attempt this move straight-on—chest facing toward the wall in a neutral position—it's far less strenuous to turn your right hip to the wall before making the reach upward. Proper positioning of the feet is critical for making this move work. Since the right hip is turning to the wall, you'll need to use the outside portion of your right foot on a hold somewhere below or in back of your body (hence the term backstep). Usually you'll find a complementary left foothold to help maintain the twist-lock body position. The feet then press in unison while the left arm pulls down and in toward your torso, creating the twist lock. Finding just the right body position is the key to providing a secure twist lock; when you do, you'll notice that a surprising lack of effort is needed to reach up and acquire the next right handhold. This amazingly efficient locomotion over steep terrain is the magic of the twist-lock technique.

Granted, skillful use of the twist lock and backstep is something that will take many hours of practice. In fact, during your initial attempts at using these moves, you might swear that they require more energy than basic straight-on moves. Trust that with practice you will develop the necessary motor skills to make these moves feel quite easy. Initially limit your practice of the twist lock and backstep to boulder problems that overhang about 20 degrees past vertical. As you acquire skill, expand their use onto even steeper boulder problems as well as overhanging toprope climbs.

Use Creative Footwork with Heel and Toe Hooks and Knee Locks

Heel hooks, toe hooks, and knee locks are real difference makers when it comes to moving over steep terrain and surmounting overhangs. Given the strength of the leg muscles, a good heel hook is often better than a handhold in helping turn the lip of a difficult roof. Similarly, toe hooks and knee locks provide terrific support when you're cranking a serious move on overhanging rock. Let's take a brief look at each.

HEEL HOOK

Heel hooks are the major go-to move when you're turning the lip of a roof, topping out on a boulder

Heel hooks can make a huge difference in pulling a tough roof or copping a shakeout on steep rock.

problem, or copping a quick shakeout while on steep terrain. In these cases you'll likely have your hands on holds at or above face level and intend to place one of your heels on a hold off to the side roughly between hip and shoulder level. Which heel you choose to hook with depends on two factors: the availability of a decent-size hold on which to place your heel, and the location of the next handhold that you hope to acquire. This next reach up is best made with the hand on the same side as the heel hook. So if it looks like the next attainable hold is set up for the right hand, it would be best to use a right heel hook. Once set, pull with the heel hook as if it were a third arm. Often it helps to think about pulling your heel toward your rear end; this will maximize use of the leg muscles and help shift your center of mass toward the heel hook. Meanwhile, the other foot should inside-edge or smear on the wall to help contribute to the upward motion. As you gain elevation, make a quick reach to the next handhold, and then switch your heel hook into a standard step-down foot placement.

TOE HOOK

The toe hook is a foot move used mostly in pulling overhangs or in navigating roofs. This technique involves simply hooking as much of the top/laces side of your shoe as possible on a large protruding hold. Sometimes you will toe hook onto a hold with a bent leg and then straighten that leg as your hands move out the roof. Ideally you'll have one foot toe hooking while the other foot pushes off a nearby hold. This opposing push–pull combination enhances the foot purchase on the holds and lowers the chance that your feet will come swinging off the roof (a common problem). Strive to keep your arms and legs in the straight position as much as possible so that your body weight is being supported more by bones than by muscles. Done properly, you can navigate a surprisingly large roof, with the limiting factor being forearm endurance. Experiment with this foot technique in the bouldering area and you'll gradually gain skill and confidence in climbing with your back to the ground!

KNEE LOCK (AKA KNEE BAR)

Knee locks are a boon on overhanging walls and roofs with large protruding holds—that is, if you know the technique and can find a position to exploit this "thank-God" move. On a severely overhanging climb with no obvious rest positions, finding a knee lock may be your only hope for a rest. Look for a place where you can step your toe onto a hold and then lock in your knee against a larger opposing hold. Such a knee lock provides surprising purchase; it will allow you to drop one hand at a time to shake out and chalk up. Occasionally you will come upon a knee lock that's so solid, you'll be able to cop a rare no-hands inverted rest! Of course, miss the knee lock and you have no choice but to sprint up the climb in the hope of reaching the anchors before the pump clock runs out.

Use Dynamic Moves When They Offer Greater Economy

Throughout this chapter I've stressed the importance of climbing with maximum economy—the goal being to climb a move, a sequence, and an entire route in a way that requires minimal energy. In most cases the hallmark of economical climbing is smooth, relaxed movement that utilizes the feet and legs over the muscles of the upper body. Such controlled, fluid movement is often referred to as static climbing. The opposite of static style is dynamic or explosive movement, and there are certain moves and sequences that demand dynamic movement to achieve maximum economy. In particular, vertical routes with tiny handholds, and overhanging routes with long reaches often require dynamic movements.

The key is to know which moves are best attempted dynamically versus statically, and this is a recognition skill that takes years to fully develop. When working a route, it's best to attempt a crux in both a static and dynamic way to determine which style yields the most economical passage; otherwise you'll never know if there was a more effective method, and you'll miss out on an important learning opportunity. Let's examine the two primary forms of dynamic movement: deadpoints and lunges.

DEADPOINTS

Consider a situation in which both hands cling to poor holds, and you would fall off the wall if either hand let go for more than an instant. It's in just such a predicament that the deadpoint move will save the day, because it allows you to make a rapid hand upgrade despite the fact you can't hang on to the wall statically with a single-hand contact point. How's this possible? It's the magic of the deadpoint!

Envision a basketball player making a jump shot. He jumps straight up and shoots the ball at the peak of his flight, a moment of apparent weightlessness before gravity returns him to the floor. This instant of weightlessness and stillness is the deadpoint. Climbers can similarly exploit the apparent weightlessness of the deadpoint to upgrade a hand position as in the desperate situation described above. But instead of jumping like our basketball player, the climber needs to use a smaller, more controlled motion to facilitate the delicate upgrading of a hand from one small hold to another.

For example, imagine a tenuous move on a vertical or slightly overhanging wall in which you want to upgrade your right hand, but you can't make a static reach for the hold. Initiate the deadpoint movement with a small droop downward (or a release outward in the case of an overhanging wall) immediately followed by a firm drawing-inward of the handholds toward your torso. This drawing-in of your body is akin to—but less dramatic than—the basketball player's jump, and there will be an instant when the motion peaks and you'll be able to flash your hand up to snag the next hold. A well-executed deadpoint is calculated and controlled such that it flows naturally in perfect economy. In extreme cases you may need to execute several deadpoint moves in a row in order to climb through a series of small handholds that you could never hang on to for a static movement.

LUNGES

Unlike the careful, controlled movement of a deadpoint, the lunge (or dyno, as it's often called) is a full-on leap for an out-of-reach hold. In lunging, the arms and legs explode in unison to propel your body upward toward the next good hold. Lunges typically end in one of two ways: Ideally you latch on to a hold and regain control of your body; however, it's also possible that you will fail to catch the target hold and end up falling on the rope or the bouldering crash pad.

Lunging is like any other skill in that it takes practice and a high level of confidence before you will be able to exploit the move in severe situations. It's also a strenuous and stressful move that has led to many shoulder injuries. Consequently, it's best to view lunging as a last-resort move that you only pull out of the bag when nothing else appears possible. In the heat of a crux sequence, though, it often comes down to a gut feeling as to whether you should try to throw a lunge or attempt a static sequence. Ideally it would be best to lunge only when climbing statically would require more energy. In fact, a perfectly executed lunge in just the right situation is a classic example of climbing with high economy, despite the apparent burly nature of the move.

Executing a lunge is very physical, but also requires good timing and a belief that you can reach the next hold. Much like a gymnast attempting her hardest move, throwing and sticking the perfect lunge requires laserlike focus and an intense belief in a successful outcome. Begin by locking your eyes on the target hold and visualize exactly how your hand will hit—and stick!—the hold. Next, look down and concentrate on maximizing an explosive launch off your four points of contact. In many cases it helps to "cock" your lunge by drooping or bouncing before you catapult upward. As you go airborne, your eyes will naturally return to a pinpoint focus on the target hold. Now stick it!

Crack Climbing

Crack climbing involves techniques and tactics far different from the skills outlined above, and therefore you need to develop completely novel motor programs and schema-rules. I advise novice climbers to consult Lisa Gnade and Steve Petro's *Crack Climbing!* for more comprehensive instruction than the primer I offer here.

Crack climbing is vastly different from face climbing, yet one fundamental remains the same: Let the legs do most of the work. Pumping laps on gym cracks is a great way to hone your technique.

FINGER- AND HAND-JAMMING TECHNIQUES

Just how your hands engage a crack depends on the size of the fissure. The narrowest cracks will accept little more than the tips of your fingers. Most often you'll place this jam with your index finger on the bottom and your elbow out to the side. This way, when you pull on that arm, the elbow will rotate downward and produce a twisting of the fingers that further anchors them into the crack. One thing you will notice in larger finger cracks (around an inch wide) is that your fingers tend to slide down instead of jamming solidly. In these situations it's vital to look for constrictions or bottlenecks along the crack and attempt to place your jams in or just above these narrower spots.

Cracks ranging from one to three inches wide are the domain of hand jams. You can execute a hand jam in the thumb-up or thumb-down position. Vertical cracks are often better climbed thumb-down, whereas cracks that slant to the side may be more easily climbed with the lower hand jamming thumb-up and the high hand jamming thumb-down. As in finger jamming, scan hand cracks for constrictions or bottlenecks that will provide the most bombproof jams imaginable. Cracks with little variance are more challenging, as they require a bit more effort to create a solid jam. The key is to cup your hand inside the crack to generate outward pressure and friction on the inside of the crack. Furthermore, jamming thumb-down exerts a twisting force on the jammed hand as you pull down, and this tends to increase the security of the jam.

Fist jamming is the optimal technique for cracks about four inches wide. The technique here is simply to insert your hand with the palm facing into the crack and then make a fist. In closing your hand tightly, the width of your fist increases, making it stick like an oversize cork stuck in the top of a wine bottle. Cracks larger than four inches require a difficult off-width technique in which your arm and leg are jammed to gain purchase.

FOOT TECHNIQUES

There are two primary foot techniques used in crack climbing: feet inside the crack and feet on the rock face. In climbing thin finger cracks, you have little choice but to search for edges on the rock surface on which you can edge or smear (as in face climbing). The exceptions are offset cracks (where one edge of the crack is set out from the opposite edge of the crack) and larger finger cracks, which occasionally afford a foot smear on the exposed edge of the crack. Look for stems, high steps, outside edges, and even backsteps in attempting to use your feet optimally.

Cracks wider than about one inch provide exceedingly solid foot placements by means of foot jamming. The simple technique involves turning your foot sideways—so that the sole of the shoe is facing inward and your knee is bent outward—and inserting as much of your foot as possible into the crack. Depending on the crack's size, you may be limited to jamming just the toe portion of the shoe (narrow hand cracks) or its entire front half (fist cracks). Once you're secured in the crack, your knee will naturally rotate back to center as you stand up on the foot. In climbing a continuous hand or fist crack, you will simply need to leapfrog one foot above the other in a series of foot jams about one foot apart.

LIEBACK TECHNIQUE

Finally, there's liebacking, a unique method of climbing cracks that are located in the vertex of a dihedral or corner. The lieback technique is fairly strenuous since it places your body in a sort of rowing position with your arms pulling and your legs pushing in a powerful opposition. Feet smear on one wall of the corner while your fingers cling to the edge of the crack and arms remain as straight as possible. Move upward by simply walking your feet up the wall and sliding (or leapfrogging) your hands up the crack. With practice you'll learn to position your hands and feet to provide the greatest leverage at the lowest possible energy expenditure. Of course, as in all kinds of strenuous climbing, moving quickly is fundamental to maximizing performance.

CRACK-CLIMBING STRATEGY

Effective crack-climbing strategy is nearly identical to optimal face-climbing strategy—climb briskly and efficiently, utilize your legs as much as possible in generating locomotion, and pause for long periods only at definitive rest stances. Just as in your clumsy first days attempting any new climbing technique, expect your initial forays at crack climbing to feel awkward and frustratingly difficult. Trust that you will rapidly acquire the unique motor skills and that crack climbing will soon become less strenuous and a heck of a lot of fun.

In your formative days of crack climbing, use the security of a toprope to experiment with different techniques and subtle variations of the basic jamming skills described above. Don't be satisfied with just thrashing up a crack to the top; instead strive to learn the best way to do each move with the goal of climbing each crack in good style and with minimal energy burn. As a practice method, climb single-pitch crack routes a few times in a row to refine your skills and learn the subtle finesse moves that will eventually make you a master crack climber!

Smart Training Drills for Enhanced Learning of Motor Skills and Strategy

Having performed the technical evaluation in table 4.1 and the self-assessment in chapter 2, you should now have a clear picture of your technical weaknesses. But knowledge is not enough; to improve you must act! Dedicate a portion of two climbing sessions per week to improving your weaknesses and you will become a better climber.

Regardless of whether you plan to climb in a gym or at the crag, it's important that you make the distinction between time spent practicing versus performing. Unfortunately, many climbers handicap themselves by constantly focusing on performance as they succumb to the natural tendency to climb as close to their limit as possible. We've all seen climbers with horrible footwork flailing repeatedly on a steep route so that they can eventually tick some impressively difficult route. While they may ultimately succeed at sending their "5.hard" climbs, they gain little in technical ability from this process—and in fact they further groove their bad habits and poor technique. I call such practices "stupid training."

Conversely, intelligent climbers will dedicate a block of practice time early in the workout when they're mentally and physically fresh. During this practice period or day (if at the crags), the goal is to seek out routes that will target their technical weaknesses. Since performance is not a goal, there is no hesitation to hang on the rope and experiment with moves, body positions, and sequences that feel awkward or difficult.

For example, if backstep and drop-knee moves are a weakness, you'll want to dedicate some time during each workout to getting onto steep routes that demand these moves. No matter your weaknesses, it's likely that the type of routes you must get on will be intimidating, since up to this point it's probably been your tendency to climb routes that favor your strengths. If you are poor at drop-knee moves, for instance, I'll bet you avoid steep routes because they feel especially hard and look overly intimidating to you. The same goes for any style of climbing—slab, thin face, cracks, roofs, what have you. You must partake in regular practice on the terrain and type of routes that target your top technical weaknesses as identified in the self-assessment and table 4.1. Excellence comes no other way.

Following are a few practice drills and games that will enhance your rate of learning new skills and correcting weaknesses, as well as make the process a little more fun. More examples of such speed learning practices can be found in my book *How to Climb 5.12*.

BOULDERING

Bouldering is often touted as the supreme method for developing sport-specific strength, but it's even more effective for learning climbing skills (motor programs) and expanding schema rules. For proof of this, consider a recent bouldering session in which you worked a difficult problem a few times before eventually succeeding. Did you ultimately succeed because your strength increased after each attempt, or did each successive attempt result in learning of the body positioning, feel, and hand- and footwork necessary to do the moves most efficiently and successfully? I think the answer is obvious.

With all the restraints of roped climbing removed, bouldering allows you to narrow your focus and partake in relaxed, repeated attempts at learning a specific skill or sequence of moves. Sports scientists call this blocked practice, because the fixed moves can be practiced over and over again until they are successfully acquired. Once a skill is perfected, however, there is little benefit to additional blocked practice of that skill. Further learning demands that you either move on to practicing a new skill via blocked practice (say, a new boulder problem with new moves and positions) or modify the original problem so that some element of it has changed (say, angle, hold size, hold position or spacing, or the like). This latter strategy is known as variable practice, and it's the gold standard for learning a skill that must be performed in a variety of positions or settings: hitting a golf ball from an infinite variety of lies, shooting a basketball from anywhere on the court, floating a deadpoint from any one of a million different body positions.

Indoor walls and home gyms are the ideal setting for variable practice. Suppose you want to gain skill at, say, using undercling holds and hip turns on overhanging cliffs. To begin, set a problem with a relatively easy sequence of underclings and hip turns. Practice the sequence several times until you feel it's 100 percent wired. Now redesign the problem with slight changes in the hold positions and locations, and repeat the practice drill until this, too, is wired. Next, reduce the hand- and foothold size and repeat the drill. Keep repeating this process until you've exhausted the possibilities.

Completion of this variable practice drill might take anywhere from a single evening to a couple of weeks. Regardless, the end result is comprehensive schemas surrounding this type of movement, and rapid recall and execution of the skill in some future performance setting. So, while bouldering outdoors on a wide range of move types and angles is best for building a diverse library of climbing skills, using the variable practice strategy on an artificial wall enables comprehensive learning of a new type of movement in a wide range of configurations. Clearly, there is great value in both formats, so get busy!

TRAVERSE TRAINING

Like bouldering, traverse training is a no-frills activity that affords focused practice on numerous technical aspects of the climbing game. Although some people find ad-lib traversing along a cliff base or at a climbing gym boring, this drill does have some major benefits when compared with working a known, graded boulder problem. When working the graded boulder problem, it's natural to want to succeed at any cost, even if your technique is sloppy and inefficient. As discussed earlier, it's difficult to develop new skills in such a performance setting.

Conversely, traversing for the sake of practicing technique and movement eliminates the pressure to perform. You can experiment with new grip positions, gentle and precise foot placements, and various body positions with no concern about whether or not you step off the wall. Maximize the benefit of this drill by carefully spotting each foot placement, concentrating on shifting your center of mass over the leading foot, relaxing your grip as much as possible, and learning to move quickly and confidently through thin, tenuous sequences. Finally, strive to remain calm and relaxed at all times, and refocus on your feet anytime you sense you're losing control.

To mix things up and increase the intensity and benefit of traverse training, you can also play around with various elimination or focus drills. For example, try doing a complete traverse using only two fingers (the index and middle fingers, for example, or middle and ring fingers) of each hand. This drill forces you to maximize the weighting of your feet (a good thing); it's also an excellent way to increase your finger strength. As another variation, challenge yourself to do a complete traverse using only open-hand finger positions. (This will be especially difficult and beneficial if you naturally favor the crimp grip.) Be creative and make up other drills, such as "side-pull only," "undercling only," or "cross-through only" elimination traverses. Beginner and intermediate climbers have much to gain from performing these drills on a regular basis.

TOPROPING AND HANGDOGGING

Toproping and hangdogging are the ideal formats for practicing difficult moves near your limit or when diving into unfamiliar terrain like pocket or crack climbing. As discussed earlier, a relaxed, low-stress environment is critical to rapid learning of new skills. Obviously, climbing on toprope or on lead, bolt-to-bolt, represents a low-stress setting where you can experiment with tricky, awkward moves without the risk of a serious fall and injury.

When attempting a route that is continuously hard or with multiple cruxes, it's best to break it down into smaller sections or chunks. This reduces the mental burden by allowing you to view and solve the route in parts. Much like working a boulder problem, you can employ blocked practice to work a sequence repeatedly. Once a problem is solved and programmed to a high likelihood of success, you can move on and begin work on the next chunk. Upon solving all the chunks (and after a good rest), your next goal should be to combine chunks. For example, on a route that you had broken down into four hard sections, you would try to link the top two chunks, and then move down and link the top three chunks. Such incremental learning will wire you for a successful redpoint or toprope ascent after another rest or on your next outing or day at that area. (Note: See chapter 5 of *How to Climb 5.12* to learn many more strategies for working and sending project routes.)

THE STICK GAME (AKA SEND ME)

This popular game is great for learning to quickly assess and execute a novel, unknown move on-sight—a vital skill when you're on-sight climbing at the crag or in competition. Best played on an indoor wall, the drill requires at least two players who take turns pointing out (with a broomstick or laser pointer) impromptu boulder problems for the other to ascend. Begin by identifying the starting hand- and footholds for the climber; then, as she pulls up on them, the course setter points to the next hold to be used. Continue in this fashion until the climber falls or the problem is done. Commonly, the game is played with open feet—that is, the climber can use any foothold she likes.

FIRST TOUCH

First Touch is a great practice drill for would-be competition and on-sight climbers—though anyone can benefit from its use. An indoor facility with a wide range of toprope routes is the ideal setting for this drill. As the name implies, you must climb a route by using each handhold in the exact way that you first grab it—no readjusting or changing your grip after you first touch it. By climbing many routes in this fashion (and, of course, obeying the guidelines completely), you will learn to examine holds more closely—both from the ground and while climbing—and thus increase the likelihood you'll use them optimally from the first touch. On lead, this skill saves you time and energy, both of which increase your odds of on-sighting a route.

TRACKING AND ELIMINATION

This drill can be used indoors when you're bouldering or on toprope. The goal is simply to climb a route by tracking your feet on the exact same holds used by your hands. It's kind of like climbing a ladder, where you press down on a rung with your right hand and make room to step on that same rung with your right foot. As a type of elimination drill, this will make a climb much harder than it would be if climbed with all the holds on the route. Therefore, if you normally practice skill by climbing 5.10 or 5.11 routes, you'll want to do this drill on routes in the range of 5.8 to 5.9.

If you climb indoors a lot, exercise your creativity and develop other elimination drills that might improve your skill, strategy, and strength. For instance, begin eliminating certain hand- and footholds from the routes you have ruthlessly wired. There's little to be gained from blocked practice of the same tired routes over and over again. So challenge yourself by eliminating the five biggest holds from the route, or by limiting yourself to grabbing the holds only as side pulls or underclings, or with only two fingers, or what have you. Not only can this make for some good fun for you and your friends, but it's also an excellent way to enhance your skill practice and overall ability.

DOWNCLIMBING ROUTES

When I'm leading or toproping indoors, it's rare that I climb a route to the top and lower off without trying to downclimb as much of the route as possible. There are many benefits to this practice beyond the obvious one of doubling the pump. If you know you are going to downclimb a route, you become a more observant and focused climber on the way up. What's more, since poor footwork is a leading handicap for many climbers, there's a lot to be gained from this practice, which demands intense concentration on footwork!

At first you will find downclimbing to be difficult, awkward, and very pumpy. But that's the MO when first attempting anything new that's worthwhile (read challenging). As your hold recognition improves, however, and as you learn to relax and fluidly reverse the route, you'll find that downclimbing a route often feels easier than sending it in the first place. This is because your eccentric (lowering) strength is greater than your concentric (pulling) strength, and due to the fact that by leading with the feet while downclimbing, you learn to maximally weight them and conserve energy. All of the above make downclimbing a killer drill—one not to be overlooked by any serious climber!

SPEED TRAINING

When the rock gets steep and the moves hard, there's no more important weapon to have in your arsenal than being able to climb fast and precisely. Climbing quickly is primarily a function of skill, not strength or power (I'm not talking about lunging wildly up a route). In fact, the less strength and endurance you possess, the more important this skill becomes.

To begin with, it's important to note that there is no benefit to climbing faster if you begin to botch sequences or if your technique degrades. Therefore, you want to practice speed climbing on routes you have completely wired and, likely, at a number grade or two below your personal best. Climb several laps on the route (rest between attempts), each incrementally faster than the previous. Attempt to climb about 10 percent faster on each successive lap, but back off the accelerator at the first sign that your technique is suffering.

Perform this drill a few times a week for several months and you'll find yourself naturally moving faster when climbing on-sight or redpoint at the crags. This new skill alone could push your redpoint ability a full grade higher over the course of a single season—a much greater gain than you'd achieve from strength training alone!

Tips for Developing Superior Technique and Movement Skills

1. Hire a climbing coach. Obtain the objective evaluation and sage guidance of a climbing coach to get on the fast track to climbing excellence. Even just one session per month will be extremely beneficial.
2. Warm up properly before every climbing session. A progressive warm-up reduces injury risk and modulates your neuromuscular system for optimal learning and performance. Spend twenty to thirty minutes on easy climbs and various warm-ups.
3. Embrace a practice perspective and resolve to always have fun. Optimize learning of new skills by maintaining a curious, carefree disposition and having fun regardless of climbing outcomes.
4. Make it your mission to develop a high level of self-awareness. Tune into your body's proprioceptive feedback and learn to really "feel" each move, including the quality of your contact with the holds, the location of your center of mass, and the various levels of tension or relaxation in your muscles. Use this information to discover the most efficient way to do each sequence.
5. Regularly experiment with new techniques and on new terrain. Challenge yourself on a wide range of wall features to expand your skill set and develop confidence. Avoid always climbing known routes and training in the same ways.
6. Push yourself, but know when to call it a day. Spend about one-third of your climbing time on routes just beyond your limit to effectively stretch your boundaries. However, focus the majority of your practice on routes just below your limit to fortify skills and confidence.
7. Get on a regular climbing schedule. Climb two to five days per week (never more) to maximize learning and improvement. Only disciplined, regular practice over the long term will yield consistent improvement and climbing excellence.

Cameron Hörst making the nearly five-foot jump to the finishing hold on Raubritter (5.14b), Frankenjura, Germany. JONATHAN HÖRST

CHAPTER FIVE

The Physiology of Climbing

If you want to climb harder, you must train smarter!

The next five chapters will describe more than one hundred exercises that will help you build a stronger, more stable and powerful, and hopefully injury-proof physique. You'll also learn how to organize your daily workouts and schedule your long-term training to get optimal results for the time and energy you have to invest. While it may be tempting to skip over this chapter on the physiology of climbing and jump right into the more enticing exercise-packed, photo-laced chapters ahead, I urge you not to!

The exercise science and training principles presented in this chapter provide an important educational foundation from which you can build long-term success in the gym and on the rocks. In possessing a 200-level understanding of exercise physiology—how muscles adapt to various training stimuli, what causes fatigue, how you can best train for strength, power, and endurance—you can go about executing an evidence-based workout and avoid getting lured into someone else's bad (and perhaps dangerous) training practices.

Here are several more reasons to read this chapter. You will learn:

- How muscle fibers are recruited in action, and how you can train for higher recruitment and more strength.
- How muscles adapt to training in order to give you more strength, power, and endurance.
- How energy is created in the muscles, and how you can train to increase power output and exercise capacity.
- What causes fatigue, and how you can train to develop a higher resistance to fatigue.
- The nine principles that build effective training and exercise programming.
- How training power, strength, and endurance are different disciplines yet intimately connected. You will learn how to improve in all three areas!
- How to recognize bogus "bro science" at the gym, call "b.s." on invalid training spray, and screen online training advice to identify the nuggets of good information amid a sea of questionable advice.

Before getting started, I want to encourage you to delve deeper into this subject, if you find that acquiring this knowledge yields a unique sense of empowerment in training. Exercise physiology is an extraordinarily interesting field, and climbing science in particular is a rapidly growing topic of research. While this chapter is steeped in sports science, no field is ever a "settled science"—new research is born each month, better training practices are constantly in development, and ever deeper and deeper levels of understanding and nuance are awaiting the curious. Read, assimilate, and apply the information in this chapter (and the entire book!), and explore the footnoted research papers and some of the books on the Suggested Reading list at the end of this book. And be sure to bookmark my website, Training4Climbing.com—visit it regularly for new articles, research updates, and a dose of inspiration!

Muscle Function and Adaptations to Training

The basics of muscle function and adaptation to exercise is a good place to begin our study of exercise physiology. First, we'll examine the type of muscle contractions and the role muscles play in generating movement. Next, you'll learn the three types of muscle fibers and how fiber recruitment varies with the type of exercise stimulus. Lastly is the critical area of muscle adaptation to exercise, and how strength and endurance training protocols produce vastly different cellular response.

Types of Muscle Contraction and Muscle Roles

The production of movement involves three different muscular actions:

Concentric contraction: Muscle action in which the tension developed produces a shortening of the musculature, as in the biceps during the upward phase of a pull-up.

Eccentric contraction: Muscle action in which the muscle resists as it's forced to lengthen, as in the biceps during the lowering phase of a pull-up.

Isometric contraction: Muscle action resulting in no shortening of the muscle (no movement), as in the musculature of the forearm while steadily gripping a handhold.

Depending on the movement being performed, muscles take on one of the three following roles:

Agonist: The muscle or muscle groups causing an action to occur. For instance, the biceps and the latissimus dorsi muscle of the back are some of the prime movers in the pulling motions common to climbing. (Reference the muscle anatomy photos in appendix A to see the location of these muscle groups.)

Antagonist: The muscle or muscles providing an opposing force to the primary muscles in action. For example, in doing a pull-up, the triceps of the lateral upper arm oppose the action of the pulling biceps.

Stabilizer: The muscle or muscle groups that help stabilize the skeletal structures so that tension of the agonist (prime movers) can produce smooth, effective movement. In climbing, some of the most important stabilizer muscles are those supporting the scapula (e.g., serratus anterior and trapezius), and the finger extensor muscles, which stabilize the wrist. Also essential to athletic movement and postural control are the many muscles of the "core" that stabilize the spine.

Muscle Fiber Types

There are two distinct types of muscle fiber: slow twitch (ST) and fast twitch (FT). Fast-twitch fibers are further subdivided into two main subcategories, Type IIa and Type IIb, as shown in table 5.1.

Slow twitch (Type I): Slow-twitch fibers make up approximately 50 percent of the total skeletal muscle, though genetic variation can range from about 20 percent to 80 percent (Bloomfield, et al., 1992). These fatigue-resistant fibers generate energy via the aerobic pathway, consuming muscle glycogen, triglycerides (fat), and lactate to generate ATP (adenosine triphosphate) in the presence of oxygen. Slow-twitch fibers have high capillary and mitochondrial density, and high myoglobin and aerobic enzyme content. Energy production and fiber recruitment are relatively slow (compared to Type II fibers), however, such that slow-twitch fibers are predominantly used during relatively low-intensity activity such as easy to moderate climbing.

Fast twitch A (Type IIa): These fibers, also called fast oxidative fibers, contract quickly and intensely, and they are relatively resistant to fatigue. Type IIa fibers are red, due to the high capillary density and myoglobin content. These fibers possess high mitochondrial density and therefore can generate ATP quickly via oxidative metabolic processes. The primary fuel source is intracellular glycogen and glucose; however, small amounts of creatine phosphate and lactate may contribute to ATP production. These fibers excel at relatively high-intensity activity lasting only a few minutes.

Table 5.1 Muscle Fiber Type and Characteristics

Characteristics	Fiber Type		
	Type I (ST)	**Type IIa (FTa)**	**Type IIb (FTb)**
Contraction Time	Slow	Fast	Very Fast
Resistance to Fatigue	High	Intermediate	Low
Functional Duration	Long	Short	Very Short
Force Production	Low	High	Very High
Glycogen Content	Low	High	High
Mitochondrial Density	High	High	Low
Capillary Density	High	Intermediate	Low
Oxidative Capacity	High	High	Low
Glycolytic Capacity	Low	High	High
Fuel Sources	Triglycerides, Lactate	Glycogen, CP, Lactate	CP, Glycogen

Fast twitch B (Type IIb): These fibers, often called fast glycolytic fibers, have the fastest contraction time and generate energy almost entirely through the anaerobic system. These white-colored fibers have low myoglobin and capillary density, and few mitochondria. Anaerobic metabolic processes prevail, converting creatine phosphate and glycogen into ATP. Resultant metabolic by-products include lactate and—more problematic—hydrogen ions (H+), inorganic phosphate, and ammonia, among other things, all of which contribute to a rapid onset of fatigue. Type IIb fibers are recruited during brief, maximum movements such as gripping a tiny handhold, locking off on one arm, and performing a powerful lunge or campus move.

Your relative percentage of FT and ST muscle fibers is genetically determined and varies little in response to training. Naturally strong boulderers are likely gifted with a higher-than-normal percentage of FT fibers (among other things), whereas gifted endurance climbers likely have a higher percentage of ST fibers. Fortunately, ST fibers can be taught to act like FT fibers (and vice versa) through use of certain training protocols (Chu 1996), and the recruitment and exercise capacity of each fiber type can be vastly improved via training. More on all these topics is upcoming!

Muscle Fiber Recruitment

Muscle fibers of the same type are organized into motor units. ST motor units innervate between 10 and 180 fibers, while FT motor units innervate up to 800 fibers (Bloomfield, et al. 1994). When a muscular contraction is triggered, motor units are recruited on an as-needed basis beginning with the smaller ST motor units. As muscular tension increases, a greater number of ST motor units will join in, and if the tension grows further, the stronger FTa motor units will begin to fire. Maximum muscular force is eventually achieved when a majority of motor units (ST, FTa, and FTb) are recruited into action (see figure 5.1).

This recruitment process explains the importance of strength training with high intensity and near-maximal weight (resistance)—it's only by recruiting the FTb fibers that you will markedly

Figure 5.1 Muscular Force Production

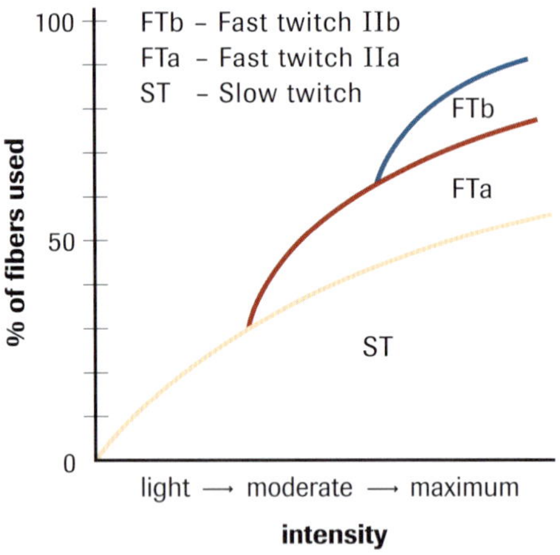

Maximum muscular force is achieved through an aggregate recruitment of ST, FTa, and FTb motor units.

increase strength and power. Thus, all the submaximal climbing in the world won't make you stronger; getting stronger at climbing requires near-maximal exercises such as hard bouldering, heavy weight lifting, hypergravity training, and such.

Later on in this chapter, you'll learn specific protocols (weights and reps) for developing maximum strength, power, and local strength-endurance, and in chapters 8 and 9 you'll learn the must-do exercises for climbers.

Muscular Adaptations to Strength Training

Two primary types of adaptations occur in response to strength training: neurological and morphological. Neural adaptations produce the initial strength gains resulting from use of a novel exercise or heighten exercises stimulus (see figure 5.2), so let's begin here.

NEUROLOGICAL ADAPTATIONS

The nervous system adapts to strength training in three ways: motor learning, motor unit synchronization, and disinhibition.

Motor learning: This first neural adaptation should sound familiar after reading chapter 4. During the initial work at a new exercise (say, uneven-grip pull-ups or even campus training), your primary limitation will be a lack of coordination and feel for the exercise. The first few workouts will yield rapid improvement as a result of motor learning and improved coordination among the prime mover, stabilizer, and antagonist muscles. Beyond this point, further strength gains will depend on other adaptations taking place.

Motor unit synchronization: Motor unit synchronization is the second neural adaptation that increases strength. Suppose you have acquired the coordination and motor skills needed for performing a given exercise—or perhaps you're adding a new exercise that requires no learning (such as hanging on a fingerboard). Initial training triggers motor units to fire in a rather random, asynchronous manner. Continued training, however, enhances motor unit synchronization; eventually most of the motor units will fire in unison, resulting in more strength and power.

Disinhibition: The final neural adaptation, disinhibition, is most important (and exciting) for intermediate to advanced climbers in search of gains in maximum strength and power. The neuromuscular system has a built-in feedback mechanism that acts as a safeguard during times of increasing force production. The Golgi tendon organ, located in the musculotendinous junction, is sensitive to the level of tension in the muscle, and in situations of high force it sends inhibitory signals that prevent further motor units from firing. In most individuals this protective response limits force production to some amount far below your absolute maximum-force-producing potential. It's like putting a restrictor plate on the engine of a race car to limit its top speed to 150 miles per hour, even though it's capable of 225. Fortunately, regular high-intensity training reduces the sensitivity of the Golgi tendon organ (disinhibition) and thus opens up a new level of maximum strength.

The difference between your maximum voluntary force and the absolute maximum capacity is called the strength deficit. Research has shown that significant gains in strength are possible by training to reduce these neural inhibitions. One study (Tidow 1990) showed that untrained individuals possessed strength deficits of up to 45 percent—that is, neural inhibition was reducing their maximum strength to almost half their absolute capacity. The study also revealed that targeted training by elite athletes reduced strength deficits to only 5 percent. Therefore, large gains in strength are possible without ever growing a larger, heavier muscle!

As a final note, the best type of training to produce disinhibition depends on the magnitude of your strength deficit. Intermediate climbers, who likely have larger strength deficits, would benefit most by training with heavy loads (weighted pull-downs and fingerboard hangs, hypergravity bouldering, HIT system, and so forth). Elite climbers with smaller strength deficits might realize further improvements only through a combination of high-resistance (hypergravity) and high-speed (reactive/plyometric) training.

MORPHOLOGICAL ADAPTATIONS

The primary morphological adaptations involve an increase in the cross-sectional area of the whole muscle and individual muscle fibers, a process called hypertrophy. As shown in figure 5.2, muscular hypertrophy contributes toward long-term gains in maximum strength.

Certainly, large muscles in the wrong place (e.g., legs, hips, chest, and shoulders) are a liability in a strength-to-mass ratio activity such as climbing. Even overdevelopment of the all-important pull muscles can be a bad thing if it's the result of exercising in a nonspecific way, such as a bodybuilding or CrossFit training program. For example, overdeveloped baseball-size biceps (a result of doing bicep curls with a heavy barbell) will have a negative biomechanical effect by preventing a tight lock-off when pulling a handhold in toward your shoulder.

Figure 5.2. Muscular Adaptations to Strength

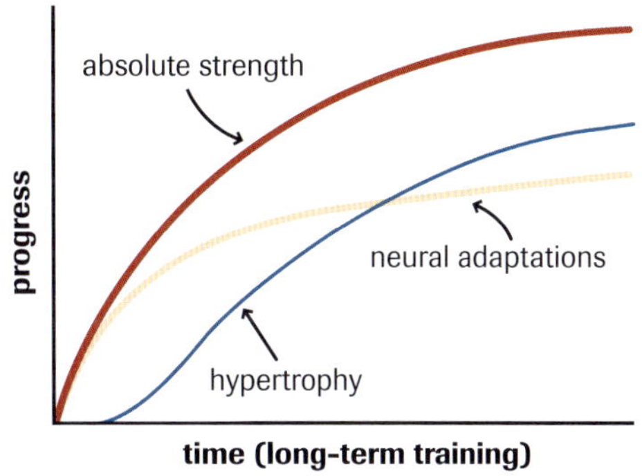

Initial gains in strength result mostly from neural adaptations, whereas long-term gains depend to some degree on hypertrophy.

Still, any muscular hypertrophy occurring in the forearms, arms, and back resulting from climbing-specific training should be viewed as a good thing. In fact, an experienced climber who has been training for a long time and doesn't realize a little hypertrophy probably isn't training effectively or eating right.

It's interesting to note that a highly trained neuromuscular system is not absolutely necessary for being a strong climber. As mentioned in chapter 1, a small number of individuals possess tendon insertion points at a larger distance from the joint (axis of rotation) than the rest of us with average genetics. These gifted people will exhibit what seems to be amazing strength given their modest body builds. Other genetic factors, such as having a slight build, a large positive ape index, or an unusually high percentage of fast-twitch fibers, may further enhance their physical prowess. With this in mind you can see why these rare climbers are incredibly strong regardless of the type of training, if any, they engage in.

Muscular Adaptations to Local Endurance Training

Muscular adaptations that result from endurance-oriented training are fundamentally different from the strength-training adaptations (described above), and are mainly confined to the FTa and ST fibers. Engaging in regular, rigorous local endurance training—"local" meaning in a specific muscle group, like the forearm flexors—produces a variety of adaptations both in the short and long term. Engaging in relatively high-intensity exercises such as Frenchies, bouldering 4x4s, hangboard repeaters, and climbing intervals will yield positive adaptations that are revealed in as little as a couple of weeks (buffering and enzymatic changes) up to many months and years (via angiogenesis). Detailed below are a few of the most significant adaptations to endurance exercise; however, there are several other more subtle cellular alterations that also contribute.

Intracellular buffering, oxidative enzymes, and glycogen supercompensation: Beginning a mesocycle of local endurance training (e.g., forearm strength-endurance and pull-muscle power-endurance) will yield noticeable improvement in only a few sessions. This initial windfall of endurance gains comes mostly by way of improved intracellular buffering of hydrogen ions ($H+$), development of beneficial glycolytic and oxidative enzymes, and glycogen supercompensation. Increases in these areas largely cease after a few weeks, so further gains in local endurance depend on other adaptations (below).

Mitochondria biogenesis: Increased mitochondria density—in both the ST and FTa fibers—is the most fundamental adaptation induced by endurance training. Mitochondria are the intracellular energy factories that convert glucose, glycogen, fatty acids, and lactate into ATP. Four weeks of endurance-oriented training (or climbing) can increase mitochondria density by up to 50 percent. Although small increases in mitochondria efficiency can continue long term, actual gains in mitochondria content approach a steady state after four to five weeks of training (Terjung 1979).

Angiogenesis: Endurance exercise increases the number of capillaries surrounding individual fibers, a process called angiogenesis. Increased capillarity improves oxygen exchange between capillary and fiber, thus enhancing the rate of energy production in ST and FTa fibers. As a relatively slow biological process, angiogenesis provides a pathway to longer-term gains in endurance.

Energy Systems

One of the many major additions to this edition of *Training for Climbing* is the concept of energy system training—that is, designing exercise protocols and workouts to target a specific energy system. This is

Table 5.2 Physiological Adaptations to Training

	Maximum Strength Training	Local Endurance Training
Muscle Fiber Size	No change or increase	No change or decrease
Fiber Recruitment	Increase	No change
Mitochondrial Density	No change	Increase
Capillary Density	No change	Increase
Cellular ATP-CP	Increase	No change
Cellular Glycogen	No change	Increase
Intracellular Buffering	No change	Increase

Adaptations from maximum strength training versus local endurance training.

Table 5.3 Energy Systems

Energy System	Energy Source	Duration of Steady-State Exercise	Power Output
Anaerobic Alactic	ATP-CP	1–12 seconds	Very high
Anaerobic Lactic	Muscle Glycogen	12 seconds–about 2 minutes	High
Aerobic	Fatty Acids, Glycogen, Lactate	2 minutes–about 2 hours	Low to Moderate

a powerful distinction that you can leverage to train far more effectively, given a sufficient understanding of the bioenergetics involved. If this sounds exciting, read on!

Energy systems refer to the metabolic pathways that produce ATP for muscular contractions. There are three major energy pathways, and all three contribute to ATP production at any given moment. Depending on the energy needs of exercise, however, just one or two energy pathway(s) dominate (see table 5.3). Let's take a closer look at each energy pathway and how they contribute toward power output in exercise and climbing.

ATP-CP (Anaerobic Alactic)

The ATP-CP system, also known as the anaerobic alactic energy pathway, provides rapid energy for brief, intense movements such as a few hard pull-ups, a powerful lunge, or a maximal contraction of the finger flexors. In maximal exercise the stored supply of ATP and CP (creatine phosphate) will diminish in just ten to twelve seconds, resulting in a drop in power output as the glycolytic (anaerobic lactic) system takes over energy production. This explains why it's virtually impossible to perform your maximum campus training movements for more than about ten seconds.

A strong anaerobic alactic energy system is important in climbing, because it's called upon to produce the maximum power output needed for a crux move or a lunge or to sustain a maximal finger grip for a few seconds. Fortunately, depleted creatine phosphate stores can recover quickly during submaximal climbing and brief rest periods. What's interesting—and relatively unknown among coaches and athletes—is that creatine phosphate resynthesis is an aerobic process. Therefore, a strong aerobic energy system will support a high rate of creatine phosphate resynthesis—important for climbing intermittent near-maximal moves separated by only a few easier moves or a brief marginal rest.

The bottom line: Your level of aerobic conditioning plays an important role in your ability to do repeated bouts of anaerobic alactic–fueled exercise or maximal moves. Recent research has confirmed this concept in showing that aerobically trained climbers (who engaged in regular nonspecific aerobic activity such as running) recovered faster than climbers who did no generalized cardiovascular training (Schöffl 2006). Furthermore, Fryer (2015) has shown that the finger flexor muscles of elite climbers use (and replenish) oxygen at a higher rate than non-elites.

Glycolytic (Anaerobic Lactic)

Sustained high-intensity exercise (or climbing) lasting between about twelve seconds and two minutes is principally powered by the anaerobic lactic energy pathway. The process of fast glycolysis can rapidly regenerate ATP in an oxygen-free (anaerobic) environment, which is the common state of the forearm flexor muscles during high-intensity isometric contractions (as in sustained gripping of difficult holds) and the large muscles of the arms and back when pulling many successive hard moves without rest. Muscle contractions of as little as 15 percent of maximum voluntary contraction (MVC) begin to impede blood flow, and contractions of more than 50 percent of MVC completely occlude blood flow (Köstermeyer 2000), so it's easy to understand why the anaerobic lactic energy system is so often called upon in climbing.

Common hallmarks of a hardworking anaerobic lactic energy system are muscular pain, the "pump," a growing shortness of breath, and increasing fatigue (and drop in power output) between thirty seconds and two minutes. At about sixty seconds into sustained near-maximal climbing, the anaerobic lactic system begins to fade quickly, and by two minutes the aerobic energy pathway becomes the dominant source of ATP, thus compelling a sharp drop in power output.

The choking off of the anaerobic energy pathway between one and two minutes of sustained, difficult exercise is due to the metabolic by-products of the anaerobic splitting of glucose to create ATP. Although a complex process (and still somewhat controversial), we know that the anaerobic metabolism of glucose generates a number of by-products including pyruvate and hydrogen ions (H+), which are generated at a rapid rate, along with lesser amounts of other metabolites such as inorganic phosphate, reactive oxygen species, and ammonia. While all these metabolites may contribute to fatigue, it's the rapidly increasing H+ concentration that most threatens homeostasis and ultimately leads to cessation of this energy pathway.

This increasing intracellular acidosis (due to H+ production) is likely the cause of the muscle burn you feel; more critical, however, rising acidosis hampers the function of glycolytic enzymes, which results in a sharp drop in anaerobic energy production. Fortunately, there are intracellular buffers that can consume H+ (for a short time) and slow the rising tide of acidosis. Interestingly, the metabolite pyruvate is one such buffer, as one molecule of pyruvate can attract two H+ ions to create lactate. Even more fascinating is the fact that lactate can pass into a nearby ST fiber and be used as fuel for aerobic metabolism. The bulk of the lactate, however, exits the cell into the blood and circulates to the liver to be converted back into glycogen, to the brain or other organs to support local energy production, or to other muscles where it can be used for aerobic energy production. This helps explain why aerobically trained climbers can recover more quickly between bouts of strenuous (anaerobic) climbing.

Aerobic

Sustained activity lasting longer than two minutes relies primarily on the aerobic (with oxygen) pathway, as energy produced via the anaerobic alactic and lactic systems quickly wanes. This transition to aerobic energy production is evident by a marked drop in power output due to the slower rate of ATP synthesis via the aerobic energy system (see figure

Figure 5.3 Muscular Energy Production

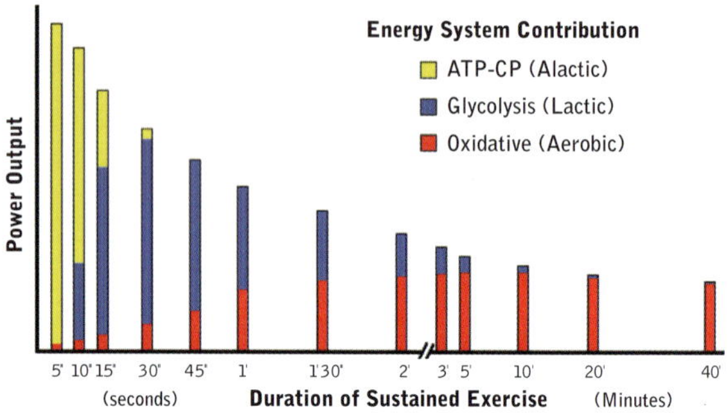

Brief, maximal muscular action is fueled by ATP-CP. After about twelve seconds, anaerobic lactic energy production becomes the primary energy source. Exercise lasting longer than two minutes depends mostly on aerobic energy production, although power output is only a fraction of maximal.

5.3). Fortunately, the only metabolic by-products of the aerobic system are CO_2, water, and heat—therefore, lower-intensity aerobic activity can continue for as long as oxygen and energy substrate are available (primarily muscle glycogen and fatty acids) and heat can be removed from the working muscle. Interestingly, the lactate produced by anaerobic glycolysis is another fuel source for aerobic energy production, and therefore lactate is a kind of molecular "holding tank" that bridges the anaerobic and aerobic energy systems.

Causes of Fatigue

After reading the previous sections on muscle fiber recruitment and the three energy systems, you should have a good understanding of some of the causes of the fatigue you experience in training and climbing. On a cellular level, depletion of ATP-CP, lack of oxygen (hypoxia), and increasing acidosis are primary causes of acute fatigue and diminished power output, while on a systemic basis, glycogen depletion and limitation of the circulatory system result in general fatigue. This textbook conceptual model of fatigue is called the Cardiovascular/Anaerobic Model. But here's where the plot thickens . . .

While all the fatigue-inducing factors outlined above are certainly at play during intense exercise, the idea that fatigue results directly and absolutely from the muscles is now being challenged. New research suggests that it is actually the brain that initiates stress signals (the pain you feel) and triggers the "stopping thoughts" that arise in the conscious mind, based on cues received from the muscles. This new Central Governor Model (CGM) of fatigue was first proposed by Dr. Timothy Noakes, a marathon runner and a professor of exercise and sports science at the University of Cape Town, and it is now gaining traction with other researchers, coaches, and athletes. (I first wrote about the possible role of the central governor in my 2010 book, *Maximum Climbing*—pick up a copy for a study of brain training for climbing!)

According to the CGM, fatigue is a sensation sent by the unconscious mind to the conscious mind to prevent loss of homeostasis. (Homeostasis is the tendency of the body to seek and maintain a condition of balance or equilibrium within its internal environment; a simple example being the body's ability to maintain an internal temperature around 98.6°F/37°C.) So what you feel during strenuous exercise—"my arm muscles hurt" or "my legs ache"—is actually the brain sending a message to slow down so as to avoid serious injury or death. Similarly, the brain involuntarily reduces neural drive (recruitment) in order to reduce power output and protect the body from irreversible damage.

The Central Governor Model remains somewhat controversial among sports scientists, but emerging research is lending support and increasing the number of advocates. As the theory goes, power output during exercise is regulated in the brain by a "central governor." Efferent control of the muscles is based upon a black box calculation that integrates afferent feedback signals from the muscles and heart, as well as sensory feedback of the external environment (weather conditions, terrain, and such), knowledge of ongoing results (competitive place or proximity of the endpoint of performance), and unconscious calibration based on past experience. Integrating all this data, the central governor is constantly assessing how the organs and muscles are faring and what modulations are needed to maintain homeostasis. So it's the brain that interprets increasing acidosis and hypoxia, elevated body temperature, and decreasing glycogen supply, among other signals, as being stressful to the body, and it's the brain that in turn issues pain sensations and stopping thoughts.

You could argue that there's little difference between the Cardiovascular/Anaerobic Model and the Central Governor Model, given that both models ultimately lead to fatigue based on what's happening in the muscles. However, the CGM's theory that the brain is the sole governor of fatigue is a crucial distinction with powerful implications.

Since fatigue is not an absolute physiological event within the muscle, but actually a brain calculation and efferent response, it is possible to extend performance in the face of the brain's distress signals!

One recent study that supports this theory tested a group of cyclists performing a rigorous one-hour time trial. Australian researchers measured power output and muscle fiber activation during a mock time trial in which the cyclists performed six one-minute maximum sprints interspersed throughout the hour of sustained exercise. The results revealed that power output and muscle activation decreased with each successive sprint (as you would expect). Surprisingly, however, the sixth sprint, performed during the last minute of the time trial, showed a significant increase in power output and muscle fiber recruitment! If the muscles themselves were the end-all in terms of fatigue signals (i.e., fatigue as an absolute result of high blood acidosis, dwindling ATP, increasing oxygen debt, and such), then the cyclists would have been physiologically unable to increase power output in the final stage of the time trial.

Per the CGM, here's what likely happened. Knowing the end of the time trial was near, the brain reassessed its estimates of energy reserves and

Figure 5.4 The Central Governor Model

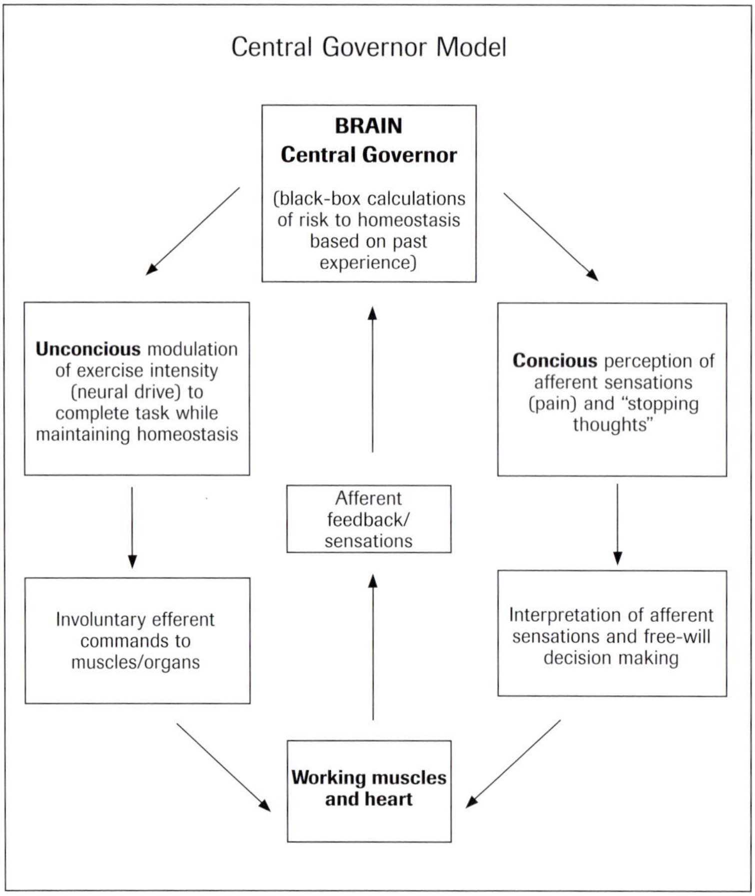

afferent signals from the muscles and heart, and determined that it could allow a higher work output during the final minute of the time trial (without loss of homeostasis and risk of injury or death). Furthermore, the cyclists' knowledge that the final sprint would be followed by cessation of the grueling exercise may have empowered some of the cyclists to overcome, by the conscious power of will, the brain's pain signals and stopping thoughts. Applied to climbing, the Central Governor Model helps explain those instances when you climbed onward through massive fatigue to successfully clip the anchors on a sport climb or realized just enough of a "second wind" to complete a multi-pitch or big-wall ascent.

It's interesting to note that two parallel pathways operate within the Central Governor Model: the objective realm of the material world governed by the forces of mechanistic determinism, and the subjective realm governed by will (see figure 5.4). As exemplified in the preceding study (and perhaps in your own experience), willpower of the mind can exert a causal influence over determinism. While I believe that extreme physical activity is sometimes modulated solely by objective physiological constraints (per the Cardiovascular/Anaerobic Model), it is likely that performance most often falters because we obey or succumb to the brain's overly conservative signals to cease physical activity. The best climbers, then, are not necessarily the absolute strongest physically—instead they likely possess uncommon mental strength and willpower that enables them to hang on longer and continue upward, in spite of the brain's rising chorus of pain sensations.

In conclusion, we can distill two important training implications from the Central Governor Model. First and foremost, you can enhance and extend performance through the power of your free will. With consistent, disciplined effort to employ greater willpower in all you do, this largely untapped power of the mind will grow stronger and more capable of carrying you through extreme situations. Secondly, engaging in high-intensity or long-duration training (and climbing) to a high level of fatigue will recalibrate the brain to be less conservative in directing work output during extreme physical activity, thus enabling you to perform longer and nearer your body's true absolute limit.

Let's take a brief look at how you might take this knowledge of the central governor and apply it to training for climbing.

Strength and Power Training to Recalibrate the Central Governor

Muscular strength and power are highly distinct functions that involve brief, intense force production. Absolute muscular strength, often called "limit strength," is the ability to exert maximum force in a single all-out effort (irrespective of time), as in crimping on a minuscule handhold or pulling hard through a strenuous move. Power is the application of force with velocity—think of it as explosive strength—as in making a fast, powerful reach upward or throwing a lunge.

Given the brief duration of maximum strength and power at work, the factors that lead to fatigue and limit performance are vastly different from those of muscular endurance. A primary limitation in maximum-strength and power output is the supply of ATP-CP stored in the muscle—the supply of these fuels limits maximal force production to less than twelve seconds (although ATP-CP is continually synthesized within the muscles and replenishes in just three to five minutes of rest).

While the central governor plays a lesser role in modulating such maximal movements, the brain is a major factor in directing application of strength and power. It's ultimately the brain that dictates recruitment of muscular motor units via neural drive (the amplitude of the impulses impelling recruitment) and by cycling motor units within a muscle in order to sustain steady force production for as long as possible. As an example of this amazing process, consider the act of holding steady a one-arm lock-off position for a few seconds. During this maximal activity, the brain cycles the firing of motor units to maintain a steady lock-off; it rests some motor units (groups of muscle fibers) while it fires others. Maximum-strength and power production are greatly influenced by the quality of coordination and synchronization of this motor unit recruitment.

Two final factors that limit strength and power production are the Golgi tendon organ (GTO) and willpower. The GTO is part of the autonomic nervous system and protects tendons by limiting the recruitment of motor units below a certain threshold amount. In a manner quite similar to the central governor, the GTO restricts power output to a level far below the likely point of catastrophic tendon damage. Unlike the central governor, however, GTO function is completely involuntary and essentially instantaneous in reaction since its neural pathway only travels from the sensory receptors in the tendon to the spinal cord and back, and not the longer round-trip to the brain and back. Still, the sensitivity of the GTO can be influenced through training. Specifically, reactive training methods (more on this later) will somewhat disinhibit the GTO, to allow a higher level of maximum strength and power output.

Muscular Endurance and Stamina to Recalibrate the Central Governor

Let's first define muscular endurance and stamina, since some people incorrectly use these terms interchangeably.

Stamina is the ability to engage in low- to moderate-intensity activity for an extended period, such as running for an hour or two, or even climbing all day. This nonspecific, general endurance is somewhat a function of aerobic capacity (VO_2 max), but it's largely influenced by available fuel supply (resident glycogen stores and carbohydrate consumption during exercise) and mental toughness (the will to endure pain and reach your goal).

Muscular endurance is the capability to sustain high-intensity anaerobic activity for a minute or more, or to maintain a high power output through several bouts of intense activity with only brief rests breaks in between. Failure on a near-limit rock climb often seems to come down to a lack of local forearm muscle endurance, as the hallmark muscle pump and burn seems to mandate an end to your effort. Local muscular endurance is a function of your level of maximum strength, your muscles' ability to tolerate acidosis, energy substrate availability, and your will to sustain strenuous activity despite painful stress signals from the brain.

Per the Central Governor Model described above, the brain limits power output and creates pain sensations and stopping thoughts so that you will terminate activity long before you risk catastrophic injury or death. Effective training, then, must not only address specific physiological constraints (aerobic and anaerobic capacity), but also train the brain to better interpret afferent feedback from the blood, muscles, and other organs and thus increase the brain's threshold for shutting down muscular activation during strenuous exercise. The key is to train in ways that closely simulate the demands of your goal climbs, and in doing so to stretch your limits in anaerobic and aerobic endurance to establish new central governor experience and fatigue set points.

In closing, top climbers—like Adam Ondra, Tommy Caldwell, Chris Sharma, Daniel Woods, and Alex Megos—have spent years training and climbing at progressively higher intensities and for longer durations. Through a combination of deep commitment to training and exercising incredible willpower, they have stretched their brains and bodies to new levels. While you and I may not possess quite as good genetics (or the time and resources) of these pros, we undoubtedly possess room to improve, both physiologically and in terms of recalibrating our central governor.

Research on Rock Climbing—The First 2,000 Years

The earliest sports science research on rock climbing primarily focused on specific sites and mechanisms of injury. The development of organized difficulty-format competitions at the World Cup level in the 1980s encouraged exploration of the climber as an athlete. Initially, scientific study focused on defining the performance model for difficult climbing—the identification of measurable factors that seemed to be common in elite climbers. Following pathways of discovery that were typical in other sports, these initial studies focused on anthropometry, or stature and body composition; muscular strength; and energy expenditure.

The first large-scale anthropometry study of elite competition climbers was published by Watts, Martin, and Durtschi (USA) in 1993. In a sample of thirty-nine international competitors, the athletes were found to be small in stature and low in body weight with very low body fat levels. It is possible this early observation of very light and extremely lean climbers at the elite level encouraged aspiring competitors to reduce body mass through special diets and borderline disordered eating. Today we know severe reductions in body weight, and body fat in particular, can negatively impact maintenance of muscular strength and health in general. With this knowledge, the dominant anthropometry of elite climbers has likely changed a bit since the 1980s. Climbing steeper, more physically demanding terrain may also be a factor in some climber anthropometry characteristics today.

Many early studies focused on strength and found elite climbers to have relatively average handgrip strength when compared with gender- and age-matched population norms. However, when grip-strength values were expressed relative to body weight, elite climbers scored in the top 10 to 20 percent. Subsequent study and observation of the hands during climbing revealed minimal use of the standard handgrip testing position where the thumb applies force in opposition to the fingers. Researchers such as Grant (Scotland), Watts (USA), Schweizer (Switzerland), Vigoroux (France), and others developed new methods to test finger flexion force through force transducers mounted in adjustable frames. Such research found climbers to be superior in sustaining repetitive contractions with the muscles that control finger force and specific hand configurations.

A developing area of research is the rate of force development (RFD) in the finger flexor muscles. Fanchini (Italy), along with coworkers in Switzerland and France, found RFD to be high in boulderers and lead climbers relative to non-climbers. Interestingly, the boulderers had significantly higher RFD than the lead climbers. There is room for more research in this area.

Muscle endurance has also been of interest. New studies by Fryer and coworkers (UK and Europe) and others have looked at factors that affect muscle contraction endurance in the hands and recovery between repeated contractions. Higher forearm blood flow and better oxygenation of forearm muscles have been found in elite climbers. These factors likely improve the climber's resistance to fatigue throughout the ascent of a route.

Bioenergetics—energy expenditure and the support systems for energy expenditure—has also been of interest in early research and continues to be explored. Billat (France) and coworkers were the first to report oxygen uptake (VO_2) values for expert climbers during climbing. Watts and Drobish used an early nonmotorized climbing treadmill (Brewer's Ledge Treadwall) to study VO_2 and energy expenditure during continuous climbing at different angles. Development of battery-powered portable metabolic analysis systems in the late 1990s and 2000s opened up the study of bioenergetics during actual climbing on indoor and outdoor terrain. Although results were specific to test protocol, climber ability level, and speed of climbing, the oxygen uptake rate during sustained climbing seemed to range between twenty-five to thirty-five milliliters of oxygen per kilogram of body weight per minute with energy expenditures of around eleven kilocalories per minute. While these studies illustrate the aerobic nature of climbing, other studies have found elevations of lactate in the blood, which can be a marker for anaerobically derived energy. Bertuzzi and coworkers (Brazil) have estimated energy to be derived 42 percent through aerobic metabolism, 22 percent from an anaerobic lactate-producing process, and 36 percent from breakdown of high-energy phosphates without lactate production during difficult climbing. Thus, climbing involves a broad range of bioenergetics.

Taken as a whole, the historical and more contemporary physiological research on difficult rock climbing yields a complex portrait—strength with endurance, peak muscular effort and rate of force development, aerobic energy expenditure with high-intensity power, explosiveness with subtle control. Researchers such as Jiří Baláš (Czech Republic) and Vanesa España-Romero (Spain), along with their coworkers, continue to pursue factors in the physiological performance model for climbing. Peter Wolf and coworkers in Switzerland have begun research with very sophisticated instrumented modular holds that should yield new information regarding the forces involved in different climbing moves and techniques.

The era of research for rock climbing is relatively young. Although the background physiological model has been refined, a lack of controlled training research requires careful application of known principles and established training theory based upon the model. Fortunately, *Training for Climbing* does this. New investigators, such as López-Rivera and González-Badillo (Spain), are starting to study climbing-specific training protocols. It is an exciting time for the science of rock climbing.

This brief overview of research does not even begin to explore the associated areas of biomechanics, nutrition, and psychological factors! Thankfully, Eric Hörst follows the contemporary research intensely and incorporates the best of our current knowledge into his website and books. Another valuable resource for tracking research is the International Rock Climbing Research Association (www.ircra.rocks).

—Dr. Phil Watts

Training Principles

Backed by the most rigorous exercise science, we can now embark on a quick study of nine training principles. Some of the nine principles presented below will sound familiar to you, while others may seem novel. Trust me, however, that they are all powerful! You might consider these as simply guideposts to effective training and exercise programming. The most pragmatic climbers—like this author!—will fastidiously abide by the principles with the goal of squeezing the maximum output in performance gains for the time-limited training input. So let's get started with the principle of specificity, the paramount of all training principles.

Specificity

The principle of specificity of training simply states that the more specific a training activity is to a given sport—in direction of force application, velocity of movement, pattern of movement, body posture, range of motion, type of contraction, and energy systems used—the more it will contribute to increasing performance in that sport. Therefore, for an exercise to be effective at producing usable strength gains for climbing (such as grip strength, lock-off strength, or lunging power), it must impart a stress on the musculature in a very climbing-specific way. The more specific the training activity or exercise, the greater the benefit on your climbing performance. Let's look at a few examples of how this rule applies to training for climbing.

Circuit training or pumping iron does not train the muscles in the slightest way similar to their use in rock climbing. Consequently, doing a health club–style workout (using machines and free weights exclusively) is largely a waste of energy in terms of improving climbing performance (the exception being individuals possessing unusually poor levels of general fitness). A better approach, according to the principle of specificity, would be to climb three days per week and design any supplemental weight training to target the important pulling and antagonist muscles, as well as the core and extension muscles of the back and legs.

Squeezing a rubber hand doughnut (or other similar spring-loaded device) is likewise unproductive for improving your finger strength for climbing. Grip strength shows a remarkable amount of specificity depending on the grip position (crimp, open hand, pinch), the positions of the wrist and elbow, the intensity of the contraction, and even the type of contraction (isometric or concentric). Furthermore, since your grip tends to fail while you are pulling down on it with near-maximum load, it must be trained in much the same way. Consequently, squeezing a rubber doughnut is basically useless as climbing training, though it does have some value as a warm-up exercise and in injury rehabilitation.

What about the basic pull-up (palms away), a most popular exercise among climbers? Obviously the motion is similar to climbing, but your posture, your degree of body tension, and the exact positions of your hands and arms do not vary randomly as they do on rock. What's more, the ability to stop or lock off your arm in some novel position is often more vital in climbing than is the simple act of pulling. Therefore, to produce the most transfer of your pull-up training to the rocks (and reduce your risk of an elbow overuse injury), you want to alter the pull-up in a variety of ways with every set. For example, you might change the distance between your hands, stagger one hand lower than the other (use a webbing loop), and include some lock-offs or stops in the motion at a variety of arm angles. This approach would be much more advantageous than just doing pull-ups in the same fixed position.

Finally, let's consider the concept of cross-training as some individuals try to apply it to climbing. Clearly, the idea that performing any other sports activity might improve climbing performance is in blatant conflict with the principle of specificity. In fact, the only sports in which cross-training seems to be practical are the aerobic endurance sports, as popularized by the triathlon phenomenon.

Individualization

This could also be called the snowflake principle, since it highlights that no two climbers—or their optimal conditioning programs—are the same. The best training program for you will target your specific weaknesses, address past or present injuries, provide sufficient time for recovery, and be structured to provide the greatest output for the available training input. Since there is no other climber quite like you, there is no other climber's training program that you'd want to copy—doing so will provide less-than-optimal results and might even get you injured. Consequently, it would be wise to develop and execute what seems to be the best program for you and ignore how others train. As a guiding principle remember that "no one is you, and that's your power!"

Progressive Overload

This granddaddy of training principles states that in order to increase physical capability, it is necessary to expose your body to a level of stress beyond that to which it is accustomed. You can achieve this overload by increasing the intensity (greater resistance), volume, or speed of training, or by decreasing the rest interval between successive sets. Depending on the exercise and which of these exercise parameters you choose to vary, the overload will effect adaptations resulting in more strength, power, anaerobic endurance, or stamina. For example, increasing exercise resistance and speed will produce gains in maximum strength and power, whereas decreasing rest intervals and increasing volume will improve muscular endurance.

While it's probably a good idea to vary the method of overload from time to time, the best method of overload for you depends on your climbing preference. If bouldering is your favorite type of climbing, then you'd want to favor training that builds strength and power (and create overload by increasing resistance and recruitment). In training for roped climbing, however, it would be best to increase volume and decrease rest intervals to improve muscular endurance. Finally, big-wall and alpine climbers looking for greater stamina should create overload by increasing total volume of moderate climbing and generalized aerobic activity.

Variation

One of the most common training errors among all athletes is the failure to regularly change their training program. This principle states that the body becomes accustomed to training stimuli that are repeatedly applied in the same way. Therefore, if you go to the climbing gym and engage in the same basic routine every time, your strength and climbing gains will eventually plateau despite what feel like good workouts. Strive to vary your training by manipulating the type of overload (per above) as well as mixing up the type and order of climbs and exercises performed.

Periodization, another form of variation, involves alternating the overall workout intensity and volume over the course of days or weeks. For example, with indoor training you might alternate workouts among "high volume" (doing many moderate routes), "high intensity" (hard, powerful bouldering), and "high, high" (climbing several near-limit routes). You could also vary your workouts every few weeks as in the 3-2-1 training cycle described in chapter 10. Bottom line: Make the Principle of Variation a cornerstone of your training-for-climbing program and you will get uncommonly good results!

Isolation

While beginning climbers typical experience steady gains in climbing ability and climbing-specific strength for up to two or three years, reaching a performance plateau is exceedingly common (often around the 5.11 or 5.12 grades). Breaking through this frustrating ceiling often requires embarking on a new training program that incorporates highly specific exercises that target the limiting constraints—most commonly, finger flexor strength and endurance, limit strength and power in the pulling muscles, and the ability to create core stiffness.

Applied literally, the principle of isolation requires targeting a single muscle group while activity in all nearby or related muscles is minimized. In reality this is very difficult to do, especially when you want to obey the principle of specificity by isolating a muscle in a climbing-specific way. Still, climbers can exercise in the spirit of this principle—and get excellent results—with quasi-isolation exercises such as fingerboard hangs, certain forms of campus training, System Wall "isolations," and various core-muscle exercises. Such isolation training provides tremendous stimulus for neural and morphological adaptations, by maximizing fiber recruitment and energy system efficiency.

Optimal Sets, Reps, and Rest Intervals Between Sets

The optimal training load (resistance), the number of reps and sets, and the rest interval between sets depend on the desired training outcome. Warm-up sets and stabilizer-muscle training (e.g., rotator cuff, wrist extensions, and scapular stabilizers) are best performed with a relatively modest resistance that allows fifteen to thirty repetitions. Similarly, antagonist-muscle exercises need only be performed at a moderately-high resistance with ten to twenty reps per set. For the purposes of developing climbing-specific strength and local endurance, however, a much higher workload (in some cases five to ten sets) is needed to produce beneficial results on the rock.

The length of rest between sets can similarly be managed to produce optimal training adaptations. A three- to five-minute recovery period is best when training for strength and power. A much shorter rest period—thirty seconds to two minutes—is optimal when training for improved local endurance. No need to be long-winded here, since chapters 8 and 9 will provide dozens of exercises and outline the best rep and set scheme and recovery interval for each.

Exercise Order

Every workout should, of course, begin with warm-up period that is gradually progressive. Once all the muscles have been warmed and "turned on," the next segment of your workout should involve actual climbing—practicing new moves, working hard boulders, rope climbing, and such—since being mentally and physically fresh is important for developing and reinforcing efficient motor and movement skills. Only upon completion of your climbing should you move on to targeted supplemental exercises such as weighted pull-ups, fingerboard hangs, campus training, and the like. Follow these activities with stabilizer and core training, and conclude with some foam rolling and stretching to jump-start the recovery process.

Any extensive antagonist-muscle training, supplemental free weight work, or aerobic exercise is best performed on a rest day from climbing. As you'll learn in chapter 6, there's no need to train the antagonists more than twice per week. Some climbers, however, may wish to do aerobic training two to four days per week, while also climbing three or four days per week and taking one full day of rest per week. The only way to schedule all this (and get one day of complete rest per week) is to do a couple of split workout days—that is, days in which you do a morning and late-day workout. The most effective way to split workouts is to do an aerobic session as early in the morning as possible, and then the climbing workout in the late afternoon or evening. Scheduling six to eight hours rest between the split sessions is essential, and you should always train general endurance early and strength/power endurance late in the day—you'll get suboptimal results the other way around.

Rest

The various muscular adaptations described earlier occur between, not during, workouts. Sufficient rest and healthy lifestyle habits (including proper nutrition and adequate sleep) are fundamental to maximizing the adaptations from your training investments. As a rough guideline, complete recovery (supercompensation) takes anywhere from twenty-four to seventy-two hours, depending on the intensity and volume of the stimulus (see figure 5.5). For example, it might only take one day to recover from a high volume of low-intensity activity

Figure 5.5 Supercompensation Cycle

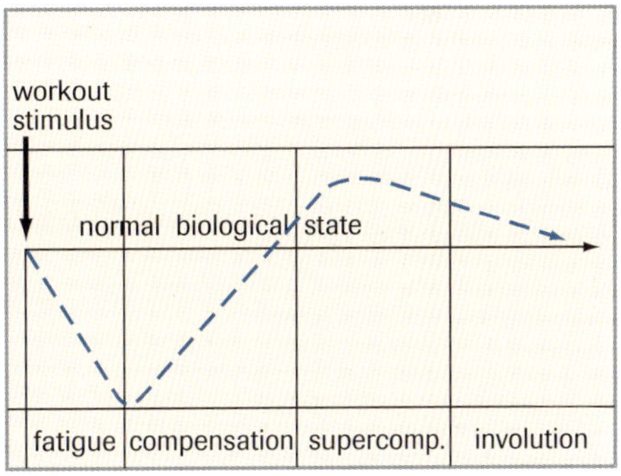

Complete recovery (supercompensation) takes anywhere from twenty-four to seventy-two hours, depending on the intensity and volume of the training stimulus.

like climbing a bunch of relatively easy routes or just hiking, whereas it will likely take two or three days to recover completely from a high volume of high-intensity exercise, such as climbing many routes near your limit, or performing a rigorous strength-training session with hypergravity pull-ups, weighted fingerboard hangs, campus training, and such.

The importance of this principle cannot be overstated, since training too often (under-resting) will eventually lead to a decline in performance and/or injury (see figure 5.6). This is known as the overtraining syndrome, and it's surprisingly common among passionate climbers. Observe how many climbers out there are whining about their nagging injuries or how they are "not getting stronger" despite their dedication to rigorous training. That's why it's called overtraining!

Another factor leading to overtraining or unusually long workout recovery is the frequent tendency of doing too high a volume of high-intensity exercise in a single session. As shown in the Supercompensation Cycle (figure 5.5), the workout stimulus results in neuromuscular fatigue and a temporary degradation in functional ability. With adequate rest the system regenerates to a level higher than before the workout. Too hard of a workout, however, creates so much neural fatigue and cellular damage that it takes much longer to recover and realize a state of supercompensation. This is an important concept to keep in mind when performing high-intensity training. Doing twelve sets of campus training probably provides no more beneficial stimulus than six or eight sets, but by doing twelve sets you dig a deeper hole from which it will take longer to recover. The same argument could be made against doing thirty sets of pull-ups or spending sixty minutes training on a fingerboard. Summing up: When it comes to high-intensity training, less is often more.

Detraining

Upon cessation of strength or endurance training (or frequent climbing), recent functional gains begin to erode in as little as seven days of rest. Local endurance diminishes more quickly than strength, and noticeable loss of endurance is likely after just seven to ten days away from climbing. Research has shown that half the mitochondria (and aerobic enzyme) gains from four weeks of training can be lost in as little as a week, and all is lost in five weeks of inactivity. Regaining the one-week loss of mitochondria content will take up to four weeks of endurance training. Realizing the remarkable plasticity of mitochondria—and how quick you'll lose your endurance—should be enough to compel you to go climbing once or twice per week! Fortunately, strength gains don't diminish as quickly—two weeks away from climbing or the gym may yield no remarkable loss in strength, although slacking much longer than this surely will.

Figure 5.6 Long-Term Training Response

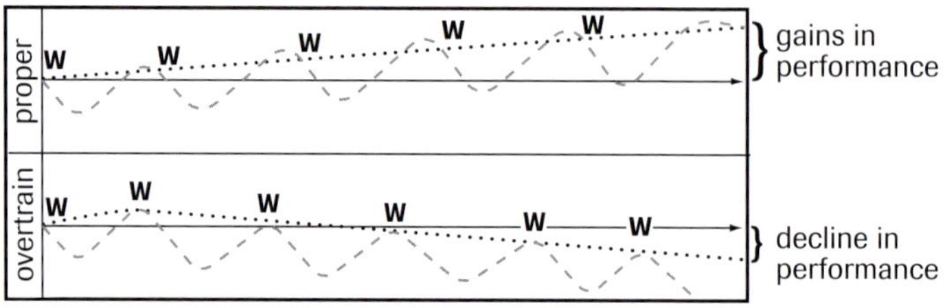

Adequate rest between workouts allows full supercompensation and long-term gains in performance. Conversely, executing workouts too close together results in a long-term decline in performance.

Tips for Effective Physical Training

1. Train specifically for climbing! While supplemental training of the antagonist and stabilizer muscles is essential, climbing-specific training holds the greatest potential to improve your climbing performance.
2. Target your limiting constraints. There are no other climbers quite like you, so performing some other climber's training program will be less than optimal. Identify what's holding you back (technically, physically, and mentally) and get busy training to improve in these areas.
3. Employ progressive overload into your weekly training. While not every workout should be the "hardest ever," it is important to occasionally expose your body to a level of training stress. This can be achieved by increasing training intensity, speed, and volume, or by decreasing the rest interval between sets or climbs.
4. Vary your workouts. Since the body adapts to training stimuli, it's essential to regularly vary training activities and workouts every few days or weeks, using either autoregulation or periodization.
5. Use muscle isolation training to break through plateaus. High-level climbers must employ isolation training to eke out small gains in strength, endurance, and power.
6. Use the optimal set, rep, and rest scheme to produce the desired gains. Write down your workouts in order to keep track of—and properly adjust—your weight, rep, and rest scheme to obtain optimum results.
7. Arrange your workouts from specific to general. Always train climbing movements (actual climbing) first, followed by climbing-specific exercises and then general strength training. Save extensive aerobic activity for a non-climbing day, or perform such training early in the day (and climb late).
8. Plan your rest days just as you plan training days. Neuromuscular adaptations occur during periods of rest and sleep, not during workouts. Therefore, sufficient rest and a healthy lifestyle are essential for making the most of your training investment.
9. Avoid long breaks from training or climbing. Taking more than a week or two off (from training or climbing) will result in a significant loss of climbing-specific endurance and strength. In other words, if you don't use it you will lose it!

Training Methodology

I'll close out this chapter with a brief, targeted look at the methodology of training strength, power, local endurance, and stamina. Founded on the exercise physiology and principles outlined throughout this chapter, the methods will then come to life in the exercises and training protocols detailed in chapters 6 through 9.

Maximum-Strength Training

In climbing, your level of maximum strength in the forearm flexor and pulling muscles (of the arms and torso) is a common physical limitation. Gripping small holds, making a powerful arm pull, and locking off with one arm all command your muscles to contract briefly with near-maximal force. Interestingly, your ability to rest effectively on a barely adequate, medium-size hold and express strength-endurance on a pumpy sequence is also a function of your maximum strength. Therefore, training for greater absolute grip and pulling strength is the single most important aspect of an effective training-for-climbing program.

So what is the best way to train this all-important attribute? For beginning climbers, simply climbing three days per week will yield some gains in climbing-specific strength. Therefore, no highly targeted training is necessary, or appropriate—it could very well lead to injury. Of course, training technique and movement skills are paramount at this stage, and any time spent strength training should be focused on the antagonist, stabilizer, and larger pulling muscles (not the fingers).

Intermediate climbers, with at least a couple of years of climbing experience, will benefit greatly from targeted strength training—and having presumably developed enough tendon strength, these mid-level climbers can begin a progressive twice-per-week strength-training program. Elite climbers are in a class of their own: With years of climbing experience and (apparently healthy) Kevlar-like tendons, these elites can embark on an ultra-intense, two- or three-day-per-week strength- and power-training regimen. Breaking through the next performance plateau depends on it.

As you learned earlier in this chapter, attaining a higher level of maximum strength is a matter of increasing neural recruitment, muscle hypertrophy, and building greater cellular stores of ATP-CP. The training goal is to maximize fiber recruitment and liberate ATP-CP at the highest possible rate for five to ten seconds. Consequently, a properly executed maximum-strength exercise will utilize a sufficiently high resistance to produce near-failure in around ten seconds. It's important to recognize that any strenuous exercise performed for more than about twelve seconds will train local endurance more than strength, as these longer efforts are fueled more by the anaerobic lactic system. Table 5.4 shows the ideal exercise duration, intensity, number of sets, rest interval between sets, and frequency of use. Chapters 8 and 9 will provide details on many strength-training exercises, but here are a few examples:

- Weighted pull-ups with enough added weight to make five repetitions difficult.
- Body weight fingerboard hangs on holds small enough to be difficult if held for ten seconds.
- Weighted fingerboard hangs on medium-size holds with enough weight to make a ten-second hang very difficult.
- One-arm lock-offs held for five seconds.
- One-arm (or one-arm-assisted) pull-ups for one to five repetitions.

A final note: Near-limit bouldering can aid in the development of maximum strength, especially in sub-elite climbers; however, more highly targeted supplemental exercises are essential to provide optimal stimuli for maximum-strength gains. Consider that failure on boulders often occurs because of movement flaws, inadequate flexibility, or lack of power, and therefore bouldering does not necessarily elicit grip or pull-muscle failure in less than twelve seconds. Shrewd, precise training—in

Table 5.4 Weight, Rep, and Rest Interval Schemes

	Intensity (% of 1RM)	Reps	Duration	Sets	Rest Interval	Frequency
Maximum Strength	90–100%	3–5	<12 secs.	3–5	3–5 mins.	2x per week
Strength-Endurance	80–90%	5–8	12–30 secs.	5–10	1–3 mins.	2x per week
Hypertrophy	70–80%	8–15	20–40 secs.	3–5	2–3 mins.	3x per week
"Local" Aerobic Endurance	50–70%	>20	>60 secs.	1–5	1–3 mins.	2–3x per week

Use these guidelines to get the best response from your strength and endurance training. Note that you may be able to avoid unwanted muscle mass gains by eschewing hypertrophy training (highlighted).

accordance with the exercise science and principles detailed in this chapter—is paramount for eking out additional strength gains over the long term. Train smarter to climb harder!

Contact Strength and Power Training

When climbers talk about "power," they typically are referring to the ability to make a swift strenuous reach, campus move, or quick latch on to a small handhold at the end of a deadpoint or lunge move. Physiologically, power is strength expressed quickly (power = strength x speed), so your level of power is closely related to your maximum strength. Both power and maximum strength involve forceful fast-twitch fiber recruitment, and both are fueled by cellular ATP-CP, which can only sustain near-maximal power (or strength) for a few fleeting seconds. Where power and strength significantly differ is in the rate at which a force is applied—sports scientists call this rate of force development (RFD).

To understand RFD, consider this on-the-rock example of how power and strength are expressed differently in grabbing on to a difficult handhold. Figure 5.7 shows hypothetical force-time curves for three climbers. Climber A possesses the greatest grip strength and can hang on very small holds, given a second or so to summon his peak strength. Climber B has less absolute strength than Climber A, but she is more powerful, because she can summon her strength more quickly (greater contact strength)—ideal for catching dynos and latching small holds when deadpointing. Climber C is neither strong nor powerful—he needs to begin a strength-training program; otherwise he'd better stick to climbing slabs!

Obviously the goal should be to maximize your strength and power, much like Climber B. Possessing a high absolute strength and the ability to recruit this strength quickly is essential for climbing hard boulders and powering through short, burly cruxes on roped climbs. While the best exercises and sample training programs will

Figure 5.7 Rate of Force Production

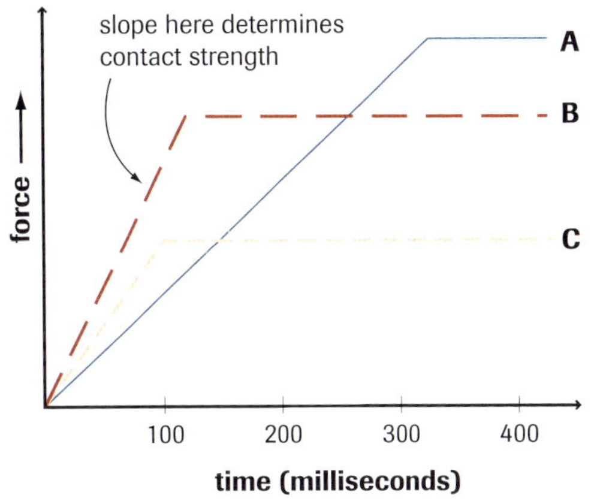

Hypothetical grip strength of three climbers. Climber A has the greatest absolute grip strength, while Climber B has the best contact strength.

be detailed in later chapters, one fundamental rule is to "develop strength before power." Therefore, no matter your current level of pulling power or contact strength, beginning a new training cycle should first focus on maximum-strength training (for a few weeks) before progressing to a mix of strength and power training.

Effective contact strength and power-training exercises must elicit extremely rapid recruitment (but always in a semi-controlled way) and focus on maximal (anaerobic) power output for one to ten seconds—continuing any longer than about twelve seconds shifts the focus to anaerobic lactic capacity, which is something completely different (see sidebar on "Energy Systems Training"). Here are a few of the many power-training exercises you'll learn in chapters 8 and 9:

- Clap pull-ups
- No-feet gym rope climbing
- Feet-off campus laddering
- Campus Board "Switch Hands"
- Double dyno campus training

Energy Systems Training

While all climbs—short or long and slab or steep—use all three energy systems simultaneously, each energy system has specific situations in which it dominates (as described on page 94). Therefore, the relative strength of your energy systems will explain some of what you experience as your physical strengths and weaknesses on the rock. While a good coach can accurately assess the state of your three energy systems, you can glean a subjective sense of where you stand with each based on the energy system characteristics shown in Figure 5.8.

A petrol-fueled automobile provides a good analogy to better understand how the energy systems apply to climbing. Think of "power" as the size of the engine—the anaerobic power system is like an eight-cylinder engine, whereas the aerobic power system is like a small four-cylinder engine. If you are climbing an extremely strenuous sequence, you need V8-like power output that only the anaerobic alactic system can provide. Much less intense climbing, say exerting only 40 percent of peak power on a climb a few grades below your limit, can readily be fueled by the less-powerful aerobic energy system.

Staying with the car analogy, the "capacity" component is like the size of the gas tank; through proper training you can increase both anaerobic and aerobic capacity (the size of each tank). It's important to understand, however, that the anaerobic "tank" will always be but a small percentage of the size of the aerobic tank; furthermore, aerobic capacity is far more trainable than anaerobic capacity. Therefore, if you want to climb a lot in a given session or day—many boulders, sport routes, or all-day gear climbing—you need a well-developed aerobic system. For boulderers and sport climbers, training aerobic power is extremely important and often overlooked. As explained earlier, it's the aerobic system that resynthesizes CP (for quick recovery of anaerobic power) and helps clean up the metabolic by-products of anaerobic glycolysis (thus refueling your anaerobic "tank" during periods of rest). This is a critical distinction that all serious climbers should recognize and apply to their training.

Figure 5.8 Energy System Characteristics—What's in Your Wheelhouse?

Which Quadrant Is Your Climbing Strength and Weakness?

Anaerobic Power • Short, severe boulders lasting <15 seconds • Big campus movements & lunges • Powerful pulls off small holds • Catching small holds on deadpoints & lunges	**Aerobic Power** • Able to recover at brief, marginal mid-climb rests • Fast recovery between strenuous, pumpy exercises • Fast recovery between boulders (as in competition, when rest is limited to 4 minutes) • Recover quickly between redpoint attempts
• Sustained, difficult boulders lasting 15 seconds – 2 minutes • Roped climbing through long, pumpy sequences • Holding isometric contractions (like hangs) for up to 2 minutes **Anaerobic Capacity**	• Climb much of the day at a relatively high level • All-day stamina on multipitch and wall routes • Able to train twice per day with a few hours rest in between **Aerobic Capacity**

Considering these energy characteristics, which quadrant seems to be the locus of your physical strength (and weakness) on the rock?

Table 5.5 Summary of Energy Systems and How They Power Your Climbing

Anaerobic Power	Aerobic Power
Role: Very high power output for less than 12 seconds. No muscle pump.	**Role:** Power low to moderate intensity exercise. Facilitates rapid recovery between bouts of anaerobic exercise.
Energy System: Anaerobic alactic	**Energy System:** Aerobic
Fuel: Cellular ATP-CP	**Fuel:** Glycogen, lactate, fatty acids
Most Important for: Bouldering, power moves, maximum strength, physical crux moves	**Most Important for:** Regenerating ATP-CP for the anaerobic alactic system, clearing excessive lactate accumulation due to anaerobic glycolysis.
How to Train: Maximum-strength exercises, brief maximal-power exercises, alactic intervals of less than 15 seconds (no pump).	**How to Train:** Alactic intervals of less than 15 seconds, Strength/power-endurance intervals of 15 to 90 seconds.
Adaptations: Greater recruitment and increased cellular ATP-CP storage.	**Adaptations:** Increased mitochondria efficiency and capillarity, increased aerobic enzymes, increased cardiac output and respiration.
Anaerobic Capacity	**Aerobic Capacity**
Role: High power output for 12 seconds to 2 minutes. Results in pumped, burning muscles; shortness of breath.	**Role:** Provides long-duration, low to moderate power output lasting many minutes to hours.
Energy System: Anaerobic lactic (glycolysis)	**Energy System:** Aerobic
Fuel: Muscle glycogen	**Fuel:** Glycogen, lactate, fatty acids
Most Important for: Long boulders and cruxes, hard sustained sequences lasting up to 2 minutes without rest.	**Most Important for:** Local endurance of more than 2 minutes, long climbs, and all-day stamina.
How to Train: Exercises and climbing intervals lasting 30 to 90 seconds with 1:4 to 1:6 work-rest ratio.	**How to Train:** Threshold intervals of 2 to 5 minutes with short rests (1:1 or 1:2 work-rest ratio), sustained easy to moderate climbing of 5 to 20 minutes, unspecific aerobic training (running, etc.)
Adaptations: Improved buffering and tolerance to acidosis, increased cellular glycogen storage, increased anaerobic enzymes, increased mitochondrial and capillary density.	**Adaptations:** Increased VO_2 max, increased cardiac output and respiration, increased liver glycogen storage, increased aerobic enzymes, increased mitochondrial and capillary density.

Strength-Endurance and Power-Endurance

Your strength-endurance and power-endurance are a direct function of your anaerobic capacity (see the "Energy Systems Training" sidebar). Training the anaerobic lactic energy system is painful and grueling, but doing the right amount of this type of training is extremely important if your climbing goals include sending difficult rope-length routes or long, sustained boulder problems.

As shown in Table 5.3 and Figure 5.3, true maximum strength and power output can only be sustained for a few fleeting moments. Strength- and power-endurance, then, relate to how long the muscles can produce high, but submaximal, power output despite frequently occluded or partially occluded local blood flow and the resultant increase in hypoxia and metabolic acidosis. A rapid decrease in anaerobic energy production will take place between thirty seconds and two minutes, depending on power output levels and a person's anaerobic capacity. Individuals with high anaerobic capacity will excel at climbing long, powerful sequences—despite a growing pump—lasting upward of two minutes without a rest, whereas a climber of similar technical ability but lesser anaerobic capacity will fail more quickly, perhaps in less than one minute.

Another important distinction relates to how long a climber can persist on a hard, sustained route with frequent brief, marginal rests. Possessing a high aerobic power will facilitate meaningful recovery in as little as five to ten seconds of shaking out at a marginal rest position. Thus, in watching a climber hang on through a long, powerful route, it's often hard to tell if they are prevailing due to a high anaerobic capacity or because they are able to benefit from very brief, marginal rests thanks to a high aerobic power contribution. Ultimately, you want to train both systems, since having high aerobic power speeds regeneration of ATP-CP and helps "clean up" the metabolic by-products of the anaerobic system.

Your anaerobic capacity is expressed on the rock in both your endurance of forearm strength (how long you can grip hard) and your power-endurance in pulling hard, deadpointing, and lunging. Therefore, you need to train anaerobic endurance using both static exercises (isometrics) and powerful movements. Furthermore, you must train using both longer-duration exercises (that significantly occlude blood flow) and short bursts of high-intensity interval training that allows blood to flow briefly between exercise bouts. Here's a sampling of the strength-endurance and power-endurance exercises you'll learn about in chapters 8 and 9:

- 20-20 fingerboard repeaters
- Pull-up Interval (10 to 20 sets of 5 to 10 reps)
- 1-minute climbing intervals (10 to 20 sets with a 1-minute rest between)
- Bouldering 4x4s
- Campus Board "Ladder Laps"
- HIT System training (strength-endurance protocol)
- Route intervals (2 minutes sustained climbing with 6 to 10 minutes of rest)

Proper scheduling of anaerobic lactic energy system training is just as important as the exercise choice. While anaerobic endurance training will yield noticeable gains in as little as two weeks, the anaerobic lactic energy system is arguably the least trainable of the three energy systems. Therefore, training gains usually cease in about four weeks, at which time the training focus should be temporarily shifted to another energy system. Another critical scheduling point—unknown by many coaches and most climbers—is that doing too much anaerobic endurance training (more than two or three sessions per week) will eventually lead to decreased endurance due to the damage chronic acidosis does to anaerobic enzymes and mitochondrial function. If you frequently train to the point of a deep, burning pump yet feel you're not gaining any endurance on the rock, you now know why.

What's More Important, Strength Training or Endurance Training?

Maximum strength, power, and contact strength (grip) are undoubtedly essential for bouldering at a high level. A recent study confirms this notion, showing that boulderers' crimp and open-hand strength was about 12 percent stronger than roped climbers. Even more remarkable, the boulderers' rate of force development in the finger flexors (contact strength) averaged 37 percent faster than roped climbers (Maurizio 2013). Interestingly, a study comparing advanced and elite rope climbers found that climbing time to exhaustion was the factor that most determined performance and on-sight level (España-Romero 2009).

These studies confirm the intuitive conclusion that boulderers should favor strength and power training, while roped climbers must focus on improving both anaerobic and aerobic endurance. But the science of climbing isn't so straightforward, and you won't get optimal long-term results by training in just one way. Earlier in this chapter I mentioned a study showing how endurance-trained climbers recovered more quickly between climbs. Another climbing study (Grant 2003) found that finger endurance (time to failure) is essentially fixed when holding an isometric grip at 40 percent of maximum voluntary contraction (MVC). Thus, increasing absolute finger strength (MVC) will yield meaningful endurance gains when carrying submaximal amounts of body weight. Another way to interpret this subtle but powerful study is that a stronger climber can rest (successfully) on smaller holds—important for pushing the limits on roped climbs!

The bottom line: While boulderers must concentrate on strength and power training, it would be beneficial to perform one or two endurance-oriented sessions per week. Similarly, a roped climber can benefit greatly from frequent strength and power training in addition to their steady commitment to training local aerobic and anaerobic capacity. See chapter 10 for specific training schedules for both boulderers and roped climbers.

Climbing Stamina and Nonspecific Aerobic Training

Stamina training and strength training are at opposite ends of the training spectrum. Fast, brief, anaerobic-powered movements are fueled by cellular ATP-CP, while the slow, steady, high-capacity aerobic system is fueled by fatty acids, lactate, and glycogen. Furthermore, powerful anaerobic movements call a large portion of FT fibers into action, whereas ST fibers dominate during lower-intensity, sustained activities. As you might expect, then, the methodology of effective stamina training is vastly different from that of training for absolute strength and power.

Effective stamina training necessarily involves a much higher volume of climbing (and aerobic exercise) than when engaging in strength or power training. In order to deeply train the aerobic energy system, it's essential to spend more time actually exercising rather than resting (the opposite is the case when strength training). Naturally, the exercise intensity of these stamina sessions is much lower and primarily targets the ST and FTa oxidative muscle fibers. No matter your choice of climbing-specific or nonspecific exercises, the ideal stamina training zone is 50 to 80 percent of maximum intensity—you can best hit this target zone by aiming for a subjective effort level (intensity) of between 5 and 8 on a scale of 1 to 10. Let's take a closer look at climbing-specific and nonspecific aerobic energy system training.

CLIMBING-SPECIFIC AEROBIC TRAINING

Effective training of the aerobic energy pathway via climbing is only possible if you set aside the desire to climb for performance (near your limit) and instead embrace the potentially boring process of climbing high volumes of moderate rock (or plastic). No matter if the climbing is done indoors or outside, this approach will naturally involve lots of submaximal climbing at varying intensities. The critical guideline to obey is that the climbing intensity never ascends deeply into the anaerobic zone, the hallmark of which is a deep muscle pump and shortness of breath. Ultimately, you want to find the margin of the anaerobic lactic zone and strive to climb mostly just below it (in the aerobic zone) while only occasionally crossing into the low end of the anaerobic zone. A light to moderate forearm pump is fine and desirable; however, a flaming pump, heavy breathing, and a growing sense of losing control is a clear sign you've climbed too deep into the anaerobic zone.

Interestingly, I've observed that many climbers who set out to train climbing stamina in this way ultimately end up crossing the line and getting massively pumped (thus training the anaerobic lactic system rather than the aerobic system as intended). It seems that wanting to get pumped while training is in the DNA of most climbers, yet this "pump lust" must be denied when training the aerobic energy pathway. Self-control and a strong intention to climb mainly in the aerobic training zone are essential to properly training this energy pathway. By keeping your perceived exertion and exercise intensity between 5 and 8 (see figure 5.9), you can rest assured that you're training the aerobic energy system. Threshold intervals (as detailed in chapter 8) requires a steady climbing exertion of 7 to 8.5 out of 10, whereas recovery "ARC training" demands you limit exertion to just a 4 to 6 out of 10.

Figure 5.9 Training Zones for Climbers

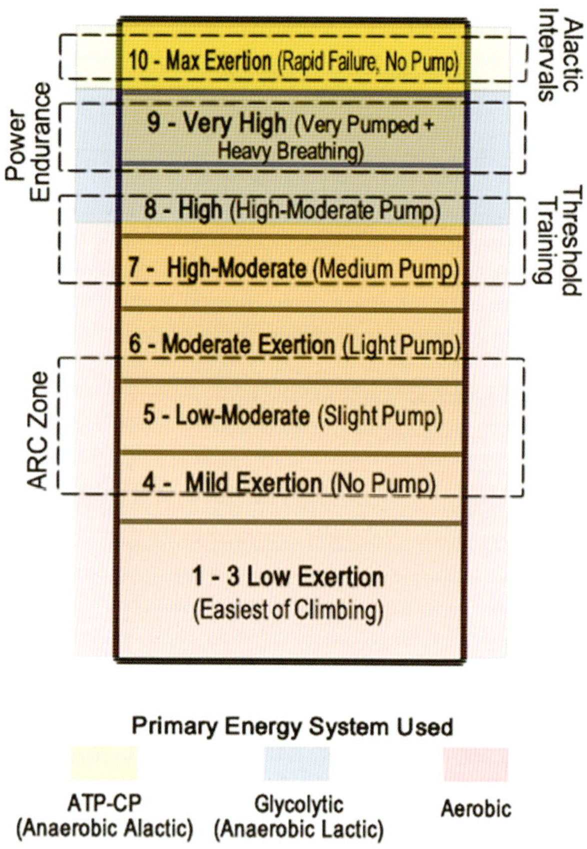

Energy system training zones for rock climbers based on subjective feeling of forearm muscle pump and perceived exertion. Effective climbing-specific aerobic training must be performed between 5 and 8.5 on the rating of perceived exertion (RPE).

Here's a preview of a few climbing-specific exercise strategies—all should be performed in the 5 to 8 training zone.

- Moderate bouldering traverses (indoors or outside) with twenty to sixty minutes of total climbing time.
- "Threshold" intervals on a Treadwall or bouldering wall, three to six minutes with near equal-length rests for a total of twenty to thirty minutes of climbing time. Strive to climb at an intensity of around 8 out of 10 on the RPE scale.
- Climb many moderate roped routes (toprope or sport lead), being sure to never get more than a moderate pump. Err on the side of selecting routes that are too easy rather than too hard.
- Long days of outdoor climbing—the goal is to get fatigued but not pumped. Doing eight to fifteen pitches that are two to four number grades below your limit is a good goal.

NONSPECIFIC AEROBIC TRAINING

While excessive nonspecific aerobic training is not a good time investment or a desired training stimulus, a moderate amount of generalized aerobic training is beneficial, especially for roped climbers. Whether your preference is running, cycling, or rowing, the many systemic and local adaptations will increase both your aerobic power and capacity. The payoffs on the rock will be faster recovery at mid-climb rests and between boulder problems, improved recovery between redpoint attempts, and stamina to climb well throughout a long day at the sport crag or on multipitch gear routes.

The "right amount" of generalized aerobic training is a tough thing to specify, since your current level of conditioning, climbing goals, and time available all factor in. As a very rough guideline, however, I suggest doing two or three sessions of moderate-intensity aerobic activity per week, each lasting twenty to forty minutes. Certainly there's no reason, or benefit, for a boulderer or sport climber to perform excessive aerobic training such as running thirty-plus miles (fifty-plus km) per week—such a program will likely hurt your climbing-specific strength and power and may leave you too fatigued to climb your best.

Another aerobic training option is sprint intervals, performed on a rowing machine or on foot (running). Alternating between twenty seconds of near-all-out sprinting (90 percent intensity) and forty seconds of easy "recovery" jogging is an excellent stimulus for gains in aerobic power and capacity. This is a rigorous way to go about your aerobic training, and it should be limited to twice per week.

Jon Cardwell on-sighting Face de Rat (5.13c), Ceuse, France. MATTY HONG

CHAPTER SIX

Mobility, Stability, Antagonist Training

To maximize your potential and reduce injury risk, it's essential to develop stability before strength, and strength before power.

Here's where the business begins! This is the first of four exercise-packed chapters that together hold the potential to transform your physique, elevate your quality of movement, and markedly increase your strength, power, and endurance. A consistent effort to properly apply the one-hundred-plus exercises presented in these chapters will literally reshape your body and undoubtedly open up a whole new level of climbing performance.

The significance of the results you obtain, of course, will depend on a number of things, including your current level of conditioning and injury history (if any), your age and genetics, and the time you have to invest in training. Far more important, however, is your willingness to engage in a comprehensive training program and do the right things right. When I talk about the "right things," it's not just about appropriate climbing-specific exercise selection (which is very important), but also about following through faithfully with the essential flexibility, mobility, stability, and antagonist exercises. For example, dedicated training on the wrist and scapular stabilizers—while not as sexy as, say, campus training—is absolutely essential as both a precursor and complement to the climbing-specific exercises. Break this guideline and, sooner or later, you will injure a finger, elbow, or shoulder—or perhaps all three!

The ubiquity of injured climbers (an alarming number needing surgery) is evidence of the prevalence of over-enthusiastic training, climbing too much (with too few rest days), and a failure to properly train arm and shoulder mobility and stability before engaging in high-end climbing and advanced climbing-specific training (such as fingerboard and campus board training). While certainly not a 100 percent preventative of injury, embracing the concept of "stability before strength, and strength before power" will vastly lower your injury risk and enable you to engage in a progressively more rigorous training program with each passing year.

Figure 6.1 presents mobility and stability as a necessary foundation to be built before progressing to strength training and, eventually, power training. Disciplined use of most of the exercises in this chapter will build a physiologically sound foundation from which you can safely execute the many climbing-specific exercises in chapter 8 and 9. Failing to regularly utilize the foundational exercises in this chapter, however, is tantamount to building your climbing physique on a foundation of sand—one that will likely fail you in a critical moment with a fateful pop, tear, or a more insidious gradual development of pain in your shoulder, elbow, or finger.

Okay, enough with my obligatory coach's warning—let's get to the details that you can put to work beginning today! First, I'll present the essential mobility and flexibility exercises that you should do each day at home, at the crag, or in the gym. The real meat of this chapter, however, are the sections

Figure 6.1 Pyramid of Training

A period of mobility and stability training is essential before embarking on serious strength training. Graduate to power training only after you've developed significant climbing-specific and stabilizer strength.

that detail the vital stability and antagonist exercises that every climber should do. Read on and you'll learn how to keep your arms and shoulders functionally sound and, hopefully, healthy throughout a long climbing career.

Flexibility and Mobility Training

First, let's distinguish between flexibility and mobility. Flexibility refers to the range of motion around a joint—for example, climbers need flexibility around the hips for high-stepping, stemming, and aggressive drop-knee positions. Flexibility is influenced by joint mechanics, tendon, fascia, and musculature, and in aggregate it's a system that will gradually respond to dedicated training. Mobility relates to functional movement patterns and how well a joint moves through the appropriate range of motion in specific physical activities. A joint's mobility is influenced by many factors including motor control, chronic movement patterns, antagonist muscle strength, soft tissue adhesions and injury, and—yes—flexibility.

For climbers, the shoulder joint is a common site of poor mobility as tight, weak, sore, and/or injured muscles diminish mobility and compromise functional movement (see figure 6.2). The forearm muscles are another common site where weak antagonist muscles and soft tissue dysfunction can contribute to poor movement patterns, undue compensatory strain, and injury. Also common are mobility and flexibility issues surrounding the hips and lower back. Though often more a result of excessive time spent sitting at a desk or in a car, the long-term effects can impact your back, core, and hip function and therefore negatively impact your climbing. The bottom line: These common problem spots can be largely corrected given daily mobility and flexibility work.

Figure 6.2 Causes of "Climbers' Posture"

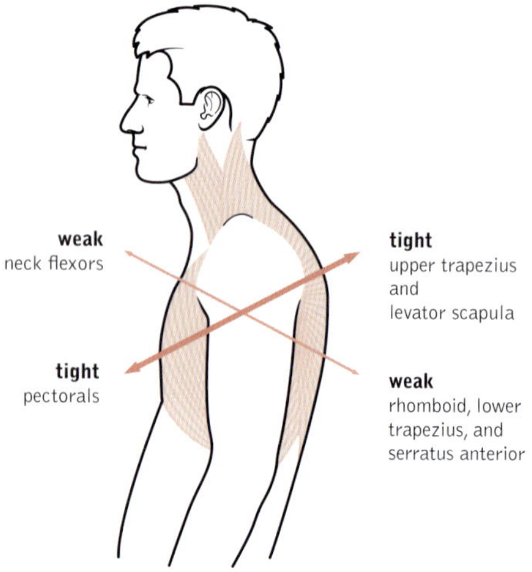

Tight pectorals and weak lower trapezius muscles are two factors that often contribute to the rounded shoulders and rounding of the upper back—this increases the risk of shoulder impingement during forceful overhead reaching and pulling.

Upcoming are seven oh-so-good mobility exercises, nine upper-body warm-up and stretching exercises, and nine core and lower-body stretches. Invest fifteen to thirty minutes per day into doing a selection of these exercises and you'll be on your way to moving—and feeling—better, both on and off the rock! (Consult the muscular anatomy photos in appendix A if you are uncertain of the location of the muscles targeted in each of these exercises.)

Foam Rolling Exercises

There are many fitness fads that come and go each decade, and many are ineffective exercises or fitness equipment promoted heavily by manufacturers and marketers. The last few years have brought the rise of foam rollers and other tools for soft tissue management, and I can tell you with complete certainty that the benefits of these devices are entirely legitimate. I'm so enamored of my foam roller and Armaid device that I take them on all my climbing trips. These tools are real difference makers in terms of subjective feelings of muscle function as well as improved mobility.

Detailed below are several techniques to address tight muscles and, more importantly, hunt out and destroy painful trigger points. Each will provide self-myofascial release (SMR) that will help lengthen muscle fibers, release trigger points, increase circulation, and perhaps even encourage fascial remodeling. Make SMR a daily habit and you will improve mobility and lower the risk of certain overuse injuries such as medial and lateral epicondylitis.

UPPER BACK AND SHOULDER ROLL

Foam rolling the upper back and shoulders with a Rumble Roller.
1. Targeting the trapezius, rhomboids, teres major/minor, infraspinatus, and posterior deltoids. 2. Rolling the latissimus dorsi.

Begin with the foam roller under your upper back and your arms across your chest. With your knees bent and feet flat on the floor, slowly roll up and down along the thoracic spine. Pause for fifteen to thirty seconds on any painful spots (trigger points) you locate in your trapezius and rhomboids. Next, tilt about 30 degrees to each side and roll along the latissimus dorsi and up across the posterior deltoid and infraspinatus. Again, dwell for a half minute or so on any sore or tight spots. Finally, return to the neutral position and extend your hands overhead. Keeping your elbows locked and maintaining butt contact with the floor, slowly roll up and down along the thoracic spine. This is excellent for improving thoracic extension and addressing the posture issues and shoulder strains common among climbers (as shown in figure 6.2).

LOWER BACK AND GLUTES ROLL

The muscles of the lower back and buttocks are common hiding spots of tightness among climbers. Anyone who spends large amounts of time sitting (commonly with a flexed lumbar spine) will find lower back rolling to be surprisingly therapeutic; it might even elicit a glorious "pop" (without dropping coin on a chiro!). Rolling lower onto the gluteal muscles of the buttock may be similarly pleasurable. Many climbers discover extremely tight gluteus medius muscles (located on the sides of buttocks, just below the hip)—this isn't surprising, since it's the gluteus medius that produces external thigh rotation when the knee is flexed (as it is in just about every climbing move).

To address the lower back, position the foam roller perpendicular to the lumbar spine and roll slowly up and down along the often tight erector spinae muscles. Add a slight roll to each side and you'll likely find soreness in the quadratus lumborum (QL). The QL connects the pelvis to the spine, and it's a common source of lower back pain.

Rolling the gluteus maximus is best done from a sitting position with straight legs and arms extended behind you. To release the often tight gluteus medius, however, you'll want to bend one leg and then lean to the opposite side—roll just a few centimeters up and down and side to side and you'll quickly locate the trigger point. Dwell there for a minute and feel the tightness release.

1. Rolling the spinal erectors, quadratus lumborum, and gluteus medius.
2. Targeting the gluteus maximus.

HIP FLEXORS AND IT BAND

The hip flexors and iliotibial (IT) band are two more common tight spots to address with a foam roller. If you spend much time in the sitting position, then you'll surely discover that you have tight hip flexors that will hurt (in a good way) when addressed with a foam roller. Assume a prone position with the foam roller under your hips and only your toes and forearms contacting the floor. Now roll just a few centimeters up and down along the hip flexors (front of your upper thighs and pelvis). Tilt slightly to the side to attack the hip flexors only on that side—this will double the pressure (more painful), but yield even more of a release. Dwell for up to a minute on each group (side) of hip flexors.

Next, proceed to rolling the IT band along the outside of each leg. Lie on your side with the foam roller under the upper outside of one leg. You'll need to support much of your weight on the floor-side forearm and position the other leg for balance. Now slowly roll along the outside of the leg, tracking the roller from just below the hip to just above the knee.

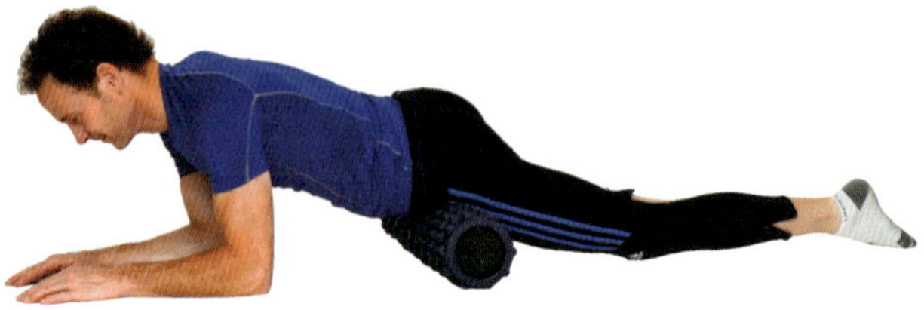

1. Rolling the hip flexors and upper quadriceps.
2. Targeting the IT band.

PRONATOR "PIN AND STRETCH"

The pronator teres is but a small muscle in the upper forearm, but for a climber it's one of the hardest-working muscles. You can easily locate this muscle by extending an arm straight to the front and then making a tight fist while you pronate the hand completely (as if pouring water from a jug). The pronator teres will bulge on the inside of the elbow just above the bony medial epicondyle. Now relax your fist and, using the thumb of the opposite hand, press deeply into the pronator muscle (the "pin") and hold for thirty seconds. Chances are you'll find this to be quite painful—a sign that you should also do the pronator strengthening exercise on page 136. Repeat the "pin" again with your thumb, but this time slowly pronate and supinate your hand to achieve a deeper massage and stretch of the pronator. Alternatively, use an Armaid on your pronator, as it provides even better leverage than using your thumb.

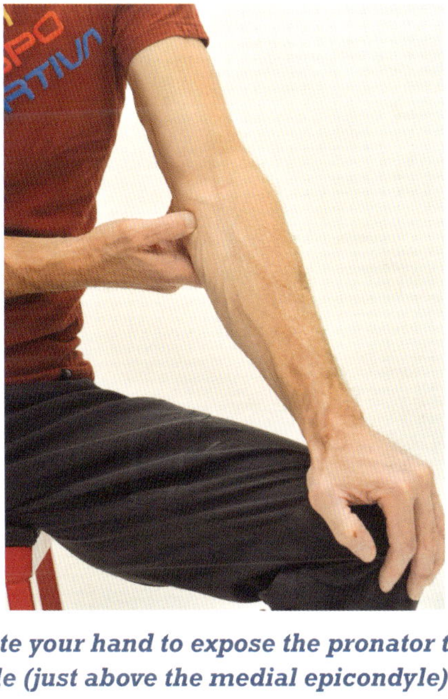

Pronate your hand to expose the pronator teres muscle (just above the medial epicondyle), then use your thumb to press deeply into this often tight muscle.

WRIST EXTENSORS "PIN AND STRETCH"

The finger and wrist extensor muscles of the lateral forearm are another common problem spot, especially among climbers who are chronic crimpers. Persistently tight extensor muscles often develop painful knots and trigger points at one or more locations from the middle lateral forearm up to within about one inch of the bony lateral epicondyle. While daily forearm stretching of the extensor muscles is essential (page 122), addressing these tight muscles with an Armaid will lessen tension, release trigger points, and ultimately reduce your chance of someday developing lateral tendinosis.

Here's how to do it: Using an Armaid (or your thumb), probe the soft tissue of the lateral forearm to locate any sore spots—when you find one, apply steady pressure and hold for thirty seconds. Next, "pin and stretch" this trigger point by making a fist and flexing your wrist as you apply increasing pressure on the sore spot. Climbers with numerous trigger points on the lateral forearm would be wise to invest at least five to ten minutes per day addressing these developing problem spots.

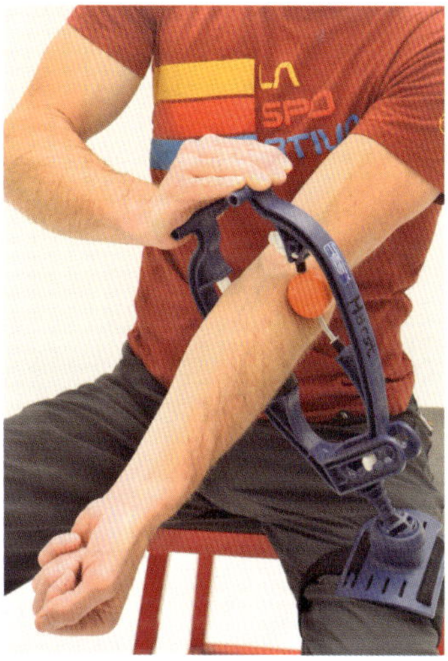

The Armaid is an excellent tool for addressing sore, tight trigger points in the finger and wrist extensor muscles.

As Essential as Your Climbing Shoes—Armaid!

We all know the feeling of sore, tight forearm muscles after a day of hard climbing or an intensive finger workout. If you climb and train frequently without taking proactive measures to address these tight muscles and trigger points, resultant muscle shortening will become chronic. Incessant tension of forearm flexor and extensor muscles produces an unwanted "pulling"—even during rest—where the muscles attach via tendon at the medial and lateral epicondyle of the elbow. Long term, this chronic irritation can eventually lead to either tendinitis (inflammation) or tendonosis (degradation of tendon collagen).

If you ever feel tendon pain near one of these epicondyles or in the attaching muscle an inch or two distal to the epicondyle, you now know what's likely part (or all) of your problem. Even if you are pain free (congrats, but let's keep it that way!), I'll bet that you can elicit some painful twinges by firmly palpating deep into the muscles of the medial and lateral forearm. By proactively addressing these trigger points with sports massage and trigger point release, you'll regain your natural range of motion and unlock a higher level of muscle function.

Here's how to do it: With a braced finger or, better yet, an Armaid or Rubbit, hold firm pressure on a sore spot (trigger point) and then stretch the muscle. Feel the tension or trigger point release over the course of a minute or two of therapy. Locate other sore spots and similarly "pin and stretch" them until they submit. This can be a painful process, but you'll quickly come to recognize and perhaps enjoy this kind of "good pain." Of course, you mustn't overdo it, or ever apply this technique directly to a tendon or epicondyle.

The bottom line: If you engage in stressful climbing or rigorous forearm training, then daily self-care of the forearm muscles is essential for reducing tension and injury risk. Furthermore, a loose, relaxed muscle is a happy, fully functional muscle possessing optimal blood flow and highest recovery ability. Armaid and Rubbit are the two best massage tools I've used, and I consider them so critical for maintaining my forearm health that I take one on all my climbing trips. You should too!

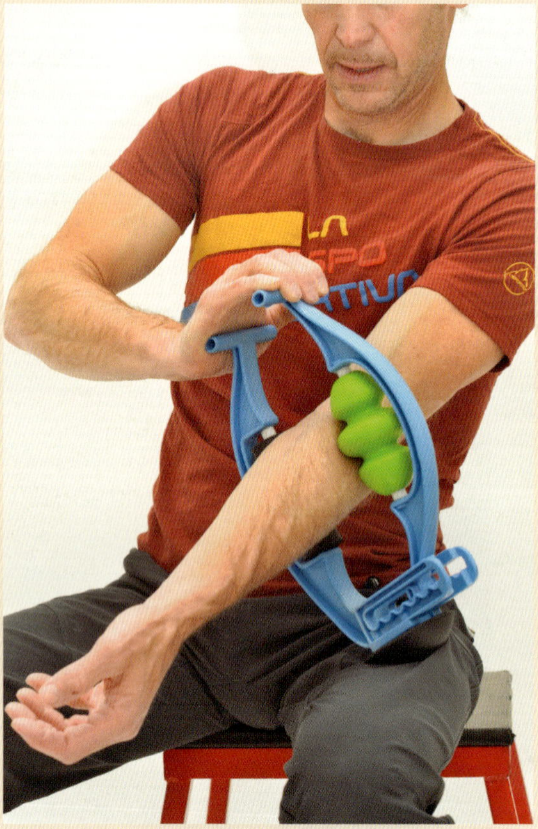

The Rubbit excels equally as a tool for massage and trigger point therapy.

ELBOW VOODOO FLOSS

Voodoo flossing is a novel technique for helping to mobilize tissues and increase circulation to cold, stiff muscles and joints, and it's been effective for improving tissue quality following a connective tissue injury. Voodoo flossing involves wrapping a tight rubbery band (available from RogueFitness.com) around a sore, stiff joint—in this case the elbow. Begin wrapping the voodoo floss about 4 inches below the elbow and tightly wrap, with 50 percent overlaps, all the way to about 4 inches above the elbow. Tuck the end of the band under the previous wraps. The goal is to wrap tight enough to occlude blood flow—your hand will turn purple or white—so shoot for a tightness of 8 on a scale of 1 to 10. Now flex and extend your elbow for about twenty slow repetitions, removing the voodoo floss after about one minute.

The effects of voodoo flossing come from the powerful reperfusion (return of blood flow) following removal of the band as well as the sliding and shearing of stiff tissues that results from the powerful compression the band provides. Long-term voodoo flossing on a chronically sore or previously injured elbow will help improve tissue mobility, increase range of motion, and enhance beneficial circulation. Also noteworthy, voodoo flossing is an excellent method of warming up the elbows before training or climbing.

PECTORAL RELEASE WITH LACROSSE BALL

The elbows and shoulders have been the focus of this section, and for good reason—next to the fingers these are the most common sites of injury among rock climbers. The last mobility exercise addresses what is, perhaps, the most overlooked muscle during climbers' warm-up and stretching

Improve circulation and tissue quality in aching elbows with regular voodoo flossing.

Many climbers have chronically tight pectoral muscles that can be readily addressed with a tennis or lacrosse ball. Here the author enjoys the good pain of some self-myofascial release.

routines. As shown in figure 6.2, tight pectorals contribute to the poor posture and shoulder dysfunction that many climbers exhibit. Releasing tight pectorals (and the upper trapezius) and strengthening the lower trapezius and rotator cuff muscles will go a long way to improving functional movement and reducing your injury risk.

While you can use a foam roller on the pectorals, a lacrosse ball or tennis ball (more forgiving) is a better match for this smaller muscle. You can best address the pecs by standing upright and placing the ball between your pectoral muscle and a wall or vertical column. You can easily move your torso position to direct the ball onto any tight spots. As with the previous exercises, pause with the ball on the sore spots and wait for the tissues to submit.

Upper-Body Stretches

While there is rarely a need for extraordinary flexibility in climbing, regular flexibility training will have a positive influence on your training and performance. Considering that movement is the very essence of the vertical dance we call climbing, anything you can do to help facilitate smooth, efficient movements will enhance your performance. Flexible agonist muscles and tendons will function better—and are more resilient—when exposed to the high dynamic force loads common to climbing. What's more, flexible antagonist muscles will levy a lower inherent resistance to the opposing agonist muscles, enabling smoother, more economical movement.

Detailed below are nine stretches that are ideal for fulfilling the above-stated goals.

Not surprisingly, stretching exercises have long been used by climbers as part of a warm-up routine before training, climbing, and competition. It's important to understand, however, that such pre-workout stretching must always be preceded by a warm-up activity that will increase muscle temperatures and spread synovial fluid through the joints and tendon sheaths. Static stretching alone can injure a cold muscle (Shrier 1999, 2000), so it's essential to engage in five to fifteen minutes of low-intensity exercise such as jogging, easy climbing (vertical walls with good holds), or foam rolling before doing this flexibility work. When climbing outdoors, the hike to the cliff base often provides the perfect lead-in to your preclimb stretching as long as it's lengthy enough to increase your breathing rate and cause a light sweat.

At the very least, do twenty-five jumping jacks followed by twenty arm circles and twenty finger flexors (as described below). Complete the prestretching warm-up with a few minutes of self-massage to the finger tendons, the palm of your hand, and the forearm muscles and biceps.

ARM CIRCLES

Arm circles provide a nice dynamic stretch that warms up your shoulder joints and increases circulation to your shoulders, arms, and fingers. Do these before you engage in any of the upper-body static stretches that follow. Stand with your arms out to the side and parallel to the floor, and begin moving your arms in small circles. Gradually increase the size of the circle until you feel slight tension in the shoulders—go no larger with the circles beyond this point, and do not wildly whip your arms or perform a rapid windmill-like motion! Complete twenty smooth, moderately paced arm circles, and then proceed to the Finger Curls.

FINGER CURLS AND MASSAGE

This is a must-do warm-up movement for climbers because it increases circulation to the forearm muscles and spreads lubricating synovial fluid in the joints of the fingers. Stand with your arms relaxed by your sides. Close your hands to make relaxed fists, and then quickly open your hands and fan out the fingers as if you're flicking water off your fingertips. Continue for thirty to forty repetitions. Use a pace that allows about two repetitions per second. Now perform a minute or two of massage on both sides of your fingers and hands—this will encourage blood flow and help warm the tendons and tendon pulleys.

FINGER ISOLATION STRETCH

This isolation stretch, along with massage of the fingers and hands, is very effective for warming up your precious digits. Work through this sequence one finger at a time. Either sitting or standing, position one hand palm-up at chest level and curl the fingers into a loose fist. Place the index finger of the other hand across the tip segment of the finger being stretched, and position the thumb under the finger near the base (hand) knuckle. Bracing with the thumb below, gradually apply pressure with the index finger to further close the bent finger and push it away from the palm. Stop when you feel mild tension in the joints. Hold the stretch for ten seconds. Release the finger for a few seconds, then repeat the stretch for another ten seconds. Repeat the stretching sequence with all eight fingers. Stop immediately if you experience any pain.

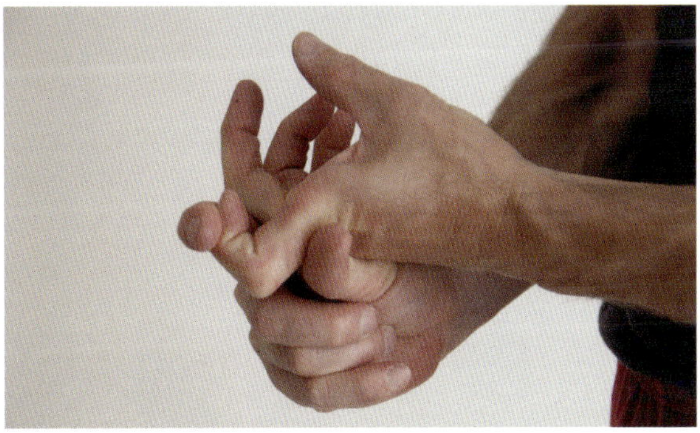

Finger isolation stretch

FINGER FLEXOR STRETCH

This rudimentary stretch targets the forearm muscles that flex your fingers and secure your grip to the rock. While in a standing position, bring your hands together in front of your waist. Straighten the arm to be stretched and lay the fingertips into the palm of the other hand. Position the hand of the stretching arm so the palm is facing down with the thumb pointing inward. Pull back on the fingers of the straight arm until a mild stretch begins in the forearm muscles. Hold the stretch for ten seconds. Release the stretch and turn the hand 180 degrees so that the stretching arm is now positioned with the palm facing upward and the thumb pointing out to the side. Again, using your other hand, pull your fingers back until a stretch begins in the forearm muscles. Hold for ten seconds. Repeat the stretch, in both positions, with the other arm.

1. Finger flexor stretch with hand pronated.
2. Repeat stretch with hand supinated.

FINGER EXTENSORS STRETCH

This important, yet often overlooked, stretch targets the numerous extensor muscles of the lateral forearm as well as the commonly sore and tight brachioradialis muscle. These muscles are especially strained when crimping with a chicken-winged

Maintain a straight elbow while flexing the wrist and fully pronating the hand.

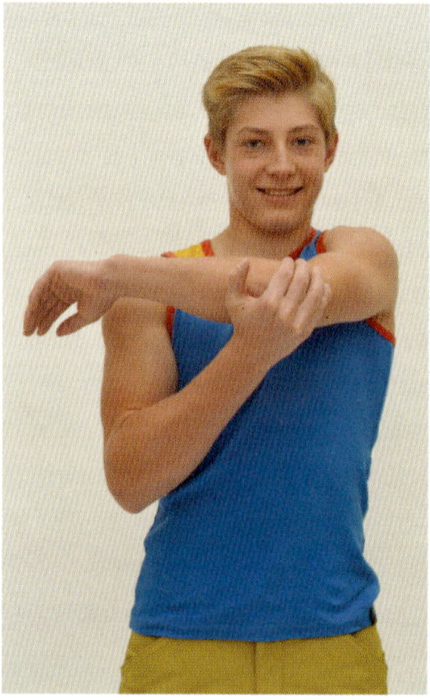

Keeping the shoulder back, gently pull the bent arm across the chest.

arm position, and so daily stretching (and Armaid use) is essential for lengthening the tissues and releasing tension that can eventually contribute to lateral epicondylitis.

With nearly straight arms, cross your hands in front of your body and interlace your fingers, palms together. While maintaining mild tension throughout the length of both arms, pull with one hand to flex the wrist of the other hand until you feel the stretch develop in the finger/wrist extensors along the outside of the forearm. Hold the stretch for about twenty seconds and then pull with the other hand to create a stretch along the other arm. Perform the stretch twice on each arm.

POSTERIOR SHOULDER STRETCH

This addresses the shoulder capsule and in particular stretches the infraspinatus and trapezius. While in a standing position, bring one arm across your chest until the hand rests on the opposite shoulder. Importantly, you must have your elbow bent (around 90 degrees) and maintain a shoulder back position—do not roll your shoulder forward. With the other hand, grasp behind the bent elbow from below. Pull on the bent elbow until you feel tension in the shoulder and upper back. Hold the stretch for ten seconds. Release the stretch for a few seconds before repeating for twenty seconds more. Repeat the stretch with the other arm.

ROTATOR CUFF STRETCH

The towel (or dowel) stretch is a great exercise to help improve the flexibility and range of motion of your shoulder, and it is a must-do before every climbing and training session. Specifically, this

Hold a towel or dowel behind your head and grasp the other end behind your back. Gently pull the dowel (or towel) upward to stretch the rotator cuff muscles.

exercise involves internal rotation and shoulder extension of the arm in the bottom position (thus stretching the external rotators) while it places the other (top) arm in external rotation and shoulder flexion. To do it, roll up a towel and hold one end above and just behind your head, and then grab the other end of the towel with the opposite hand (palm facing backward) behind your back. Pull up on the towel with the top hand until you feel the light stretch; hold this position for ten to twenty seconds. Perform the stretch two or three times on each side.

ANTERIOR SHOULDER, CHEST, AND BICEPS STRETCH

This exercise provides a global stretch to improve shoulder mobility and, specifically, shoulder extension. This stretch is my personal favorite for the upper body because it addresses all my common tight spots—the biceps, pectorals, and shoulders. Sit on the floor with feet flat and knees bent about 90 degrees. Position your arms just behind your hips with the elbows straight, palms flat on the floor, and fingers pointing back. Slowly walk your hands away from your hips until you feel mild tension in your shoulders, pecs, and biceps. Be sure to keep your shoulders back (do not let them roll forward)—thinking about extending your lumbar spine and pushing your chest forward will provide a nice stretch into the pectorals. Hold this position for twenty seconds. Walk your fingers back a bit farther to enhance the stretch. Hold this position for twenty to thirty seconds before releasing the stretch.

Walk your hands backward while keeping the lower back straight, chest out, and shoulders back.

LATISSIMUS, SHOULDER, AND TRICEPS STRETCH

This stretch will improve range of motion and shoulder mobility in the overhead, externally rotated arm position common to most climbing movements. Stand erect with arms overhead and bent at the elbows. Grab one elbow and gently pull it toward the back of your head until you feel a stretch in the back of the upper arm. Hold the stretch for ten seconds. Release the stretch for a few seconds and then perform a secondary stretch for about twenty seconds. You can extend this stretch down through the latissimus dorsi muscle by leaning slightly sideways in the direction of the pull. Repeat the stretch with the other arm.

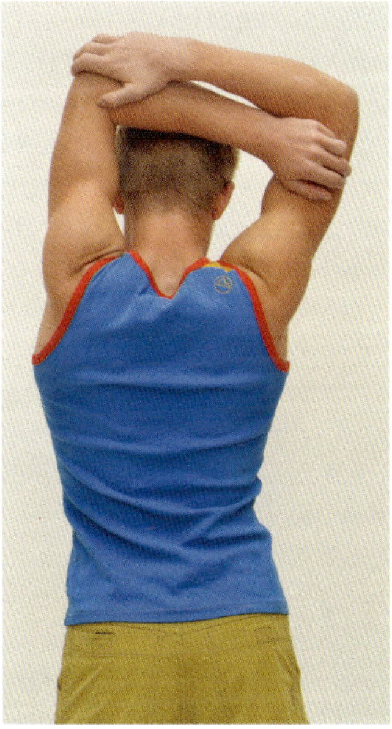

Pull the elbow toward the back of your head until you feel tension in the shoulder and lats.

Tips for Safe and Effective Flexibility Training

1. Always engage in five to fifteen minutes of jogging, jumping jacks, easy climbing, or foam rolling before beginning flexibility training. Stretching a cold muscle can lead to injury.
2. Stretch in a slow, gradually progressive manner. Stretching should produce mild discomfort, but never sharp pain.
3. Perform a primary stretch of ten to thirty seconds. Release the stretch for a few seconds before performing a secondary stretch of twenty to thirty seconds.
4. Direct slow, deep breathing throughout the stretch. Inhale through your nose and exhale through your mouth.
5. Maintain a neutral back position—neither rounded nor hyperextended—to maximize the stretch and avoid injury.
6. Limit "gain" stretching to the legs and hips. Be conservative in stretching the shoulders.
7. Using foam rolling in conjunction with stretching will have a synergistic effect. Roll first, stretch second.
8. Refrain from excessive stretching of the forearm flexors prior to climbing, since this may affect the nervous system in a way that reduces your maximum strength and power for up to one hour. Favor light stretching, Armaid use, and sports massage prior to performance climbing.

Lower-Torso and Leg Stretches

The legs, hips, and lower back are areas where many climbers benefit from improved flexibility. Increased hip turnout, wider stemming, and better ease at high-stepping will markedly improve center-of-mass positioning and quality of movement—the upshot, of course, is a conservation of energy. While your ultimate degree of flexibility is largely a function of genetics, dedicated daily stretching and mobility work will produce some gains in functional range of motion. Consequently, engaging in a modest amount of lower-body stretching is a smart thing to do, not only as part of a pre-performance warm-up, but also as part of some before-bed mobility work and rest-day flexibility training. Here are nine stretches to put to use beginning today.

BUTTOCKS AND LOWER-BACK STRETCH

This stretch will improve hip flexion and help facilitate high-stepping. Lie flat on your back with both legs straight. Bend one leg and grasp it behind the thigh or around the upper shin and pull it toward your chest. Hold the stretch for ten seconds and

Pull the bent leg toward your chest and hold.

then release it for a few seconds. Pull the bent leg toward your chest again for a secondary stretch of about twenty seconds. Repeat with the other leg.

HAMSTRINGS STRETCH

The hamstring muscles, along the back of the thigh, are chronically tight in many climbers, thus restricting stem and high-step movements. Lie flat on your back with one leg straight and the other bent with the foot flat on the floor. Lift the straight leg upward, grab it behind the thigh or calf, and pull gently forward until you feel the stretch down the back of the leg. (Alternatively, you can keep the

Pull the straight leg forward and hold.

non-stretching leg flat on the floor as shown in the photo.) Hold this stretch for ten seconds and then release it slightly for a few seconds. Pull the leg once again for another twenty to thirty seconds. Be sure to maintain a straight leg throughout, and perform this stretch equally on both legs. You can also work this stretch by looping a fitness band or towel over your foot and regulating the stretch by pulling on the band.

ADDUCTOR STRETCH

This wall stretch is one of the very best lower-body stretches for climbers. Lying on the floor eliminates strain on the lower back and allows you to relax and

Separate legs, relax, and let gravity extend the split.

let gravity do the work. Wearing socks will reduce friction between your heels and the wall, helping maximize the range of the stretch. Lie on the floor with your buttocks about six inches from a wall and your legs extending straight up it with about a 90-degree bend at your hips. Slowly separate your legs by sliding your heels out to the sides. Concentrate on relaxing throughout your body, and allow gravity to extend the split until you feel mild tension in your legs and groin. Hold this position for twenty to thirty seconds. Try to split your legs farther apart; if needed, press on your thighs to apply some downward pressure to extend the stretch. Hold this position for a minute or two.

GROIN STRETCH

This is an excellent stretch for improving hip turnout. Flexibility gains from this stretch will allow you to move your center of mass in closer to the wall—

1. Gently press elbows down on thighs.
2. Lie flat and allow gravity to pull knees downward.

more over your feet—on near-vertical climbs. Sit upright with your legs flexed and knees out to the sides so that you can bring the soles of your feet together. Grasp your ankles and rest your elbows on the inside of the thighs. Press down with your elbows to apply light pressure on both thighs until you feel mild tension in your groin and inner thigh. Hold this stretch for ten seconds and then release it for a few seconds. Apply pressure for a secondary stretch of twenty to thirty seconds. Next, lie flat on your back while keeping your feet together. Relax and allow gravity to pull your knees toward the floor for another minute or two. To enhance the stretch, have a partner apply light downward pressure on your knees.

PIRIFORMIS

The piriformis muscle lies deep beneath the gluteal muscles and assists in lifting and rotating the thigh laterally. In climbing, this muscle is used to position your foot on a hold that's up and out to the side. If you have trouble reaching out your foot to engage distant edges, a tight piriformis is likely part of the problem. The piriformis stretch may also provide some relief for individuals experiencing mild sciatica. Here's how to stretch it.

Gently lower your hips and torso toward the bent leg.

Kneel on the floor with your hands positioned under your shoulders. Shift your upper-body weight onto your arms so that you can position one leg in front of you with the knee acutely flexed so that the outside of the foot contacts the floor near the opposite hip. Slide the other leg backward until it's nearly straight with the kneecap and toes touching the floor. Maintaining a straight torso, lower your hips toward the floor to increase the stretch. Hold this position for ten to twenty seconds and then raise your hips slightly to release the stretch for a few seconds. Lower your hips again for a secondary stretch of thirty to sixty seconds; repeat the stretch with the other leg. **Warning:** Perform this stretch with caution, and ease up at the first sign of any pain in the knees, hips, or lower back.

HIP FLEXORS AND QUADRICEPS

The hip flexor muscle group is commonly tight, not only because of the critical role they serve in running, hiking uphill, and lifting the legs in climbing, but also because they can readily shorten during extended periods of sitting. This makes the hip flexors, including the powerhouse psoas, a prime muscle group to target with foam rolling and stretching. Here's how to do it.

Kneel on the floor with one leg forward and bent at near 90 degrees, while the other leg is nearly straight and extended behind you. Resting your hands on the knee for balance, shift your hips forward while maintaining a flat or slightly extended spine—this should create some tension in the hip flexors atop the straight leg. Hold this position for ten seconds and then raise your hips slightly to release the stretch for a few seconds. Now, shift your hips forward again and, if you can maintain balance, extend your arms straight overhead. This will enhance the stretch and perhaps elicit a "pop" from the lumbar zone. Hold the stretch for thirty seconds. Release the stretch and then flex your rear leg so that you can grab it with the opposite hand.

1. ***Shift hips forward until you feel tension in the front of your hip.***
2. ***Pull foot upward with opposite hand to stretch the quadriceps.***

Now do a final stretch in which you both shift forward and pull gently on the rear foot. This will provide an excellent stretch of the quadriceps.

CALF STRETCH

There are many ways to stretch the calf muscles of the lower leg, so there's no reason not to give these hard-working muscles a few stretches throughout the day. By elevating the front part of the foot, on a small step or other object, and keeping your heel on the floor, you simply need to lower your hip level and flex your knee forward to elicit a good stretch. Hold the stretch for twenty seconds, release it for a few seconds, and then resume the stretch for another thirty seconds. Repeat the stretch with the other leg.

Elevate your forefoot and shift your knee forward while maintaining heel contact with the ground.

ABDOMINAL STRETCH

While strong abdominals that can stiffen on demand are highly coveted, it's equally important to be able to quickly relax the abs and extend the torso. Most people find it relaxing and pleasurable to stretch the abdominals and extend the spine before and following a workout. Begin in a prone position with your arms bent and palms flat on the floor next to your shoulders. Slowly press your shoulders away from the floor until you feel mild tension in your abdominals. Keep your legs and pelvis in contact with the floor for the duration of this

Keeping your hips and legs grounded, push your shoulders away from the floor until you feel a stretch in the rectus abdominus.

Gently rotate your torso toward the bent-leg side.

stretch—it helps to contract your buttocks in order to maintain the position and reduce stress on your lower back. Hold the stretch for ten seconds and then return to the starting position for a few seconds. Press up for a secondary stretch of twenty to thirty seconds. Relax and allow the curve of your spine to extend up through your upper back and neck. Look forward, but not up toward the ceiling. Do not be overly aggressive with this stretch—proceed with caution, especially if you have a history of back problems. Stop immediately if you experience any pain in the lower back.

OBLIQUES, HIPS, AND BACK STRETCH

This final global stretch—of the hips, torso, and back—will help prepare your body for the torso-twisting, hip-turning, drop-kneeing movements that are so common on steep sport climbs and boulder problems. Sit erect on the floor with one leg straight and the other bent and crossing over the opposite knee. Slowly turn your body toward the side of the bent leg until you feel mild tension in your lower back, hips, and the side of your torso. Maintain a level head position and fix your eyes on the wall to the side of the bent leg. Hold the stretch for ten to twenty seconds and then return to the starting position for a few seconds. Perform a secondary stretch for twenty to thirty seconds. If needed, you can increase the stretch by levering your elbow against the thigh of the bent leg. Repeat the stretch in the other direction. Be sure to switch leg positions.

Stabilizer and Antagonist Muscle Training

This section on training the stabilizer and antagonist muscles may be the single most important in the entire book. While few climbers need additional motivation to train their finger or core strength, it's my experience that the majority of climbers spend too little time training the crucial muscles that support the wrist and shoulder during strenuous climbing moves. Left untrained, these "supporting cast" muscles, which stabilize the wrist and scapula, will eventually let you down in critical moments of fatigue—the result could be insidious slow-onset elbow tendinitis or shoulder impingement, or a more acute rotator cuff tear.

As common as injuries are in this sport, it surprises me that so few climbers are dedicated to regular training of the antagonist muscles. No doubt, training these smaller muscle groups lacks the excitement of bouldering or campus training, and low-information climbers might view it as unnecessary, boring, or a waste of time. It's my opinion, however, that every climber should train their stabilizers and antagonists twice per week. Furthermore, the harder a person trains and climbs, the more indispensable these exercises become for preventing injury and ensuring longevity in the sport. So shelve the excuses, and make the commitment today. Coach Hörst insists!

The three subsections that follow will provide rich details on training the wrist stabilizers, the scapular stabilizers and rotator cuff, and the larger push muscles that oppose and provide balance to the many climbing-specific push muscles. (Consult the anatomy photos in appendix A if you are unfamiliar with any of the muscle groups mentioned.)

Training the Wrist Stabilizers

The musculature of the forearms is some of the most complex in the body. For example, at first blush it seems that the forearm flexor muscles are almost single-handedly (pun intended) responsible for securing a tight grip to the rock. Consequently, exercises that target the forearm flexor muscles—such as the fingerboard, HIT System, campus board, or others—are the focus of most climbers' training programs. The problem is that developing strong fingers and forearms that are also resistant to injury demands that you also regularly train the muscles that extend the fingers and wrist. Here's why.

The finger flexors suffer from a sort of functional insufficiency in that they are much weaker when the wrist is flexed and the muscles are short. As an experiment, flex your wrist as much as possible (wrist angle around 90 degrees) and pinch your middle finger as hard as possible against the thumb. It's hard to create much force, right? Now, while still pressing your middle finger against the thumb, slowly extend your wrist to a straight position and then an over-extended position. What did you notice? If you tried to squeeze hard throughout this range of motion, you likely discovered that your finger strength increases as the wrist extends.

Biomechanically, there are a couple of reasons that finger strength is greater with an extended wrist position. First, muscles can contract more forcefully when they are elongated, as the finger flexors are with an extended wrist position. More interesting, however, is how the fingers naturally assume a hook-like position when the wrist is over-extended. Try it right now—over-extend your wrist and you'll see the meat hooks revealed!

Now you know why fatiguing climbers lift their elbows into the chicken-wing position—it puts their wrist into a position that enables their pumped forearms to grip a little longer. Done chronically, however, such chicken winging stresses the extensor muscles and puts added stress on the tendon pulleys in the fingers. The result can be gradual onset of lateral epicondylitis and/or finger tendon problems.

The training "fix," then, is to dedicate a modest amount of time to training the finger/wrist extensor muscles. No, you can't just extend your fingers against a rubber band and call it good. You need to do some serious training in multiple ways, just as you train the finger flexors in a comprehensive manner! It's paramount to train the wrist in both a neutral and extended position, as well as in a wide pinch grip position—this is the single most overlooked and important position to train it. While you don't need to do all the exercises every workout, at minimum I suggest doing reverse wrist curls, wide pinches, and pronator isolation. Do one set of these three exercises (with a light resistance) as part of your warm-up for climbing (or training), and then do two more sets with higher resistance toward the end of your workout.

FINGER EXTENSION AGAINST RUBBER BAND

Okay, let me get this one out of the way first. Use of a rubber band (or similar) to extend your fingers

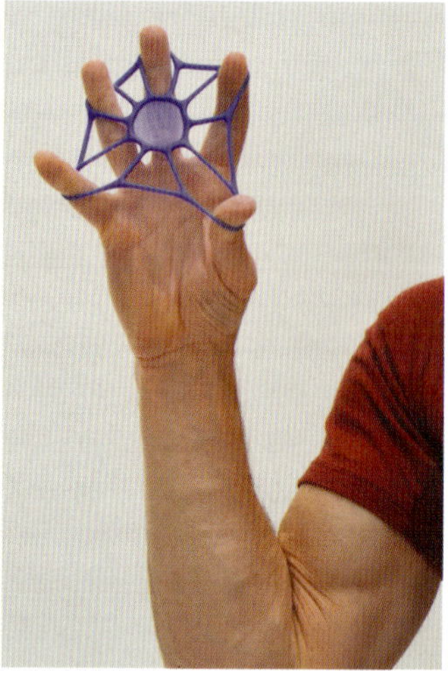

Powerfingers are an excellent tool for warming up and rehabbing the extensors.

against is sufficient only for the purposes of warm-up and rehabilitation from injury. I recommend use of Powerfingers to warm up before advancing to the exercises below.

REVERSE WRIST CURLS

Just as the name implies, this exercise involves curling a dumbbell upward with your palm facing down. Fix your forearm in a stable, horizontal position using a bench, table, or on your thigh (if sitting) and grasp the dumbbell with your hand overhanging the supporting surface. Begin with the dumbbell in the top (over-extended) position and lower it to the neutral (straight wrist) position, then curl the dumbbell back to the top position. Continue with slow, controlled reverse curls at a rate of about one rep per second. I recommend doing two sets with progressive resistance. For the first set select a weight that allows twenty to twenty-five repetitions, but stop the exercise before complete failure. Rest three minutes before doing a second set with a heavier dumbbell that allows only ten to fifteen reps. Initially you may need to use only a five-pound dumbbell; advanced climbers may need as much as a twenty-five- to thirty-pound dumbbell for the high-resistance set. Do some

1. ***Start in the top position.***
2. ***Stop at neutral position and return to top position.***

mild stretching of the extensors during each rest period.

Note: Anyone with elbow pain or recent history of lateral tendinosis should do only the negative phase of this exercise—that is, use your free hand to grab the dumbbell-holding hand and aid its return to the top position after each negative (lowering phase).

WRIST EXTENSION ISOMETRIC

I love this exercise! You'll need a clock (with a second hand) in view or a timing app to train against. The setup is the same as in the reverse wrist curl, but you'll be using a lighter-weight dumbbell. The difference here is that there's no lowering phase—you'll simply hold the dumbbell in the up (over-extended position) for a long isometric contraction. Select a dumbbell light enough to allow an isometric hold in the over-extended position for forty-five to sixty seconds. Do two sets with each arm with a three-minute rest in between. Long term, strive to hold the over-extended position for a full two minutes. It'll feel good to do some stretching of the forearm extensors during the rest period.

WIDE PINCH WITH WRIST EXTENSION

This novel exercise is absolutely essential, as it strengthens the extensor muscles with the fingers fully extended to mimic grabbing open-hand and wide pinch holds in climbing. It may seem like a small distinction, but the wrist extensors function a bit differently when the fingers are straight (extended) compared with when the fingers are flexed, as in crimping or holding a dumbbell. So it's important to do this exercise in addition to one of the previous.

Until there's a commercially available device for training the wide pinch grip, you'll need to kludge something that will work. Screwing together two or three pieces of 2x4 wood blocks is a cheap,

Wide pinch with wrist extension.
1. Using a bumper plate.
2. Using wood blocks.

effective solution—consider making two sizes, wide and extra-wide. Another option is pinching a thick bumper weight plate. Anyway, the exercise is straightforward: Standing upright with good posture, pinch the wood block or bumper plate with a straight arm and extended wrist; hold this position for ten to thirty seconds.

Initially, I suggest training for endurance, which will require a light weight that allows a full thirty-second hold. Do three with each hand with at least a minute rest in between. Longer term, consider using a heavier weight that allows only a ten-second hold. In this case, do three consecutive ten-second pinches with the same hand, resting only thirty seconds between each one. Do a total of three sets of three reps with each hand, resting for about three minutes between sets.

PRONATOR ISOLATION

Arm-pulling movements naturally result in supination of the hand. If you perform a pull-up on a free-hanging set of Pump Rocks, you'll discover that your hands naturally turn inward, or supinate, as your biceps contract. Consequently, training forearm pronation is an important antagonist exercise for climbers to maintain muscle balance across the forearms. While a well-equipped gym may have a machine for training forearm pronation, most folks will need to find a creative training solution. My preference is using an ordinary three-pound sledgehammer!

Sit on a chair or bench with your forearm resting on your thigh, hand in the palm-up position. Firmly grip the sledgehammer with the heavy end extending to the outside and the handle parallel to the floor. Turn your hand inward (pronation) to lift the hammer to the vertical position. Stop here. Now slowly lower the hammer back to the starting position. Stop at the horizontal position for one second before beginning the next repetition. Continue lifting the hammer in this way for twenty to twenty-five repetitions. Choke up on the hammer if this feels overly difficult. Perform two sets with each hand.

Alternatively, you can cut a sixteen-inch length of one-inch-diameter dowel and mount a two-and-one-half pound weight on one end.

1. Palm up. 2. Lift hammer to vertical.

PRONATOR ISOLATION WITH AN EXERCISE BAND

As an alternative to the sledgehammer exercise above, you can train the pronator with an exercise band. In a sitting position, anchor one end of the band under your foot and then wrap the other end of the band around your hand. Remove all the slack between your hand and foot so that there's tension when holding the band palm up with the back of your forearm resting on your thigh. Keeping your forearm in a fixed position, turn your hand inward (pronation) to reach the palms-down position. Return to the starting position and continue for twenty-five repetitions. Make sure there's enough tension in the band to provide moderate resistance throughout the full 180-degree range of motion. Do two sets with each hand.

***1.** Anchor one end of the band under your foot and grasp the band palm up.* ***2.** Rotate your forearm inward until palm is facing down.*

REVERSE ARM CURLS

The reverse arm curl is one of my favorite warm-up exercises. While it obviously activates the biceps, more importantly, it demands an isometric contraction of the wrist extensors and calls into play the often overlooked brachioradialis to stabilize and flex the elbow. In elbow flexion the brachioradialis is most active when the hand is pronated, as in the majority of climbing moves—therefore

With a palms-down grip (pronated forearms), curl the barbell upward while keeping your elbows fixed.

strengthening the brachioradialis means a stronger wrist and a more stable elbow and forearm while gripping and pulling down on the rock.

Do this exercise with a barbell or bent E-Z curl bar (see photo), not with dumbbells. Take an overhand grip and, with elbows fixed at your side, curl the bar upward to reach full elbow flexion. Continue for fifteen to twenty repetitions, being sure to contract your core, glutes, and spinal erectors throughout the duration of the exercise. I suggest doing one set with light weight as part of your warm-up, and another moderately heavy set or two with your antagonist training.

Training Rotator Cuff and Scapular Stability

The rotator cuff is arguably the most stressed group of muscles in the body of a climber. While the forearms get all the attention—and pump—the rotator cuff and scapular stabilizers are the real heroes as a climber repeatedly pulls with his arms from a wide range of angles, both statically and dynamically applying force of varying intensity. Climbing on overhanging walls, at times with jumping, lunging, and campusing moves, challenges the small rotator cuff muscles to keep the humeral head in place; similarly the scapular stabilizers must work hard to move the scapula into the proper position for each given arm position in climbing. Even in vertical climbing the crimp grip and the chicken-wing arm position stress the rotator cuff, and, not surprisingly, shoulder pathology will weaken your grip. Hence, dysfunction anywhere along the chain of force application—fingers, wrist, elbow, or shoulder—will negatively affect performance of the entire system.

If you still aren't motivated to train the cuff and scap, roll this over in your mind: Weak rotator cuff muscles are a common, yet unrecognized, limiting constraint in your maximum pulling strength, lunging power, grip strength, and contact strength. So if you're a hard-training climber frustrated by a lack of strength/power gains on the rock, it may be that your central governor is limiting power output due to afferent feedback from your weak, unstable shoulder joints. This is why it's essential to develop stability before strength, and strength before power (per figure 6.1).

Well-developed middle back muscles, as Anna Davey displays here, are essential to stabilize the scapula during strenuous arm movements common to hard climbing and campus training.
THERON KIRKMAN

Anyway, I trust you'll agree that the shoulder is a truly wondrous and remarkably dynamic joint, and therefore it's essential that you are proactive in training (and addressing weaknesses in) the many muscles involved. By using both the aforementioned mobility exercises and the strength exercises that follow, you will improve movement patterns and function, even when climbing in a state of high fatigue (when injury risk is highest). First, I'll detail two exercises that isolate the four muscles that comprise the rotator cuff: the supraspinatus, infraspinatus, teres minor, and the subscapularis. Next, I'll reveal four exercises that work the supporting cast of muscles, including the upper, middle, and lower trapezius, rhomboids, and serratus anterior, that move the scapula into proper position for overhead arm movements. Then, in the next section (antagonist training) I'll present three pushing exercises that work the entire system, including the larger role players of the pectorals, deltoids, and latissimus.

DUMBBELL INTERNAL ROTATION

Of the four rotator cuff muscles, only the subscapularis contributes to internal rotation. It does get substantial help, however, from the deltoid, teres major, latissimus, and pectorals—this helps explain why many climbers find they are stronger at internal rotation than external rotation. Still, you want to do this exercise twice per week since it (partially) isolates and strengthens the subscapularis.

Lie on your side with your bottom arm in front of your waist; place a rolled-up towel under your head to support your neck. Rest your other arm along your hip and upper thigh. Hold a five- to fifteen-pound dumbbell in the hand of your bottom arm, positioning this forearm perpendicular to your body. Lift the weight up to your body and hold for a moment before lowering it back to the floor. The upper portion of your arm should remain fixed throughout the range of motion—think of the upper arm and shoulder as a door hinge that allows your forearm to swing "up and down."

***1.** Starting position.* ***2.** Ending position.*

Continue in a slow but steady motion for a total of twenty to twenty-five repetitions. Do two sets on each side, with a three-minute rest between sets. Select a weight heavy enough to make you work, but not so great that you have to strain hard or compromise technique. Increase weight in two- to five-pound increments, as needed.

An alternative method of training the internal rotators is to anchor an exercise band to a waist-high object and, while standing, grip the band and pull it across your body. The key is to keep your elbow and upper arm in a fixed position and only move your hand and forearm across your body. Repeat this twenty-five times, adjusting resistance as needed by changing your distance from the anchor point or by using a different exercise band. In my opinion, such exercise band training, while good for rehab, doesn't cut it for serious training of the rotator cuff. Therefore I recommend using the dumbbell exercises detailed here.

DUMBBELL EXTERNAL ROTATION

The infraspinatus and teres minor are the primary external rotators, although they get some help from the deltoid. Many climbers are surprised to discover that they have weak external rotators and thus may be able to use only about one-half as much weight as when doing the internal rotation exercise above. Strengthening the external rotators should be a high priority, as this will provide additional protection of the cuff when grabbing the rock with the stressful above-the-head Gaston positions common to hard climbing.

Lie on your side with your bottom arm in front of your waist and a rolled-up towel under your head to support your neck. Alternatively, you can bend your bottom arm and use it as a headrest. Hold a five- to ten-pound dumbbell in the hand of your top arm. Rest the upper arm and elbow on the top side of your body, and then bend at the elbow so that the forearm hangs down over your belly and the weight rests on the floor. Keeping

1. Starting position. 2. Ending position.

your elbow and upper arm fixed, lift the weight upward toward the ceiling and stop when you feel the resistance ease as you move past the horizontal position. Return the weight to the starting position and continue for twenty to twenty-five repetitions. Do two sets on each side with a three-minute rest between each set. Increase weight in two- to five-pound increments. Initially you may need to use as little as five pounds. With long-term training, however, you should be able to improve to using a ten-pound dumbbell; especially fit climbers may be able to use up to fifteen pounds. This is a difficult exercise, and using proper technique is essential for isolating the external rotators. Err on the side of using too little weight, rather than too much.

If you don't have access to dumbbells, you can use an exercise band as an alternative, though perhaps less effective, training method. With an exercise band anchored to a waist-high object, stand with your side (opposite the arm to be trained) facing the band anchor spot. Grab the free end of the band with your forearm across your belly and upper arm at your side. Keeping your elbow and upper arm in a fixed position, pull outward on the exercise band with your forearm opening up away from the body like a swinging door. Repeat this twenty-five times, adjusting resistance as needed by changing your distance from the anchor point or using a different exercise band.

"T" EXERCISE

This exercise targets the middle trapezius and rhomboids, the muscles that produce scapular retraction. You can do the Ts in a standing position

Ts with TRX Sling trainer.
1. Starting position. 2. Finish position.

with a TRX trainer or prone on a bench. Using the TRX, grasp the handles with straight arms extended forward and palms facing each other. Now contract your core, glutes, and leg muscles and lean backward to weight the TRX; you can also walk your feet slightly forward (farther forward is harder). Maintaining a tight torso and straight arms, pull your hands apart until your arms are straight out to your side in a T position—think about squeezing your shoulder blades as close together as possible. Slowly lower back to the starting position and continue for ten to twenty repetitions. Do two sets. If you don't own a TRX trainer, you can still train Ts in an effective way by assuming a prone position on a bench with your arms hanging straight down. Contract your core and glutes, and lift straight arms out to the side until raised just above horizontal. Feel your shoulder blades come together, and actively squeeze them at the top position. Continue for twenty repetitions. You can progress to using very light dumbbells (a few pounds max).

"Y" EXERCISE

This exercise is only slightly different from the Ts described above, but the Y motion specifically targets the lower trapezius. The lower traps produce scapular depression and upward rotation, which is essential to avoid shoulder impingement when doing overhead movements. Among climbers, the lower traps are commonly a weak link and thus a potential contributing factor to shoulder injury. If you frequently engage in campus training and lunge moves, then a strong mid and lower trapezius are vital to facilitate proper scapular positioning (to avoid trashing your shoulders).

Ys with TRX trainer.
1. Starting position. 2. Ending position.

Set up in the same way as when doing Ts, but the motion is up and outward to form a "Y." Stop pulling when your arms come in line with your body—at this top position your arms should be just beyond shoulder width apart. Be sure to contract your core, glutes, and legs to maintain rigidity throughout the range of motion. Think about drawing your scapula downward as you reach the top of the Y position. You can also do the Y exercise lying prone on a bench with just arm weight or a one- or two-pound dumbbell in each hand. Begin with your arms straight and hanging down under the bench below your face. With a stiff core and tight glutes, lift straight arms up into the Y position with your hands just beyond shoulder width at the top position. No matter which method of Y training you select, do two sets of ten to twenty repetitions with a three-minute rest in between.

SCAPULAR PUSH-UP

The scapular push-up isolates the serratus anterior muscle, which is vital for scapular stability and protraction. You can do this simple exercise from a straight-arm push-up position or from a plank position with your elbows and forearms flat on the floor. I suggest using the plank position for learning the feel of this exercise. Assume the classic plank position with elbows under your shoulders, a neutral spine, and tight abs and spinal erectors. Keeping your torso stiff and straight, allow your chest to sag downward between your arms. Now drive your elbows and forearms into the floor to return to the top position—feel your scapula slide around your rib cage as the serratus anterior contracts. The range of motion is only a few inches, but it's a great isolation exercise if you do twenty or so repetitions. This movement is not meant to be heavily loaded, so there's no need to use additional weight. Do one or two sets.

SCAPULAR PULL-UP

This last exercise is anything but the least—the scapular pull-up is perhaps the best climbing exercise that almost nobody does! Keeping your shoulders healthy and developing proper movement patterns in pulling motions demands the ability to depress, rotate, and retract the scapula. Regular use of this isolation exercise will develop better kinesthetic awareness of your scapula position and enable you to climb harder and longer with good form, despite growing fatigue. Furthermore, being able to quickly and forcibly engage the lower trapezius and lats will empower you to keep your scapula in proper position when campus training and lunging.

Strong climbers can do this exercise with full body weight, but I suggest learning with less resistance by keeping your feet on the floor and flexing your knees enough to hang with straight arms from a pull-up bar. Either way, the range of motion is

1. Begin in a fully extended push-up position with scapular protraction. 2. Maintaining straight arms, allow your chest to sag downward (scapula retraction) and immediately press back to the starting position.

only a few inches—from a full hang with somewhat shrugged shoulders, the desired action is to draw the scapula down and together. The best learning cues are to try to "bend the bar," and think about doing a reverse shrug (i.e., shoulders drawn downward). Do this and you'll feel your head shift backward and your chest raise upward, as your scapulas pinch together. Hold the top position for one second, then return to the starting position. Do eight to twelve reps, keeping straight arms and tight spinal erectors and glutes throughout. At first you may find this to be a difficult exercise (a sign that you've found a critical weakness to correct!), but resist the urge to overdo it. Add a second set to your workout only after you've mastered the exercise.

1. Begin from an ordinary pull-up starting position. 2. Maintaining nearly straight arms, depress and downwardly rotator your scapula by pressing down on the bar—think about pushing your chest out and trying to bend the bar.

Antagonist Training

The previous sections presented the must-do isolation exercises for strengthening your rotator cuff and scapular stabilizers. This chapter concludes with three vital multi-joint exercises that target the large climbing antagonist muscles, including the three heads of the deltoids, the pectoralis, and the triceps. The importance of doing these exercises cannot be overstated, considering the need to balance out all the pulling you do in climbing with some quality push movements. As in training the stabilizer muscles, you want to train the antagonists with a moderate resistance and relatively high number of repetitions. Keep in mind that performing a high-weight hypertrophy or maximum-strength program is unnecessary and, in fact, could be detrimental if it causes unwanted gain in muscle mass.

While the three following exercises can all be performed on standard health equipment (Cybex, Olympic weights, and so forth), I would advise against purchasing a health club membership just to gain access to the necessary machinery. Instead, I recommend a one-time investment in a few pairs of dumbbells (only $100 to $200)—they'll last you a lifetime. Alternatively, you might ask the climbing gym you patronize to purchase a few dumbbells or a set of free weights for the purpose of training the antagonist, rotator cuff, and stabilizer muscles. Of course, it's also possible to do some of these pushing exercises with a sling trainer such as the TRX.

SHOULDER PRESS

The shoulder-press motion is almost exactly opposite that of pulling up while climbing—therefore, no exercise is more central to antagonist-muscle training. Although you can execute this exercise with a common health club overhead-press machine, performing dumbbell shoulder presses provides a more complete workout, including some extra work for the cuff and scapular stabilizers.

Sit on a bench with good upright posture and feet flat on the floor. Begin with bent arms, palms

1. Beginning position. *2. End with dumbbells touching end-to-end.*

facing forward, and the dumbbells positioned just outside your shoulders. Press straight upward with your palms maintaining a forward-facing position. As your arms become straight, squeeze your hands slightly inward until the dumbbells touch end-to-end. Lower the dumbbells to the starting position. The complete repetition should take about two seconds. Continue this motion for fifteen to twenty repetitions. Strive for smooth, consistent motion throughout the entire set. Rest for three minutes and perform a second set.

Women should start with five-pound dumbbells and advance to ten- or fifteen-pounders when they can do twenty reps. Most men can begin training with fifteen- or twenty-pound dumbbells and then progress to twenty-five and thirty pounds as they are able to achieve twenty-five repetitions. Over the long term it's best not to progress beyond about 40 percent of your body weight (total weight lifted), since frequent use of heavier weights may build undesirable muscle bulk.

BENCH PRESS (OR PUSH-UPS)

The bench press is a staple exercise of power lifters and bodybuilders, but it's also useful to climbers striving to maintain stable, healthy shoulders. The key is to use only moderate resistance—begin with a total weight equal to about 30 percent of your body weight and progress up to about 75 percent (no need to go higher). For example, a 160-pound climber would begin training with two 25-pound dumbbells (50 pounds total) and progress up to

1. Beginning position. *2. End position.*

training with, at most, 50-pound dumbbells or 120 pounds with an Olympic bar.

Lie flat on a bench with bent legs and your feet flat on the floor. Using an Olympic bar or two dumbbells, begin the exercise with your hands just above chest level and palms facing your feet. If you're using a bar, your hands should be a few inches wider than your shoulders. Press straight up with a slow, steady motion. If using dumbbells, squeeze your hands together to touch the ends of the dumbbells together upon reaching the top position. Return to the starting position, pause for a moment, and then begin the next repetition. With a bar, be careful not to bounce the bar off your chest. The goal is slow, controlled movement that takes about two seconds per repetition. Continue for fifteen to twenty repetitions. Rest for three minutes before performing a second set.

As an alternative, push-ups provide a workout similar to the bench press. Begin with your hands shoulder width apart and build up to doing two sets of twenty-five repetitions. If necessary, move your hands closer together to increase training resistance. Conversely, beginners should do the push-ups with their knees on the floor until they are able to progress to the normal feet-on-floor position.

DIPS

Dips are an excellent exercise for strengthening the many muscles of the upper arms, shoulders, chest, and back. What's more, the dip motion is quite similar to the mantle move in climbing and thus provides a very sport-specific benefit! Some health clubs and gyms possess a parallel-bar setup ideal for performing dips. Alternatively, you can use the incut 90-degree corner of a kitchen counter, or set two heavy chairs in a parallel position. A set of free-floating Pump Rocks or gymnastics rings are my personal favorite, as they provide a more dynamic (and difficult) workout.

Position yourself between the parallel bars, rings, or similar apparatus. Jump up into the straight-arm starting position with your hands drawn in near your hips. Slowly lower until your arm is bent 90 degrees—do not lower beyond this point! Immediately press back up to the starting position. Continue this up-and-down motion, with each repetition taking about two seconds. Strive to complete eight to twenty (hard) repetitions. Perform two or three sets with a three-minute rest between each set. Don't rush or bounce through this exercise, and never lower beyond a 90-degree arm bend.

If you are unable to do at least eight dips, enlist a spotter to reduce the resistance as needed so that you can reach this goal. The spotter should stand behind you and lift around your waist or, more easily, pull up on your ankles (bend your legs and cross them at the ankles to facilitate this).

1. Begin with a straight-arm start.
2. Lower to a ninety-degree elbow angle, then immediately press back up to starting position.

Alex Puccio sends Unshackled Low (V11), Lincoln Lake, Mount Evans, Colorado.
CHRIS NOBLE

CHAPTER SEVEN

Core, Legs, and Aerobic Training

No one is you, and that's your power!

Core, legs, and aerobic training are three things that seem relatively unrelated and, perhaps, even could be viewed as unnecessary for rock climbing. Think again!

The core muscles of your torso are called into play for every climbing movement, and they are especially important in climbing vertical to overhanging terrain. A stronger core will enable you to step higher, hang onto slopers better, position your hips for optimal center-of-mass placement, and create torso tension and torque for hard, powerful movements.

Intimately related to the core muscles are the upper-leg and hip muscles that almost always co-contract with the core muscles. You can prove this to yourself by doing a simple plank or a front lever—notice how the glute muscles of your rear end contract with these exercises. In this way the hip flexors and extensors are active players in all climbing movements. Even more dramatic are deadpoint and lunging moves, which require rapid, forceful recruitment of the entire posterior chain—interestingly, these are muscle groups that few climbers ever target for specific training. I hope this chapter will increase awareness of the importance of the posterior chain in climbing, and hopefully you'll take some of the exercises for a test drive and recognize how they will help you climb with more motor control and power.

The closing sections of this chapter examine the topic of body composition and how it relates to performance in a strength-to-weight ratio sport such as climbing. We'll also examine the somewhat controversial subject of "running for climbers"—should you or shouldn't you run? Obviously, doing a modest amount of aerobic training can help improve your body composition, but will it directly improve your climbing performance? (Hint: For roped climbers the answer is definitely "yes!"). In this chapter we'll sort this out once and for all, so let's get started!

Core and Posterior Chain Leg Training

In climbing, the core muscles of your torso play a key role in enabling your arms and legs to maximize leverage and transfer torque from hand to foot and vice versa. Furthermore, the core muscles are essential in providing the stability you need to stand up on a small foothold and pull on a small crimp hold. But it's on overhanging routes that the core muscles activate most forcefully—twisting your hips, stiffening up on a long reach, throwing and sticking a deadpoint, and keeping your feet on during a super-steep sequence is not possible without total core involvement.

For the average John Doe, the quest for six-pack abs is what comes to mind when speaking of core training. Of course, most climbers know better—there are many muscles that contribute to core strength and the ability to create the stiffness needed for hard movements. To understand how to better train the many core muscles, it's helpful to dig a little deeper and distinguish between the inner core and outer core.

As a conceptual model you can think of the inner core as a protective cylinder that stiffens to stabilize the spine. This cylinder is composed of the abdominals in the front, the spinal erectors on the back, and the obliques on the sides; the diaphragm sits atop the cylinder and the pelvic floor muscles form the bottom of the cylinder. It's these muscle groups that are conventionally viewed as the "core," and they are the target of common exercises such as crunches and Supermans.

All the muscles of the torso—from shoulders to hips—comprise the outer core. For example, the pectorals, trapezius, rhomboids, latissimus dorsi, quadratus lumborum, gluteals, hip flexors, hamstrings, abductors, and adductors are all outer core muscles that provide torso stiffness and drive macro movements.

Proper core training must target both the muscles of the inner and outer core, and importantly, equally strengthen the anterior and posterior muscles. Climbers who just climb, however, tend to be disproportionately stronger in the anterior core muscles—this is one reason for the common "climbers posture" of rounded shoulders, flexed torso, and a flat lower back. Therefore I believe most climbers can benefit from diligent training of the posterior chain of muscles, as detailed in the section on total core and leg training (page 154).

To help facilitate appropriate exercise selection, I've divided the core exercises into three categories according to the area of training focus: anterior core, posterior core, and total core. Performing two exercises from each of the three categories will comprise one excellent core workout.

Anterior Core Muscles

This first group of exercises target the anterior core—that is, pretty much all the muscles you see between your shoulders and hips when you look in the mirror. While the abdominals are the hallmark of the anterior core, there's much more to effectively training this zone than simply cranking out a hundred crunches. Give the Windshield Wipers exercise a try—it's uniquely effective and my personal favorite!

ABDOMINAL CRUNCH

Okay, let's get this one out of the way. No, it's not a bad exercise, but it often gets too much focus, and occasionally people don't even do it correctly. Here's how to do crunchers that truly isolate the abdominals. Lie on the floor with your legs bent at about 90 degrees and your feet flat on the floor. Cross your arms over your upper chest or place your hands behind your head (harder), but do not interlace your fingers behind your neck. Now lift your shoulder blades off the floor and exhale as you "crunch" upward. The range of motion is small—lift your shoulder blades off the floor, but do not ascend all the way as you would in doing old-school sit-ups. Continue up and down at a brisk pace that takes about one second per repetition, but don't go so fast that you are bouncing off the floor. Perform as many crunches as possible. Your long-term goal is to be able to do fifty to one hundred crunches in a set. As your conditioning improves further, you can perform a second set after a three-minute rest.

1. Starting position.
2. Top position with shoulder blades off the floor.

HANGING KNEE LIFT

This strenuous exercise targets the lower abdominals and hip flexors in a very climbing-specific way—much like lifting your legs on an overhanging route. Do these hanging from a pull-up bar, the bucket holds of a fingerboard, or a set of Pump Rocks with your palms facing away—be sure to engage your scapular stabilizers and maintain tension in your shoulders throughout. Briskly lift your knees up to chest level, allowing your legs to bend naturally with the motion. Pause for a moment, and then lower your legs slowly until they return to a slightly bent position. Immediately begin the next upward repetition, and continue these knee-lift movements at a steady pace until you can no longer perform the full range of motion. Your long-range goal is fifteen to twenty repetitions, at which time you can add ankle weights to increase resistance. Rest for at least three minutes before performing a second set.

1. Starting position. 2. Top position.

ONE-ARM ELBOW AND SIDE PLANK

There are dozens of plank variations, but this is one of the best because it trains the obliques and hips as well as the anti-extension capabilities of the abdominals. Begin in the standard elbow plank position with only your toes, elbows, and forearms touching the floor. Now lift one arm and continue to open up fully in order to raise the free hand to a vertical position. Contract your inner and outer core muscles as needed to remain stable, and hold this top position for two seconds. Return to the starting position and lift the other arm, opening up to the side and extending the hand to the ceiling. Again, hold the top position for two seconds. This

1. Starting position.
2. Alternate raising each arm.

is a good exercise to train endurance, as some core muscles relax and other contract as you alternate sides. Continue for one to two minutes.

ONE-ARM, ONE-LEG PLANK

This strenuous exercise calls into play almost every muscle from your hands to your feet, and as a result it's remarkably hard and tiring! Assume a push-up position with your torso straight and in line with your feet. Spread your feet shoulder width apart, with your toes in contact with the floor. Keeping your arms, back, and legs straight, lift one foot and the opposite hand off the floor for approximately five seconds. Contract the muscles of your arms, shoulders, core, and legs as needed to maintain balance. Switch foot and arm positions so that your other arm and leg are now supporting your weight. Hold this position for about five seconds. Continue alternating the supporting arm and leg every five seconds. End the exercise after one minute, or earlier if you cannot maintain balance on the single arm and leg. Rest for three minutes and perform a second set.

1. Lift one hand and the opposite foot. 2. Then the other.

TRX "MARINE CORE"

With a name like "marine core," this is surely a must-do exercise! Adjust your TRX sling trainer or rings to hip height when you are in a kneeling position. Kneel about one to two feet away from the handles and extend straight arms to grip the handles or rings with a palms-down grip. Now stiffen up from knees to shoulders and push your hands forward until your arms and torso form a straight line—hold this position for two seconds, and then return to the starting position. This is a strenuous exercise, so proceed with caution; stop if you can't maintain proper form. The goal is six to twelve (hard) repetitions. Do two or three sets with at least a three-minute rest in between.

1. Starting position. 2. Ending position.

WINDSHIELD WIPERS

Along with marine core and the front lever, this is one of my favorite core exercises. Initially it may take you a few workouts to get the hang of this exercise—but trust that you'll quickly gain the feel and strength to do it like a champ. Begin hanging palms away from a pull-up bar, and then lift your legs upward until your back is more or less parallel to the ground and your shins are near the level of the bar. It helps to bend your arms slightly and think about "bending the bar" with your hands throughout the entire exercise—this will put your shoulders and scapula in the best position for this exercise. Now lower your legs to the side, then immediately raise them back to the top position and lower to the other side. The side-to-side motion is, of course, like windshield wipers—try to "wipe" from 9 o'clock to 3 o'clock and back again. Continue for six to twelve (hard) repetitions. Do two or three sets with adequate rest in between.

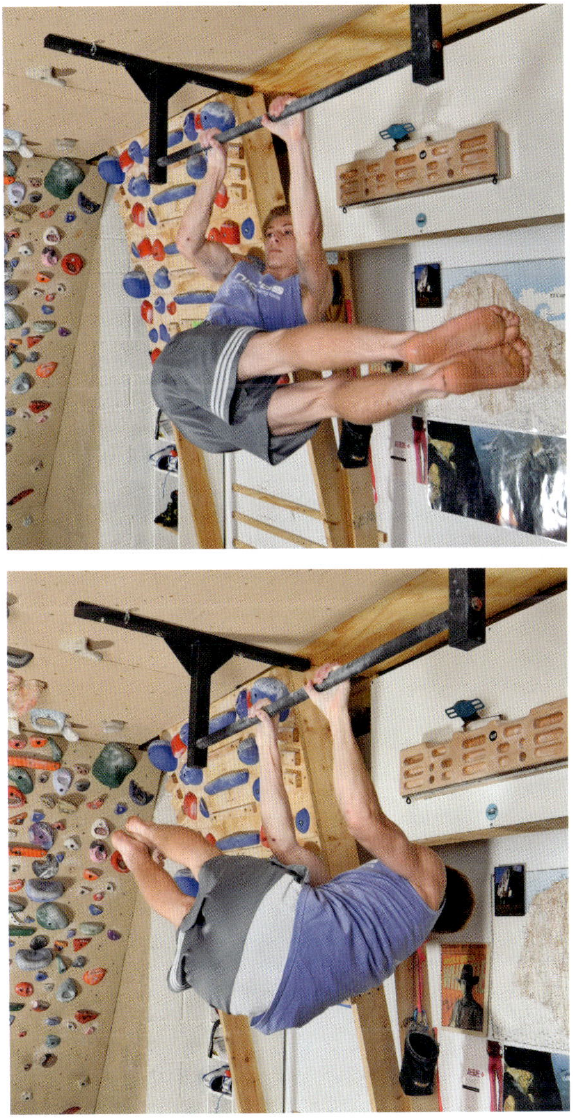

Begin with shins pulled up to the bar. 1. Drop to 9 o'clock position. 2. Pivot past the starting position and down to a 3 o'clock position.

FRONT LEVER

Introduced to climbing by the legendary boulderer John Gill, the front lever is the gold standard of core-muscle strength. It is a very difficult gymnastics move, so expect this exercise to feel hard—or even impossible! Fortunately, you can make it a bit easier by simply bending one leg or having a spotter hold your feet. Begin by hanging straight-armed from a bar or a set of rings (harder). Pull up halfway, then push your hands forward, drop your head backward, and lift your legs. Do all this in a single quick motion while attempting to position your entire body—head to toe—parallel to the ground. Squeeze tightly throughout your shoulders, torso, buttocks, and legs to hold this position for two seconds (if you can). It helps to think about pushing your hands toward your hips, even though you'll be in a stationary position. Lower yourself slowly to the starting position and immediately pull up into a front lever again and hold for two seconds. Perform two to five (hard) total front levers. Rest for a minimum of three minutes before performing a second set.

Bent-leg and straight-leg (harder) front lever.

Safety note: The front lever places a great deal of stress on your shoulders and elbows (just like steep climbing), so it is inappropriate for novice or out-of-shape climbers or anyone with ongoing elbow or shoulder problems.

Posterior Core

Exercises that target the posterior core are missing from many climbers' training programs. Taking a few minutes to do a couple of the following exercise would be a wise thing, as would be doing a couple of the total core and leg exercises described in the next section. Do these twice per week for a few months and you'll improve posterior chain proprioception, motor control, and discover a new ability to extend powerfully on steep climbing terrain.

REVERSE PLANK

As the name implies, this is pretty much the reverse of the standard plank described earlier—it strengthens anti-flexion muscles rather than anti-extension as in the downward-facing plank. You can do this exercise with either your elbows or hands as support—either way, you'll work many of the muscles of the shoulders, upper and low back, hips, and hamstrings. Begin in a sitting position with legs extended, then lean back and support your upper body with your elbows and forearms on the floor. Now lift your hips off the floor by driving your elbows and heels into the floor. Attain a position with your shoulders, hips, and knees all in line. Think about squeezing your glutes and lower back muscles to prevent your hips from sagging downward. Hold the reverse plank for twenty to sixty seconds (hard). Do one or two more sets with three minutes rest in between.

Reverse plank.

SUPERMAN

The Superman is an isolation exercise that targets the commonly weak muscles of the lower back. Lie face down on the floor with your arms extended overhead, your legs straight with pointed toes, and your head in a neutral position. Begin by simultaneously raising one arm and the opposite leg as high as is comfortably possible. Hold the top position for a moment, and then return to the starting position. Repeat by raising the opposite arm and leg off the floor simultaneously. Again, pause for a moment in the top position before returning to the floor. Continue this alternating exercise motion for a total of twenty repetitions or until you can no longer perform a slow, controlled movement. Rest for three minutes before performing a second set.

1. Raise one arm and leg. 2. Then the other.

BACK BRIDGE

There are a number of different ways to back bridge, but this simple version was a favorite of legendary martial artist Bruce Lee for developing a strong lower back and explosive hip extension. Here's how to do it: Lie on your back with arms out to the side, legs bent about 90 degrees, and feet flat on the floor. Press down simultaneously with your feet and shoulders in order to raise your hips and lower back off the floor as far as possible. Strive to explode upward to the top position, hold there for a second and then return slowly to the starting position. Continue this motion for fifteen to twenty reps. Rest for three minutes before performing a second set.

1. Starting position. 2. Top position.

SIDE HIP RAISE

This surprisingly difficult exercise works the oblique muscles along the side of your torso, as well as the quadratus lumborum, gluteus medius,

1. Start/end position. 2. Lowered position.

abductors, and adductors. Lie on your side on the floor and press up with the floor-side arm straight and supporting your weight so that your body forms a triangle with the floor. Rest the free arm along the other (top) side of your body. Keeping the supporting arm straight, lower your hip until it touches the floor and then immediately raise it back up to the starting position. Repeat this lowering and raising of the hip in a slow, controlled manner for ten to twenty (hard) repetitions. Rest for one minute and then switch sides to perform another set.

Total Core and Posterior Chain Leg Training

Why would any climber want to do leg training? The legs are never the primary cause of failure in rock climbing, and added leg muscle mass would surely be a bad thing. Move on—there's nothing important in this section, right?

Read on and apply, that's my message to you! Unless you campus up every route, you do indeed employ forceful leg movements in climbing. Furthermore, the muscles of the posterior chain—spinal erectors, quadratus lumborum, glutes, and hamstrings, among others—are extremely important in providing the core stiffness necessary for steep, powerful moves. Finally, it's rapid rate of force development throughout the posterior chain that adds explosive power to big deadpoint and lunge moves.

Detailed below are four exercises that will fortify your core from shoulders to hips, strengthen the posterior chain, and, in fact, also train your rotator cuff and scapular stabilizers to turn on quickly. Doing these exercises, therefore, is a win, win, win proposition. Furthermore, if you follow the exercise guidelines exactly, I can almost guarantee you won't gain any unwanted muscle mass—neurological strength gains are a wonderful thing for a strength-to-mass ratio athlete!

DUMBBELL SNATCH

An important physical capability in sports is being able to quickly turn on (and off) the core muscles. In climbing, sticking a difficult deadpoint or lunge move demands lightning-fast recruitment of your core, from shoulders to hips, at the instant you hit the destination handhold. So in this example your core muscles would be moderately turned on at the launch, relax for a moment while in flight, recruit rapidly and with high force at the catch, and then return to a semi-relaxed state as you gathered yourself after the hard move. While all this happens in just a second or so, it's a critical neuromuscular trait to train both on the bouldering wall and with exercise.

Enter the one-arm dumbbell snatch. While far from a climbing-specific exercise, the dumbbell snatch is beneficial in two ways: (1) It trains explosive triple extension of ankles, knees, and hips (as in a climbing jump move), and (2) It demands a rapid, near-maximal firing of the entire core as you initiate the lift and again when you stick the finish position with the dumbbell straight-arm-locked overhead. Here's how to do it.

Stand with feet just over shoulder width apart and toes pointed about 20 degrees outward. With the dumbbell positioned between your feet, bend equally at your knees and hips to grab onto the dumbbell. At the starting position your lower back should be flat and the working arm hanging straight down from the shoulder; extend the free arm out and backward for balance as needed. The snatch is then executed in one coordinated, continuous, and explosive motion. It begins with knee extension, then hip, knee, and ankle extension simultaneously (the triple extension); the arm remains straight initially and you want to keep the elbow over the dumbbell as long as possible as you jump off the floor. As your shoulders shrug at the end of the jump, allow the dumbbell to launch upward and then drop your body underneath the dumbbell to attain a partial squat position with the dumbbell locked out overhead. Stand up into the finish position with the dumbbell overhead, shoulders, hips, and feet all in line. Contract your core completely to stick the finish position and hold for one second. Lower the dumbbell and push your hips backward to return to the starting position. This is a technical lift, so begin with a moderate weight (fifteen or twenty-five pounds) and build from there. I suggest pausing for a few seconds between each snatch—let go of the dumbbell, stand tall, and relax for a couple seconds before repeating the lift. Do five to ten repetitions.

1. Starting position. 2. Ending position.

SUMO DEADLIFT WITH DUMBBELL OR KETTLEBELL

The dumbbell sumo deadlift is an excellent gateway exercise for the more difficult barbell deadlift described next. Both forms of deadlift are excellent for training the posterior chain, core stiffness, the trapezius, and the rotator cuff. I believe that every serious climber should do either this exercise or the barbell deadlift twice per week. The training time investment is small, but the benefits are multiple.

1. Starting position. 2. Ending position.

The starting position is somewhat similar to the dumbbell snatch described above, except that you are using two hands to grasp the ends of the dumbbell (or matching hands if using a kettlebell) and your feet are one and one-half shoulder widths apart with toes angled out about 20 degrees. With flexed knees and hips, a straight back, and arms hanging straight down from the shoulders, tighten your abs and begin the lift by extending the knees. The hips should quickly begin to extend too; however, the knees should extend fully before the hips reach full extension. During the final third of the lift, think about driving your hips forward and then pulling your shoulders back (and scapula together). Finish standing tall, like a soldier at attention, at the top position, but do not hyperextend your back and do not shrug your shoulders. Lower the dumbbell by pushing your rear end back and bending at the hips (maintain a straight back) and then at the knees. Face more or less forward throughout the lift, but with a slight downward gaze near the bottom position.

Train this lift twice per week, favoring a lighter weight and good technique over going super heavy. Many people begin with a fifteen- to thirty-pound dumbbell or kettlebell and build to twice this weight over a year or so. Do two sets of fifteen repetitions. Advanced lifters can do one set of dumbbell sumo deadlifts as a warm-up before doing the barbell deadlift described below.

BARBELL DEADLIFT

It took me until almost age fifty to discover the benefits—and joy!—of deadlifting. As an aging climber with a "bad" lower back, I began a slowly progressive program of deadlifting, stretching, and foam rolling in hopes of erasing decades of abuse. In under two years of training, I went from a fifty-year-old climber with chronic back pain (and in need of back surgery, according to one neurosurgeon) to a rejuvenated, nearly pain-free fifty-two-year-old climber sending 5.13 routes that I might have struggled on at age thirty! During this two-year ramp-up at deadlift training, I progressed from barely being able to lift 135 pounds to, two years later, deadlifting 300 pounds. But what really matters isn't the weight I can lift, it's that my core muscles are now way stronger than ever before, my posterior chain muscles have awoken from a decade-plus of amnesia, and I'm nearly pain-free and climbing much harder than a couple of years ago—talk about a win, win, win! (And, in case you are wondering, I didn't put on a single pound of body weight.)

The bottom line: Regardless of your age and ability, I strongly recommend some deadlifting if you have access to the weight equipment. No, you shouldn't be deadlifting like powerlifters (i.e., many heavy sets) or like CrossFitters, who commonly do many high-rep sets with a more moderate load. The protocol I recommend, after a light warm-up set of six reps, is three sets of deadlifts with reps of five, four, and three per set, respectively. Take a three- to five-minute rest between sets, and add ten to twenty pounds with each successive set. The weight used should be heavy enough to make each set difficult, but not so heavy that your technique is compromised. Do this twice per week and you'll be amazed at how strong you get while gaining little or no muscle mass. Furthermore, I believe you'll be pleasantly surprised to discover that deadlifting makes you feel very good, and you'll likely climb better!

The starting position is somewhat similar to the dumbbell sumo deadlift except that your feet should be parallel and a bit less than shoulder width apart. Set up with the bar over the middle of your feet and about one and a half inches from your shin, and then push your rear end back and flex at the hips and knees in order to grab onto the bar with an overhand grip. At the starting position check that your arms are just outside of your legs, your scapula are above the bar, and your knees are over the bar. Now think about squeezing your chest up by engaging the muscles in the mid-back and then

Table 6.1 Deadlifting Protocol for Rock Climbers

Set	Weight (% of 1RM)	Reps/Set	Rest
Warm-up	50–60%	6	3–5 minutes
1	70%	5	3–5 minutes
2	80%	4	3–5 minutes
3	85–90%	2–3	3–5 minutes

This deadlift protocol will maximize neurological strength gains without triggering significant hypertrophy. 1RM (one rep max) is your estimate of the heaviest weight you could deadlift for one repetition.

letting the contraction continue down into the lower back until it is tightened into contraction too. Fix your eyes on the floor at a point twelve to fifteen feet in front of you to maintain a neutral neck position. Before you begin the pull, get the weight back off your toes and onto your mid-foot. Take a deep breath, tighten your abs, and drive your feet

1. Starting position.

2. Ending position.

your feet into the floor—think about dragging the bar up your shins. Focus on driving your hips forward and then pulling your shoulders back (and scapula together) as you approach the top position—your lower back must be kept in extension throughout the lift (not over-extended or rounded). Finish standing tall, like a soldier at attention, but do not hyperextend your back and do not shrug your shoulders. Lower the barbell by pushing your rear end back and bending at the hips (maintain a straight back) and then at the knees. Face more or less forward throughout the lift, but with a slight downward gaze near the bottom position. Pause at the bottom for one second before beginning the next repetition—it's not a deadlift if you bounce the bar off the platform!

Warning: This is a technical lift, and I recommend consulting a coach on your initial forays into the wonderful world of deadlifting. Furthermore, do not deadlift if you have an active back problem; do not deadlift more than twice per week; and do not increase your weights so fast that your form is compromised. But do stretch and foam roll your hamstrings, glutes, and lower back muscles at the end of your workout and before bed on the eve after your deadlifting. I recommend wearing a weight belt when lifting near your 1RM.

BARBELL SQUAT

The squat is another excellent full-body exercise that, like the deadlift, lights up the core muscles in addition to working leg and hip extension. Doing two brief sets (five to eight reps) with moderately heavy weight is a great workout, and it's unlikely to lead to any gain in muscle mass. Learning to squat with proper technique is important—if possible, enlist a coach to help you get started. The lift requires a free weight set and squat rack, so it may not be an option unless you belong to a gym with the necessary equipment; as an alternative, buy a few dumbbells and train with the sumo deadlift described earlier.

1. Starting position. 2. Ending position.

To begin the lift, stand under the racked bar and position it across your mid to upper trapezius, taking a grip wider than shoulder width. Take a deep breath and unrack the bar—carefully back up a step or so to clear the hooks (that were holding the bar). Set your feet about shoulder width and with an outward flare of around 20 degrees. Take another deep breath and contract your inner core, then begin the descent—think about sitting in a chair behind you rather than going straight down. Knees should track over your toes and not collapse inward. Your chest will naturally tilt down as you descend, but strive to keep your weight back on your feet as if sitting down. For a full squat, descend until your thighs are parallel to the floor; beginners may want to stop short of this (three-quarter squat). At the bottom, immediately reverse direction by driving your feet into the floor and extending simultaneously at the knees and hips—think of pushing your head toward the ceiling to quickly regain the top position. Breathe out as you near the top of the lift. Pause for a moment in the top position before taking another deep breath and beginning the next repetition. Be sure to maintain a flat lower back throughout the lift. A final pro tip: Try to bend the bar over your shoulders throughout the lift. While you won't likely bend the bar, this action will maximally recruit your outer core including the latissimus dorsi, pecs, rotator cuff, and trapezius.

Begin squatting with a modest weight, say, around 40 percent of your body weight. Do two sets of five to eight reps (never more), twice per week. Over the course of a year or two, you can work toward squatting your body weight—in my opinion, there's no reason for a climber to train with weights any heavier.

Optimizing Body Composition

Strength-to-weight ratio is the physical metric that most accurately correlates to climbing performance. How small a hold you can pull on, how far you can lunge, and how long you can pull down before pumping out are all physical capabilities that are influenced by your strength-to-weight ratio. Recognizing this strong correlation, it's not surprising that avid climbers have an insatiable appetite for more strength and power. Interestingly, a climber with less-than-ideal body composition can increase his strength-to-weight ratio most quickly by decreasing weight, not by increasing strength. This is a powerful concept, and for some climbers it points the way to a source of some very fast gains in climbing performance.

A prevailing theme throughout this book is the importance of training smarter, which does not necessarily mean training harder. With regard to the subject of physical training, the smart approach is to pursue near-optimal body composition before delving deeply into a serious strength- and power-training program. Every serious climber should ponder whether or not body composition represents a significant limiting constraint.

Measuring Your Percentage of Body Fat

Most health clubs and some universities have the equipment necessary to measure percentage of body fat, so getting your body fat measured may be just a phone call and a few miles away. A study of athletes in a variety of sports reported that males possess body fat ranging from 4 percent in wrestlers to 8 to 12 percent in runners and 16 percent in football players, with an elite average of below 12 percent (Wilmore 1983). The same study revealed that female athletes possess between 8 and 25 percent body fat, with an elite average of 15 percent. Therefore, a percentage of body fat near these elite average levels (12 percent men, 15 percent women) is a good initial target for most climbers. Given that climbing performance is directly correlated to strength-to-weight ratio, however, your ultimate goal should be a few percentage points lower—perhaps 6 to 8 percent for men and 10 to 12 percent for women. One study (Watts 1993) revealed that some elite male and female climbers possess body fat as low as 4 percent and 9 percent, respectively.

However, extremely low body fat is neither desirable nor advised, since it will adversely affect your energy levels and recovery ability, as well as cause numerous health problems (especially among women).

If you are unable to get a professional body fat measurement, you can always employ the highly economical at-home method—that is, pinch a fold of skin just above your hip! If you can pinch an inch or more (thickness of the fold), you definitely need to drop some body fat. A fold between one-half and one inch thick indicates you may be slightly overweight for a climber. If you pinch less than one-half inch of fat, then your body fat is likely at or below the target averages stated above.

In addition to optimizing your percentage of body fat, you should consider the size and location of the muscles you carry. For instance, it is indisputable that possessing hulking leg muscles is as bad or worse for a climber as carrying a spare tire around the waist (especially since muscle weighs more than fat per unit volume). Since the legs muscles are never the weakest link while climbing, you must be careful how you train the legs and be sure to avoid training in the hypertrophy zone. The same goes for any weight-lifting exercise or practice that produces a bulking-up effect in any other part of the body. Traditional bodybuilding exercises such as biceps curls, heavy-duty leg training, or excessive push-muscle training are of no benefit and likely counterproductive.

Strategies for Optimizing Body Composition

Certainly there are genetic limitations to how much you can change your body composition through diet and exercise. Some people are naturally going to carry a little more body fat; others inherently have a larger frame and bulkier muscles. Still, many novice climbers can improve their body composition significantly in a way that will benefit their climbing. The two key strategies are improved dietary surveillance and increased aerobic training.

Performance nutrition will be discussed in depth in chapter 11, but for now let me state the obvious—reducing body fat is possible only if you create a net calorie deficit over the course of many days and weeks. Crash dieting is unhealthy and dangerous, especially for a serious athlete. Instead strive for, at most, a 500-calorie deficit per day. Over the course of a week, this will add up to a 3,500-calorie deficit and equal the loss of one pound of body fat.

Your daily calorie deficit is best created by a combination of reduced calorie intake and increased energy expenditure. For fat burning, nothing beats aerobic activities such as running, biking, and rowing. Given a healthy back and knees, select running as your activity of choice since for most people it will not result in muscle hypertrophy (growth in size) in the legs. A Concept II rowing machine is another excellent aerobic activity that activates a large amount of muscle mass. Moderate-intensity swimming and biking (on relatively flat terrain) are the next best alternatives. No matter your fat-burning activity, the goal is to perform a minimum of thirty minutes of sustained moderate-intensity aerobic activity at least four days per week.

If your schedule is too busy to accommodate this two-plus hours of aerobics per week, recent research indicates you can get a similar fat-burning effect from shorter, high-intensity interval training (King 2001). For instance, after a three-minute warm-up jog, alternate twenty seconds of high-intensity running (about 90 percent intensity) with forty seconds of jogging for an additional twelve minutes. While this vigorous fifteen minutes of interval training will certainly burn less fat than the thirty minutes of slower steady state running, the metabolism-elevating effects of the sprint intervals will burn more calories in the hours that follow. A final fat-burning tip: A few studies seem to indicate a better fat-burning effect when aerobic activity is performed in a fasting state, as in running first thing in the morning (before breakfast).

Upon reaching your desired percentage of body fat, cut back somewhat on the aerobic training and

Tips for Optimizing Body Composition

1. Use a combination of dietary surveillance and exercise to lower your percentage of body fat.
2. Strive for four thirty-minute (or more) aerobic workouts per week.
3. Adjust calorie intake to produce approximately a 500-calorie-per-day deficit. See chapter 11 for more nutritional tips.
4. Reduce aerobic training activity (and reinvest the training time in climbing-specific exercises) as you approach your optimal percentage of body fat.
5. Do not obsess over body composition—do the best you can given your genetics, and remember that climbing is two-thirds mental and technical. You can climb at a high level despite less-than-ideal body composition.

refocus your training time and effort on climbing-specific activity. Slowly reintroduce more calories incrementally and watch your waistline and body weight. The goal is to find a level of calorie consumption equal to your daily energy use and thus maintain a steady body weight.

In summary, I want to emphasis that while optimizing body composition is an important aspect of training for climbing, it is not everything. Obsessing over body weight and depriving yourself of nutrients—and occasional pleasure foods—is no way to live, and it's certainly not optimal for your climbing performance.

Generalized Aerobic Training

Many climbers shun aerobic training based on the belief that high-end rock climbing is primarily an anaerobic sport. This is understandable given the common experience of pumped-out forearms when failing on a difficult route. The climbing performance puzzle is extremely complex, however, and it would be a mistake to jump to the simple conclusion.

As detailed in chapter 5, any sustained climbing lasting in excess of two minutes is fueled principally by the aerobic energy pathway rather than the anaerobic. Furthermore, it's the aerobic system that drives the recovery process, no matter if it's at a brief mid-climb rest, between boulders and redpoint attempts, or between workouts. Consequently, aerobic training cannot simply be written off as unnecessary or irrelevant. Engaging in a moderate amount of generalized and climbing-specific aerobic training will benefit your climbing performance and accelerate recovery. The focus of this section is generalized aerobic conditioning (local aerobic training of the forearm and pulling muscles will be covered in chapters 8 and 9).

Aerobic Training for Boulderers and Sport Climbers

Excellence at bouldering and cragging requires abundant strength and power, precise technique and efficient movement, and a killer instinct, but much less in the way of stamina. As explained in chapter 5, however, research has shown that climbers who engaged in some generalized aerobic training recovered faster than those who did not. Therefore, doing a modest amount of aerobic training is a smart thing if recovery is important to you.

There's no need for high-volume aerobic training as performed by road racers, bike racers, or triathletes—this would be a foolish investment of training time and would negatively impact your climbing strength and power, due to the catabolic effects of high-volume aerobic training. Furthermore, actual climbing time and climbing-specific training must always take precedence over aerobic training. Therefore, climbing three days per week—and performing some climbing-specific and antagonist strength training—must always take priority over any aerobic training. But if you are getting all your climbing sessions in and still have time available for additional training, then performing two or three aerobic workouts per week will be beneficial. Let's examine two approaches.

STEADY STATE AEROBIC TRAINING

Tempo runs and Concept 2 rowing are the two best steady state activities for climbers. The goal is to run (or row) at a moderately high intensity that not only stresses the ST muscle fibers, but also begins to recruit some of the FTa (oxidative) fibers. Some people call this a "threshold" workout, since you are exercising near the anaerobic threshold at which lactate and H+ ions begin to accumulate. Running at this pace for twenty to thirty minutes not only provides stimulus for favorable cardiovascular adaptations, but it also trains the large exercising muscles (in the legs, hips, back) to better metabolize lactate for energy. The upside, when on a strenuous climb, will be improved processing of lactate and H+ released into the bloodstream from the pulling muscles of the upper body. This is one of the reasons climbers who do generalized aerobic training recover faster—and perhaps can persevere longer—on long, pumpy anaerobic climbs.

Sussing out the right intensity of running (or rowing) is the key—you don't want to exercise at too low an intensity (as in a "long slow distance" running pace) or at a high intensity that produces deep fatigue and creates a large acid load on the body. Aim for a rating of perceived exertion of 8 out of 10, or a heart rate around 85 percent of maximum (220 - age x 0.85). Two twenty- to thirty-minute runs per week are enough to get favorable adaptations. If you desire a third aerobic session each week, I suggest doing an easy "recovery" run with your heart rate nearer 75 percent of maximum.

RUNNING INTERVALS

The most common interval-training program is to run alternating fast and slow laps on a track. Although you can also run intervals on a road or trail, the ease of setting a goal and gauging distances makes running on a track preferable. For initial training sessions, set out to run two miles (aggregate distance of fast and slow laps). As a rough gauge, your rating of perceived exertion on the fast laps should be about 9 out of 10—hard enough to get significantly winded. Try to hold the fast pace for a complete lap, and then pull back to an easy jog or fast walking for the "slow" lap. Continue alternating fast and slow laps for a total of eight. If road or trail running, alternate between one minute of hard running and two minutes of easy running for about twenty minutes.

This workout will tap significantly into the anaerobic pathway during the fast segments, but the slow segments offer the opportunity to metabolize lactate and buffer H+. As described above, aerobic activity that trains the large muscles of the body to increase consumption of blood lactate for energy will hasten the return of homeostasis (in the pumped arm muscles) at rests during (or between) strenuous boulders or roped climbs. The benefits of doing a moderate amount of aerobic training haven't been overlooked by some of the best climbers. Sasha DiGuilian, one of the best endurance sport climbers, and Alex Megos, one of the world's best on-sight climbers, both run regularly as part of their training. Perhaps you should too!

Aerobic Training for Multipitch and Big-Wall Climbers

If your climbing preference is all-day multipitch climbs or big walls, then aerobic training is essential for performing your best in these endeavors. The physical trait you are training for is stamina—the ability to resist fatigue while engaging in sustained or intermittent physical activity for an extended period of time (all day or longer). A regular commitment to long-duration aerobic training will yield local and central adaptations that increase your glycogen stores, improve use of fatty acids for fuel, and strengthen your cardiovascular system. Equally important, however, is the gradual recalibration of the central governor that results from longer-duration exercise. This sort of "brain training," a result of pushing to new limits year after year, is the magic behind the training of world-class endurance climbers such as Alex Honnold, Hans Florine, and, of course, Kevin Jorgenson and Tommy Caldwell.

As in other types of conditioning, there are sport-specific and general ways of stamina training. The most specific—and therefore most effective—approach is to train as you will perform. To develop greater stamina for long days at the crags, then, you would train by frequently climbing all-day with the goal of squeezing in as many pitches as possible. Obviously, this approach is not an option for many recreational climbers who only climb outside once per month due to career, school, and family commitments. A more practical training alternative is regular high-volume aerobic activity, such as running and biking, coupled as often as possible with high volumes of climbing at the gym or crag. Let's take a brief look at these two best ways for training stamina.

ALL-DAY CLIMBING

This is the classic train-as-you-will-perform strategy. If you have the resources nearby, then no training is more specific than chalking up many long days on the rock. You could do this by climbing as many routes as possible from sunrise to sunset at a cragging area or by racing up a Grade IV or V big-wall route in a day. Do this two days per week (or three or four, if you're already a badass wall rat!) for a few weeks to two months, and you'll develop amazing climbing stamina! For many climbers, however, it may only be possible to train this way once or twice per month. As a training surrogate, then, put in a few thirty- to fifty-route half-day sessions at the local climbing gym. The routes will need to be fairly moderate (two to four number grades below your limit), and you should employ liberal use of toproping to speed up the process of sending one climb and moving on quickly to the next. To meet the two-day-per-week, long-duration training goal, you may also need to engage in some generalized aerobic training as well.

HIGH-VOLUME GENERALIZED AEROBIC TRAINING

The goal here is to engage in two to four, forty-five-minute to two-hour aerobic workouts per week that focus on mileage over speed. This could be any combination of running, swimming, cycling, and trail running. As your conditioning improves, consider doubling up sessions one or two days per week. For example, you might go for a long run in the morning and then an hour-long bike ride or trail run in the evening. If you engage in such two-a-day workouts, it is best to take at least a six-hour break between the two. This is clearly an advanced aerobic training program, but it might be just the ticket in the months and weeks leading up to a big-wall or alpine climbing adventure.

Aerobic Training Tips

1. All climbers can benefit from a modest amount of aerobic training. Boulderers and crag climbers will realize accelerated recovery between attempts and ascents, while multipitch and big-wall climbers will gain valuable general endurance for ultralong days and ascents at elevation.
2. Boulderers and sport climbers will benefit the most from twice-per-week interval training or tempo runs near the anaerobic threshold, although aerobic training should never be done at the expense of climbing time.
3. The most effective stamina training for multipitch and big-wall climbers is putting in frequent dawn-to-dusk days on the rock. Alternatively, regular long-distance aerobic activities (running, cycling, hiking, and such) lasting forty-five minutes to two hours will yield substantial gains in aerobic capacity.
4. Two-a-day stamina workouts are effective preparation for single- and multiday wall ascents.

Alex Megos cruising up Action Directe (5.14d), Frankenjura, Germany. CLAUDIA ZEIGLER

CHAPTER EIGHT

Finger Training for Strength and Endurance

There's no such thing as too much strength.
—*Wolfgang Güllich*

This chapter on training grip strength and forearm muscle endurance will likely be the most referred to in the book and understandably so, because the fingers are usually the epicenter of fatigue and failure in rock climbing. Of course, the self-aware climber will always analyze whether failure on a given route was actually the result of an underlying problem in sequencing, technique and tactics, or mental control. This distinction aside, gaining more finger strength and endurance is obviously central to taking your climbing to the next level. Read and appropriately utilize the exercises in this chapter, and you will undoubtedly improve in this area—perhaps massively—and crush at a higher level in the months and years to come!

While beginning climbers will get stronger simply by climbing a few days per week, more experienced climbers need to engage in some targeted training of the finger-controlling muscles of the forearms. As detailed in chapter 5, effective training must zero in on a specific functional aspect and exercise the fingers flexors in a precise way to target the related fiber type and energy system. Accordingly, this chapter is broken into four sections that detail exercises for training maximum grip strength, contact strength (power), strength-endurance, and local aerobic endurance.

The exercises in each section are organized roughly by relative difficulty, beginning with the easier exercises and ending with the more advanced. Exercise difficulty and the appropriateness of an exercise for a given ability level is a most vital distinction. A novice climber could be injured in attempting an advanced exercise such as feet-off campusing, whereas an advanced climber would gain little outside a warm-up by performing an entry-level exercise. Consult table 8.1 for a classification of the exercises that will help guide you in proper selection.

As you engage in finger training over the months and years to come, it's important to recognize that strength and endurance gains will not come in a steady, linear fashion. While initial gains will be realized quickly, long-term improvement will be harder to recognize as apparent performance plateaus develop. Breaking through these frustrating plateaus demands training both smarter and harder. You just can't do more of everything (a trap that many passionate climbers fall into) hoping to make a breakthrough; instead you must identify your limiting constraint and make it the focus of your training. For most climbers, long-term gains demand a more polarized approach that focuses equally on increasing absolute strength (anaerobic alactic) and developing greater aerobic power and endurance. Ironically, many climbers do just the opposite in worshipping the false idol of "the pump" (anaerobic lactic training) as the ultimate validation of an effective workout. Certainly you must do some training of anaerobic capacity, but as presented in chapter 5, this is the least trainable

Table 8.1 Classification of Finger/Forearm Training Exercises

	Exercise	Beginner	Intermediate	Advanced
Maximum Strength (anaerobic alactic)	Bouldering	X	X	X
	Hypergravity Bouldering		X	X
	Fingerboard "Minimum Edge" Hangs		X	X
	Fingerboard "Maximum Weight" Hangs			X
	HIT System with Max Weight			X
Contact Strength & Power (anaerobic alactic)	One-Arm Lunging (feet on)		X	X
	Campus Laddering (small holds)		X	X
	Campus Board "Bumps" (small holds)		X	X
	Campus Board "Switch Hands"			X
	Campus Board Double Dynos			X
Strength-Endurance (glycolytic/ anaerobic lactic)	Fingerboard Repeaters (short duration)	X	X	X
	Fingerboard Repeaters (long duration)		X	X
	Bouldering 4x4s	X	X	X
	HIT System—Strength-Endurance Protocol		X	X
	System Wall "Repeaters"		X	X
Local Aerobic Endurance (aerobic/oxidative)	ARC Traverses ("Recovery Climbing")	X	X	X
	Fingerboard Moving Hangs		X	X
	Campus Board "Hand Play" (feet-on)		X	X
	Threshold Treadwall Intervals		X	X
	Route Climbing Intervals	X	X	X

energy system and the most likely to lead to overtraining (and negative results).

A final comment from Coach Hörst before we dig into the exciting exercise details: The number one rule of finger training is *Don't get injured!* While this rule is presumably self-evident, a surprising number of enthusiastic climbers get injured (fingers, elbows, shoulders) by training too much or in attempting advanced exercises for which they are not ready. Here are some important finger-training guidelines that will reduce your risk of injury:

- Train wrist and shoulder stability (see chapter 6) before and concurrent with targeted finger exercise training.
- Always perform a progressive warm-up that gradually builds from easy full-body activity to difficult, climbing-specific exercises.
- Make a conscious effort to avoid the most painful and stressful holds (such as a sharp, small-radius edge or a pocket that feels tweaky). No move or boulder problem is worth getting injured over!
- Limit training redundancy by using a few different exercises each session. Don't just train for an hour on a single apparatus (such as the fingerboard or campus board).
- Don't try to train everything—maximum strength, contact strength, strength-endurance, and local aerobic endurance—in a single session. Always train with a specific focus.
- Immediately end an exercise at the first sign of any tendon or joint pain. Stop training for a few minutes (or days) to assess the cause of the pang and severity of the potential injury.
- Rest more than you think you need to—your muscles, tendons, and precious digits will thank you! Three to five days of aggregate training and climbing per week is enough, and any more tempts injury.

Training Maximum Strength

"There's no such thing as too much strength" is a now iconic quote of the late, great Wolfgang Güllich, and it's a good prime directive for your training. But what's the best way to train for greater finger strength?

According to the principle of specificity, effective finger training must necessarily target the neuromuscular system in ways that are specific to climbing. Therefore, fingerboard hangs, campusing, and bouldering are all valid ways to train finger strength for climbing, whereas a hand-held squeeze device is a waste of time as anything other than a warm-up exercise. The degree to which a given exercise will produce gains in functional grip strength for climbing can be estimated by considering the following requirements—the more of these requirements that are met, the more effective the exercise will be at producing usable gains in climbing grip strength.

1. The exercise must be near maximum intensity throughout the entire set. In climbing-specific finger training you can increase intensity by decreasing hold size or adding weight. Of course, there's a definite limit to how small a hold you can train on comfortably—holds smaller than about 10mm (⅜ inch) deep are often painful to train on. A popular alternative, then, is to use a somewhat larger hold (14 to 20mm or ⅝ to ¾ inch is ideal) and add weight to your body to increase intensity.

2. The exercise must produce muscular failure in less than twelve seconds. As detailed in chapter 5, maximal exercise is powered by the anaerobic alactic energy system, so this energy system must be the training focus. Exercising any longer than about twelve seconds per set trains strength-endurance (the anaerobic lactic energy system), not maximum strength—this is a critical distinction!

3. The exercise must be specific to climbing grip positions and movements. Obviously

Self-Testing of Finger Strength and Endurance

As a climbing coach with deep background in science, I'm enamored with fitness testing—that is, using a specific exercise with a fixed protocol to measure a physical capability and track changes over the long term. Following are three simple, yet effective methods of testing limit strength and strength-endurance of your forearm flexors (primary limiting constraints for many climbers). Perform these tests every few months (or training cycle) to track you gains and modify your program appropriately, year over year. See chapter 9 for six tests to track your pull-muscle limit strength, power, and endurance.

Finger strength test: Determine the maximum amount of weight you can add to your body (via weights hanging from the belay loop of a harness) and hang for five seconds from a fingerboard 10mm (one-half finger pad size) edge using a half-crimp grip (no thumb lock). Finding the maximum weight will take a few attempts. Be sure to perform an extensive warm up beforehand, and rest a minimum of three minutes between hangs. In case you're wondering, elite climbers can typically hang five seconds with an added weight of at least one third of their body weight—this is a good long-term (multi-year) goal to train toward. (**Note:** Small differences in hold size will lead to large differences in weight you can hold, so it's important to test on the same 10mm hold each time.)

Finger endurance test #1: Determine how long you can endure through series of repeated five-second hangs, with exactly five seconds of rest between each hang, on a 10mm fingerboard edge. After a thorough warm up, have a training partner direct you through a series of precisely timed five-second intervals—rests between hangs must never exceed five seconds. The test ends when you can no longer hang for five seconds. Use only half-crimp, open-crimp and/or open-hand grips, and strive to maintain good fingerboard technique throughout. This test closely simulates how the forearm flexors work (intermittent blood-flow occlusion and recovery) when climbing a difficult route.

Finger endurance test #2: Determine the longest you can hang from a fingerboard 20mm (or similar) edge using the half-crimp or open-hand grip. Your results will likely be somewhere between twenty seconds and two minutes and, therefore, this testing protocol provides a good measure of your anaerobic lactic energy system. Warm up extensively—be sure to

exercises such as fingerboard and campus training will carry over to climbing better than nonspecific exercises such as finger rolls, squeeze devices, and the like.

4. The exercise must focus on a specific grip position for an entire set. In climbing, the rock dictates a random use of varying grip positions. Since strength is grip-specific, such cycling of grip positions allows you to climb longer than if you used the same grip repeatedly. That's great if you are climbing for performance, but it's ineffective for building maximum grip strength. (This helps explain why a full season of climbing builds local forearm endurance but often leaves you with about the same maximum grip strength as before.) Effective grip-strength training must target a specific grip position to near failure—I recommend training the half crimp (or open crimp), open hand, wide pinch, and the three two-finger pocket grips.

Keep these four requirements in mind as you execute the maximum-strength finger exercises detailed below, especially the second requirement: Be sure to scale the exercise resistance to be near maximal (near failure in under twelve seconds).

get through the flash pump phase—before taking this test. Ask a partner to give you verbal encouragement, and do feel free to pull up with your arms, if needed, to obtain a true maximum-length hang. Do two tests with at least a fifteen-minute rest in between.

The Zlagboard finger training system (see photo) is an excellent testing—and training—platform for coaches and serious climbers. This patented system incorporates a niffy switching mechanism that marries your smartphone to the Zlagboard, thus providing precise hands-free operation that directs and records hang-time measurements, archives past hang tests, provides professional training programs, and allows you to compete with climbers locally and globally.

Based on recent Zlagboard Contest results, the median hang-time is about forty-five seconds—a respectable time that is commonly achieved by accomplished climbers who climb at a moderately high level. Using the Zlagboard 20mm "contest holds," hang times between sixty to ninety seconds are common among advanced climbers, typically capable of climbing 5.13. Hangs of more than ninety seconds indicate elite-level strength-endurance (often 5.14 climbers). And if you can hang more than two minutes . . . then you're likely a famous climber already! The current world-record hang (as of March 2016) is an incredible 2:44 by Spanish rock star (and two-time world champion) Ramon Julian Puigblanque. Learn more at: www.ZlagboardUSA.com.

BOULDERING

Bouldering is the most straightforward way to train grip strength. Without the constraints of a rope and gear, bouldering allows you to focus on climbing the hardest moves possible. Inherent to hard bouldering, however, are some limiting factors that diminish the potential to build maximum grip strength. Consider that technical difficulties may prevent you from climbing to near the point of muscular failure. Furthermore, the rock or plastic dictates the use of many different grip positions, thus making it difficult to isolate a single grip position and work it to failure.

Despite these limitations, bouldering should be a staple of your training program. It will build some functional strength and, at the same time, develop your mental and technical skills. Consequently it's a good training strategy to couple bouldering with one of the other finger-strength-training exercises described in this section. Use the following training strategy to best stimulate gains in finger strength via bouldering.

Select a short boulder problem that appears to be strenuous, but not technically difficult. Favor overhanging problems, which will place more weight on your hands and maximize the training effect. When bouldering indoors, try to locate (or consider setting) problems that isolate a specific grip position; for example, a problem that possesses a lot of crimp holds will be best for training crimp strength. The ideal boulder will be climbable in under fifteen seconds, since the goal is to target the anaerobic alactic energy system—if you're getting seriously pumped, then the problem is too long (bringing the anaerobic lactic system deeply into action). Attempt to climb the problem three times with sufficient rest (two to three minutes) between each ascent to allow a good effort. Doing a problem three times makes one "set."

Move on to another strenuous-looking problem that appears to target a different grip position, such as wide pinch, two-finger pockets, open hand, and such. Ascend this problem three times (one set), with adequate rest (two to three minutes) between attempts. Continue bouldering in this way for thirty to sixty minutes (three to ten total sets), and then finish your finger training with one of the isolation exercises described later in this section.

HYPERGRAVITY BOULDERING

Advanced climbers with several years of bouldering under their belt eventually reach a point where they no longer achieve significant gains in finger strength despite regular, hard bouldering. Fortunately, hypergravity bouldering, weighted fingerboard hangs, and the HIT System workout (all detailed below) are potent training methods that will yield further gains in high-end finger strength. To do this, you'll need to invest in a five- or ten-pound weight belt (twenty pounds for an advanced climber) or fill a fanny pack with five to ten pounds of scuba divers' weights. Here is the best protocol for engaging in hypergravity bouldering—this is an indoor training strategy only!

Complete a general and specific warm-up—that is, work through various warm-up and mobility exercises, and then move on to some moderate climbing and bouldering lasting at least thirty minutes. Now clip on your weight belt and predetermine a target number of hypergravity bouldering sets (repeating a problem three times makes one "set") that you will perform. As a guideline, limit yourself to two sets on your initial session, then build to five to seven sets as you gain confidence and strength.

Select short, overhanging boulder problems that possess small- to medium-size holds but no tiny and tweaky features, and no dynamic or highly technical moves. Since you are climbing with a weight belt, favor problems that are a couple of grades or more below your limit—you should be able to ascend the

Hypergravity bouldering with weight belt.

Grip Positions

Although rock dictates a wide range of gripping positions, we can best train maximum grip strength by addressing the six primary grip types. Let's take a quick look at each grip position and the training considerations.

Full Crimp

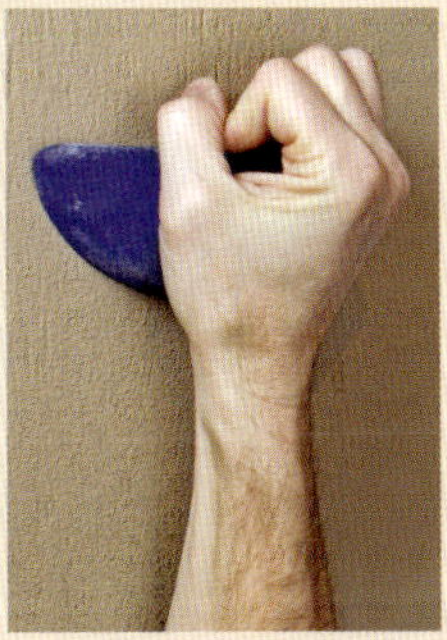

The full crimp is favored by many climbers because it provides what feels like the most secure lock onto small handholds thanks to its hallmark thumb lock over the top of the tip of the index finger. The full-crimp grip excels on small, square-cut edges, shallow flakes, and any hold that possesses a small incut edge. Unfortunately, the full-crimp grip is the most stressful on the tendons and joints due to the hyperextension of the first (distal) joint of each finger and the sharp flexion of the second finger joint. Chronic use of this grip can lead to various tendon injuries in the fingers and elbows, especially among individuals who frequently chicken wing their elbows. It's best not to specifically train in this grip position, but instead focus on the half-crimp grip (sans thumb lock) since it's a bit less stressful on the joints and tendons, and the training gains will largely transfer to the full-crimp position.

Half Crimp

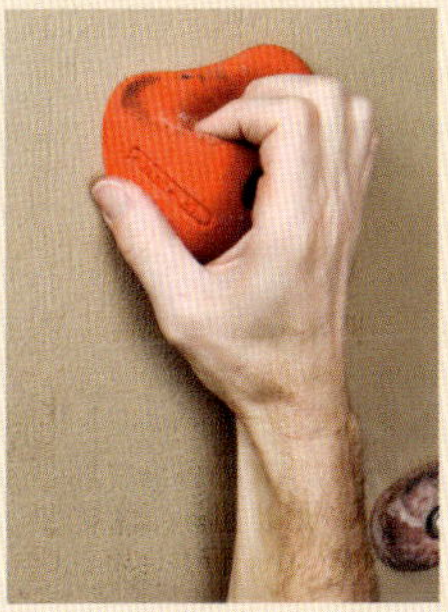

The half-crimp grip is a slight variation of the full crimp in which you do not thumb-lock over the index finger. This reduces tendon stress and softens the aggressive angles on the fingers' first and second joints, but at the expense of a slightly less secure feel. Fortunately, targeted training of the half-crimp grip will yield large increases in strength that will make a huge difference on the rock, especially when crimping on small edges, incut pockets, and narrow pinches.

Open Crimp

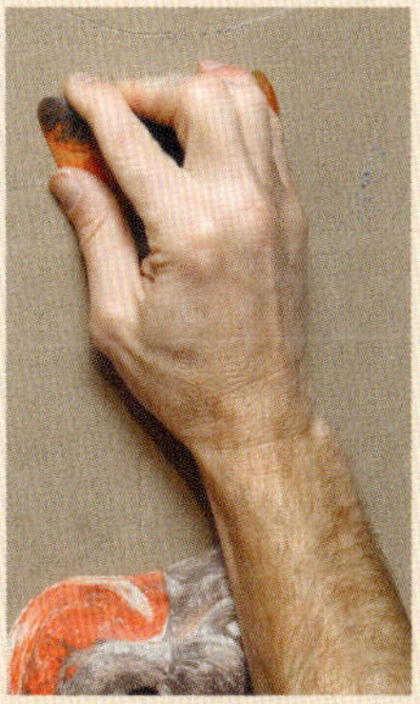

The open crimp is a hybrid grip characterized by the two middle fingers clinging in a half-crimp fashion, while the shorter index and pinky fingers assume the extended open-hand grip. The open crimp is often used in fingerboard training and in climbing crimpy endurance-oriented routes.

Open Hand

The open-hand grip has distinct advantages over the crimp grip. First, the open-hand position is much less stressful on the finger joints and tendons—one study (Vigouroux 2006) revealed that the force on the A2 pulley is thirty-six times lower in the open-hand grip than in the crimp grip. Furthermore, despite its less secure feel, the open-hand position can be trained to become your strongest grip position on all but the smallest crimp and incut holds (which require a crimp grip). This grip is most effective on deep, rounded or sloping holds, and particularly when pulling on pockets. If you're unfamiliar with the open-hand grip, it will feel quite awkward and difficult at first. But rest assured that your open-hand grip strength will improve quickly with targeted training.

Pocket Grip

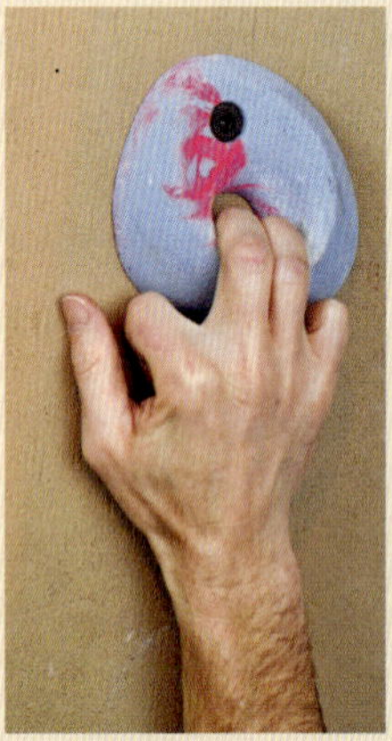

This is not really a unique grip, but it's worth including here since the pocket grip deserves some dedicated training. While shallow or incut pockets will require a half-crimp-like grip, most pockets (deeper and rounded) are best engaged with fingers extended in the open-hand position. Train the open-hand pocket grip with all three pairs (or "teams") of fingers. Advanced climbers (solid 5.13 and seven-plus years' experience) can ease into training one-finger pockets with the middle finger.

Pinch Grip

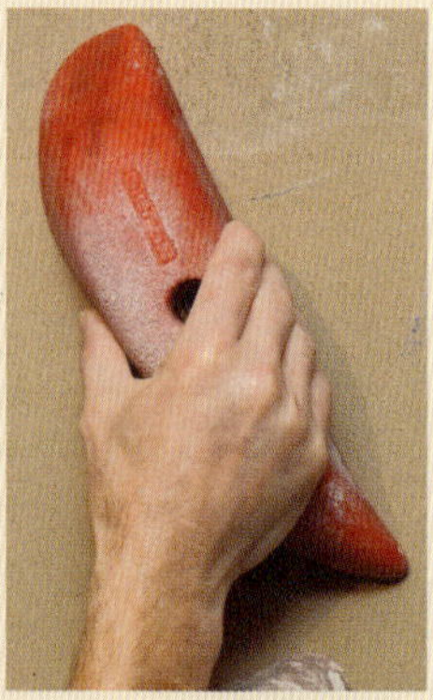

The pinch grip is vital for latching on to protruding holds such as pebbles, tuffas, aretes, and opposing edges. Due to the protruding nature of indoor climbing holds, use of the pinch grip is far more common indoors than on natural rock faces. Fortunately, our hands are designed to excel at pinching thanks to strong thumb muscles that help anchor this grip. An important distinction is the difference between narrow and wide pinch grips. Pinches of less than about three inches in width place the fingertips in a half-crimp-like position (hyperextended distal interphalangeal [DIP] joint), whereas wider pinches extend the fingers into an open-hand position with an over-extended wrist. While it would be smart to train both narrow and wide pinches, it's the wide pinch grip that should be your primary focus.

route in less than fifteen seconds (anaerobic alactic system). Climb the problem three times with a rest of at least two to three minutes between ascents—these three ascents (or attempts) make one set.

Move on to another strenuous problem that appears to target a different grip position. Consider taking the time to set "theme problems" that possess only holds of a certain shape and size—this is the best way to target and train a weak grip position. Do one set of three ascents of each problem, always resting for at least two minutes between each ascent.

FINGERBOARD "MINIMUM EDGE" HANGS

The following training protocol, loosely based on research by Eva Lopez-Rivera (2012), is what I recommended as an entry-level fingerboard program. A few multiweek cycles will bring noticeable gains in finger strength for intermediate climbers, as well as serve as preparation for delving into weighted fingerboard hangs (described next).

You'll need a fingerboard with many different-size edges and pockets, and then you'll need to experiment a little to identify what features you can hang on for just fifteen seconds or so. Actual training hangs should terminate a few seconds before failure of the grip, so I recommend making each hang exactly twelve seconds in length (the terminus of the anaerobic alactic energy pathway). Initial fingerboard workouts should focus on training with either the half-crimp or open-crimp grips, although you can eventually add in some open-hand pocket

Fingerboard train only with the open-hand, open-crimp, and half-crimp grips. Eva Lopez-Rivera's Transgression board is pictured.

and pinch grip training, if your fingerboard allows. Never fingerboard train with the full-crimp (with thumb lock) grip!

The training protocol is simple: Do a series of five, twelve-second hangs with exactly three minutes rest in between. Each hang should be near-maximal (rating of perceived exertion of 9 to 9.5 out of 10), but not quite take you to failure—as mentioned above, use a feature that you can barely hold for fifteen seconds with maximum effort. Begin by doing just two sets, but more advanced climbers can do two or three additional sets to isolate other grip positions. Always rest five minutes between sets (see table 8.2).

By design, this training protocol will produce little or no muscle pump, as it primarily targets the anaerobic alactic energy system.

FINGERBOARD "MAXIMUM WEIGHT" HANGS

A period of dedicated "minimum edge" fingerboard training will eventually lead you to the point of needing to train on tiny, painful edges to keep with the protocol detailed above. Enter the "maximum weight" protocol, which involves using larger, more

The author maximum weight training with eighty pounds hanging from the belay loop of his harness.

Table 8.2 "Minimum Edge" Fingerboard Protocol

Duration of Each Hang	Rest Between Hangs	Hangs per Set	Intensity (scale of 1 to 10)	Number of Sets	Rest Between Sets
12 seconds	3 minutes	5	9–9.5	2–5	5 minutes

Note: Select holds that you can barely hold for 15 seconds, although all hangs must terminate at 12 seconds.

Table 8.3 Maximum Weight "10-Second" Protocol

Duration of Each Hang	Rest Between Hangs	Hangs per Set	Intensity (scale of 1 to 10)	Number of Sets (aggregate of all grips trained)	Rest Between Sets
10 seconds	3 minutes	5	9–9.5	2–5	5 minutes

Note: Your training weight should be heavy enough to cause failure in 13 seconds, although all hangs must terminate at 10 seconds.

Table 8.4 Maximum Weight "7-53" Protocol

Duration of Each Hang	Rest Between Hangs	Hangs per Set	Intensity (scale of 1 to 10)	Number of Sets (aggregate of all grips trained)	Rest Between Sets
7 seconds	53 seconds	3	9–9.5	2–5	5 minutes

Note: Your training weight should be heavy enough to cause failure in 10 seconds, although all hangs must terminate at 7 seconds.

comfortable holds, but with added weight to create sufficiently high intensity for maximum-strength adaptations. The ideal size edge for weighted fingerboard hangs is between 14mm and 20mm (⅝ to ⅞-inch), or a little less than one finger-pad depth—this moderate depth lessens skin pain, reduces strain on the distal (DIP) joint, and has been proven effective to develop maximum-strength gains that will carry over to different-size edges on the rock.

Tables 8.3 and 8.4 present two maximum weight training protocols that really work. The first is adapted from Eva Lopez-Rivera's research, whereas the second is my own advanced protocol to train both maximum strength and aerobic power (increased rate of CP resynthesis between hangs). Do two to five sets of one or the other—not both!—focusing mainly on the half-crimp or open-crimp grips, although advanced climbers may want to dedicate one or two sets to pocket or wide pinch grips. The amount of weight added will be significant (generally between twenty-five and one hundred pounds), so you'll need to invest in a large weight vest, several weight belts, or hang a combination of free weight plates from the belay loop of your harness. The latter is the best solution since you can easily unclip the weights to de-load your body between hangs and sets.

Record your training details in a notebook, including hold size, weight used, and the number of hangs and sets. In the months and years to come, you'll undoubtedly document some significant gains in finger strength!

HYPERGRAVITY ISOLATION TRAINING—MAXIMUM-STRENGTH PROTOCOL

Hypergravity Isolation Training (HIT) is a cross between hypergravity bouldering and weighted fingerboard hangs. The unique HIT System provides a platform on which you can target a specific grip position for a single set of wall climbing. Since HIT System training involves actual climbing (unlike fingerboard training), it calls into action the entire

Overview of Fingerboard Training

Since its advent in the mid-1980s, the fingerboard has become the most used type of training equipment among climbers—and for good reason: The straight-armed, weighted hang is the single most effective isolation exercise a climber can do. What's more, the fingerboard is economical, and it can be mounted in just about any apartment or home.

The obvious strengths of fingerboard training are its ease of access and the ability to isolate a wide variety of grip positions. While not appropriate for beginners, experienced climbers can progressively add weight to their body to train maximum grip strength with a series of brief, high-intensity hangs. The strategy for training strength-endurance is to use lighter loads and a higher number of hangs, but with less rest in between.

Being able to vary the training load is an important aspect of effective fingerboard training. While you can indeed adjust intensity up and down by using smaller and bigger holds, respectively, it's also important to be able to adjust resistance while training on a specific hold such as the common 20mm (3/4-inch) edge. To increase resistance, simply wear a weight vest or hang free weights from the belay loop of your climbing harness. For resistances less than body weight, you can employ a pulley system with counterweights—especially useful for training one-arm hangs and learning one-arm pull-ups.

Always train with good hangboard technique: Maintain moderate tension throughout your shoulders and upper torso by engaging your scapular stabilizers (think about pushing your chest out); relax from the hips downward and avoid lifting your knees excessively; and most important, do not relax your shoulders and allow them to elevate into an extreme shrug position near your ears. Also, it's vital to do preparatory and concurrent training of the scapular stabilizers and rotator cuff muscles—select from exercises detailed in chapter 6.

Two-finger pocket pull-up training on a NICROS Nexgen fingerboard.

A word of caution: Misuse of the fingerboard has contributed to tendon injuries in countless climbers. Fingerboard training should be limited to just two days per week and, ideally, as a supplement to climbing rather than a replacement for actual climbing. A gradual warm-up is essential beforehand, including a general activity to elevate heart rate, followed by various mobility exercises and some self-massage as outlined in chapter 6. Complete your warm-up with some pull-ups on large holds. It's also a good idea to conclude your fingerboard training with a few sets of antagonist training of the wrist stabilizers.

chain of climbing muscles, from the finger flexors to the arms to the many core muscles of the torso. This novel exercise is unquestionably one of the best pathways to becoming a stronger climber.

It's ideal to use the HIT workout as part of a training cycle or an off-season program; however, you can also use HIT once weekly during your climbing on-season. As part of an off-season (winter) program, you might do four to six HIT workouts over the course of a two- or three-week maximum-strength mesocycle, and then switch to another training modality (aerobic or anaerobic endurance) for a few weeks. Given its stressful nature, it's best to cycle on and off this exercise every couple of weeks. Learn more about the HIT System in the sidebar on page 191.

The maximum-strength HIT System protocol (Table 8.5) trains six basic grip positions in sets lasting a maximum of fifteen seconds—no set should go longer, otherwise the training focus becomes anaerobic lactic. The grips trained are half crimp, pinch, open hand, and the three "teams" of two-finger grips. There will be enough near transfer from these fundamental positions to make your fingers stronger in any configuration on the rock. Perform one or two sets for each grip position—those new to the HIT workout should begin with one set—starting with the most difficult grip position for you. Most people work through the grips in this order: pinch, two-finger "third team" or outside pair (pinky and ring finger), two-finger "second team" or inside pair (index and middle finger), two-finger "first team" or middle pair (middle and ring finger), half crimp, and open hand. The entire HIT workout is done "open feet," meaning that you can place your feet on any holds on the wall.

Here's how you would perform a HIT set on the pinch holds: Sitting below the first HIT Strip, begin by gripping the first set of right- and left-hand pinch holds, then pull up and grab the next higher left-hand pinch hold. Continue climbing with the next higher right-hand pinch hold and the next higher left-hand pinch hold until both hands are on the top two pinch holds. Begin descending immediately, alternating left and right pinch holds back down until you are holding the bottom two pinch holds—this will take you nearly fifteen seconds, so end the set now. Upon stepping off the wall, use a stopwatch or phone app to time a rest of exactly three minutes before beginning the next set. Meanwhile, record the total number of "reps" (hand movements) and weight used in your training notebook. Use weight belts to add weight, since having the extra weight near your center of mass will have the least impact on your climbing technique; above about thirty pounds you'll need to use a weight vest.

Training on the HIT System pinch holds with a twenty-pound weight belt.

Table 8.5 HIT System—Maximum Strength Protocol

Grip Position	Weight Used HIT "Novice"	Weight Used HIT "Advanced"	Set Duration (reps/set)	Number of Sets	Rest Between Sets
Pinch	None	20 lbs.	<15 seconds (8–15 reps)	1–3	2–3 minutes
2-Finger "3rd Team"	None	20 lbs.	<15 seconds (8–15 reps)	1–3	2–3 minutes
2-Finger "2nd Team"	6 lbs.	30 lbs.	<15 seconds (8–15 reps)	1–3	2–3 minutes
2-Finger "1st Team"	8 lbs.	40 lbs.	<15 seconds (8–15 reps)	1–3	2–3 minutes
Half Crimp	10 lbs.	40 lbs.	<15 seconds (8–15 reps)	1–3	2–3 minutes
Open Hand	10 lbs.	40 lbs.	<15 seconds (8–15 reps)	1–3	2–3 minutes

* Weights are approximations for a 160-pound climber. Use similar percentages of your body weight.

After your three-minute rest, proceed immediately with a second set of pinch grip (advanced) or begin training the next grip position (two-finger "third team") by utilizing the identical two-finger pocket holds on each HIT Strip. Once again climb up and down the HIT Strips one time using only this grip position. The commonly weak two-finger third team and pinch grips may require little or no additional weight, but if doing one full up-and-down lap is easy, then you will need to add weight next time. Ideally, you want to add enough weight to make ten consecutive hand moves difficult (effort of 9 out of 10). Rest for two to three minutes before performing the second set with this grip (advanced) or moving onto the next grip position. Continue in this manner until you've trained all six grip positions—a hardy workout, for sure!

Contact Strength Exercises

Contact strength is your ability to quickly latch onto a hold. This trait is directly related to the speed at which you can recruit the forearm muscle's motor units and summon peak strength—a capacity called rate of force development (page 109). While the maximum-strength exercises described earlier will yield some improvement in contact strength, reactive training exercises that emphasize speed and shock loading is the optimal method for increasing contact strength. Since fast, dynamic movements are fundamental to effective reactive training, the resistance used (training load) must be significantly less than in the maximum-strength exercises. For many climbers the resistance will need to be less than body weight to allow for the rapid movement and turnover (change in direction) that's essential for effective reactive training.

Why Do Strong Fingers Matter?

Let me count the ways…

1. **Stronger fingers can grip smaller holds.** Duh! Seriously, though, all the climbing in the world won't do much to improve your ability to grip small edges and pockets. Improvement at gripping smaller and smaller holds—essential for climbing harder—depends on building a higher level of absolute (limit) grip strength. Fingerboard training (with the right training protocol) is unquestionably the best method of training maximum grip strength.
2. **Stronger fingers can endure longer when climbing on submaximal holds.** As explained earlier, when your fingers are gripping at just 20 percent of maximum voluntary contraction (MVC), blood flow through your forearm flexor muscles begins to slow … and at a contractile force of about 50 percent of MVC, the blood flow is occluded completely. When blood flow is reduced or stopped completely, power output declines precipitously after about ten seconds and, depending on the difficulty of the sustained grip (percent MVC), failure will follow in a matter of seconds to, at best, a minute or two if the finger flexors are contracting at a force far less than 50 percent MVC.

   Anyway, lack of blood flow and oxygen supply is the crux of the matter, since oxygen is required for CP resynthesis and blood flow is needed to remove metabolic byproducts of anaerobic lactic energy production. Thus, when resistance climbing through a long sequence of relatively difficult, yet submaximal holds, the greater the perfusion (delivery of blood to the capillary bed) the longer you will endure. Given the above understanding of blood flow occlusion as a function of percentage of maximum voluntary contraction (MVC), it's now easy to understand that in gaining a higher level of maximum grip strength (a greater MVC) you will be able to support your body weight (or whatever part your feet aren't supporting) with a smaller percentage of MVC. This is a powerful concept and a critical guiding principle for effective training!

   Summarizing: Increasing the MVC of the finger flexor muscles enables contraction at a lower percentage of maximum (compared with the weaker fingers of the "old you") when climbing on similar submaximal terrain, thus allowing for increased blood flow (and use of the aerobic energy system) and improved endurance.
3. **Stronger fingers can rest and recover on smaller holds.** I'm sure you've seen videos of rock stars, such as Chris Sharma and Adam Ondra, pausing in the middle of some long, steep, and ridiculously hard climb to shake out and somehow rest on a small "finger bucket" that would in no way be a rest hold for the mass of climbers. Yet somehow

Reactive training is appropriate only for intermediate and advanced climbers with no recent history of finger, elbow, or shoulder injury. Begin with the tamer feet-on exercises (less than body weight) and progress gradually to the feet-off exercises over the course of months or years. A few sets of reactive training will impart all the stimuli necessary for favorable adaptations—resist the urge to perform additional sets. Remind yourself that such neural training does not produce extreme fatigue, so if you train to the point of high fatigue, you are doing far too much and tempting injury.

Following are five reactive training exercises listed in order from least stressful (lowest force load and injury risk) to most severe (highest force and injury risk). Controlled one-arm lunging is the ideal icebreaker exercise for climbers wishing to these guys can stop and catch their breath and recover enough power reserve to push on and finish the climb. What is their secret to resting on holds so small they'd pump out an average climber? Strong fingers, of course!

As explained in #2, blood flow is the key to resynthesizing CP (essential for brief, high power movements) and removing fatiguing metabolic byproducts of the anaerobic lactic energy system (the predominant energy system when climbing hard, sustained sequences lasting between twelve seconds and a minute or two). For a rest hold to be good enough to hang onto for a significant rest (thirty to sixty seconds or more), you must be able to grip the hold using less than 50 percent of your MVC—only this way will there be any rejuvenating blood flow. Therefore, a climber with "average" grip strength may require a four-inch deep hold to recover (the smallest size hold he can grip for an extended time at <50 percent MVC) whereas the 5.15 climber can likely rest on a one-inch hold (with feet on the rock, of course) thanks to their incredible grip strength that allows them to grip this small hold with less than 50 percent of MVC.

4. **Stronger fingers have more stamina.** Occasionally you hear a mind-boggling media report of some pro climber on-sighting or redpointing multiple 5.14 routes in a day and then doing it again the next day . . . and the next! How is that even possible?

Let me tell you a story about a climber named Alex who does this with regularity. I've climbed with Alex a few times in recent years, and in October 2015 I was with him at the New River Gorge when, in the matter of a few hours, he warmed up on a couple 5.13+ routes and then proceeded to do a first ascent of a 5.14b and a second-go second ascent of another 5.14b. Sounds like a fatiguing day of climbing, right? Not for Alex. In fact, he climbed other routes at the 5.14 grade both the day before and the day after!

How is this possible? Before I embellish further on the importance of getting stronger, I must point out that Alex possesses world-class technique and a very strong mind. That said, the master key is that Alex is really strong! (See the front cover photo of this book.) We have yet to see what Alex's true climbing limit is (but it will be fun to watch in the coming years), but I can tell you that climbing 5.13+/5.14- routes are nowhere near his limit. So for Alex to climb at this level on successive days is similar to a 5.12b climber doing 5.11 routes on successive days or a 5.14a climber sending multiple 5.12+/5.13- routes.

The bottom line: By increasing your limit strength and advancing your high-end climbing ability, the submaximal level at which you can climb with relative ease and aplomb—and in high volume—is elevated. Therefore, by making a long-term training commitment to getting stronger (and improving your mental and technical game), you may someday find your current maximum climbing level to be "moderate" and achievable in volume.

add some reactive training to their routines, as each one-arm catch involves a slight shock loading of the forearm muscles. Contact strength gains achieved through this form of feet-on "reactive light" training are limited, however—beyond a certain point you will need to graduate to feet-off campus training, which produces a much higher shock load, to stimulate further gains.

ONE-ARM LUNGING (FEET-ON)

One-arm lunging with feet fixed on good holds (or the floor) is the easiest reactive training exercise. You can do this exercise using the bottom two large holds on a campus board or two juggy holds at the base of a slightly overhanging section of climbing wall. Ideally you can set a few modular holds specifically for performing this exercise. Set two footholds

1. Grip the higher handhold.

2. Drop down to the lower.

3. Lunge back to the higher.

about a foot off the ground, and then set two large, rounded holds that fit your hand nicely (open-hand grip), one in front of your face and the other about ten to eighteen inches above that. If training on a campus board, you'll need to lunge between the two lowest large holds on the board with your feet on the floor below and slightly behind the board.

Either way, balance your weight evenly on both feet and then grip the higher of the two jug holds with both hands. Now let go with one hand and hold the arm by your side or behind your back. Begin with an inward pull with the engaged hand, and at the deadpoint (moment of quasi-weightlessness on that hand) let go and drop the hand down to catch the lower jug hold with a partially bent arm and engaged rotator cuff and scapula (think about keeping your chest out). Absorb the downward energy and immediately recoil upward to catch back on to the starting handhold. Continue with brisk up-and-down lunging for six to twelve total hand movements—total duration of exercise is ten seconds or less.

After a brief rest, step back up on the wall and perform an identical set of one-arm lunges with the other hand. Perform two or three total sets with each hand.

CAMPUS LADDERING

As the name implies, this exercise involves climbing in a hand-over-hand, ladderlike motion up the campus board with no aid from the feet. Unlike double dynos (described later), this laddering exercise uses controlled dynamic movements that are less likely to result in injury. Consequently, this is a better staple exercise for regular use, and it is the

Figure 8.1 Campus Laddering

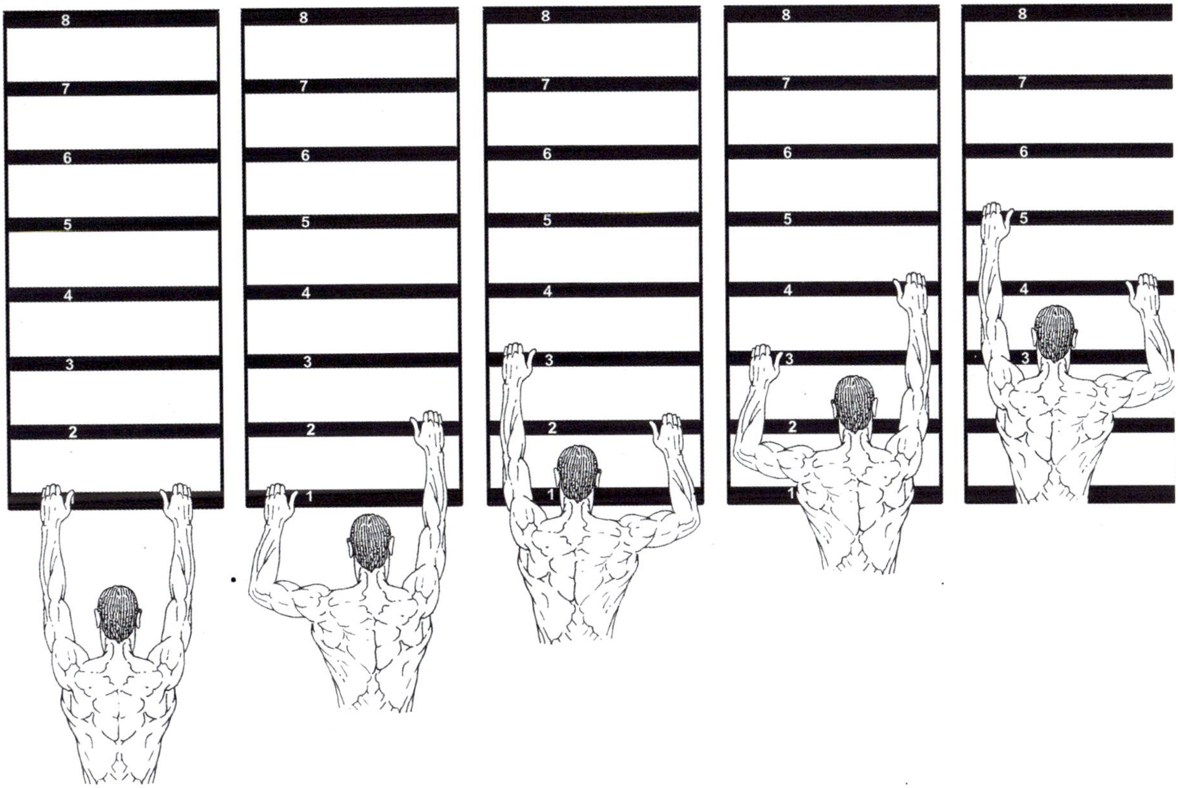

perfect icebreaker exercise for climbers new to campus training. An important distinction when ladder training: Using smaller holds and shorter reaches trains contact strength whereas using larger holds and longer reaches trains pulling power and lock-off strength (the subject of chapter 9). The focus here is on contact strength, so you should use the smallest size holds that you can ladder without skipping rungs.

Hang with nearly straight arms from the bottom rung of the campus board. Your hands should be about shoulder width or slightly less apart. Striving for brisk, fluid motion, climb hand-over-hand up the campus board using alternating rungs for your left and right hands. Your goal is to ascend the board as fast as possible and, upon reaching the top, jump off. Most campus boards feature at least eight rungs, so your training goal is to make eight hand moves as quickly as possible. Increase difficulty by using smaller rungs or adding five to ten pounds of weight around your waist rather than skipping rungs.

Think of this exercise as an alactic sprint—laddering eight rungs should take just three to six seconds. Initially, rest two to three minutes between sets; however, you can train aerobic power by decreasing the rest interval to just thirty to sixty seconds between sets. Begin by doing just three sets, but build toward a maximum of ten sets.

CAMPUS "BUMPS"

As the name implies, this exercise involves bumping one hand up successive rungs while the other hand remains fixed on the bottom rung. Like most campus board exercises, you'll be using momentum to assist with the upward hand bumps—still, each rung "catch" will elicit a high rate of force development in the finger flexors, which is of course the training goal here. Begin by hanging from the bottom rung with shoulders engaged (not shrugging) and arms just slightly bent, and then proceed to pull upward and "bump, bump, bump, bump" the active hand as fast as possible while the other arm pulls down into a lower and lower lock-off position.

Given a campus board with normal-size rungs, you'll likely be bumping the active hand just three or four times before you jump off and call it a set. Importantly, your highest bump hold must not be with a straight arm and shrugged shoulder—this is a critical distinction, as many shoulder injuries occur when individuals repeatedly campus with fully extended arms and elevated scapula. As with the previous exercise, increase difficulty by using smaller holds or adding a small amount of weight rather than skipping rungs; make the exercise easier by placing your feet on holds fixed below the campus board. Initially do just two or three sets on each side, although in the long term, advanced climbers can progress up to ten sets each side. Resting two minutes between sets is usually sufficient; however, advanced climbers can reduce rests to just thirty seconds to train aerobic power.

Figure 8.2 Campus Bumping

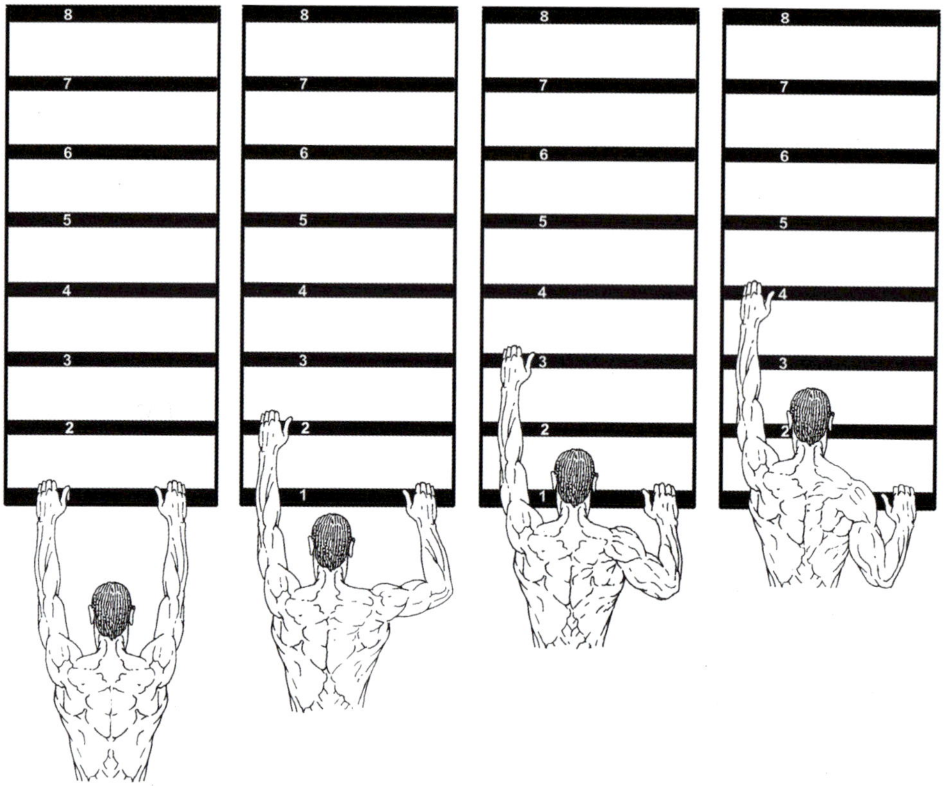

Overview of Campus Board Training

Developed in the late 1980s by Wolfgang Güllich at the Campus Center in Nürnberg, Germany, campus training is the gold standard for training upper-body power and contact strength for climbing. The campus board is a unique training platform that allows for various reactive training and quasi-plyometric exercises that train recruitment and rate of force development in the finger and arm flexors. This type of dynamic training is a real boon for high-end sport climbers and boulderers.

While feet-off "campusing" is the most common method of training among elite climbers, feet-on campus training with the toes resting on small holds or wooden strips is the preferred method for more intermediate climbers wanting to dabble on the campus board. An ideal campus board rig will include at least three different-size strips (roughly 20mm, 40mm, and 60mm "jug" or open-hand sloper) and foot strips at a few different heights under the board.

Sadly, the campus board is widely misused, both by individuals not strong or experienced enough for the high dynamic loads and by some elites who overutilize this training platform. No one with less than two years climbing experience should use a campus board—their tendon strength is unlikely to be ready to carry the load. Even elite climbers should limit campus training to less than 10 percent of total training time. Finally, anyone wanting to campus train should first engage in several months of scapular stabilizer training (see chapter 6) and continue with this training indefinitely. Here are several more guidelines for safe and effective use of the campus board.

Engage in campus training only if you are an advanced-intermediate (leading 5.11 or bouldering V5) to elite climber with no recent history of finger or arm injury. Favor feet-on exercises and feet-off laddering and bumps. The most stressful double dynos exercise must be reserved for only highly conditioned, elite climbers (5.13/V8 climbers).

Warm up thoroughly. Spend at least half an hour performing various warm-up activities and bouldering to fully warm the finger, arm, shoulder, and back muscles.

Use only the open-hand or open-crimp grip when doing feet-off campusing.

Never engage a rung with a completely straight arm and shrugged shoulder—this will wreck your shoulders in short order! Upward grabs should always be done with a slight elbow bend and a well-secured scapula (think about keeping your chest up/out rather than caved in).

Emphasize quality over quantity—it's better to do a few perfectly executed explosive sets rather than many reckless sets with poor technique (straight arms and shrugged shoulders).

Do not campus train while in a state of high fatigue or if you have any doubts about the health of your fingers, arms, or shoulders.

Immediately terminate your campus training at the first sensation of pain in your fingers, elbows, or shoulders (common among people who campus with poor technique and weak scapular stabilizers).

Campus no more than twice per week, and cycle on and off campusing every couple of weeks.

Youth climbers should abstain from campus training, especially during peak growth velocity (ages thirteen to sixteen) when growth plates are most easily injured.

The famous Café Kraft campus board in Nürnberg, Germany, the birthplace of campus training!

CAMPUS "SWITCH HANDS"

Whereas the previous campus training exercises all involved advancing one hand while the other hand remained engaged on a rung for support, the Switch Hands exercise escalates to moving both hands simultaneously, albeit for just a small distance of about ten inches. Still, this dynamic movement demands more rapid rate of force development in the finger flexors to successfully re-grasp the rungs after the double release move. The Switch Hands exercise, therefore, is a good segue toward eventually performing the most difficult double dynos exercise (below).

Do Switch Hands using positive medium to large-size rungs (not slopers) and an open-hand grip. Begin with your hands on successive rungs (either the first and second, or the second and third), and then tighten down your scapula (think chest out) and bend your arms slightly to gain a good starting position before lifting your feet off the floor. Begin the exercise with a short but sharp pull—only a few inches—to create upward momentum and then, at the deadpoint, quickly switch hands to the opposite rungs. You'll latch back on to the rungs as your center of mass begins to descend, so you'll need to momentarily absorb this energy with your pulling muscles before initiating the next upward pull and hand switch. Continue switching hands as fast as possible, for up to ten or twelve total hand switches.

Campus Switches

There's a little bit of timing involved in doing this correctly, but if you're strong enough to rightfully employ this exercise you'll quickly acquire the skill and be able to do about ten to twelve successive switches in only about five seconds. This is a bang-bang exercise that, if done correctly, involves very little upward and downward movement of the torso. The exercise itself is pure anaerobic (alactic) power; however, it's also excellent for developing aerobic power (for faster resynthesis of CP) if you do several sets in a row with only short rests. Begin with just two sets per session with a two-minute rest in between, but gradually build toward six sets with just thirty to sixty seconds between sets (advanced).

CAMPUS DOUBLE DYNOS

The double dyno exercise is the pinnacle of campus training with its double-handed, fully airborne flight between rungs. Done on smaller rungs and without skipping (rungs), this exercise focuses more on finger flexor recruitment, whereas using large rungs and greater flight distance (skipping rungs) equally trains finger and pull-muscle power. The focus now is on developing finger contact strength via more synchronous motor unit recruitment and neural disinhibition, so the protocol here is smaller rungs and no rung skipping.

Every climber must acknowledge, however, the extremely stressful and potentially injurious nature of this exercise. Are your fingers tendons, rotator cuff, and scapular stabilizers ready for this level of stress? It's my belief that the answer is "no" for over 95 percent of climbers. I discourage use of this exercise if you've been climbing less than four

Complex Training

Complex training is a cutting-edge training method used by elite athletes in many sports, including most power-oriented Olympic events. Applied to climbing, the complex training protocol described below is one of the most advanced strength-training concepts available. Since introducing complex training in the first edition of *Training for Climbing* in 2002, I have heard from countless climbers around the world who have leveraged this technique to increase their grip strength and upper-body power. You can, too, as long as you are an intermediate-advanced climber (solid at 5.11 and V5 or harder) with no recent history of finger, elbow, or shoulder injury.

Complex training involves a coupling of a maximum-strength exercise with a reactive power-oriented exercise. Research has shown that performing these two very different exercises back-to-back—and in the order of strength first, power second—produces gains in strength and power beyond those achieved by performing either exercise alone. While no studies have been done with climbers, there is compelling research in the use of complex training to increase vertical jump that shows phenomenal gains in absolute ability (Adams 1992). In this study six weeks of strength training produced a 3.3-centimeter increase in the vertical jump, compared with a 3.8-centimeter increase after six weeks of reactive (plyometric) training. The group performing complex training (strength and reactive) for six weeks experienced an incredible 10.7-centimeter increase in jumping ability!

Incorporating complex training into your program can be done a number of ways—the key requirement is a coupling of a maximum-strength exercise and a power exercise with minimal rest in between. Here are a few common training complexes:

- Do a fingery near-maximal boulder problem followed immediately by one set each hand of one-arm lunging (feet-on) on a campus board or climbing wall.
- Do a hypergravity boulder problem (with, say, a twenty-pound weight belt on) coupled with a set of Campus Laddering (sans weight belt).
- Do a max-strength set on the HIT System (with weight belt) followed immediately by a set of Campus Switch Hands (no added weight).
- Do a max-strength set of fingerboard hangs (with weight) followed by a set of campus board double dynos. This training complex is one of the most powerful for elite climbers, and it may represent the single best training protocol for pursuing absolute genetic potential for contact strength. Elites can build to doing up to eight coupled sets (complexes) with three to five minutes rest between sets.

Cautionary note: Complex training is, obviously, an advanced technique that produces both high passive and dynamic stress on the finger tendons and joints, the elbows, and the shoulders. This protocol should be used only by well-trained climbers with no recent history of injury. Furthermore, limit use of training complexes to once every three or four days and primarily during the maximum-strength and power mesoscale.

years, don't climb 5.13 or V9, can't do at least five hypergravity pull-ups with one-third of your body weight added, and can't easily ladder up and down the campus board in a 1-3-5-7-7-5-3-1 sequence.

Begin by hanging from one of the middle rungs, with slightly flexed arms and engaged shoulders. Simultaneously let go with both hands and drop to catch the next lower rung with flexed arms and engaged shoulders. After a brief amortization phase of energy absorption in the pull muscles, explode upward with both hands to catch the starting rung. This is one full repetition, but

Campus Double Dynos

don't stop! Without hesitation, drop down to again catch the next lower rung, and explode back up to the starting rung. Continue for three to five repetitions (six to ten total hand moves), and then dismount. The turnaround time must be as fast as possible—ideally less than one-half second—and the total exercise time is less than ten seconds. This exercise is almost fully alactic powered, so you should get hardly a hint of pump in doing it. Do two to five sets with two to three minutes rest in between each set.

Warning: End the exercise prematurely rather than risk a failed downward catch (but have a bouldering pad in place just in case). Terminate your campus training at the first sign of pain in your fingers, arms, or shoulders. Remember rule number one: *Never get injured training!*

Strength-Endurance Exercises

As detailed in chapter 5, your ability to climb many hard moves in a row is largely a matter of your anaerobic capacity. Specifically, it's strength-endurance of the finger flexor muscles and power-endurance of the larger pulling muscles of the arms and torso that are being tested in doing long, sustained boulder problems and roped "resistance" climbs. The burning muscle pump is the hallmark of the anaerobic lactic (glycolytic) energy system being pushed to near its limit, and of course many redpoint attempts end accordingly, with a Hindenbergian forearm pump that makes climbing to (or clipping) the chains impossible.

In an attempt to improve anaerobic capacity, many climbers make strength-endurance of the fingers (and power-endurance of the pulling muscles) the primary focus of their training. While a few weeks of targeted anaerobic-capacity training will often bring favorable adaptations and some noticeable gains on the rock, many climbers train this energy system too frequently and too long without variation. It's interesting to note that climbing (or training) to the point of a blistering pump more than about two or three days per week over the long term often leads to decreasing endurance, possibly due to the damage of chronic acidosis to mitochondrial function and related enzymes. If you have ever engaged in frequent high-volume strength/power-endurance training, only to discover that you're pumping out even faster on the rock, you now know why. So what's the best strategy for training anaerobic capacity?

I've pointed out several times that the anaerobic lactic energy system is the least trainable of the three energy systems, and therefore making significant year-over-year gains in anaerobic capacity demands getting stronger (anaerobic alactic training) and increasing aerobic power and capacity. The best training approach, then, is to partake frequently in anaerobic alactic and local aerobic energy system mesocycles, and then to perform a two- to four-week mesocycle of pumpy anaerobic lactic training prior to a climbing road trip or competition. This approach will boost all three energy systems, prevent overtraining, and provide you with the important anaerobic lactic system adaptations (cellular buffering and increased anaerobic enzymes) in the final weeks before your event.

With this understanding, you can think of your actual strength-endurance (and power-endurance, covered in chapter 9) workouts as mostly training "tolerance" to the acidosis and high lactate levels that result from pushing your anaerobic lactic system to the limit. This energy system is predominant in sustained, high-intensity exercise lasting fifteen seconds to about two minutes—thus each exercise presented in this section must be performed in a way that roughly meets this duration criteria . . . and gets you pumped!

SHORT-DURATION FINGERBOARD REPEATERS

Repeaters are the standard fingerboard exercise for developing strength-endurance and improving the ability to climb onward despite a building pump. There are many different repeater protocols in the public domain, but below I will outline what I feel are the two most effective approaches. First I'll present short-duration repeaters, then I'll outline the benefits of also training with long-duration repeaters.

Table 8.6 presents four difficult levels of short-duration fingerboard repeaters. While each level involves doing a set of six ten-second hangs, each higher level of difficulty affords a shorter rest between each hang. Each set of six hangs is followed by a one-minute rest, after which you commence with the next set of six repeaters. Do up to five sets of six hangs. If doing these five sets with the Level 1 protocol isn't difficult, then use the Level 2 protocol for the next workout. If you eventually come to find Level 4 training less than difficult, then you can add a ten-pound (or more) weight belt or use a pair of smaller holds

The beauty of short-duration repeaters is that the alternating periods of contracting and relaxing the forearm flexor muscles roughly approximates how we climb on the rock. The frequent rest periods allow blood flow to reoxygenate the working muscles and remove metabolic by-products—functional gains in the biological processes involved that will directly translate into improved performance on the rock!

A final distinction with regard to the grips you will train here: Research has determined that two primary muscles using in gripping the rock, the flexor digitorum profundus (FDP) and the flexor digitorum superficialis (FDS), contribute to force generation in crimp gripping at a ratio of 3:1, respectively. When open-hand gripping, however, force generation from these two muscle groups comes at nearly a 1:1 ratio (Vigouroux 2006). Given this knowledge, you can understand the importance of training both the crimp and open-hand grips; of course, you must always train the crimp position as a half crimp, *not* a full crimp with thumb lock. Applying this to repeater training, it would be a good idea

Table 8.6 Short-Duration Fingerboard Repeaters

Difficulty Level	Duration Hang/ Rest (seconds)	Number of Hangs per Set	Number of Sets	Rest Between Sets
Level 1	10/30	6	3–5	1 minute
Level 2	10/20	6	3–5	1 minute
Level 3	10/10	6	3–5	1 minute
Level 4	10/5	6	3–5	1 minute

to alternate between half-crimp and open-hand grips with each successive set performed.

LONG-DURATION FINGERBOARD REPEATERS

Long-duration repeaters are a bit less specific to how we generally climb, although they may roughly simulate the longer-duration forearm contractions common to shaking out at a mid-climb rest position. This point aside, the extraordinary benefits of long-duration repeaters are first, that longer-sustained contractions occlude blood flow—this ischemia results in an increasingly hypoxic and acidic cellular environment. Then, during the rest periods, forceful reperfusion (restoration of blood flow) develops throughout the forearm flexor muscles, as you recognize the "pump" feeling develop. This cycle of ischemia and reperfusion is an apparent stimulus for beneficial adaptions, although the mechanisms responsible are not fully understood. Furthermore, training that yields a reduction in intracellular pH (acidosis) will result in improved cellular buffering—an important adaptation in the final weeks of a training cycle before the pre–road trip or pre-competition training taper.

Once again, I am presenting you with four difficulty levels of long-duration repeaters in table 8.7. Begin with Level 1 and advance to the next level when you can complete five sets at the current level. Long-duration repeaters can become quite painful, so you may also benefit from mental (pain tolerance) and central governor recalibration. **Warning:** Good fingerboard technique is essential for repeater training—maintain engaged shoulders

Fingerboard repeater training with guidance from the Zlagboard training app.
ZLAGBOARDUSA.COM

Table 8.7 Long-Duration Fingerboard Repeaters

Difficulty Level	Duration Hang/ Rest (seconds)	Number of Hangs per Set	Number of Sets	Rest Between Sets
Level 1	30/30	4	3–5	1 minute
Level 2	30/15	4	3–5	1 minute
Level 3	60/30	4	3–5	1 minute
Level 4	60/15	4	3–5	1 minute

(chest out!) throughout each set, and end a hang early if you sense your shoulders beginning to loosen and shrug upward.

BOULDERING 4X4S

The bouldering 4x4 is a common indoor climbing method of training strength-endurance in the finger flexors and power-endurance in the larger pulling muscles of the arms and torso. Physiologically, 4x4s are kind of a climber's equivalent of "gassers" sprint training performed by speed-endurance athletes such as soccer, hockey, and football players. This increasingly difficult workout trains both anaerobic capacity and aerobic power, if you follow the protocol outlined below. The short recovery periods are just as important as the brief spells of bouldering—so use a timing app or stopwatch to get it right.

There are many different ways of doing 4x4s, but Table 8.8 presents the most straightforward and my personal favorite—and it's a great protocol to do with a training partner. The 4x4 involves doing four ascents (each) of four different boulder problems. Selecting the right problems is a bit tricky, as you want each to be hard enough to push you but not so hard you'll fail (except, perhaps, on the fourth pass). Obviously, you'll need to choose problems a few grades below your maximum level—for example, if your current (this season) hardest boulder ascent is a V9, then you should select problems in the V4 to V6 range for your 4x4s. For the purpose of finger training, it would be best to select boulders with smallish holds, but void of any big stopper reaches. Climbing each problem should only take thirty seconds, so don't pick long and involved problems or any that require stopping to rest. The training protocol is this: You have one minute for each boulder ascent (including post-climb rest), and then you'll take four minutes of rest after every fourth climb. So beginning on the first problem, let's say it takes twenty-five seconds to ascend; you'll then rest for the remainder of the first minute (thirty-five seconds). Do a second, third, and fourth lap on the first boulder problem using the same climb-rest scheme that adds up to exactly one minute. Upon completing the fourth ascent (actually, at the end of the fourth full minute), take four minutes of complete rest—if you're training with a partner, you can now time her set of four climbs. Next, you'll repeat this process on the second of your four chosen boulder problems. Again, you have one full minute of climb-rest time per lap, after which you get four minutes of rest. Repeat this process with the third and fourth boulder problems. All totaled this 4x4 protocol takes about thirty minutes. This is a powerful anaerobic endurance

Table 8.8 Bouldering 4x4 Protocol

	Boulder 1		**Boulder 2**		**Boulder 3**		**Boulder 4**	
	Climb	Rest	Climb	Rest	Climb	Rest	Climb	Rest
Ascent 1	~30"	~30"	~30"	~30"	~30"	~30"	~30"	~30"
Ascent 2	~30"	~30"	~30"	~30"	~30"	~30"	~30"	~30"
Ascent 3	~30"	~30"	~30"	~30"	~30"	~30"	~30"	~30"
Ascent 4	~30"	~30"	~30"	~30"	~30"	~30"	~30"	~30"
Rest	4 minutes		4 minutes		4 minutes		4 minutes	

training technique—so get a partner, use a smartphone timing App, and get pumped!

HYPERGRAVITY ISOLATION TRAINING—STRENGTH-ENDURANCE PROTOCOL

Performed exactly as described in the HIT System Maximum-Strength Protocol (page 174), here you will be using lighter weights and climb for a much longer duration to train strength/power-endurance (anaerobic capacity). The acceptable extremes for duration of each set are twenty seconds and two minutes, although I believe thirty to ninety seconds is ideal (see table 8.9). Consider taping your fingers (figure-8 method) for skin protection so that you can push hard throughout each set, rather than needing to terminate early due to skin pain. This very grueling workout creates significant fatigue—full recovery may take up to seventy-two hours, so plan accordingly.

SYSTEM WALL "REPEATERS"

A System Wall is a specialized training platform with a large assortment of differing holds organized in a way that each half of the wall is a mirror image of the other. System Walls typically overhang anywhere from 20 to 45 degrees past vertical, and they are often only six to eight feet wide and nine to, at most, fifteen feet high. The utility of a System Wall is the ability to train a specific finger grip, arm position, movement, and body position in a very precise and repeatable way for both arms and sides of your body.

Common uses of a System Wall include working undercling arm strength and reaches, one-arm lock-offs and hand bumping, deadpoint moves, compression moves, and twist-lock moves, among many other possibilities. A well-outfitted System Wall with dozens of different holds can offer a really good targeted workout of the forearm (gripping) muscles, the larger pulling muscles of the arms and torso, and the many core muscles of the torso.

In terms of training strength-endurance of the forearm flexors (and power-endurance of the pulling muscles), you'll want to use a protocol very similar to the HIT System strength-endurance protocol outlined in Table 8.9. Initially it will take a little experimentation, but develop four to six different

Table 8.9 HIT System—Strength-Endurance Protocol

Grip Position	Weight Used HIT "Novice"	Weight Used HIT "Advanced"	Set Duration (reps/set)	Number of Sets	Rest Between Sets
2-Finger "3rd Team"	None	5 lbs.	20–40 secs.	1–3	3 mins.
Pinch	None	5 lbs.	20–40 secs.	1–3	3 mins.
2-Finger "2nd Team"	None	10 lbs.	30–60 secs.	1–3	3 mins.
2-Finger "1st Team"	None	10 lbs.	30–60 secs.	1–3	3 mins.
Half Crimp	None	20 lbs.	45–90 secs.	1–3	3 mins.
Open Hand	None	20 lbs.	45–90 secs.	1–3	3 mins.

* Weights are approximations for a 160-pound climber. Use similar percentages of your body weight.

The History of Hypergravity Isolation Training (i.e., HIT System Training)

In the mid-1990s I set out to develop a climbing-specific method for training functional strength in the important finger and arm flexor muscles, as well as the vital muscles of the shoulders and core. Much experimentation with equipment designs and training protocols led to what I call Hypergravity Isolation Training (HIT). While similar to the more variable System Wall Training, HIT workouts are highly focused on training specific grip positions while pulling and twisting up a severely overhanging wall. Since I first promoted this exciting training method in my book *How to Climb 5.12* in 1997, HIT workouts have been utilized by thousands of climbers around the world. The effectiveness of HIT (not to be confused with the popular weight lifters' "HIT workout") is a result of its fulfillment of the four fundamental requisites for training grip strength detailed on page 167.

The adjacent photo depicts me training on the third-generation HIT Strips and HIT Pinches (available at www.Nicros.com), a unique platform I developed for optimal HIT workouts. Each HIT Strip possesses identical crimp edges and two-finger pockets that are ideal for laddering up and down until failure, although in lieu of the HIT Strips you can also arrange pairs of identical crimp, pocket, and pinch holds to train on. The ideal wall angle for HIT training is 45 to 55 degrees past vertical. Weight added around the waist is increased or decreased to produce near failure of the finger flexors in the required amount of time—fifteen seconds if using the HIT maximum-strength protocol and thirty to ninety seconds when using the HIT strength/power-endurance protocol. Here are a few more tips for effective HIT System training.

- Use a snug-fitting weight belt(s) or a weight vest, and adjust the weight for each grip position. Record weights used in a training notebook.
- Climb briskly and without hesitation—no stopping or chalking mid-set. Always step off the wall as opposed to risking an uncontrolled fall while climbing with added weight.
- Climb with normal foot movements and body turns. Small- to medium-size footholds are best, because too much thought on footwork will slow you down.
- Rest breaks between sets must be exactly two or three minutes; more advanced climbers should use the former. Use a stopwatch and stick to the planned order and schedule of exercises.
- Keep a training notebook in which you log each set, weight added, the number of reps (hand moves) performed, and the length of rest intervals. This way you'll always know what weight you need for a given set, and you can quantify and track your gains in finger strength!
- Tape your fingers using the Figure-8 method (page 286) to reduce skin pain, especially when training with high weight loads.
- Visit www.Training4Climbing.com for more information on building a dedicated HIT System Wall.

The author (plus twenty pounds) on a HIT System.

System Wall Repeaters isolating the same movement on both sides. KRIS HAMPTON COLLECTION

"theme repeaters" that you can climb up and down through—using identical left and right hand/arm positions—for between thirty and ninety seconds without stopping. Since System Walls are short, you'll likely need to lap up and down through the sequence several times to reach the desired training time and level of fatigue. On a less steep System Wall (closer to just 20 degrees past vertical), you may be able to climb for sixty to ninety seconds for each set, whereas a steeper wall may limit your training set to just twenty to forty seconds. Either way, take a three-minute rest between each set.

Do one or two sets on each of four to six different "theme repeaters" for a total of four to twelve sets in aggregate. Long term, you can increase difficulty by using smaller holds, larger arm moves, and more difficult and strenuous body positions, as well as by adding a weight belt. In chapter 9 we'll examine using a System Wall to train arm and core strength in a variety of arm and body positions.

Training Forearm Local Aerobic Endurance

Effective training of the aerobic energy pathway via climbing is possible only if you set aside the desire to climb for performance (near your limit) and instead embrace the potentially boring process of climbing high volumes of moderate rock (or plastic). No matter if the climbing is done indoors or outside, this approach will naturally involve lots of submaximal climbing at varying intensities. The critical guideline to obey is that the climbing intensity never ascends significantly into the anaerobic

Figure 8.3 Training Zones for Climbers

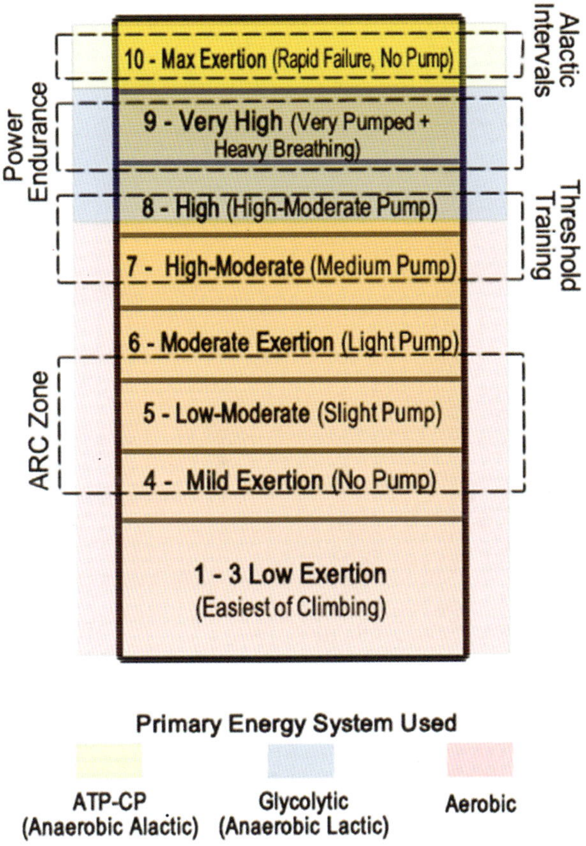

Effective climbing-specific aerobic training must be performed between 5 and 8.5 on the rating of perceived exertion.

zone, the hallmark of which is a deep muscle pump and shortness of breath. Ultimately, you want to find the margin of the anaerobic lactic zone and strive to climb mostly just below it (in the aerobic zone), only occasionally crossing into the low end of the anaerobic zone. A light to, at times, moderate forearm pump is fine and desirable; however, a flaming pump, heavy breathing, and a growing sense of losing control are clear signs you've climbed too deep into the anaerobic zone.

Self-control and a strong intention to climb mainly in the aerobic training zone are essential to properly training this energy pathway. By keeping your perceived exertion and exercise intensity between 5 and 8.5 on a scale of 1 to 10 (see figure 8.3), you can rest assured that you're getting it right. Detailed below are five methods of training local aerobic endurance.

ARC TRAVERSES ("RECOVERY CLIMBING")

ARC is an acronym for aerobic, recovery, and capillary training. The goal of ARC training is to enhance recuperative blood flow via an extended period of lower-intensity climbing. Such a training protocol—if you can stick to it—singularly targets the aerobic energy system and therefore yields little (or no) muscle pump. Done right, this light climbing workout will generate no fatigue to recover from and, in fact, will help accelerate recovery from the previous day's intense workout. The problem, however, is that the typical enthusiastic climber has a tough time visiting a climbing gym and refraining entirely from doing more difficult routes or boulder problems, but even a small sampling of more challenging routes or boulders will sink the ARC.

Rather than calling it ARC training, I prefer the term "recovery climbing," since this unambiguously expresses the actual mission of the activity: Easy climbing that will enhance recovery rather than get in the way of it. The modus operandi we are after is similar to that of a runner going for a "recovery run"—the climbing (or running) pace must be so casual that you can hold a conversation throughout. On a perceived exertion/intensity scale of 1 to 10, the ideal recovery-training zone is between a 4 and 6 (see figure 8.3); go any higher and it's no longer an ARC/recovery session.

Recent Research on the Importance of Local Aerobic Endurance Training of the Finger Flexors

Strength and endurance of the finger flexors is now considered to be one of the key determinants of sport climbing performance. Current studies have focused on understanding the open-crimp position on plastic holds. When sport climbers are placed in groups characterized by on-sight and redpoint abilities, several significant physiological differences have been found. It has now become evident that these differences are training adaptations that affect the muscle structure of the forearm flexors, and these may influence the way we ascend and rest on a route.

Given our understanding of rock climbing physiology, there are some training modalities that are likely to enhance sport climbing performance—for example, climbing-specific training that focuses on improving the aerobic capacity of the forearm flexors (not to be confused with training whole body aerobic capacity (VO_2 max), such as running). Although we recognize that VO_2 max is important for sport climbing, the aerobic capacity that is specific to the forearm flexors appears to be more important. Our laboratory has found that after sustained and intermittent contractions to failure, higher-level sport climbers have a greater forearm aerobic capacity, as they can off-load and recuperate oxygen faster and to a greater extent than lower-level sport climbers. Interestingly, the speed of this oxygen recovery has been strongly correlated to creatine phosphate resynthesis (replenishing our short-lived but powerful anaerobic energy system). As such it is important to include training that stresses the aerobic metabolism in the forearms—that is, a high number of repetitions at a relatively low intensity, as this is likely to improve the ability to recover between holds on a route.

Based on the relationship between sport climbing ability and oxygen recovery (and creatine phosphate resynthesis), the physiological benefits of resting on a route are going to be of paramount importance to a successful ascent. This would be particularly important for sections on a route that come just before the crux move. Further, as we have found that the nondominant finger flexor muscles recover oxygen slower compared to the dominant, it will be worth spending a little extra time resting (and training) the nondominant side to ensure maximal performance. This will be particularly important if the route requires a lot of workload to be placed on the nondominant forearm.

—Dr. Simon Fryer, School of Sport and Exercise,
University of Gloucestershire, UK

For the purpose of seriously developing the aerobic energy system, however, the ARC/recovery climbing protocol misses the mark—it's just too low-intensity. Therefore, save this type of recovery training for occasional use the day after a hard maximum-strength or strength-endurance workout. Traversing along the base of a large indoor climbing wall, using mainly large holds, is the easiest way to go about this—without the tether of a belay you can easily step off the wall at the first sign of a developing pump. Two common approaches are to simply traverse around the gym until you get bored, or to do a series of five-minute traverses with two- to five-minute rests in between. Aim for a total climbing time of around thirty minutes, and don't get pumped!

FINGERBOARD MOVING HANGS

If you do a lot of your training at home by way of a fingerboard, then the "moving hang" is your ticket to getting a decent local aerobic endurance

Fingerboard "moving hang" with feet on the wall.

workout. Yes, this is an exceedingly boring way to train, and you should take every opportunity to train at a climbing gym instead. Still, a motivated climber can do a lot of beneficial training at home, including antagonist training, mobility work, generalized aerobic training, and fingerboard training, the latter of which is as specific as home training gets outside of having a climbing wall.

As the name implies, moving hangs involve circulating your hands around the board in a semi-continuous fashion for several minutes while keeping your feet fixed on a chair (or footholds fastened to the wall) to de-load your body and reduce the intensity as needed. It helps to visualize being on an actual rock climb as you hang, pinch, pull, and cross-through in a climbing-like way. When you start to get pumped, move onto the jug holds for a brief shakeout before proceeding with more "climbing." Continue in this way for three to six minutes, being sure to stay in the aerobic training zone of between 5 and 8.5 (figure 8.3). Do this right and you will get a moderate pump, but not a deep, painful pump (a sign you're training anaerobic capacity, not the aerobic system). Do three to six moving hangs with a climb-rest ratio of between 2:1 and 1:1. Consider doing some core or antagonist training during the rest periods.

CAMPUS BOARD "HAND PLAY"

This exercise is basically the same as the moving hangs described above except that it's performed on a campus board. It's important to note that this is a feet-on campus exercise, so you'll need to place your feet on a chair or on wooden strips or climbing holds bolted onto the wall below. It's important to recognize that this is not a dynamic exercise, so it's in no way like the campus board exercises used to develop contact strength. The goal here is aerobic endurance training by way of easy to moderate hand movements around the board and liberal use of shakeouts from the largest holds available. Depending how much body weight is shifted onto the feet, you should be able to "hand play" around the campus board for at least three to five minutes. Keep the pump under control, and step off the board before attaining a deep, painful pump—a sign of cellular acidosis as a result of anaerobic energy production becoming predominant. Err on the side of too little pump and shorter sets, rather than developing deep fatigue and the need for longer rests. Do four to six sets with nearly equal periods of climbing and resting.

THRESHOLD INTERVALS ON A TREADWALL OR BOULDERING WALL

A Treadwall is an expensive piece of equipment, but to a climber-for-life type (like me) it's worth every penny. Depending on the size of holds used and the amount of weight added via weight belt (if any), a Treadwall can be effectively used to train anaerobic and aerobic power (via brief, intense intervals lasting less than twenty seconds), anaerobic capacity and the lactic system (hard, pumpy intervals lasting thirty seconds to two minutes), or the aerobic energy system by way of longer (three to six minutes) moderate-intensity intervals with equal or shorter rest periods. The focus here, of course, is the latter application of training local aerobic capacity. If you don't have access to a Treadwall, you can also execute the following training protocol on a bouldering wall.

As with all the previous exercises in this section, the fundamental requirement is to climb mainly in the aerobic training zone—that is, between 5 and 8.5 (see figure 8.3). A steep Treadwall or bouldering wall (more than 30 degrees past vertical) may make this a challenging endeavor, however, in which case you'll need to use large, juggy holds and frequent shakeouts. End a climbing interval early (say at three minutes) rather than push deeply into the anaerobic zone—if you get a painful pump, experience shortness of breath, and need to fight to stay on the wall, then you're well beyond the target training zone. If there's one liability to owning a Treadwall or home bouldering wall, it's the ease of use (and overuse) and the difficult-to-resist tendency to always climb into the anaerobic zone. Climbers who succumb in this way inevitably end up getting lackluster results (despite all their hard training) and often end up victims of overtraining syndrome.

As you can probably surmise by now, the threshold interval protocol is to climb a series of moderate-intensity intervals lasting three to five minutes. The ideal training intensity is between a 7 and 8.5 out of 10 on the RPE scale—this puts you right at the anaerobic threshold, where the aerobic system is taxed to its limit. Do four to eight intervals with a 1:1 climb-to-rest ratio. Err on the side of too little pump and only a few sets rather than push it too hard, for too long, and acquire too deep of a pump.

Threshold interval training on a Brewer's Ledge Treadwall.

ROUTE CLIMBING INTERVALS

This is by far the best local aerobic training protocol if you're lucky enough to have membership at a large climbing gym. You will need to exert self-control in not getting drawn into climbing for performance—the goal here, as with all the aerobic training exercises, is to engage in sustained climbing that yields just a light to moderate pump. This is an excellent partner exercise, so enlist someone who also understands the value of doing a high volume of moderate climbing. Take equal turns climbing and belaying and you'll have a nice 1:1 climb-to-rest ratio.

To maintain a proper intensity level, choose routes that are two to four number grades below your limit. Accordingly, if you are a 5.12 redpoint climber it's best to train only on routes in the 5.8 to 5.10+ range—yes, these routes will seem really easy, but the training goal is to climb lots of volume and never get more than a moderate pump. Check your hard-climber ego at the door and assume a new mind-set and mission—to climb three times as many pitches as anyone else in the gym! To do this, you'll likely need to climb twenty or more toprope or lead climbs. By keeping the routes easy and the pump "light," both you and your partner should be able to complete between six and twelve routes per hour, depending on length. If you develop a deep muscular pump or labored breathing, immediately move onto easier routes rather than allow your training focus to shift into the anaerobic zone.

Daniel Woods on the first ascent of one of the world's hardest boulder problems, The Process (V16), Buttermilks, California. DAVID CLIFFORD

CHAPTER NINE

Pull-Muscle and Power Training

You have a finite amount of time and energy to dedicate to training—invest wisely!

While the previous chapter provided explicit details on strengthening your fingers' grip on the rock, the following pages will divulge more than twenty exercises for strengthening the important pulling muscles of the arms and torso. Specifically, you will learn how to train for greater strength, power, and endurance in the muscles that both enable upward movement and help facilitate the static postural positions needed to advance hand and foot engagement.

According to the Principle of Specificity, training gains in strength, power, and local endurance will transfer favorably to climbing only if the exercise is markedly similar in direction of force application, movement patterns, and body position. Based on this principle we can dismiss the common proposition that CrossFit training or bodybuilding exercises are useful for improving rock climbing performance. (These training strategies are certainly legitimate for improving general conditioning and "getting in shape," but they are not valid as a primary method of training for climbing.) Yes, I do advocate limited use of common barbell exercises—bench press, deadlift, and various dumbbell exercises—for the purpose of antagonist, stabilizer, and posterior chain training, but I do not endorse spending long hours pumping iron or doing vast amounts of other nonspecific training. The bottom line: You have a finite amount of time and energy to dedicate to training, and so you must invest your time wisely—climbing-specific exercises and actual climbing are where the money is.

In chapter 8 I set forth increasing finger strength as the training-for-climbing prime directive. In this chapter on pull-muscle training, I will likewise stress the importance of increasing maximum pulling strength and power. The standard pull-up, performed with a palms-away grip on a bar, has long been a staple exercise for climbers, and the maximum number of pull-ups performed in a single set is often (incorrectly) viewed as the best measure of pulling strength (see the "Self-Testing Pull-Muscle Strength, Power, and Endurance" sidebar). Upon reaching a modest proficiency at doing pull-ups, however, effective training—and long-term gains in strength—requires more advanced exercises that involve greater resistance than body weight and demand higher rates of force development. Fortunately for you, the pages that follow will detail more than twenty highly specific and effective exercises for increasing your pulling power, lock-off strength, and pull-muscle endurance. Let's get started!

Maximum-Strength Exercises

American free-climbing legend Tony Yaniro famously pointed out that "if you cannot pull through a single hard move, then you have nothing to endure." So it's with this sentiment that you must resolve to acquire higher and higher levels of maximum strength with each passing training cycle and climbing season. Not only will greater absolute

Self-Testing Pull-Muscle Strength, Power, and Endurance

I'm often asked, "What is the best metric of pull-muscle strength?" Beyond a modest level of climbing fitness (i.e., being able to do only ten or fewer pull-ups), the body weight pull-up is not a good measure of strength; in fact, the maximum number of pull-ups you can do in a single set is a better measure of pull-muscle endurance. For the typical intermediate to advanced climber, then, the best metric of maximum strength is how much weight you can add to your body in doing a pull-up. Here are six pull-muscle tests to track your level of pull-muscle strength, power, and endurance—use them at the beginning and end of a training cycle, or about once quarterly, to track your training gains.

Maximum-strength test #1: What is the most weight you can add and still do a compete pull-up? Clip free weights to the belay loop of your harness, and increase in ten-pound increments to determine the maximum load. The drawback of this test is the large amount of weight needed to accurately test an advanced climber (likely in excess of one hundred pounds).

Maximum-strength test #2: Similar to the previous test except that you're testing to determine the maximum weight you can add in doing five complete pull-ups. (This may take a few workouts to figure out via trial and error.)

Power test #1: A timed twenty-foot gym rope climb is my preferred test of pulling power. Use a 1.5-inch-thick gym rope and time how long it takes to climb to the top—this usually requires between six and twelve arm pulls, depending on your strength and power. Have a partner time from "first movement" (from a standing position with flat feet) until you touch the clasp at the top of the rope. Advanced climbers can begin from a sitting position.

Power test #2: The time needed to ladder up the 1-3-5-7 rungs on a campus board. Use the largest-size rungs and begin with both hands on the first rung. The stopwatch begins on first movement and ends when both hands match on rung 7.

Power test #3: Beginning with both hands on the lowest large rung of a campus board, pull-up hard (no feet) and slap as high as possible with one hand (but do not engage a high rung with the slapping arm at full extension). Do three slaps with your dominant hand and measure the distance from the top of the starting rung to your high point.

Strength-Endurance test: After a throughout warm-up, do one maximal set of pull-ups—how many full repetitions can you do before failure? Each pull-up should begin with nearly straight arms (but not completely straight with shrugged shoulders) and end with your chin above the bar.

strength help you pull harder single moves, but it will also contribute toward higher power output and improved endurance.

As in building maximum finger strength, training to increase pulling and lock-off strength requires high-intensity stimulus that will produce rapid muscular failure. This is a vastly different workout strategy from that described for building anaerobic endurance (as detailed later in this chapter). Revisit the exercise physiology presented in chapter 5 if you need clarification of the ideal protocols for training maximum strength, power, and endurance. Described below are seven exercises for training maximum strength—employ just two or three of these exercises in any given workout.

Table 9.1 Classification of Pull-Muscle Exercises

	Exercise	Beginner	Intermediate	Advanced
Maximum Strength (anaerobic alactic)	Weighted Pull-Ups	X	X	X
	Square Pull-Ups		X	X
	Steep Wall "Lock-Offs"		X	X
	System Wall "Isolations"	X	X	X
	Uneven-Grip Pull-Ups		X	X
	One-Arm Lock-Offs			X
	One-Arm Pull-Ups			X
Power (anaerobic alactic)	Big Move Bouldering	X	X	X
	Gym Rope Climbing (no feet)		X	X
	Campus Board Laddering (skipping rungs)		X	X
	Boulder Campusing (aka Monkey Business)		X	X
	Clap Pull-Ups			X
	Campus Board Double Dynos			X
Power-Endurance (glycolytic/ anaerobic lactic)	Pull-Up Intervals	X	X	X
	Frenchies	X	X	X
	"Square Dance"		X	X
	Bouldering 4x4s		X	X
	Campus Board "Ladder Laps"		X	X
Local Aerobic Endurance (aerobic/oxidative)	Roped Route Intervals	X	X	X
	Threshold Intervals		X	X
	Concept 2 Rowing Machine	X	X	X
	Endless Rope Machine	X	X	X

WEIGHTED PULL-UPS

Upon being able to do about eight solid body weight pull-ups, you will need to add resistance to continue training maximum strength in the pulling muscles—the best way to do this is simply by adding weight via a weight belt, weighted vest, or by hanging free weights from the belay loop of your harness.

After doing a thorough warm-up, including some basic mobility and stability exercises, the maximum-strength-training protocol is to do three to six sets of weighted pull-ups with enough added weight to make doing five pull-ups challenging. Explode upward as fast as possible with each repetition, but lower in a slower, more controlled fashion and stop just short of a straight-arm hang position (which must be avoided when training with added weight). Rest for at least three minutes between sets.

Melissa Le Neve pull-up training with free weights suspended from the belay loop of her harness. CLAUDIA ZEIGLER

If you are new to weighted pull-ups, you will discover that adding just ten or twenty pounds makes for a much more difficult pull-up—you will also discover remarkable gains in pull-up strength in just a few weeks of training! Long term, the amount of weight you need to add may be upward of 50 percent of body weight to make doing five pull-ups a near-maximal exercise. I suggest using a training weight that would allow just seven repetitions if you were doing a single maximal set of weighted pull-ups.

SQUARE PULL-UP

This pull-up variation is a bit more climbing specific since it emphasizes lock-off positions and uneven arm force application. Grip a pull-up bar with hands about 50 percent wider than shoulder width, and begin by doing a pull-up to reach the top position. While maintaining the top position, shift to the left by pulling your left hand in against your chest as you push your right hand out to the side as if trying to straighten your arm. Now lower slowly until your left elbow reaches an angle of about 120 degrees, and then immediately shift your torso rightward to a position under the right hand so that the right elbow is now flexed at an angle of about 120 degrees. Pull-up to the top position with your right hand locked off against the right side of your chest and your left arm extended in a nearly straight position. Hold the top position, with chin over the bar, and shift left until your left hand is once again touching your chest—this completes the square pull-up, but keep going!

Do two sets of four to six square pull-ups with a three-minute rest between sets. Do the second set in the opposite direction, and add weight when you find doing two sets of six repetitions to be easy.

How to Pull-Up Train If You Can't Do a Pull-Up?

Pull-ups are the most obvious exercise for a climber to do, but how can you effectively train pull-ups if you can barely eke out one or two repetitions? Here are three excellent assisted pull-up variations that will help you advance to body weight and hypergravity pull-up training in just a few weeks or months.

Pull-Up Negatives: Use a chair, box, or other object to step up into the top position of a pull-up with your chin above the bar and hands pulled in tightly near your armpits. Now step off the chair and lower as slowly as possible—subvocalize a five-second count, and try to make the pull-up negative last this long. Upon reaching the bottom position, step back up to the top position and do another slow pull-up negative. Do a total of three sets of five repetitions. Rest for three minutes between sets.

Aided Pull-Ups: The strategy here is to do three sets of five pull-ups with the aid of a training partner or Theraband removing a portion of your body weight. With a Theraband, simply girth hitch one end over the middle of the pull-up bar and then place your feet through the other end. Alternatively, you can have a partner stand behind you and lift around your waist to remove enough weight so that you can do five pull-ups. Either way, pause for a moment at the top position, and then lower to a two-second count. Do three sets of five repetitions with at least a three-minute rest between sets. Use this exercise three days per week, and soon you'll be doing pull-ups on your own!

Counterweight Pull-Ups: Using a pulley system and counterweights clipped into the belay loop of your harness, do three sets of five to eight pull-ups with a three-minute rest between sets.

Regardless of your chosen technique for assisted pull-up training, it's essential to use proper technique and to do concurrent training of the rotator cuff and scapular stabilizers. Although you can eventually advance to doing pull-ups with your hands at different widths apart, you should initially do them with hands shoulder width apart—and always with a palms-away grip. **Warning:** Avoid bottoming out in the straight-arm position between repetitions, and never hang with straight arms and shrugged shoulders to rest between repetitions.

Square pull-up progression.

STEEP WALL "LOCK-OFFS"

This is an excellent exercise for developing lock-off strength and climbing-specific core stiffness. You can do steep wall lock-offs on an overhanging bouldering wall, a HIT Strip or System Wall, or a campus board with foot strips. Begin with matched hands on a pair of good holds (or large campus rung) and both feet on a toe board or footholds, and then pull into a tight lock-off position with one hand and reach as high as possible with the other hand. Touch the wall for two seconds with the free hand while maintaining a solid lock-off with the other—twist and stiffen your body as needed to maximize your reach. Return to the starting position and immediately pull into a tight lock-off with the other arm. Again, reach as high as possible with the free hand and touch the wall for two seconds. Do not engage any holds with the "touch hand." Continue for a total of four to six lock-offs on each side. Do two to five sets with a rest of three minutes between sets. Increase difficulty by using a steeper wall or adding a weight belt, but not by using smaller handholds—the focus here is training lock-off strength, not finger flexor strength.

1. Beginning position.

2. Lock-off position.

SYSTEM WALL "ISOLATION"

The utility of a System Wall is in being able to isolate and fatigue a specific combination of grip and arm positions while performing actual climbing movements and body positions. While the fingerboard and campus board are better tools for training of finger strength and strength-endurance, the System Wall excels at building pull-muscle strength across a wide range of arm positions. With a well-equipped System Wall, you can isolate a variety of undercling and side-pull positions, pulling and twisting Gaston moves, and compression moves between widely spaced holds. Ultimately, your imagination is the only limitation when it comes to training unique arm and body positions. You can even create a System Wall isolation that mimics a crux move on some outdoor project you're working—that's functional training of the highest degree!

Given access to a good System Wall, you may want to reduce time spent bouldering (by ten to twenty minutes) in order to dedicate a little time to isolation training. While you can certainly use small (difficult) handholds to train finger strength on a System Wall, it my belief that it's best to use a fingerboard to train the fingers and a System Wall to train arm positions, body positions, compression, and other specific movements. Each System Wall session should have a focus—what arm and body positions seem to be your weakness on the rock? For many climbers huge functional gains are possible via System Wall Training that isolates long reaches from undercling and side-pull positions, extending reach off a lock-off hold (by pressing it down), twist-locking acutely and deeply for maximum reach, and compressing and slapping up a series of distant holds. Pick two or three different System Wall isolations and do three to five identical repetitions of each, taking only a brief rest in between.

Strive for tight body positions and full extension with each repetition—there's little benefit to doing incomplete movements with sloppy technique and poor body position. Be sure to perform identical isolations on each side of your body. Increase resistance by doing longer moves or by adding weight (via weight belt) rather than using holds so small and poor that you can't bear down and fully recruit the core and pulling muscles that you intend to train.

Kris Hampton training hard on his System Wall.
KRIS HAMPTON COLLECTION

UNEVEN-GRIP PULL-UPS

This excellent exercise develops one-arm and lock-off strength. As the name implies, doing uneven-grip pull-ups requires a setup that offsets one hand twelve to twenty-four inches lower than the other. You can do this by simply looping a sling or knotted rope over a pull-up bar or extending one of a pair of free-floating rings or similar setup.

It's best to learn the exercise with an opposing grip—do this by standing under the pull-up bar facing longways with the high hand gripping the

1. *Starting positon (top).*
2. *Top position—hold for one second (bottom).*

bar palm inward (thumb pointing backward) and the low hand gripping the sling with a deep two-finger pocket grip or pinching the knotted rope. From this bottom position initiate upward movement by pulling with both hands; however, focus on pulling hardest with the higher hand. As you ascend past mid-height, begin pushing downward with the low hand to aid the pulling of the high hand. Finish by pulling the bar down along the side of your head to achieve a tight lock-off position. Hold the top position for one second before beginning a controlled descent. Stop short of reaching a straight-arm position and immediately begin the next repetition. Do three to five reps, then dismount and rest for a minute before doing three to five reps with the other hand gripping the bar. Perform two or three sets on each side.

Begin uneven-grip pull-up training with your hands offset by just twelve inches; increase the displacement when you can do more than five reps. Advanced climbers can do this exercise with both hands in a palms-away grip position.

ONE-ARM LOCK-OFFS

The ability to hold a steady one-arm lock-off is vital for hard bouldering and roped climbing. This exercise is obviously very specific to this need, but it does demand a high level of base strength for proper execution. If you cannot hold a solid one-arm lock-off, it would be best to train with weighted pull-ups or uneven-grip pull-ups rather than attempt this exercise. Twice-a-week training with one-arm lock-offs is a perfect gateway exercise to eventually being able to do a one-arm pull-up.

You can do one-arm lock-offs using a pull-up bar or a single free-floating ring. Begin with hands side-by-side and in opposing grips (palms facing each other). The beginning position for each repetition is with hands extended overhead, but not completely straight. Let's train the right arm first: Pull up with both arms to reach a high lock-off position with the bar or ring pulled in tightly near your

One-arm lock-off.

right cheek. Immediately let go with the left hand and hold the static lock-off position as long as possible—when you begin to lose the lock-off, lower as slowly as possible, but do grab back on with the other hand before your elbow reaches an angle of 120 degrees. Immediately commence with another pull-up, this time locking-off in the top position with the other arm. Do two repetitions on each side. Rest for two or three minutes before doing another set or two on each side. **Warning:** Be sure to lower in a slow, controlled manner and never drop forcefully into a fully straight-arm position.

ONE-ARM PULL-UPS

The one-arm pull-up is a benchmark exercise for elite climbers. Amazingly, some of the world's top climbers can do more than five consecutive one-arm pulls (really hard), and a few ridiculously strong individuals can do a one-arm pull-up while holding twenty pounds (or more) in their free hand! This is obviously not an exercise to rush into training—doing so tempts injury and may be demoralizing—but it is worth playing around with if you've been climbing at a high level for a few years and already possess a high level of base pull-muscle and stabilizer strength. If you can do a few weighted pull-ups with 50 percent of body weight added and a solid one-arm lock-off, then you are likely ready.

First you'll want to learn a one-arm pull-up using a palms-inward grip and by pulling in a neutral position with the bar finishing in a lock-off near the cheek of the pulling arm side. Over time you'll learn to do a one-arm pull-up with the palm facing away and the bar finishing below your chin. The best transition into one-arm pull-up training is by way of a counterweight pulley system; this way you can gradually reduce the amount of counterweight help over the course of many weeks of training. (Alternatively, you can stand in a Thera-band looped over the pull-up bar—stand using the leg opposite the pulling hand.) Either way, do three to five one-repetition sets of aided one-arm pull-ups, using the least amount of counterweight support as possible. Rest for two or three minutes between each one-rep set.

When you sense you are ready to attempt your first body weight one-arm pull-up, I suggest you stand on a box that allows you to begin with just the slightest bend in your pulling arm. Before initiating the one-arm pull-up, it's vital that you tighten your shoulder muscles (engage the rotator cuff and scapular stabilizers), and then think about screwing your forearm inward (supination) as you perform the pull-up motion. Concentrate on pulling the bar down past your cheek (working arm side) and finish in a tight lock-off position—hold a solid finish like a champ, and then take pride in having done your first one-arm pull-up!

Power-Training Exercises

When climbers talk about power, they are typically referring to the need to make quick, strenuous reaches or lunges on steep terrain. This type of movement is the stuff of steep sport climbs and V-hard boulder problems.

Physiologically, your ability to move powerfully is a function of how fast muscle motor units can be called into play and how well they are trained to fire in unison. Effective power training, then, must target the nervous system with fast, dynamic motions that are far different from the strength- and endurance-training exercises covered in this chapter. Inherent to power training are high dynamic force loads, which provide beneficial training stimuli but also threaten the joints and tendons of the fingers, arms, and shoulders. For this reason the following power-training exercises are inappropriate for beginner or recently injured climbers, as well as anyone lacking the maturity and discipline to follow the training and rest guidelines.

Adequate rest between power exercises and workout sessions is also crucial. As a rule you should not engage in more than two power workouts per week. Furthermore, individual workouts should be relatively brief: Training intensity and speed are more important than training volume. In fact, performing a high volume of power-training exercises (or training power in a state of high fatigue) is a prescription for injury. Constantly remind yourself that it's exercise quality, not quantity, that matters most in power training.

BIG-MOVE BOULDER PROBLEMS

If you are an avid boulderer, then you are likely already using this training strategy. The goal is to climb several six- to ten-move boulder problems that involve numerous powerful arm movements between relatively good holds. The ideal boulder will feature mainly positive medium- to large-size holds that will not challenge your grip strength, and lengthy reaches that demand tight lock-offs, powerful hand movements, and an occasional all-out dynamic move or lunge. When you find the right route, try to send it five times with about a three-minute rest between ascents. Strive to refine your movement and improve climbing economy with each successive ascent—this way you'll learn to climb more accurately and effectively through strenuous movements, despite growing fatigue. If you own a home wall, consider setting a few moderately difficult, big-move boulder problems that you can climb a few times each and every workout.

GYM ROPE CLIMBING

Gym rope and inverted ladder climbing is one of the very best ways to develop awesome upper-body power. Legendary boulderer John Gill used rope climbing as a staple training exercise, and years later John Bachar popularized inverted ladder training among climbers. The Bachar Ladder, as it became known, was a popular training exercise of high-end climbers throughout the 1980s. Since the advent of indoor climbing walls and the campus board, however, rope and ladder climbing have fallen largely out of use. Still, serious climbers would be wise to incorporate some arm-only gym rope climbing into their training program—"campusing" up a 1.5-inch-thick gym rope is, in my opinion, one of the best arm-power-training exercises a climber can do!

After a lengthy warm-up of pull-ups and mild upper-body stretching, begin from either a standing or sit-down (harder) position and grip the rope with both arms at near full extension. Begin with an explosive two-arm pull and then continue upward as fast as possible using quick, crisp arm-over-arm movements. The goal is to maintain smooth, steady upward movement for the duration of the ascent, although it may take some time to develop the necessary arm strength and power. Upon reaching the top, slowly lower back down with controlled arm-over-arm movements—do not drop down in a fast, jerky manner that will

Gym rope training in the Hörst home!

shock-load the elbows and shoulders. If you sense a loss of control, in ascending or descending, immediately clamp down on the rope with your feet rather than risk falling.

Perform three to eight (an elite alactic-power workout) total laps on the rope, always taking at least a three-minute rest between ascents. Optimal adaptations (and gains) to power training come from high-quality, full-speed efforts—think of each ascent as a sprint! Therefore, it's better to do four full-speed sprint ascents, rather than eight low-powered "jogs" up the rope.

Two technical tips: Think about pulling the engaged hand down to meet your upper chest and, in reaching up, grab the rope with your arm less than fully extended (an elbow angle of between 120 and 150 degrees is good, the latter being much harder).

CAMPUS BOARD "LADDERING"

Chapter 8 presented campus laddering up small holds and without rung skips as an effective method of training contact strength. In the context of training pulling power, however, the effective approach is using larger rungs and longer, more powerful pulls. Most campus boards have at least three different-size rungs (you want to use the largest), with each stack numbered from 1 to 8, and perhaps higher.

The most basic ladder sequence is 1-3-5-7, beginning with both hands on rung #1 and ending with both hands on rung #7 (figure 9.1). As with all power-training exercises, it's essential to move as fast as possible. In the case of a 1-3-5-7 ladder sequence, it should take but a few seconds to make the ascent. Think of this exercise as a sprint—if you need to pause or break sequence, then you're either too tired or too weak to be doing this exercise. Begin by doing just three sets per workout, but build toward a maximum of ten sets over months and years. Rest for at least three minutes between sets, so that you can make a quality effort with each alactic sprint up the board. Elite climbers, however, can train aerobic power by decreasing the rest interval to just thirty seconds between sets.

A more advanced ladder sequence is 1-4-7, although this isn't something you should be in a rush to train. If you regularly fail in attempting the 1-4-7 sequence—or if you engage the #4 or #7 rungs with fully extended arms—then you simply aren't strong enough to do this exercise. **Warning:** Regularly engaging campus rungs with a fully extended arm and an elevated (shrugged) shoulder will quickly lead to shoulder pain and, perhaps, injury. Please heed my advice on this—I can name

Figure 9.1 Campus Board 1-3-5-7 Ladder

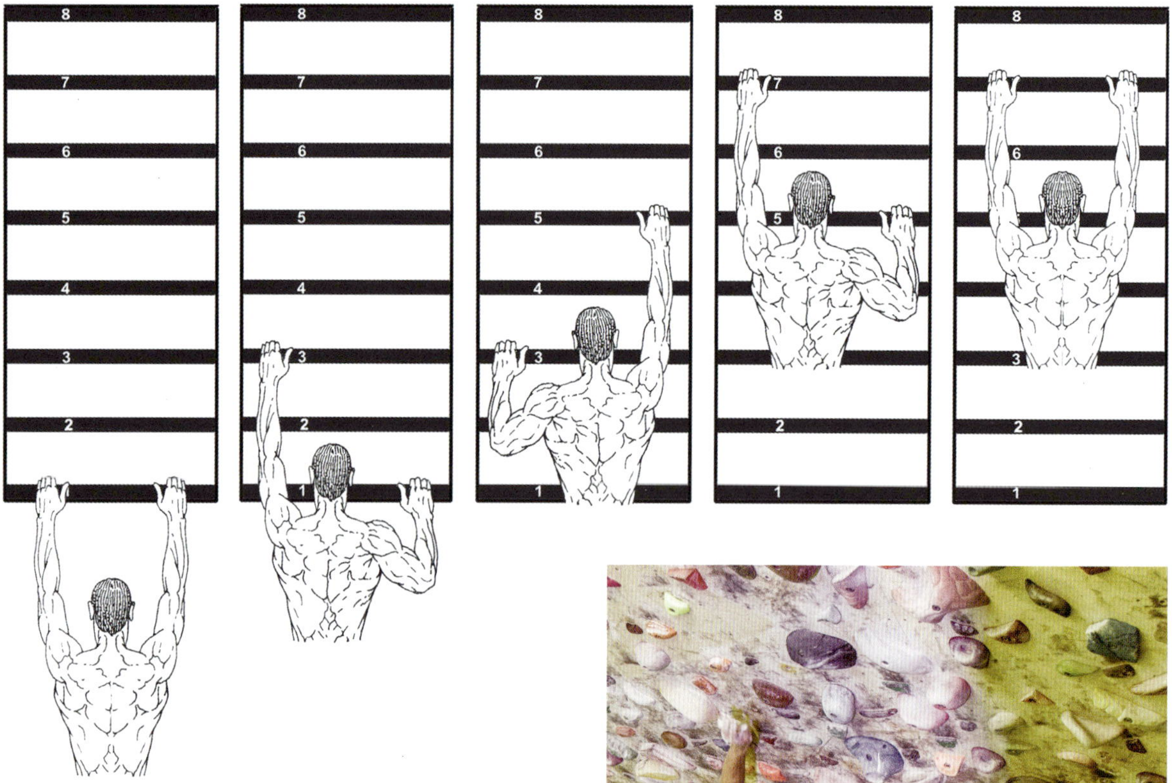

more than a few climbers who have wrecked their shoulders due to overuse and misuse of a campus board!

BOULDER CAMPUSING

Boulder campusing is a popular indoor training exercise among advanced climbers—it's also a heck of a lot of fun if you're strong enough to do it right! The goal is to ascend a section of overhanging wall by simply climbing hand-over-hand with no aid from the feet. This exercise is similar to campus laddering, and the same injury warnings apply: Boulder campusing with straight arms and shrugged shoulders will get you injured, likely sooner than later.

They call it "Monkey Business" at Germany's famous Café Kraft gym. Here Alex Megos exhibits excellent boulder campusing technique—no straight arms allowed! HANNES HUCH

Select three- to eight-move routes with medium- to large-size holds that you can engage with an open-hand grip. When you find a boulder with the perfect hold combination, do it three to five times with about a three-minute rest between ascents. Use of good campusing technique is essential—your reaching arm must engage each hold with some observable bend in the elbow and a secured scapula. Have a friend shoot a short video of your boulder campusing, to self-assess the quality of your technique. Favor boulders with fewer moves and moderate reaches to ensure use of good campusing technique.

CLAP PULL-UPS

The clap pull-up is an excellent power-building exercise and a good alternative if you don't have access to a campus board. The huge training benefit of a clap pull-up is that you accelerate all the way to the bar, whereas a standard pull-up requires a deceleration into the bar. This is a difficult exercise, however, and it may take some time to develop the power and timing to release the bar long enough to make the clap.

A good learning progression is, first, to simply release and re-grab the bar without moving your hands at the top of each pull-up. Next, try to release the bar and touch index fingers together before re-grabbing the bar. It helps to lean your head and shoulders back slightly and think about pulling the bar to your chest with each repetition—of course, you must accelerate into the top position and release the bar just before the deadpoint (i.e., the moment of stillness at the top of the movement). Your long-term training goal is two to three sets of three to eight repetitions. Rest for at least three minutes between sets.

CAMPUS BOARD DOUBLE DYNOS

The double dyno exercise, performed on small rungs, was described in chapter 8 as an advanced finger-training method for developing contact strength (page 109). When done using larger rungs and greater flight distance (skipping rungs), the double dyno trains pull-muscle power in addition to contact strength.

Double dynos with rung skips is a most difficult—and potentially injurious—campus training exercise. This is an advanced-only exercise!

Using the largest stack of rungs, begin hanging from one of the middle rungs (say #3), with slightly flexed arms and engaged shoulders. Simultaneously let go with both hands and drop to catch the next lower rung with flexed arms and engaged shoulders. After a brief amortization phase of energy absorption in the pull muscles, explode upward with both hands to catch one rung above the starting rung. This is one full repetition, but don't stop! Without hesitation, drop down to again catch the next lower rung, and then explode back upward to catch two rungs higher. Continue for three or four repetitions. The sequence of rungs engaged, as described above, is 3-2-4-3-5-4-6-5-7. A more advanced double dyno sequence is 3-2-4-2-4-2-4-2-4. Do one to five (advanced) sets with at least a three-minute rest between each set.

As with all power-training exercises, high-speed and high-quality movements are paramount to getting the most out of your double dyno training. The turnaround time in "rebounding" off the low rung must be less than one-half second—if you need to fight to stick the rung or pause to gather yourself, then you're either using too small a rung or you're too tired (or weak) to be doing the exercise. Please review the campus training guidelines (see the "Overview of Campus Board Training" sidebar in chapter 8).

Power-Endurance Exercises

The ability to sustain high power output for thirty seconds to two minutes is largely a function of your anaerobic capacity. More physiologically complex, however, is the capability to prevail through many intermittent bursts of high power output, which depends on the aggregate development of anaerobic power, anaerobic capacity, and aerobic power. (Return to chapter 5 for a review of exercise physiology behind effective training of these energy systems.) Most climbers refer to the above-mentioned traits as power-endurance—an okay term for the ability to sustain powerful locomotion with the arms, although strength-endurance is a better term in reference to the fatigue resistance of the finger flexors. But I digress.

The focus of this section is training to increase power capacity in the larger pulling muscles, which will provide what you'll perceive to be better power-endurance in climbing. While actual climbing, be it a bouldering 4x4 or a series of short, pumpy climbs, is obviously the most specific training method, there are a few isolation exercises that will directly target the pulling muscles of the arms and torso. Regular use of these exercises—twice weekly is ideal for most climbers—will yield significant gains in this area. Of course, you don't want to train with these grueling exercises too often or without a break every few weeks, as intensive training of the anaerobic lactic (glycolytic) system can often lead to overtraining and performance declines. Consult chapter 10 for guidance on periodizing your training and the need to occasionally taper and break from extensive gym training.

PULL-UP INTERVALS

This is a great exercise that trains the pull muscles to persevere through the fatiguing effects of acidosis (and other by-products of anaerobic glycolysis), as well as strengthens the recuperative influence of the aerobic system (aerobic power). The training goal is to complete twenty pull-up intervals, each exactly one minute in length, composed of a set number of pull-ups performed and a rest period for the time remaining in each interval. For example, if you are doing five pull-ups per interval, it may take ten seconds to complete the five pull-ups, and thus you have the remaining fifty seconds to rest before beginning the next interval (see table 9.2). Use a stopwatch or timing app to stay on a tight schedule for all twenty intervals.

Train using a pull-up bar or the largest holds on a fingerboard. Increase the difficulty by adding one pull-up per interval, rather than using smaller handholds or adding weight. Conversely, reduce the

Table 9.2 Sample Pull-Up Interval Protocol

Interval	# of Pull-ups	Approx. Work/Rest	Interval	# of Pull-ups	Approx. Work/Rest
1	5	10/50 secs.	11	5	10/50 secs.
2	5	10/50 secs.	12	5	10/50 secs.
3	5	10/50 secs.	13	5	10/50 secs.
4	5	10/50 secs.	14	5	10/50 secs.
5	5	10/50 secs.	15	5	10/50 secs.
6	5	10/50 secs.	16	5	10/50 secs.
7	5	10/50 secs.	17	5	10/50 secs.
8	5	10/50 secs.	18	5	10/50 secs.
9	5	10/50 secs.	19	5	10/50 secs.
10	5	10/50 secs.	20	5	10/50 secs.

number of pull-ups per set, as needed, to complete the full twenty-minute interval workout. This is an excellent home training exercise, requiring only a pull-up bar, for individuals without a home wall or easy access to a climbing gym.

FRENCHIES

While it's been more than twenty years since I first coined the name "Frenchies" and popularized this exercise in my book *Flash Training*, this exercise is

1. Lock off at top position.

2. Lock off at 90 degrees.

3. Lock off at 120 degrees.

no less grueling and effective in developing power-endurance in the large pulling muscles.

Begin with a single pull-up (palms away, hands shoulder width apart) and lock off in the top position for a four-second count. Now lower to the bottom (starting position) and pull up to the top again, but this time immediately lower yourself halfway down to an arm angle of 90 degrees. Hold a solid lock-off here for a four-second count, then again return to the bottom position. Immediately crank another pull-up, but this time lower to a lock-off with an arm angle of about 120 degrees—hold this lock-off for four seconds before returning to the bottom position. This sequence of three lock-offs constitutes a single cycle, and it will take about fifteen seconds (assuming it takes one second for each pull-up)—but don't stop yet! Continue on with another cycle (or more) until you can no longer endure the pain and fatigue, or hold a four-second lock-off. Record the number of cycles (or partial cycles) in your training notebook.

Each set of Frenchies should last between thirty seconds (about two cycles) and ninety seconds (six cycles, which is really badass!). If you can't complete two full cycles, stand in a Theraband girth hitched to the pull-up bar or enlist a spotter to remove some body weight by lifting around your waist. Conversely, you can add a ten- or twenty-pound weight belt once you are able to do five or six full cycles in any given set. Do a total of two or four sets with a rest of at least five minutes between sets.

SQUARE DANCE

This exercise is best performed on a System Wall or campus board with foot strips. Since you'll be training pull-muscle and lock-off endurance, it's important to use large handholds so that your forearms don't pump out. The goal is to "square dance" for between forty-five seconds and ninety seconds.

The exercise is simple, albeit quite boring: Beginning with matched hands on a large low hold, pull-up with both hands and then reach up to grab a large high hold. Next, match hands on the high hold, and then immediately drop the leading hand back to the starting hold. Finish by matching both hands on the starting hold. Hang here for a few seconds, if you like, before repeating the sequence with the other hand leading the way. Keep your feet fixed on the same holds throughout the "square dance." Modulate exercise intensity by varying the distance you reach with each upward movement. Continue in this way for up to two minutes, but step off the wall before reaching complete failure. Do two to four sets with only partial recovery between each set—a work-to-rest ratio of 1:2 or 1:3 is ideal.

Campus board "square dance" using large holds and with feet on large holds or foot strip.

BOULDERING 4X4

In chapter 8 I detailed a highly effective bouldering 4x4 protocol (see table 8.8) for training strength-endurance in the finger flexor muscles. The bouldering 4x4 protocol for developing power-endurance in the pulling muscles is identical, except that you must select boulder problems with better handholds and longer, more powerful arm and body movements. The ideal boulder will demand that your large pulling muscles and core work hard, while not fatiguing the finger flexors to the point of failure. If you fail on one or more of your sixteen boulder ascents, it should be due to fatigue in the pulling muscles (a failed big move, lunge, or lock-off) and not due to failure of the finger flexors (inability to maintain your grip). Therefore, it's best to err on the side of doing routes with handholds that are too large, rather than too small, for the purpose of training power-endurance in the pulling muscles.

In my opinion, it's best to discriminate between strength-endurance training of the finger flexors and power-endurance training of the pulling muscles, instead of training them both at the same time. You can certainly train both in the same workout, but it's best not to do them at the same time. One effective approach is to do a bouldering 4x4 that targets the pulling muscles (as described above) and then, after a rest break of at least twenty minutes, do another bouldering 4x4 that targets the finger flexors (as described in chapter 8). You might conclude your workout with a couple of isolation exercises to further target power-endurance of the pulling muscles (such as a couple sets of Frenchies) and strength-endurance of the finger flexors (as in doing some fingerboard repeaters).

LADDER LAPS

This popular power-endurance exercise involves doing a few laps up and down the largest holds on a campus board. To deeply train the anaerobic lactic energy system, however, requires that you are strong enough to ladder continuously for thirty to sixty seconds. Since the goal of this exercise is to target the large pulling muscles of the arms and back (not the finger flexors), it's essential to use large handholds—ideally deep rounded edges or large sloper rails—that are easy to grip for the duration of this exercise. Strong climbers will be able to ladder

Perform ladder laps using large holds—the goal is to fatigue the pulling muscles, not the finger flexors.

No Train,
No Gain.
TREADWALL M6
WARNING: Keep Hands Out

lap the campus board with a 1-3-5-7-7-5-3-1 sequence. A somewhat easier approach is to ascend via 1-3-5-7 (skipping rungs) and then descend using every rung (7-6-5-4-3-2-1). Each up-and-down lap will take ten to fifteen seconds, so strive to do between two and four laps per set in order to reach the desired exercise duration of thirty to sixty seconds. Do two to five sets with at least a three-minute rest between sets. Advanced climbers can reduce the rest break to sixty seconds to train aerobic power (recovery ability of CP resynthesis) in addition to anaerobic capacity.

Local Endurance Training

Often overlooked in training-for-climbing programs is local aerobic endurance training. Hopefully the exercise physiology presented in chapter 5 was enough to convince you of the importance of doing some training of the aerobic system, especially if your preference is route climbing.

As detailed in chapter 8's section on aerobic training of finger flexor muscles, the critical training guideline is to climb primarily at a moderate intensity and to avoid developing a deep, painful pump. Ultimately, you want to find the threshold of the anaerobic lactic zone and strive to climb mostly just below it (in the aerobic zone) while only occasionally crossing into the low end of the anaerobic zone. By keeping your perceived exertion and exercise intensity between 5 and 8.5 on a scale of 1 to 10 (see figure 8.3), you can rest assured that you're training in the proper zone to acquire the desired adaptations.

The specific exercises to aerobically train the pulling muscles are the same as those detailed in chapter 8. Rather than rehash all the fine details here, please consult pages 192–197 for the instruction on local aerobic training via roped climbing intervals and threshold intervals.

Two other nonspecific exercises that offer a solid aerobic workout for the pulling muscles are the Concept 2 Rower and the Endless Rope machine. If you're lucky enough to have access to either one of these machines, then consider adding three sessions per week into your aerobic-training mesocycle and one aerobic maintenance/recovery session per week throughout the remainder of the year. One approach to using these machines is to exercise for three to five minutes at an intensity of 8 out of 10. Do two to four such intervals with a work-to-rest ratio of 2:1 (i.e., two minutes of rest for every four minutes of sustained exercise).

Aerobic endurance training via submaximal Treadwall intervals involving mainly large-hold climbing.

Sasha DiGiulian sending Golden (5.14b), Cathedral, Utah. CHRIS NOBLE

CHAPTER TEN

Designing Your Training Program

No matter how much you climb and how hard you try, you cannot just climb your way to someday reach your genetic potential. Climbing your best requires a rigorous, nuanced training program.

Perhaps no sport can match rock climbing for the dramatic increase in the mean level of performance of its participants in recent years. Today's average climber is capable of a standard that few climbers dreamed of achieving when I began climbing in the late 1970s. Furthermore, many weekend warriors are able to progress to the lofty levels of 5.12 and 5.13—grades that hardly existed a few decades ago. The reasons for these incredible improvements include sport-climbing tactics, improved climbing shoe technology, and, more than anything else, the advent of climbing gyms and a growing focus on climbing-specific training.

Still, there is much disagreement among climbers and coaches about the best way to train, and people frequently tell me that they are confused by the often conflicting training information published in various books and on the Internet. What's more, the occasional magazine article describing the training practices of some 5.15 pro climber, while titillating, is of little use for average climbers—it might even get them injured. Other popular generalized training approaches, such as P90X and CrossFit, are similarly red herrings for a serious climber in search of the higher grades.

For a training-for-climbing workout that makes a difference, nothing beats a climbing gym with a large bouldering area, a wide variety of toprope and lead walls, and a well-equipped training area. If there's such a facility within about a thirty-minute drive of your home, then join it! Visiting such a gym two to four days per week will enable you to engage in comprehensive training of all aspects of the climbing performance triad (skill, mind, body). Alternatively, building a home bouldering wall and training area is a wise investment if you're short on free time, due to a busy work schedule or family life, or if you live in a town without a commercial climbing gym.

Knowing what to do when you train at a climbing gym or on a home wall is what this chapter is all about. While a novice climber can steadily improve simply by going to the gym and "just climbing," intermediate and advanced climbers must engage in a more elaborate, smartly designed program that targets known performance constraints with climbing-specific exercises. No matter how much you climb and how hard you try, you can't just climb your way to someday reaching your genetic potential. The purpose of this chapter, then, is to help you craft an intelligent, safe, and effective training program given your current fitness level and climbing ability.

First, you will learn the value of premeditating your workout and how to structure your long-term program to include microcycles, mesocycles, and an annual macrocycle—employing some form of periodization is essential to making the most of your daily workouts and obtaining maximal gains season after season. The real meat of the chapter are the sections on designing a personalized training program, including sample workouts for beginner, intermediate, and advanced climbers. The chapter then concludes with coverage of important training considerations for youth, female, and over-fifty climbers—three classes of climbers uniquely equipped to excel in the vertical extreme!

Keys to an Effective Training Program

The premise of this book is that a well-informed, motivated, and mature individual can grow to climb at an exceedingly high level in just a few years. The preceding chapters provided a comprehensive look at the fundamental elements of climbing performance—mental, technical, and physical—and you've also been armed with the knowledge of an introspective self-assessment test (see chapter 2) and a basic understanding of exercise science (chapter 5). You are now in a position to execute an uncommonly effective training program—one that will help you outperform the mass of climbers who either train in a disorganized way or simply go climbing as their "training." To be effective, the program must be designed to optimize your body composition, improve flexibility and mobility, strengthen the important stabilizer and antagonist muscles, enhance stamina and recovery ability, and increase climbing-specific strength, power, and endurance (as shown in figure 10.1).

Figure 10.1 Training Goals

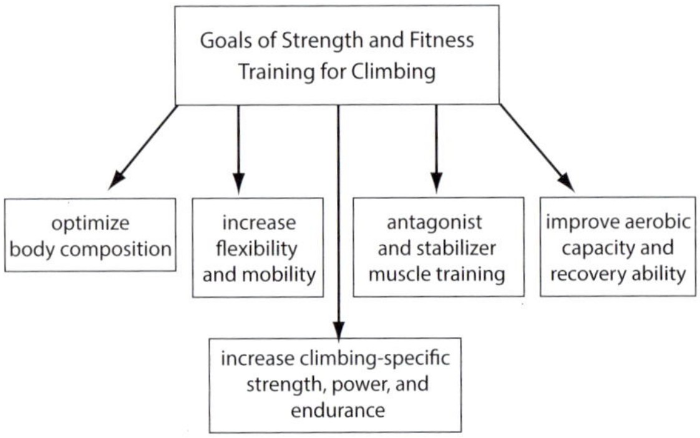

An optimal training program will address all five areas.

Premeditate Your Training

The mass of people who engage in some form of training program do so in a haphazard, ad-lib manner. There is little or no method to their madness other than to "climb a lot" and "get pumped." This unsystematic approach will produce mediocre results and can often end in injury.

Conversely, savvy climbers are proactive in designing and modifying their training program for maximum effectiveness. Wisely, the program targets their weaknesses, is modified regularly to stave off mental or physical stagnation, and is crafted in a way to produce a peaking effect for an upcoming road trip or competition.

TARGET YOUR WEAKNESSES

Several times throughout this book, I've highlighted the importance of training the weakest link. For many climbers this weakest link involves poor technique, tactics, and mental control. While the ill-informed climber trains only for more physical strength, you know that it's paramount to train your weaknesses in all aspects of the performance triad. The amount of time you dedicate to training technique, the mind, and physical strength depends on both the results of your self-assessment and your current ability level.

As a rough rule of thumb, beginner and intermediate climbers should spend a majority of their training time on improving technique, tactics, and the mental game (via climbing), while only about one-third of training time is spent doing general and sport-specific training. Advanced climbers, however, must invest much more time in the pursuit of increasing maximum strength, power, anaerobic endurance, and aerobic capacity. With already highly honed technique and mental skills, these more-veteran climbers will improve season-over-season primarily as a function of taking their physical capabilities to higher and higher levels.

REGULARLY VARY THE WORKOUT TO SUSTAIN MOTIVATION AND PHYSIOLOGICAL ADAPTATIONS

Chapter 5 explained the importance of regularly modifying your training for climbing. Sadly, many individuals go through the same basic workout ritual week after week and get frustrated with their lack of progress. Furthermore, engaging in the same weekday training or weekend at the crags will slowly quell your motivation to work hard and push beyond your current limits.

A more effective and mentally stimulating approach is to alternate your training focus every few weeks and to switch your climbing focus every few months. In the gym you can vary your training modality to target different energy systems every few workouts or weeks. Furthermore, long-term motivation, grand achievements, and the most memorable experiences in the great outdoors often come in proportion to your willingness to try new types of climbing, visit new areas, and test the limits of what is possible (given your current ability). Later in this chapter you will learn how to leverage a training mesocycle and an annual macrocycle to optimize the effectiveness of your training and help sustain improvement and psych year after year.

PRODUCE A PEAKING EFFECT FOR A ROAD TRIP OR COMPETITION

Olympic and professional athletes design their training schedules to produce a peaking phase around the time of a major event or competition. No doubt some of the best competition climbers also use peaking strategies; however, it's my observation that the majority of climbers do not deliberately plan their training in order to produce a peaking effect. Worse yet, some climbers intensify and lengthen their workouts in the days leading up to an important climb or project send day, as if they were cramming the night before an exam in school. This is a grossly counterproductive approach—when it comes to effective training, you simply can't "cram"!

Fortunately, it's really not that difficult to structure your workout schedule to peak for a road trip or to send a major project route or hardest-ever route. If you currently train and climb a few days per week, you're already doing the hardest part—the magic of peaking comes from properly tapering training volume and getting enough rest in the days leading up to the event. Details on all the above are forthcoming.

Structuring Your Workout Schedule

In this section you will learn how to manipulate your workout schedule over the time frame of several days, a few weeks or months, and a full year in order to gain optimal results. In the lexicon of sports scientists, these crucial time frames are known as the microcycle, mesocycle, and macrocycle, respectively.

MICROCYCLE

A microcycle relates to the structure, content, and volume of your training over the course of a week and for a given workout. It's essential to plan out your microcycle at least a week or two in advance—only this way can you integrate your outdoor climbing plans and your indoor training, while being sure to get enough rest days for optimal performance outside and to realize gains from your training investment. Maximizing effectiveness requires training the right things, in the right way, and in the right order during a given training session. If you've read through the preceding chapters, then you likely have a good understanding of the optimal workout hierarchy, but here's a recap:

1. Warm-up activity followed by some mobility exercises.
2. Actual climbing to develop skills and technique.
3. Performance climbing—near-maximal bouldering or roped climbing.
4. Climbing-specific exercises and energy system training.
5. Antagonist-muscle, stabilizer, core, and posterior chain training (best done on a non-climbing day).

Tapering Your Training for a Peaking Effect

For an enthusiastic, hard-training climber, nothing can be more disappointing than a poor competition performance or a "flat," weak-feeling period of outdoor climbing following a dedicated training cycle. While illness, mental stress, and poor nutrition and sleep habits sometimes contribute to lackluster performances, an inadequate end-of-cycle training taper is often to blame. If you engage in a regular three- to five-day-per-week training program, then a deliberate tapering of training activities is essential in the days leading up to a competition, road trip, or important weekend of performance climbing. Do it right and you'll be gifted with an increase in strength, power, and endurance. Conversely, a climber who tries to "cram" before an event—training more, rather than less—will likely end up feeling weak and heavy, and ultimately underperform on the rock.

The goal of tapering is to decrease accumulated fatigue from recent extensive training, while retaining hard-earned gains in strength, power, and endurance. And, if you hit the taper just right, you will likely experience a spike in maximum strength and strength/power-endurance—just want you want heading into a competition or road trip. Taper-induced adaptations that help amp up endurance include increased oxidative enzyme activity, red cell production, and supercompensation (increased intramuscular glycogen stores), whereas strength and power gains likely result from biomechanical and neural adaptations that can finally "catch up" following many weeks of intensive training.

Research shows that athletes engaged in extensive training benefit most from a one- to two-week taper. A longer tapering scheme, composed of an exponential reduction in training volume, is best for endurance athletes logging massive mileage (Bosquet 2007), whereas a shorter (one-week) taper is generally sufficient for strength/power athletes, such as climbers. Here's how to do it.

Engage in a normal training cycle (or self-directed Daily Undulating Periodization scheme) up to one week before the event or first day of performance climbing. Then, during the final pre-performance week, progressively reduce training volume while maintaining exercise/climbing intensity. For example, if your typical climbing session lasts about three hours, then five days pre-event you want to train just two hours, and then three days pre-event you'd train just one hour. The final day or two of the taper is all about active rest and mobility work—no climbing-specific training is advised.

It's important to understand that you want to taper training volume and frequency, but not intensity. Doing a small amount of maximum-strength and power training is essential during the training taper, but you mustn't overdo it. Scale down the number of sets performed (say, on the bouldering wall, fingerboard, or campus board) by 50 percent around five days pre-event and a total of 75 percent by three days pre-event. Thus, if you normally do eight sets on the campus board, you'd cut to four sets and then two sets for the workouts five and three days before the event, respectively.

To round out your pre-performance taper, strive to nail your diet and sleep just right to help create a well-rested, light, and energetic state and, ultimately, an amazing low-gravity day of climbing!

6. Generalized aerobic training (best done in a separate workout earlier in the day or on a non-climbing day).

Determining what to do (and what not to do!) each day of the week is the real art of program design. While a climbing coach can be a big help in scheduling your microcycle and mesocycle, this chapter will equip you with the knowledge to self-coach effectively. Creating a written training game plan, at least a week or two in advance, is essential, especially if you plan to do some outdoor climbing. If you desire to be 100 percent fresh for your outdoor climbing, then you need to schedule the two prior days to be free from strenuous climbing (although a modest bout of antagonist, aerobic, and ARC training is okay two days prior).

With the possible exception of some elite climbers, a typical microcycle will include just two intensive workouts—these are the most stressful workouts composed of high-load maximum-strength and power training (weighted fingerboard hangs, campus board and such) or a high volume of strength/power-endurance (which inflicts a high acid load on the muscle cells). Other workout days will include antagonist and stabilizer training, generalized and specific aerobic training, and supplemental nonmaximal climbing. At least one day per week should allow for complete rest from training; if you climb on weekends, then Friday is typically the day of complete rest.

MESOCYCLE "PERIODIZATION"

The Principle of Variation states that you must regularly vary your workouts in order to avoid long-term training plateaus, and it's in the mesocycle that you can best manipulate your schedule toward this end. You can leverage the proven strategy of periodization by changing your training focus, intensity, and volume every few days or weeks. Since adaptations to a specific type of workout (and training protocol) begin to flatten out after just two to four weeks, it's essential to somehow change your training focus and workout every few weeks. Described below are three approaches to periodizing your workouts over a mesocycle. The 4-3-2-1 and 3-2-1 cycles are best used during off-season training or in multiweek gaps between road trips, whereas the Daily Undulating Periodization (DUP) scheme is perfect for in-season use, when you are climbing outside nearly every weekend.

THE 4-3-2-1 TRAINING CYCLE

This is the training cycle that I advocate for the "average climber," and it's particularly appropriate if your climbing preference is roped routes. The first three phases of this cycle individually target each of the three energy systems (as shown in figure 10.2) and include a lot of actual climbing time to maximize skill development. The one-week fourth phase involves a "training taper," composed of reduced training/climbing volume and active recovery activities. Let's take a brief look at each phase of this cycle.

Phase 1: The four-week climbing skill and stamina phase involves, well, lots of climbing! This climbing can be done indoors, outdoors, or a combination of both. You must, however, faithfully obey an important distinction of this phase—that is, minimize time (less than 20 percent)spent maximal climbing and "projecting," and instead log lots of mileage on a wide variety of routes that are one to three number grades below your maximum ability. The result of this four-week phase will be improved technique and tactics, acquisition of new motor programs (climbing skills), and the development of local endurance and general stamina. Climbing four days a week is ideal as long as you are not climbing at your limit or to extreme levels of fatigue. You can also engage in general conditioning exercises and stamina-building activities (specific and nonspecific aerobic training) during this phase.

Phase 2: Three weeks of maximum-strength and power training is the next step in the cycle, and therefore hard bouldering, weighted exercises (e.g., fingerboard hangs and pull-ups), and reactive training are ideal choices since powerful movements and short, near-maximal efforts are hallmarks of this phase. Given the high intensity and physical stress of such training, it's important to take plenty of rest between boulder problems, exercises, and workout days. Moreover, you should avoid training hard on consecutive days, although doing some moderate-intensity aerobic "recovery" climbing and antagonist training is okay on the day after a maximum-strength/power day.

Phase 3: The two-week strength/power-endurance phase is the most fatiguing and grueling portion of the cycle. Training at moderately high intensity and with reduced rest between exercises and climbing sets will produce the telltale muscular pump and "burn." Interval training is the cornerstone method of triggering adaptations of the anaerobic lactic energy system. Chapters 8 and 9 present many exercises for improving strength-endurance in the finger flexors and power-endurance in the pulling muscles. I recommend three hard anaerobic endurance workouts per week with a fourth aerobic recovery climbing session. This grueling phase is best limited to just two weeks (three at most), since the anaerobic lactic energy system is the least trainable and the most stressful (most likely to lead to overtraining, excessive fatigue, and a drop in performance).

Phase 4: The final phase of the ten-week cycle is a training taper that allows for a peak in strength, power, and endurance to be revealed upon completion of the taper. Climbing and specific training must be limited to just two or three days and with a significant reduction in volume (see the "Tapering Your Training" sidebar). A small amount of high-intensity exercise is essential, so a brief (twenty-minute or less) bouldering session or two, a few sets on the hang board or campus board, and a couple of pump runs on a short route should be spread through the first five days of the week. The sixth and seventh days must allow for complete rest from climbing—only modest mobility work is advised.

Figure 10.2 The 4-3-2-1 Training Cycle

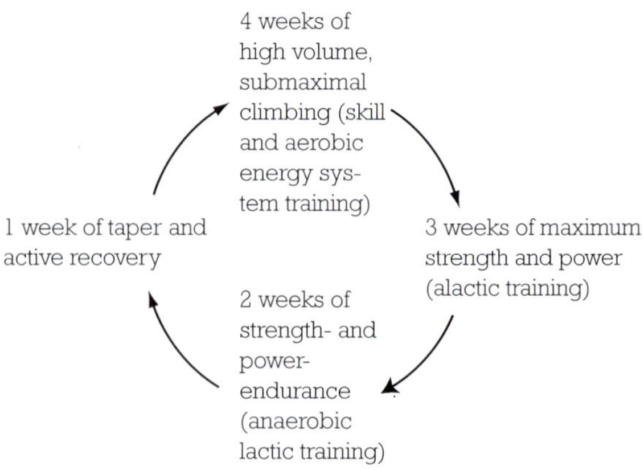

THE 3-2-1 TRAINING CYCLE

This training cycle is ideal for climbers with a preference for hard bouldering, as it deemphasizes aerobic energy system training by eliminating the first phase of the 4-3-2-1 cycle. This can also be used during the climbing on-season, given a six-week gap between significant weekend climbing trips. As shown in figure 10.3, the 3-2-1 cycle follows the same workout strategy as the aforementioned 4-3-2-1 cycle, except for the elimination of the four weeks of skill and stamina training. Still, one day of aerobic climbing (threshold or ARC) is recommended each week

Figure 10.3 The 3-2-1 Training Cycle

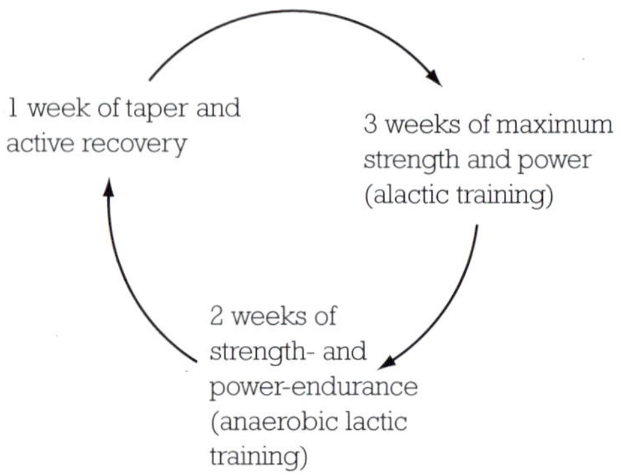

DAILY UNDULATING PERIODIZATION (DUP)

This nontraditional form of periodization is a good microcycle strategy for more-advanced individuals engaging in regular outdoor performance climbing. Weekend warriors and pro climbers alike can employ DUP to help maintain all three energy systems during a period of several weeks up to a couple of months, although this approach is unlikely to yield any significant long-term gains (which requires a more focused cycle such as the 4-3-2-1 or 3-2-1).

Here's how to do it: Each one-week DUP cycle must include one or two training or climbing sessions targeting each of the three energy systems. Therefore, if you go bouldering outdoors two days per week, it's these two sessions that serve as your two maximum-strength/power workouts for the week—the remainder of your week's training should include only one aerobic climbing session and one pumpy anaerobic capacity session. Conversely, if you engaged in two days of hard, pumpy route climbing over the weekend (two days of strength/power-endurance training), then your weekday training should involve only a maximum-strength/power (bouldering) session and a threshold or ARC aerobic climbing session. The bottom line: Regardless of your climbing preference, the goal of DUP is to engage in at least one hard workout of each energy system each week. Of course, you must also incorporate two brief sessions per week of core, antagonist, and stabilizer training—consider the latter to be mandatory.

MACROCYCLE

The macrocycle is your annual game plan of off-season training, on-season training and climbing,

Table 10.1 Sample DUP Microcycles for Boulderers and Route Climbers

Sample DUP Microcycle for Boulderers

Monday	Tuesday	Wednesday	Thursday	Friday	Saturday	Sunday
S/AA*	Aerobic Climbing & CE (AeEnd) & TC	Anaerobic Climbing (4x4s, etc.) & CE (S/P End) & TC	S/AA*	R	Hard Bouldering Outside	Hard Bouldering Outside

KEY: C=Climbing; CE (S/P End)=Strength/Power-EnduranceClimbing Exercises; CE (AeEnd)=Aerobic Endurance Climbing Exercises; S=Stabilizer & Antagonist Training; TC=Total Core & Leg Exercises; AA=Nonspecific Aerobic Activity; R=Rest (*Optional)

Sample DUP Microcycle for Route Climbers

Monday	Tuesday	Wednesday	Thursday	Friday	Saturday	Sunday
S/AA*	Aerobic Climbing, CE (AeEnd) & TC	Bouldering & TC/CE (Str/Power)	S/AA*	R	Hard Route Climbing	Hard Route Climbing

KEY: C=Climbing; CE (Str/Power)=Strength & Power Climbing Exercises; CE (AeEnd)=Aerobic Endurance Climbing Exercises; S=Stabilizer & Antagonist training; TC=Total Core & Leg Exercises; AA=Nonspecific Aerobic Activity; R=Rest (*Optional)

and break periods away from training/climbing. In traditional sports the macrocycle is planned around the competitive calendar, with the goal of peaking for a major competition or sustaining near-peak conditioning throughout a sports season. In climbing, however, the goal is to structure a training program to produce a peaking effect for a major road trip, a competition, or the best climbing season in your region.

You can loosely map the macrocycle on a calendar by identifying the months of your on-season road trips or competitions, the months you expect to perform off-season training, and any time off from climbing you plan to take during the year. Note that indulging in a multiweek annual break (or brief seasonal breaks) from climbing is essential for recharging your motivation and healing any known (or unknown) injuries that may have developed during the course of the climbing season. For many climbers, taking off the latter part of December makes the most sense, as this offers the reward of holiday parties and relaxing with family after a year of dedicated training and tight dietary surveillance. Another popular option is taking a couple weeks off during the peak of midsummer heat, before beginning a late-summer training cycle that leads into prime autumn climbing season.

Figure 10.4 depicts a typical macrocycle. Note that a couple of 4-3-2-1 training cycles are fit into the off-season training period, along with another during the midseason. The fall months are targeted as the peaking period, followed by a couple of weeks off to conclude the year. A blank fifty-two-week macrocycle is contained in appendix B for your use—you can also download a blank macrocycle spreadsheet at www.Training4Climbing.com.

Targeting Training on Your Preferred Subdiscipline

In chapter 1 you learned the importance of obeying the SAID Principle (specific adaptation to imposed demands) in optimizing your training for your favorite subdiscipline of climbing. Figure 1.7 depicts how the demands of these subdisciplines vary over

Figure 10.4 Sample Macrocycle

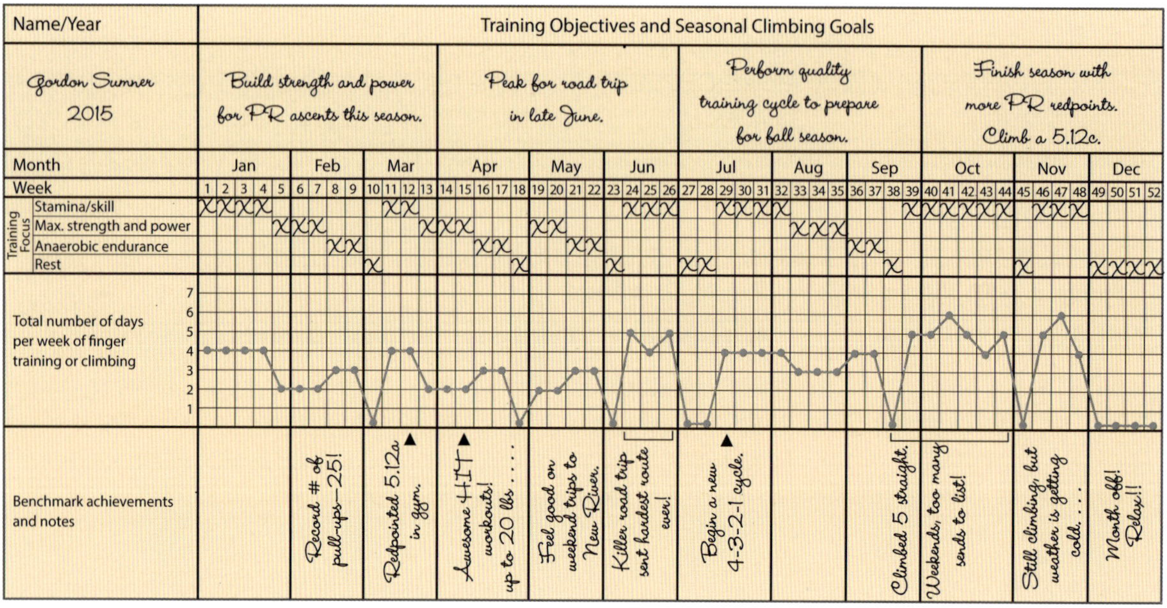

a continuum from bouldering to alpine climbing. Maximizing the effectiveness of your training requires designing your workouts accordingly.

Most climbers reading this book participate in the three subdisciplines of bouldering, sport climbing, and multipitch climbing, and this text is obviously focused on helping these climbers improve their performance. Still, big-wall and alpine climbers should be able to glean plenty of useful information. For instance, in accordance with the SAID Principle, a serious alpine climber would benefit much more from high-volume endurance StairMaster training and trail running than from bouldering on a home wall or hanging on a fingerboard. Of course, the most specific and effective training for alpine climbers is to engage in frequent, high-volume climbing and nonspecific aerobic training.

Conversely, building a home wall or joining a climbing gym is the single biggest advantage that boulder, sport, or multipitch climbers could give themselves. Time spent training in the gym should mimic the performance demands of their preferred focus. Boulderers must dedicate more time to maximum-strength and power training, while multipitch and big-wall climbers should focus more on climbing-specific aerobic training and generalized endurance exercise. Sport climbers possessing a high degree of technical skill, however, would do best to cycle their focus between maximum strength/power, anaerobic capacity, and climbing-specific aerobic capacity.

Clearly, the best training program for you will change over time as your technical ability and your physical strengths and weaknesses change. For this reason active self-coaching, with regular self-assessments and course correction, is critical in maintaining a successful training program. The time invested in plotting your program intelligently and striving to stay on course over the long term will pay huge dividends in how far and how fast you progress in this sport. You might also consider hiring a climbing coach to help guide your training—the objective analysis and expert guidance can be a real wild card in obtaining the most rapid gains in ability possible.

IMPORTANCE OF A HOME WALL OR GYM MEMBERSHIP

Regardless of your ability, nothing beats indoor climbing for sport-specific, time-efficient training, any time of the day or year. Hopefully, there is a good commercial facility within a reasonable distance of your home or workplace. If so, join the gym and use it at least twice per week—this is the number one thing you can do to improve climbing ability and fitness. Many of us are less fortunate (the climbing mega gym nearest to my home is more than an hour away), however, so it's vital to invest in a home wall or some basic exercise equipment (fingerboard, TRX trainer, dumbbells) in place of that gym membership.

If your space is tight, simply build an eight-foot by eight-foot, 50-degree overhanging wall with a small section of ceiling climbing atop it. While this setup has obvious limitations (physical and mental), it will enable you to get an excellent upper-body workout as well as help improve some aspects of climbing movement and body position. If a larger space is available, it would be wise to construct three additional sections of wall: a less overhung wall (20 to 30 degrees past vertical is ideal, especially if you want to make a System Wall), a super-steep, 65-degree overhanging wall, and a slightly overhanging (about 5 degrees past vertical) traverse wall. A garage with a high ceiling offers a good location for your home wall, especially if there is a way to control the climate in the summer and winter; however, many homeowners feel it's more practical to build their home gym in the basement or spare room.

Another excellent strategy is organizing a community wall. Recruit five or ten energetic climbers to pitch in a few hundred dollars each. Rent a garage or some similar structure that has room to build several hundred square feet of climbing surface with a variety of angles, and then complete your facility with a campus board, pull-up bar, gymnastic rings, HIT System, Treadwall, and fingerboard.

Designing an Effective Personal Training Program

A powerful central tenet of this book is that you must train in the manner best suited to you and not do as others do. Obviously, there is a limit to how precisely I can prescribe an optimal training program for you via the static format of a book. On the pages that follow, however, I will lay out the basic, fundamentally important guidelines that you should follow in developing your own training program. Do so and you will be far better off than the typical climber who trains in a haphazard, trial-and-error manner.

Most important, you must adopt the appropriate training template for your current ability level. Over time you can tweak this program according to the results you experience and in line with the good training sense you've developed from reading this book. As long as you act in ways consistent with the principles and concepts described throughout this text, you will remain on course toward your goals. The starting point of your program design will be one of the three workout templates—beginner, accomplished, and advanced—detailed on the pages that follow. Consult table 10.2 to determine which classification best describes your current climbing ability and experience.

Table 10.2 Climber Classifications and Training Program Overview

	Beginner	Accomplished	Advanced
Classification of Ability	• Less than one year climbing experience • Toprope ability 5.10 and under • Little or no lead-climbing • Boulder V3 and under	• Actively climbing more than one year • Toprope 5.11 to 5.12+ • Lead climbing up to 5.10+ trad or 5.12 sport • Boulder V4 to V8	• More than three years' climbing experience • On-sight lead ability of 5.12 sport or 5.11+ trad • Redpoint climbing 5.13 and above • Boulder V9 or harder
Training Program Overview	• Climb: 2–4x per week • General conditioning and stability/antagonist training: 2x per week • Generalized aerobic conditioning: 1–4x per week	• Climbing and climbing-specific exercises: 3–4x per week • Stability/antagonist training: 2x per week • Generalized aerobic conditioning: 1–3x per week	• Climbing and climbing-specific exercises: 3–5x per week • Stability/antagonist training: 2x per week • Generalized aerobic conditioning: 1–2x per week

Beginner-Level Workout

PRIMARY MISSION

Learn climbing skills and techniques for efficient movement, optimize body composition, and improve general conditioning, including exercises that target the antagonist and stabilizer muscles. Time spent climbing will provide a rigorous climbing-specific (muscle and tendon) workout, and thus little or no additional climbing-specific training is needed. Also of high importance is a conscious quest to develop basic mental skills such as hold/move identification, mental rehearsal and sequencing, visualization, arousal control, fear management, and goal setting.

Figure 10.5 Workout Time—Beginner

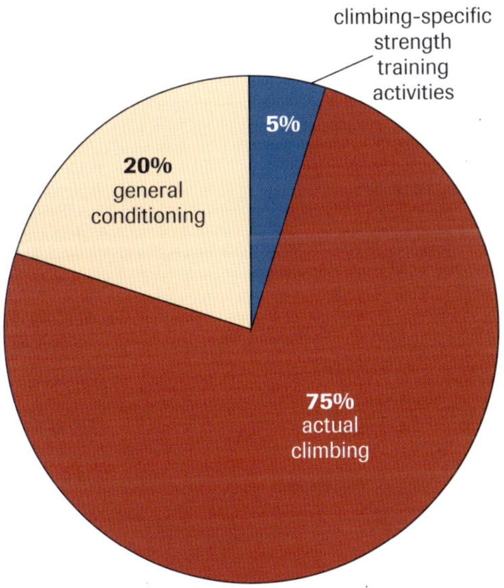

Beginners should invest the majority of their training time in actual climbing. Time spent fitness training should mostly focus on general conditioning.

WORKOUT GUIDELINES

Climb up to four days per week, including outdoor climbing days whenever possible. Reduce body fat, if needed, via improved dietary surveillance and up to four days of aerobic training per week. Train the antagonist, stabilizer, and core muscles twice per week using the exercises described in chapters 6 and 7. If you cannot climb during the workweek, you should instead engage in some of the entry-level finger flexor and pull-muscle exercises described in chapters 8 and 9. Time spent training and climbing should break down according to figure 10.5. An overview of beginner workouts, with and without climbing wall access, is shown in table 10.3. Visit www.Training4Climbing.com for detailed workouts available as free downloads.

SAMPLE MICROCYCLES

Two slightly different microcycles are shown in table 10.4—one for those able to climb during the workweek (home or commercial gym, or outdoors) and the other for those unable to climb except on weekends.

SAMPLE MESOCYCLE

I do not advise the use of a formal training mesocycle (such as the 4-3-2-1 cycle) for a true novice, nor do I suggest you attempt to climb at maximum difficulty or push excessively hard on the rock. Instead, your medium-term goals should be to increase your volume of climbing as well as the diversity of techniques used. If you climb regularly, it's prudent to take a few consecutive days off from climbing every few weeks to allow for systemic consolidation of skills and strengthening of tendons (which take much longer than muscles to strengthen).

SAMPLE MACROCYCLE

A thoroughly designed and executed macrocycle is less important for beginners than it is for

Table 10.3 Beginner Workout Guidelines

Beginner's Workout with Climbing	Beginner's Workout with No Climbing
• 10–15 minutes of general warm-up activity including a few mobility exercises. • 20–40 minutes submaximal practice climbing—focus on learning new skills, efficient movement, and mental skills. • 10–30 minutes strenuous bouldering or near-limit roped climbing. • 3–5 sets pull-muscle exercises (see table 9.1). • 15–30 minutes of core, antagonist, and stabilizer muscle training, doing an aggregate of 8–12 sets; although this can be done on a separate day. • 5–15 minutes cool-down—foam rolling and mild stretching.	• 10–15 minutes of general warm-up activity including a few mobility exercises. • 5–8 sets pull-muscle exercises (see table 9.1). • 4–6 total sets of various core exercises. • 2–4 sets of fingerboard repeaters. • 15–30 minutes of antagonist and stabilizer muscle training, doing an aggregate of 8–12 sets. • 5–15 minutes cool-down—foam rolling and mild stretching.

Visit www.Training4Climbing.com for additional workouts as free downloads.

Table 10.4 Beginner Sample Microcycles

Four-Day-Per-Week Climbing

Monday	Tuesday	Wednesday	Thursday	Friday	Saturday	Sunday
R or S/AA*	C/CE/TC	S/AA*	C/CE/TC	R	C/AA*	C/CE/TC*

KEY: C=Climbing; CE=Climbing-Specific Exercises; S=Stabilizer & Antagonist Training; TC=Total Core & Leg Exercises; AA=Nonspecific Aerobic Activity; R=Rest (*Optional)

Weekend-Only Climbing

Monday	Tuesday	Wednesday	Thursday	Friday	Saturday	Sunday
R or AA	CE/S/TC	R or AA	CE/S/TC	R	C/AA*	C/CE/TC*

KEY: C=Climbing; CE=Climbing-Specific Exercises; S=Stabilizer & Antagonist Training; TC=Total Core & Leg Exercises; AA=Nonspecific Aerobic Activity; R=Rest (*Optional)

accomplished and elite climbers, though you can still benefit from some long-term planning relating to possible road trips and multiweek breaks from climbing. Still, you can use the blank macrocycle in appendix B to plot your training and climbing schedule as it evolves.

Summary of Training for a Beginning Climber

- Climb up to four days per week—and outdoors as often as possible. Climb for volume over difficulty—maximum learning of a wide range of skills and tactics is far more important than the grade of routes sent.
- Engage in conditioning exercises that focus on optimizing body composition, improving flexibility, and strengthening the important antagonist, stabilizer, and core muscles. Improved dietary surveillance is crucial for improving body composition.
- Climbing-specific strength training should be limited to the beginner exercises (tables 8.1 and 9.1), and actual climbing should be generally given preference over doing these exercises.
- Strive for awareness of your thoughts and emotions throughout the day and while climbing. Practice the mental techniques described in chapter 3, and begin using them as part of your preclimb preparations and while on the rock.

Accomplished Climber Workout

PRIMARY MISSION

Maximize economy of climbing movement with constant focus on refining mental and technical skills. Expand technical skills and on-sight climbing ability with experience on many different rock types and by avoiding specialization as long as possible. Increase intensity of climbing-specific training exercises with twice-weekly finger flexor training on a fingerboard and a similar amount of focused pull-muscle and core training—getting stronger year-over-year must be the prime directive of your training-for-climbing program. Concurrent stabilizer and antagonist training is a must to maintain muscle balance and prevent injury.

WORKOUT GUIDELINES

Every intermediate-level climber has a different "perfect" training program depending on his or her unique physical, technical, and mental weaknesses, as well as time available and climbing goals. Still, actual climbing is the most essential part of this workout program for all accomplished climbers. Climbing three to four days per week (indoors and/or outdoors) is the backbone of this program. For most people, this will require joining a climbing gym or building a home training wall to help facilitate weekday climbing. Strive to climb outside as often as possible—one or two days each weekend, if possible—to enable learning of the diverse skills and techniques not represented by human-made walls.

Serious strength training can be scheduled via the DUP scheme and, when feasible, according to the 4-3-2-1 or 3-2-1 training cycles.

Figure 10.6 Workout Time—Accomplished

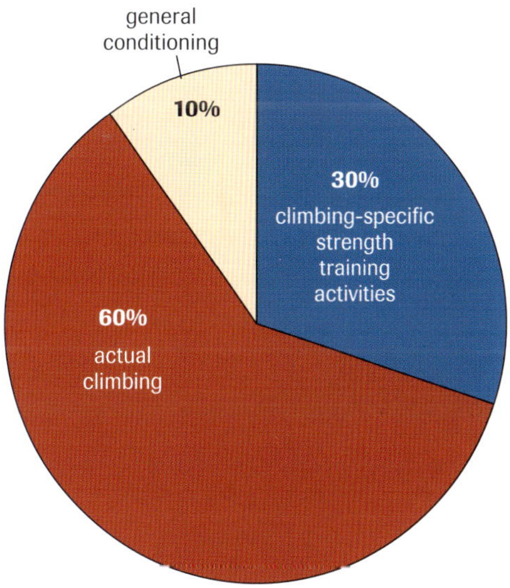

Accomplished climbers should spend about one-third of total training time on climbing-specific exercises, but time spent climbing rock and plastic remains the top priority.

Table 10.5 Accomplished Climber Workout Guidelines

Sample "Skill and Stamina" (Aerobic Energy System) Workout (2–4 hours)

- 10–15 minutes of general warm-up activity including a few mobility exercises.
- 75–120 minutes practice climbing and lapping moderate (submaximal, no-fall) routes. Build up to 1,000 feet of climbing; if the gym's routes average 30 feet in length, you'll need to climb 30+ routes (or up and down 15+ times).
- 10–30 minutes strenuous bouldering or near-limit roped climbing.
- 15–30 minutes of antagonist and stabilizer muscles training, doing an aggregate of 8–12 sets—ideally, do this on a rest day from climbing.
- 5–15 minutes cool-down—foam rolling and mild stretching.

Sample "Maximum-Strength/Power" Workout (1.25–2.5 hours)

- 10–15 minutes of general warm-up activity including a few mobility exercises.
- 30–60 minutes maximal bouldering and hypergravity bouldering.
- 20–40 minutes maximum-strength and power-training exercises. Select appropriate forearm exercises (3–7 total sets) and pull-muscle exercises (3–7 total sets) from tables 8.1 and 9.1, respectively.
- Conclude with 3–6 sets of core exercises.
- 20–40 minutes of posterior chain and antagonist/stabilizer muscles training, doing an aggregate of 8–12 sets—ideally, do these exercises on a rest day from climbing.
- 5–15 minutes cool-down—foam rolling and mild stretching.

Sample "Strength/Power-Endurance" Workout (1.5–2.5 hours)

- 10–15 minutes of general warm-up activity including a few mobility exercises.
- 30–60 minutes interval training on rope routes or a Treadwall, or bouldering 4x4s or similar. You should get deeply pumped, yet strive to avoid complete muscle failure until late in the session.
- 20–40 minutes strength/power-endurance exercises. Select appropriate finger flexor exercises (5–10 total sets) and pull-muscle exercises (5–10 total sets) from tables 8.1 and 9.1.
- Conclude with 3–6 sets of core exercises.
- 20–40 minutes of posterior chain and antagonist/stabilizer muscles training, doing an aggregate of 8–12 sets—ideally, do these exercises on a rest day from climbing.
- 5–15 minutes cool-down—foam rolling and mild stretching.

Visit www.Training4Climbing.com for additional workouts as free downloads.

Actual climbing should be done before doing any climbing-specific exercises, and never climb or do climbing-specific exercises more than a total of four days per week. Train the antagonist, stabilizer, and core muscles twice per week, on either climbing or nonclimbing days (ideal). Maintain close dietary surveillance during the latter portion of off-season training and during on-season training/climbing. Your time spent training and climbing should break down in the proportions shown in figure 10.6.

Use the three sample workouts in table 10.5 as templates from which you can build the optimal workout for you, or visit Training4Climbing.com for detailed workouts available as free downloads. Modify and vary the program over the mesocycle and macrocycle and also in accordance with the principles of training detailed in chapter 5. In the context of the 4-3-2-1 training cycle, use the stamina and skill template for four weeks, the maximum-strength and power for three weeks, and the strength/power-endurance for two weeks.

SAMPLE MICROCYCLES

Your discipline at planning and executing quality workouts over a seven-day microcycle is a primary factor in determining the results you obtain. Integrating climbing days, hard training days, and sufficient rest days is the crux of the matter. Train too little or rest too little, and you will shortchange yourself. Table 10.6 provides four microcycles to help guide your scheduling. Depending on your access to a climbing wall or rock, select either the weekend-only climbing microcycle or the four-days-climbing microcycle. Use the microcycle as a template for planning your weekly schedule, but recognize that you may need to adjust or deviate from the schedule depending on travel or the need for additional rest.

MESOCYCLE DESIGN

Dedicated periods of serious strength training for gains are best scheduled according to the 4-3-2-1 cycle. Figure 10.2 shows a highly effective ten-week program that allows for adequate rest and thus produces maximum-strength gains with low risk of overtraining or injury. High-end accomplished climbers may benefit more by using the 3-2-1 mesocycle (see figure 10.3) or DUP scheme.

Peak climbing season (when you most often climb for performance) will make it difficult to follow a strict ten-week mesocycle. At these times you may deviate from the schedule by taking two full rest days before a weekend climbing trip and at least one active rest day after the weekend climbing. Often the best in-season training strategy is to develop a seven-day microcycle that best accommodates your weekend climbing while still allowing for at least one "maintenance" climbing-specific strength-training workout and one stabilizer and total core session—in doing this you're more or less engaging in a DUP program. Regardless, when you find a weekly schedule that works, stick with it for several weeks or until you can commit to a more structured 3-2-1 or 4-3-2-1 regimen.

SAMPLE MACROCYCLE

The average accomplished climber gets outdoors twenty or more weekends per year and may go on as many as two to four extended road trips per year. Therefore, careful macrocycle planning is vital to optimize preparation for these trips and to help produce peaking for an extreme project or personal-best ascent. Use the blank macrocycle in appendix B to fashion an effective long-term training plan that accounts for your travel plans, the best outdoor climbing season, and when you choose to take your month off from climbing.

Table 10.6 Accomplished Climber Sample Microcycles

Four-Day-Per-Week Climbing—Schedule #1

Monday	Tuesday	Wednesday	Thursday	Friday	Saturday	Sunday
R or S/AA*	C/CE/TC	S/AA*	C/CE/TC	R	C/AA*	C/CE/TC*

KEY: C=Climbing; CE=Climbing-Specific Exercises; S=Stabilizer & Antagonist Training; TC=Total Core & Leg Exercises; AA=Nonspecific Aerobic Activity; R=Rest (*Optional)

Four-Day-Per-Week Climbing—Schedule #2

Monday	Tuesday	Wednesday	Thursday	Friday	Saturday	Sunday
R or S/AA*	C/CE/TC (Str/Power)	C/S/CE (AeEnd)	TC/AA*	R	C/AA*	C/CE/TC*

KEY: C=Climbing; CE (Str/Power)=Strength & Power Climbing Exercises; CE (AeEnd)=Aerobic Endurance Climbing Exercises; S=Stabilizer & Antagonist Training; TC=Total Core & Leg Exercises; AA=Nonspecific Aerobic Activity; R=Rest (*Optional)

Weekend-Only Climbing—Schedule #1

Monday	Tuesday	Wednesday	Thursday	Friday	Saturday	Sunday
R or AA	CE/S/TC	R or AA	CE/S/TC	R	C/AA*	C/CE/TC*

KEY: C=Climbing; CE=Climbing-Specific Exercises; S=Stabilizer & Antagonist Training; TC=Total Core & Leg Exercises; AA=Nonspecific Aerobic Activity; R=Rest (*Optional)

Weekend-Only Climbing—Schedule #2

Monday	Tuesday	Wednesday	Thursday	Friday	Saturday	Sunday
R or S/AA	CE (Str/Power)/TC	CE (AeEnd)/S	TC/AA*	R	C/AA*	C/CE/TC*

KEY: C=Climbing; CE (Str/Power)=Strength & Power Climbing Exercises; CE (AeEnd)=Aerobic Endurance Climbing Exercises; S=Stabilizer & Antagonist Training; TC=Total Core & Leg Exercises; AA=Nonspecific Aerobic Activity; R=Rest (*Optional)

Summary of Training for an Accomplished Climber

- Climb up to four days per week and gain exposure to as many different types and styles of climbing as possible. Refine mental and technical skills to maximize economy of movement—the fastest way to becoming a better, stronger climber.
- Engage in regular, scheduled, climbing-specific strength training to increase maximum grip strength, upper-body power, and endurance. Focus primarily on the intermediate exercises listed in tables 8.1 and 9.1. During a particular workout, always perform actual climbing before engaging in strength-training exercises.
- Commit to training the antagonist and stabilizer muscles twice per week—critical for maintaining muscle balance and lowering injury risk.
- Work on becoming a more mental climber, on a mission to always climb and train smartly. Plan your workouts and then work your plan—follow-through is critical to long-term improvement. Practice using mental-training strategies throughout the week, and then strive to leverage all your mental and tactical techniques when you step onto the rock.

Advanced Climber Workout

PRIMARY MISSION

Identify and correct any technical weak spots or energy leaks (no matter how small) that compromise climbing performance. Constantly evaluate and refine mental skills—there's always room for improvement in this area, even among top pros! Work to eliminate subtle forms of self-sabotage by narrowing your focus onto the process of climbing and letting go of any outcome-oriented thinking.

Figure 10.7 Workout Time—Advanced

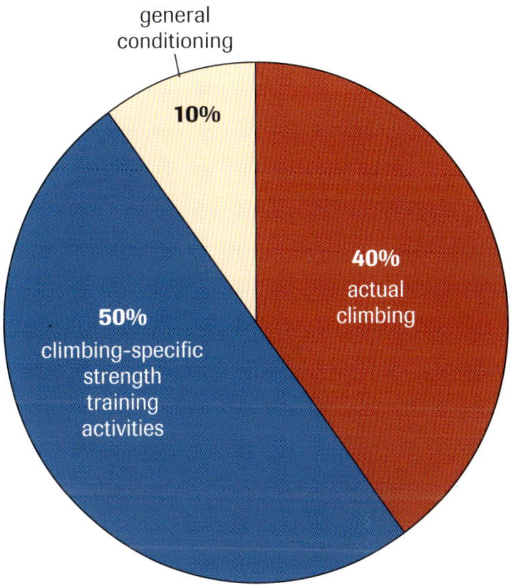

Only advanced climbers need to focus extensively on climbing-specific strength-training activities—getting stronger, season-over-season, is priority number one. Design workouts to target a preferred subdiscipline, a specific energy system, or simulate a current project route.

Exercise workouts must be highly specific to your preferred climbing subdiscipline (bouldering, sport climbing, multipitch, or big walls), and they must stretch the limits of what you are currently capable of doing, in order to eke out further neuromuscular gains and central governor recalibration. Sound nutrition and sleep habits are critical for accelerating recovery and obtaining optimal adaptations from your hard workouts.

WORKOUT GUIDELINES

Unlike the mass of climbers, the elite performer needs to spend a disproportionate amount of training time on strength training (see figure 10.7). For boulderers and sport climbers, several weeks or even a month or two at a time may be dedicated to strength/power training and hard bouldering

Table 10.7 Advanced Climber Workout Guidelines

Maximum-Strength/Power Workout (1.5–2.5 hours)

- 10–15 minutes of general warm-up activity including a few mobility exercises.
- 30–60 minutes maximal bouldering and hypergravity bouldering.
- 30–45 minutes maximum-strength and power-training exercises. Select appropriate forearm exercises (7–10 total sets) and pull-muscle exercises (7–10 total sets) from tables 8.1 and 9.1, respectively.
- Conclude with 4–8 sets of total core.
- 20–40 minutes of posterior chain and antagonist/stabilizer muscles training, doing an aggregate of 8–12 sets—ideally, do these exercises on a rest day from climbing.
- 5–15 minutes cool-down—foam rolling and mild stretching.

Strength/Power-Endurance Workout (1.5–2.5 hours)

- 10–15 minutes of general warm-up activity including a few mobility exercises.
- 45–60 minutes interval training on near-limit rope routes or a Treadwall, or bouldering 4x4s or similar. You should get deeply pumped, yet strive to avoid complete muscle failure until late in the session.
- 30–45 minutes strength/power-endurance exercises. Select appropriate finger flexor exercises (7–10 total sets) and pull-muscle exercises (7–10 total sets) from tables 8.1 and 9.1.
- Conclude with 3–6 sets of core exercises.
- 20–40 minutes of posterior chain and antagonist/stabilizer muscles training, doing an aggregate of 8–12 sets—ideally, do these exercises on a rest day from climbing.
- 5–15 minutes cool-down—foam rolling and mild stretching.

Aerobic Capacity Workout (2–4 hours)

- 10–15 minutes of general warm-up activity including a few mobility exercises.
- 90–180 minutes of intermittent climbing (submaximal, no-fall) routes. Build up to 1,200 feet of climbing; if the gym's routes average 30 feet in length, you'll need to climb 40+ routes (or up and down 20+ times). Alternatively, climb large holds on a Treadwall for 3–5-minute intervals at an intensity of between 5 and 8.5 out of 10. Do up to 8 intervals with approximately 1:1 climb-to-rest ratio.
- 3–6 sets of core exercises.
- 15–30 minutes of antagonist and stabilizer muscles training, doing an aggregate of 8–12 sets—ideally, do this on a rest day from climbing.
- 5–15 minutes cool-down—foam rolling and mild stretching.

Visit www.Training4Climbing.com for additional workouts as free downloads.

with little or no actual roped climbing. Multipitch and big-wall climbers must invest a large amount of time into actual climbing—climbing for volume, exercising to build strength/power-endurance, and stamina-training activities are what it's all about. Frequent training with the advanced-level exercises in chapters 8 and 9 is essential to achieving further physical gains. Elites with several years of strength and power training under their belt must also train to develop higher aerobic power and aerobic capacity—essential for reaching your genetic potential for sustained, near-limit ascents.

Access to an indoor climbing wall, boulders, or crags is absolutely necessary for advanced-level training. Use of the 3-2-1 cycle can be highly effective for both on- and off-season training, although many advanced climbers will train intuitively via autoregulation and the DUP scheme. Still, the microcycles, mesocycles, and macrocycle described herein offer a framework for such intuitive training. Finally, brief but regular bouts of stabilizer, antagonist, and posterior-chain training will lower injury risk and help optimize climbing posture for maximal application of force to the rock. Abundant rest and proactive performance nutrition are vital to accelerate recovery and help stave off injury and overtraining.

Table 10.7 provides three highly focused workout templates, one each for training maximum strength and power, strength/power-endurance, and climbing-specific aerobic capacity. You will need to modify the volume of training as well as exercise selection based on your capabilities, time available to train, and your climbing preference. Design and vary your workouts according to the training principles outlined in chapter 5.

SAMPLE MICROCYCLES

The appropriate amount of training stimulus (workout length, frequency, and intensity) will vary greatly among elite climbers based on climbing preference, quality of nutrition, genetic factors, and age, among other things. Some individuals may do best by training hard just twice per week, while others do better by training and climbing a total of four days per week. Given the tendency of elite climbers to push their limits, however, it is often necessary to take forced rest days instead of training or projecting while sore. As a guiding principle, advanced climbers should "train hard when training, and rest completely when resting." While many elites will choose to train intuitively via DUP, you can also adopt one of the accomplished climber weekly programs detailed in table 10.6.

SAMPLE MESOCYCLE

As in planning weekly training and climbing, many advanced climbers will intuit their multiweek mesocycle. Even so, it's critical that you consider your outdoor climbing and travel plans, then build a workout schedule around these dates. One planning strategy is to schedule rest and workout days backward from your climbing days—for example, allow for at least forty-eight hours of rest before a weekend of performance climbing and then plan a workout day or two prior to these rest days. On a calendar, mark in your climbing days and trips, then mark the preceding rest days, then fill in your training days. Advanced climbers preferring a more structured schedule will do best by planning their workouts according to the 3-2-1 mesocycle shown in figure 10.3.

SAMPLE MACROCYCLE

Advanced climbers tend to be very goal-oriented and compulsive long-term planners. It's in the macrocycle that you need to book long road trips, competitions, and an annual month off from climbing, so that you can plan the most effective training schedule to produce a physical peaking for key events. You can plot your own macrocycle using the blank chart found in appendix B.

Summary of Training for an Advanced Climber

- Plan and execute an optimal—not maximum—strength-training program that targets your personal weakest link. The goal is to increase grip strength, upper-body power, and anaerobic endurance season over season.
- Constantly evaluate your technique and mental performance to identify subtle flaws that are preventing further gains. Economy of climbing movement is paramount, and it's your mental, technical, and tactical skills that determine your fuel efficiency. Make the mental strategies described in chapter 3 into life skills that you employ daily.
- Err on the side of over-resting instead of over-training. Use performance nutrition and generous amounts of sleep and rest to enhance recovery and maximize gains from training.
- Be a compulsive planner of training, travel, and rest. Try to leave nothing to chance, and avoid trial-and-error training or getting drawn into some else's (flawed) training routine.
- Evaluate all you do in your daily life with this question: *Is it helping me reach my goals or holding me back in some way?*

Training Considerations for Female, Over-Fifty, and Youth Climbers

This final section takes a look at special considerations for female climbers, those over age fifty, and youth climbers. I've intentionally kept this section brief, because I feel that these groups are particularly gifted for climbing—there are only a few things they need to consider or do differently compared with others.

Unique Issues for Female Climbers

Female climbers differ from males both physiologically and psychologically. While the psychological differences are more difficult to measure, there are clear physiological differences that may be an asset or liability in terms of climbing performance. The average female is about five inches shorter, thirty-five pounds lighter in total body mass, and forty-five pounds lighter in lean body mass (due to a higher percentage of body fat) than the average male. This large difference in lean body mass (muscle) is largely attributed to greater levels of the hormone testosterone in males (Bloomfield 1994).

Consequently, the average female possesses approximately 40 percent of the upper-body strength and 70 percent of the lower-body strength when compared with men. In terms of strength-to-lean-body-mass, however, the ratio is notably less—females possess about 55 percent of the upper-body strength and about the same in lower-body strength as men (Wilmore 1974). Thus, it's clear that the greater level of adipose tissue in females has a negative effect on physical performance, especially in sports requiring a high strength-to-weight ratio. The female climber, therefore, will benefit much more from regular aerobic training (to lower her percentage of body fat) than her male counterpart—running for twenty to forty minutes a few days per week will effectively increase strength-to-weight ratio in many females (due to changes in body composition).

Though females are naturally weaker than males (less testosterone and lean mass), they do respond to strength training in the same ways as men. Consequently, the serious female climber should not hesitate to engage in the climbing-specific strength-training exercises described in chapters 8 and 9. In particular, the focus should be on increasing maximum strength in the finger flexor and pull muscles and general conditioning of the core, antagonist, and stabilizer muscles.

The first few weeks or months of training will produce marked improvement thanks to neural adaptations. Beyond that, strength gains will come more slowly as hypertrophy (muscle growth) becomes a more significant player in producing strength gains. For this reason it's vital that strength training for the female climber be just as focused as for the male. The typical health club workout is no more appropriate for female climbers than for males, and in the long run could have a negative effect on climbing performance.

Technically and mentally, the beginning female climber is often a better performer than her male counterpart, and this is something that every female climber should recognize and leverage to the greatest possible extent. More flexibility, a lower center of mass, less body weight, shorter fingers, and a more measured approach to climbing can all help a female climber outperform her male counterpart despite possessing less strength. So while sport-specific strength training is a must for any serious female climber, she should not overlook her gifts of style, strategy, creativity, and finesse.

As a final note, it's a common misconception that physical performance tends to be worse during menstruation. While the menstrual cycle's effect on performance varies widely among individuals and from sport to sport, at least one study has shown that grip strength was greater during the actual menstrual phase (Davis 1991). Ultimately, you need to develop an awareness of just when is your best performance time of the month. You can then plan your training and climbing to exploit this period, whether it's for a few high-intensity workouts or making a personal-best ascent!

Conditioning for Over-Fifty Climbers

As adult climbers age, numerous physiological changes combine to form an increasing constraint on performance, especially beyond the age of fifty. A few of the unfortunate changes include reduced VO_2 max (aerobic capacity), decreased muscle mass, a lower proportion of fast-twitch muscle fibers, and reduced recovery. Despite these inevitable life changes, you can still climb at a very high level given a renewed focus on the mental and technical aspects of climbing and a steady dose of strength training. I know of more than a few fifty- and sixty-somethings who regularly climb 5.12 and 5.13 (at age fifty-two, I'm now one of them—yikes!), ascend big walls, and trek in the mountains. You can too, given a three-pronged approach of injury avoidance, physical conditioning, and mastery of skills.

INJURY AVOIDANCE

Compared with the resilient bodies of young adults, older climbers' muscles, tendons, and joints are more susceptible to injury during rigorous workouts and near-limit climbs. Common issues range from muscle pulls to dislocated shoulders, torn tendons, and a variety of other joint and spinal problems. Fortunately, you can significantly reduce your risk by engaging in a comprehensive warm-up before every training and climbing session. Younger climbers might rush through a warm-up in just a few minutes, but older climbers would be wise to complete a full thirty-minute warm-up of general aerobic activity, light exercise, stretching, mobility activities, and easy climbing. Such a progressive warm-up will markedly decrease injury risk by warming and lengthening the muscles and spreading synovial fluid to lubricate the joints. While thirty minutes of non-climbing exercise might not be your idea of a good time, it will enhance the quality of your climbing and reduce the risk of muscle or joint injury that might lay you up for months or even knock you out of climbing completely.

Another way the mature, disciplined climber can avoid injuries is simply by avoiding potentially injurious moves while climbing. The goal is to foster a level of kinesthetic awareness at which you can assess—or often intuit—the risk potential of a given move. Whether it is an awkward-feeling drop-knee, a tweaky-feeling pocket, or an improbable-feeling lunge, your discipline to heed the sensory feedback and rapidly evaluate the situation before forging onward can save you. Ultimately, you will need to make a quick decision as to whether you should retreat from the risky-feeling move, test the move once to see how it feels, or just push onward in the belief that you will succeed without incident. As a rule the older you get, the more you should view such a risky-feeling move as a stop sign instead of a caution sign.

PHYSICAL CONDITIONING

Physical conditioning for over-fifty climbers is not all that different from the program I prescribe for the mass of climbers. You can safely employ many of the exercises contained in this book. Most of your limitations relate to dynamic, forceful training exercises, which become increasingly dangerous with advancing age. Climbers over fifty years of age would be wise to not engage in the most dynamic forms of campus training, one-arm lock-offs or one-arm pull-ups, frequent lunging, and V-hard bouldering. Of course, every climber possesses different genetic encoding, experience, and physical capabilities, so there are surely a few senior climbers who prevail through the most stressful endeavors. But for the vast majority of older climbers, dynamic training is dangerous training. Otherwise, your fitness-training goals are similar to those of every other climber: optimize body composition, improve aerobic capacity and stamina, and increase muscular strength and endurance.

Preplanning workout and rest days is of great importance for the older climber. Too many back-to-back workout (or climbing) days, too little rest, and poor nutrition over just a few consecutive days will crack open the door to possible injury or illness. Compound this over several weeks and it will fling the door wide. Once an older climber is injured and sick, reduced immune efficiency and changing hormone levels mean slower recovery and a faster drop-off of physical conditioning than for a younger climber. The bottom line for over-fifty climbers: Train, rest, and eat on a calculated schedule that will reduce injury risk, and do nothing to tempt injury.

TECHNICAL AND MENTAL MASTERY

The best older climbers are usually Zen masters who leverage the fact that climbing performance is two-thirds technical and mental and only one-third physical. By exploiting superior skill and wisdom, and bringing many years of experience to the table, older climbers can become true masters of rock by climbing very near their maximum capacity. Whether that top capability is 5.8 or 5.14, you can spot these elder masters by their measured approach, smooth sailing through scary terrain, and even the occasional calculated lunge or grunt that shows they are still willing to pull out all the stops to send.

Developing such mastery takes many years; in fact, in a complex sport such as climbing you can still acquire and refine mental and technical skills after ten, twenty, or even thirty years' experience. So while your physical capacities may be steady or waning, you can often compensate by improving mentally and technically. Consequently, you should strive to strike a balance between strength training—still an important part of the equation—and going climbing at one of the myriad wonderful crags around the world. And, after all, isn't that the bottom line? Simply by moving over stone, you tap into the life force that climbing provides, which transcends ability, gender, and age. That's the power of climbing!

Training for Junior Climbers

Kids can unquestionably learn complex sports skills more rapidly than adults, and in recent years we've seen numerous "wonder kids" take the sport-climbing world by storm. Clearly these young, generally prepubescent climbers possess the slight physique ideal for difficult climbing. There are numerous other physiological traits that work in their favor to enhance function and rate of recovery. Unfortunately, these young climbers often lack the maturity, self-awareness, and life experience to transfer their sport-climbing prowess to a wide range of climbing pursuits. They are also not prepared for the rigors of serious climbing-specific training as outlined in this text. Let's take a look at the appropriate type of activity and training for youth climbers.

With the growing popularity of youth climbing competitions and the recent press of preteen

Ashima Shiraishi climbed 5.15a before she was old enough to drive! CLAUDIA ZEIGLER

climbers sending V12 and 5.14 routes, many parents—and some coaches as well—are suspicious that these elite youth climbers must be involved in some secret, arduous strength-training program. The truth is, however, that elite youth climbers develop as the result of an early introduction to climbing (often between ages four and seven), high-quality coaching, dedicated practice, and a slight (often prepubescent) physique.

So what is the best way for a youth climber to train, and what can a coach or parent do to foster a youngster's interest in climbing, while at the same time keeping it safe and fun?

As both a parent and coach of two elite youth climbers, I've spent much time the last decade researching and developing a youth climbing philosophy that I feel is safe, effective, and appropriate. On the pages that follow I'll present—for coaches and parents—this philosophy for training youth climbers, including guidelines for training skill and strategy, cognitive development, physical fitness training, and injury prevention.

SKILL DEVELOPMENT

Climbing is first and foremost a skill sport, and it should always be treated as such, especially when dealing with youth climbers. Much like golf, climbing requires proficient use of a wide range of skills, while strength and power are secondary. Consequently, skill development is paramount for novice climbers (of all ages), while extensive strength training is unnecessary and inappropriate early on. Interestingly, preteen brains are predisposed to prolific learning of motor skills, and so they have a time-limited gift to develop and refine climbing skills at a much higher rate and with greater ease than adults.

While climbing in general is extremely intuitive—and many youngsters might seem to be able to successfully teach themselves—there are in fact many complex techniques and skills that novices are unlikely to discover on their own. This is where knowledgeable climbing coaches are indispensable, since they can present new skills to be learned with proper form and in a logical progression, all the while keeping the climbing activities safe and fun.

A good coach will have a lesson plan of sorts that begins with a warm-up activity and then progresses through several periods focused on learning new skills, practicing previously learned skills, engaging in some form of "performance climbing" (attempting to climb entire roped routes or "limit" boulder problems), and concluding with some basic conditioning exercises and cool-down stretching. All the while the coach will engage the students, actively correcting lackluster form and inefficient movement patterns.

Feedback is essential to the learning process—the coach must help direct effective practice that will encode fundamentally correct movement skills into the brain and foster a high level of climbing efficiency, rather than allowing youth climbers to muscle through a move with poor technique and call it "okay." As in learning any physical skill, it's paramount that young climbers avoid encoding sloppy, inefficient ways of moving that will be more difficult to correct once they are firmly wired in the brain.

(Again, golf is a good analogy: Many adult golfers futilely struggle to overcome technical flaws that were deeply encoded during their formative days.)

Longer term, youth climbers should be encouraged to explore unfamiliar terrain. An early focus on slab climbing should expand to the more challenging terrain of overhanging walls and bouldering caves. When they've achieved a high level of proficiency at face climbing, youths should be exposed to cracks and corners, which demand acquisition of new skill sets. An early focus on bouldering and toprope climbing should eventually progress to an introduction to lead climbing, although this is obviously a risky, headier form of climbing that is not to be rushed into prematurely. Some strong, talented youth climbers will develop the skill and confidence to begin lead climbing by age eight or nine, while others may take years longer. There are no rules (no specific age) for when a climber is ready to lead—obviously this is a critical decision for the coach and parent to make together, and not something the youth climber should unilaterally decide.

A final and most important coaching matter involves climbing frequency and degree of dedication to the sport. Understandably, many youths fall in love with climbing—to the point that they would like to make it their one and only recreational/sporting activity. It's my opinion, however, that single-sport specialization should be discouraged before the age of thirteen and, ideally, until after age sixteen. Research has identified a finite "golden period" of accelerated acquisition of motor abilities that lasts only through the early teenage years. This period of heightened neurodevelopment should be used to learn a wide range of sports skills that include running, jumping, flipping, throwing and/or shooting a ball, swinging a club or racquet, and swimming, among many other wonderful and pleasurable ways to engage in skilled movement. A youth's brief opportunity to learn at hyperspeed should be invested in learning more than just how to dance and pull up a rock wall. It's my experience that young athletes can come to climb at a national-class level (or higher) while at the same time participating in—and perhaps excelling at—one or two other sports, and in school, as well!

COGNITIVE DEVELOPMENT

My advice on cognitive training for youth climbers parallels almost everything I've outlined above on training technical skills. Start with the most basic mental challenges—developing confidence and poise in climbing hand-over-hand up juggy vertical routes—and gradually introduce more challenging terrain that requires visualization of sequences and the vertical chess match of reading several moves ahead while on a climb. For some kid climbers the process is a natural and apparently simple one to learn, as they quickly solve climbing wall puzzles on the fly. Other kids will require more coaching input to help them solve the puzzle and "see" the moves to be performed. (A laser pointer is a must-have coaching tool for helping a young climber see and mentally rehearse a tricky sequence.)

For younger climbers—say, under age nine—it's important to treat a climbing session as more a playground experience than a training session. A good coach will present climbing games that keep the focus on having fun, with learning of climbing skills and strategies a by-product.

Climbers between the ages of nine and thirteen can be presented with more complex instruction on critical cognitive skills such as mental rehearsal, visualization, arousal and fear control, risk management, and such. With good instruction, it's within this age range that many youth climbers, usually those with several years of experience, put together the complex technical and mental puzzle that is hard climbing and suddenly break into the lofty grades of bouldering V8 and/or lead climbing 5.12 (or harder).

Given a growing mastery of the fundamental technical and mental skills, some youth climbers between ages eight and thirteen are ready to be introduced to the challenges and joys of outdoor climbing. As with the introduction to lead climbing indoors, however, taking youths outside is a big step that should not be rushed. The earliest transitioners to outdoor climbing will be those youths whose parents are experienced climbers themselves—this way the parent can be responsible for making the tough calls on what climbs are safe or unsafe for a youth to attempt. For those kids without a climbing parent, it's best to wait until at least thirteen to venture outdoors—and even then, to do so only in the presence of a mature, qualified climbing coach and/or instructor.

No matter if the outdoor climbing adventure is bouldering, toproping, or lead climbing, the game is pretty much the same as it is indoors, although the technical and mental demands are far greater on the infinite playing field of Mother Nature's rock walls. Given a good coach or experienced parent, however, climbing outdoors offers an extraordinarily rich environment for learning and experiencing the wonders of nature. The bottom line: Outdoor climbing can be nearly as safe as indoor; however, some outdoor climbs are more complex, and this may increase the potential for climber and belayer error, in addition to the common objective dangers that come into play in the great outdoors. Proceed with caution.

Just as outdoor climbing will stretch a youth climber's cognition in new and exciting ways, so will competition climbing—which, for many youths who don't venture into outdoor climbing, offers an excellent way to add a more challenging cognitive aspect to the game. Many climbing gyms hold local youth competitions, which serve as a great introduction to the unique challenges and pressures of competition climbing. More formalized regional competitions for both bouldering and roped climbing are professionally organized and sanctioned by the governing body USA Climbing. Youths between the ages of eight and eighteen compete in five different age divisions for medals and to qualify for a national championship event. Learn more at USAClimbing.org.

AGE-APPROPRIATE STRENGTH TRAINING

The increasingly widespread push for early specialization in youth sports has led to an unnecessary and, in some cases, inappropriate application of advanced strength-training techniques among young athletes. Regardless of the sport—soccer, baseball, running, or rock climbing—early specialization and use of adult-like training programs has sadly led to a rapid increase in overuse injuries. It's now well documented that some of the hardest training/climbing youths, both in America and Europe, are suffering growth plate fractures in the fingers—a few top climbers have had multiple fractures, some leading to permanent disfiguration.

It's interesting to note, however, the countless youth climbers who "climb their age" without engaging in dangerous, age-inappropriate training practices. While some form of physical training is certainly necessary, there's really no need for an intensive strength/power-training program—the risk is far greater than the reward. By simply climbing three or four days per week for several years, many youth climbers quickly advance into the higher grades of sport climbing—the wild card seems to be easy access to a climbing gym and high-quality coaching.

Given a regular schedule of climbing, a limited amount of supplemental strength and conditioning exercises is okay and, likely, beneficial for building a complete, well-balanced athlete. Disregard any old wives' tales you've heard that "strength training is not for kids" or that "strength training will stunt a youth's growth." The American Academy of Pediatrics and the American College of Sports Medicine both support basic strength training for kids, as long as the exercises are age appropriate and not overly dynamic or stressful, and youths are coached to exercise with proper form. So what are the age-appropriate exercises for youth climbers? Let's take a look at three general classifications: ages six through nine, ten through fifteen, and sixteen through eighteen.

AGES SIX THROUGH NINE

Prior to the adolescent growth spurt, most apparent gains in strength come from motor learning, not hypertrophy (muscle growth), and so any manner of extensive strength training is unnecessary and largely a waste of time at this age. Motor learning comes when adaptations of the nervous system—specifically, improved coordination and synchronization of muscular motor units (groups of muscle fibers that fire together)—lead to a greater expression of strength and power. Therefore, movement-oriented training should be the backbone of every workout. Developing climbing-specific strength, then, is simply a matter of following through with a consistent schedule of climbing (which will yield measurable gains in strength despite little or no change in muscle size).

Use of a few supplemental climbing-like exercises is fine, as long as it doesn't take away from movement training and climbing-for-fun time. Body weight exercises such as pull-ups, push-ups, various core training exercises, and other similar gymnastic movements are the only strength-training exercises needed at this age.

AGES TEN THROUGH FIFTEEN

Given a year or more of climbing experience and assuming a solid command of technical skills, it is not inappropriate to introduce a moderate amount of strength training for climbers ages ten through fifteen. These are the years of the adolescent growth spurt, with peak height velocity occurring at age 11.5 for girls and age 13.5 for boys. Changing hormone levels will lead to a noticeable growth of the muscles as weight velocity peaks between ages twelve and fifteen.

It's during this period that some fast-growing youths perceive a disturbing decrease in strength-to-weight ratio as their weight gain outpaces their strength gains. Once again, quality coaching is critical so that concerned youth climbers understand why they are apparently getting weaker despite a consistent climbing schedule. Some misguided youths will react by beginning a strict diet or extensive strength- or power-training program (or both) in an attempt to regain their physical capabilities. This response is unfortunate and, in fact, unhealthy, and it often ends in injury, anorexia, or burnout.

A good coach will explain the changes that all youth climbers face during puberty, and how the end result will undoubtedly be a physique that is stronger, taller, more powerful, and supremely capable of climbing at a very high level. The coach should direct a gradual introduction of general and climbing-specific strength-training exercises that will train the newly gained muscle to be more efficient and effective for performing in the vertical plane, as well as reduce injury risk as the growing youths attempt harder climbs.

With the overriding training emphasis remaining on the development of outstanding climbing technique and mental fortitude, youth climbers can engage in twenty to forty minutes of strength training, three days per week. Climbing-specific exercises such as pull-ups, lock-offs, open-hand-grip fingerboard hangs on medium-size holds (in small doses), slow, controlled campus laddering (never double dynoing!), and various core-strengthening routines should be executed on climbing days, not rest days. Most important, the youth should forgo most advanced and stressful exercises (as used by older elite climbers), such double-dyno campus training and weighted fingerboard hangs—these can lead to growth plate fractures in the fingers and a necessary withdrawal from climbing for an extended period.

Perhaps the most important addition to a youth's training program is a small number of exercises to target the muscles that oppose the prime movers in climbing. A regular schedule of climbing (even without use of climbing-specific strength exercises) will lead to significant gains in strength of the pull muscles that are the prime movers for the vertical athlete. Maintaining stable joints and proper posture, reducing injury risk, and pursuing peak performance in climbing demands a steadfast commitment to training the antagonist push muscles of the upper body. Specifically, the training should target the extension-producing muscles of the chest, shoulders, and arms, the scapular stabilizers, and the small muscles of the rotator cuff. A modest investment—twenty to thirty minutes, two or three days per week—will strengthen these important yet often overlooked muscles, and vastly lower the risk of the elbow and shoulder injuries common among avid and expert climbers alike.

Most of the necessary climbing-specific and antagonist-muscle-training exercises are described earlier in this book For the antagonist muscles I suggest beginning with two sets of push-ups and reverse wrist curls, TRX trainer Ys and Ts, one or two sets of dumbbell shoulder presses, two sets of dips (with assistance, if needed), and two sets each of external and internal rotations of the shoulder. Each exercise should be performed with a relatively light weight that allows fifteen to twenty repetitions. These exercises can be performed at the end of a climbing workout or on rest days from climbing.

A final facet of effective training for youth climbers is flexibility training. While most climbing moves do not require extraordinary flexibility, quickly growing bones and muscles can lead to an increasing sense of tightness that may somewhat limit movement on the rock. A moderate amount of daily stretching can go a long way toward maintaining smooth, flexible movement. Gentle stretching of the arms, torso, and legs should be performed as part of a more comprehensive warm-up before engaging in maximal climbing. Furthermore, engaging in ten to fifteen minutes of stretching each evening (while watching TV or during quiet time before bed) is highly effective in helping relax and lengthen the tired, growing muscles of a hard-training youth climber.

AGES SIXTEEN THROUGH EIGHTEEN

As youth climbers approach their adult height, they can begin a gradual transition into a more intensive climbing-specific training program. Still, growth plates remain vulnerable to injury; they may not fully fuse until around ages eighteen to twenty. What's more, increases in training volume and magnitude can lead to overuse and acute injuries of the fingers, elbows, and shoulders. For these reasons, among others, a fully engaged coach or climbing parent is highly beneficial during this transition into becoming astute, self-directed adult climbers.

Many of these late-teen climbers will already be highly accomplished, and a few will be proven to possess world-class capabilities. Elite-level training techniques, such as one-armed pull-ups, weighted fingerboard hangs, campus training, and weighted bouldering (say, with a ten-pound belt), can be added incrementally during this multiyear ramp-up period. However, hold off on fully dynamic double-dyno campus training and advanced hypergravity-training protocols until after the eighteenth birthday (and even later in the case of a late bloomer). Strengthening the antagonist muscle groups remains essential for muscle balance, proper posture, and reducing the risk of elbow and shoulder injuries—all potential issues for hard-training late-teen and twenty-something climbers.

All the while, it's imperative that the training program remain focused on improving the complete climber—including mental and technical training—rather than a narrow, impulsive quest for greater strength and power as the sole pathway to improvement. Teenage climbers should be reminded frequently that sharp advances in ability often result from mental breakthroughs, and, furthermore, that becoming a true master of rock comes only by way of gaining vast experience on a wide range of climbing walls and rock types. Toward this end, a good coach will constantly dovetail physical training with ongoing instruction on advanced climbing techniques, tactics, and the many facets of the mental game. The most thoughtful and introspective teenagers will be ready to begin a study of the book *Maximum Climbing: Mental Training for Peak Performance and Optimal Experience*—a challenging text that explores powerful metacognitive skills that will enhance performance in climbing as well as many other life endeavors.

Drew Ruana powering through Lucifer (5.14c), Red River Gorge, Kentucky.
SAVANNAH CUMMINS

CHAPTER ELEVEN

Performance Nutrition

Life is subtle—only through improving on the little things will you succeed in the big things.

The foods and beverages you consume play a primary role in determining your mental acuity, physical energy, and ability to recover from vigorous training or climbing. Therefore, a thoughtfully designed diet will provide a noticeable edge in performance, whereas engaging in a "see-food diet"—you see food and you eat it!—will continue to hamper your performance in a covert way that you may never recognize.

While it's impossible to say exactly how big a part diet plays in climbing performance, I estimate that most climbers can realize a 10 to 20 percent improvement in their training, recovery, concentration, energy, and overall climbing performance if they dedicate themselves to improved dietary surveillance.

As a dedicated athlete and performance coach, I follow the changing trends in nutrition with great interest. In the late 1980s high-carbohydrate, low-fat diets were the rage; in the mid-1990s high-protein diets were in vogue; in the 2000s the high-fat, low-carbohydrate diets sold the most books and got the greatest hype; and now in the 2010s the Paleo diet has become somewhat popular. Interestingly, all these diets seem to have some scientific backing, yet it's often hard to separate science from dogma. Fortunately, performance nutrition is not that complex a subject—if you make sensible food choices, eat moderately, and avoid excessive amounts of sugar, alcohol, and unhealthy fats, then you'll be eating more healthfully than most folks.

I was fortunate to realize the causal connection between nutrition and performance many years ago. Though I occasionally relax my dietary surveillance, I credit sound nutrition—about forty-eight weeks per year—for my ability to train exceedingly hard, avoid injury, recover quickly, and still climb at a high level into my fifties—despite decades of climbing abuse to my joints, tendons, and muscles. Follow the guidelines presented in this chapter, and I trust that you can do the same as well!

Macronutrients

There is no single perfect diet for climbers, just as there is no single perfect training program. To some extent the amount and best type of foods for you depend on your climbing preference. For instance, alpine climbers have significantly different nutritional needs and energy requirements than folks who partake in cragging or bouldering.

Our study of performance nutrition begins with a look at the three macronutrients: protein, fat, and carbohydrate. As in the prior chapters, the focus will remain on the best strategies for rock climbers, with only general information for alpine climbers.

Protein

Protein has many functions in the body, including building and repairing tissue, acting as a major component of the immune system, and making up enzymes, which facilitate every reaction that goes on in the body. Growing individuals need more protein than adults do simply because they are actually laying down large amounts of new tissue.

Healthy adults have a fairly extensive protein pool to draw on—that is, the proteins we consume are recycled several times for different functions in the body. For this reason daily protein requirements for adults are modest, even if they are training to increase muscle mass. Successful training is much less a factor of consuming a lot of protein than of using the appropriate training strategy and eating enough carbohydrates to fuel your training.

DAILY REQUIREMENTS

Between 1.2 and 1.5 grams of protein per kilogram of body weight per day is adequate for most climbers. For a seventy-two-kilogram (160-pound) individual, this translates to 86 to 108 grams per day. This is higher than the 0.8 to 1.0 gram per kilogram recommended for sedentary individuals by the FDA. Some studies have shown a slightly higher need in athletes, not just to increase muscle mass but also to facilitate recovery from exercise and compensate for the catabolic (tissue-consuming) effects of long, intense exercise. Still, I (and most nutritionists) do not buy in to the massive protein-intake guidelines (as much as 2.0 to 3.0 grams per kilogram per day) prescribed by some.

BEST PROTEIN SOURCES

Low-fat dairy products such as skim milk and yogurt, plus grilled chicken and fish and lean red meats provide you with the best protein value for your calorie. For example, a three-ounce piece of lean red meat such as tenderloin contains only 180 calories and twenty-five grams of high-quality, complete protein. A glass of skim milk contains about ten grams of complete protein and almost zero fat. If you prefer not to eat much meat (like me) or dairy products, whey protein powder mixed into skim milk, 100 percent pure fruit juice, or water is an excellent source of high-quality protein. Incomplete proteins—sources that do not contain all twenty amino acids—are also useful when eaten in combination. This is of particular importance to vegetarian athletes, who, by the way, are more likely to be protein-deficient.

Table 11.1 Caloric Content of Macronutrients

Macronutrient	Calories/gram
Carbohydrate	4
Protein	4
Fat	9

Fat

It's true that most Americans eat far too much fat, which contributes to our high incidence of heart disease, cancer, hypertension, and obesity. Still, getting too little fat has serious implications as well. Dietary fat is necessary as a source of essential fatty acids, which are involved in critical physiological processes such as the functions of the immune system and hormone production. Furthermore, our cell membranes consist largely of phospholipids (fatty acid derivatives), without which we would not be able to make healthy new cells, including muscle cells. A dietary fat deficiency in female athletes has been shown to cause amenorrhea (menstrual cycle irregularities), which may affect the development and maintenance of bone tissue.

DAILY REQUIREMENTS

On average the body's minimum fat requirement is fifteen to twenty-five grams per day. Usually fat-intake recommendations are expressed in terms of percentage of total calories consumed daily. For climbers, 15 to 30 percent of total calories should come from fat, depending on your climbing preference.

For cragging and bouldering, where a low percentage of body fat is desirable and the energy demands are largely anaerobic, fat intake should be restricted to 15 to 20 percent of total calories consumed. Alpine climbers, however, may be better off consuming up to 30 percent of daily calories from fat. These endurance climbers place great demands on the larger muscles of the body (especially the legs) and expend much more energy per day than, say, sport climbers. Fat is more calorie-dense than carbohydrate and protein (see table 11.1), and it's a good fuel for long, slow aerobic activities. Both these attributes make foods with a higher fat content more advantageous for alpine climbers than for crag climbers.

FOUR TYPES OF FATS

In consuming your daily requirement of fat, it's important to know which of the four types of fat—saturated, monounsaturated, polyunsaturated, and trans fatty acids—are "good" and "bad." Although each contains the same nine calories per gram consumed, they are not all created equal in terms of their role in performance nutrition. Consequently, it's important not only to eat the optimal amount of fat but also to have the best ratio among the different types of fatty acids.

- **Saturated fats** are most common in animal products such as milk and dairy, meats, and poultry. They are also present in significant amounts in some nuts, including Brazil and macadamia. Although excessive saturated fat intake does increase serum cholesterol, in particular the LDL or "bad" cholesterol, a certain amount is needed by our bodies to be made into fatty-acid-containing compounds such as hormones and phospholipids.
- **Monounsaturated fatty acids** are found in vegetables and oils including canola, olive, peanut, and avocado. These "monos" are thought to be the most beneficial in protecting against heart disease because of their ability to lower LDL without reducing HDL (the "good" cholesterol).
- **Polyunsaturated fatty acids** are common in fish, especially tuna, mackerel, salmon, and trout, and in corn, sunflower, and soybean oils. The omega-3 "polys" found mainly in fish and flaxseed are currently being investigated for their roles in fighting inflammatory diseases such as arthritis and other illnesses, including migraine headaches and heart disease.
- **Trans fatty acids** are found in trace amounts in almost all sources of natural fats, but most of those in our diet come from hydrogenated oils. During the process of hydrogenation, liquid vegetable oils are converted into solids by bombardment with hydrogen atoms (as in the making of margarine and shortening). Hydrogenation in effect converts unsaturated fatty acids into saturated fatty acids largely through the formation of trans bonds. Recent studies have raised concerns about these bonds because they produce effects similar to those of saturated fats and may, in fact, be cancer causing.

While most well-trained athletes have a very healthy cholesterol profile (unless they smoke or have a genetic predisposition to problems), it's wise to limit your intake of trans fatty acids. Unfortunately, hydrogenated oils and partially hydrogenated oils are found in such a wide range of foods that they are hard to avoid. For instance, many of the breads, cookies, and snack foods you buy off the shelf at the grocery store contain high amounts of these harmful oils. (Read the labels—you'll be surprised how many foods you eat daily contain them!) Many commercial fried foods are cooked in oils that contain trans fatty acids. Surprisingly, even some health foods and energy bars contain partially hydrogenated oils.

In terms of fat consumption, the best approach is to consume about equal amounts of saturated, monounsaturated, and polyunsaturated fatty acids and minimize intake of trans fatty acids. Try to eliminate hydrogenated oils from your diet, and in doing so you will reduce your consumption of these unhealthy fats to acceptable levels. (Unfortunately, it's very difficult to escape them completely in this world of highly processed and prepackaged foods.)

Examine the labels of the foods you eat most regularly and determine which items are doing you the most nutritional damage. Chances are you can make huge strides by eliminating just a handful of killer items like french fries, fried meats, snack cakes and muffins, salty snacks (buy baked chips and crackers instead), and any highly processed food designed for maximum shelf life (no doubt high in hydrogenated oils).

Carbohydrate

Although fat and protein can be used to provide energy, carbohydrate is the most efficient and effective source of energy for the muscles and brain. A high-carbohydrate diet is also important for athletes due to its protein-sparing effect. If you do not consume enough carbohydrates to meet your energy needs, muscle protein will be broken down for energy—the last thing any strength or power athlete would ever want! Consequently, the popular low-carbohydrate diets (Atkins, Zone, Ketogenic, and so forth) are inappropriate for most active climbers.

Carbohydrates come in two forms: sugars and starches. The sugar foods include fruit, sugar, soda pop, jam, honey, and molasses, while common starches are breads, rice, and pasta. Because these are the best sources of energy for high-intensity training and climbing, I'm sure you are already consuming plentiful amounts of these foods. Not all carbohydrates are created equal, however: Different carbohydrates release sugar into the bloodstream at different rates. The very best athletes know how to leverage this information to maintain stable energy throughout the day and to significantly increase the rate of recovery after a hard workout or day of climbing. If you are serious about climbing better, this subject should be of great interest to you. Enter the glycemic index.

GLYCEMIC INDEX

Historically, nutritionists classified carbohydrates only into the two basic groups of simple carbohydrates (sugars) and complex carbohydrates (starches). Simple sugars were said to produce a rapid rise in blood sugar and quick energy, while complex carbohydrates were said to provide slow, steady energy. Although this concept holds true in general, recent studies have found that there is a large variability in the rise in blood sugar following the ingestion of various foods from both the sugar and starch groups.

To investigate and more accurately classify the metabolism of carbohydrates, researchers developed the glycemic index (GI)—a powerful nutritional tool I first introduced to climbers in my 1994 book *Flash Training*. This index determines how the ingestion of a particular food affects blood sugar levels in comparison with the ingestion of straight glucose. Consumption of high-GI foods causes a rapid increase in blood sugar and a large insulin response. Low-GI foods produce more subtle changes. Climbers can use knowledge of the glycemic index to control energy levels and to speed recovery after a workout. Here's how.

Stable insulin levels are optimal for long-duration stop-and-go activities such as all-day climbing and long training sessions. Experts also agree that a steady insulin curve promotes muscle growth and discourages fat storage. This makes low- to medium-GI foods preferable for climbers in most situations. High-GI foods produce large swings in blood sugar and an insulin spike. One minute you are jonesing to crank another hard route and the next you're yawning and feeling strangely weak.

Figuring the glycemic index of certain foods is more difficult than it might seem at first. For instance, most foods classified as simple carbohydrates (cereal, candy, some fruit juices) are high-GI foods. However, so are potatoes, white rice, bread, and bagels—all considered complex carbohydrates. Low-GI foods include vegetables, whole grains, brown rice, and milk (see table 11.2).

As a general rule, the more processed and easily digestible a food, the higher its glycemic index (for instance, liquids have a higher index than similar food in solid form). High-fiber foods tend to elicit

Table 11.2 Glycemic Index of Common Foods

High (> 70)		Medium (50–70)		Low (< 50)	
Sports drinks	70–85	Banana	55	Balance Bar	30
Clif Bar	70+	PowerBar	65	Peanuts	14
Bagel	72	Raisins	64	Apple	38
Carrots	71	Granola bars	61	Orange	43
Corn chips	73	Macaroni	64	Pear	36
Cornflakes	77	Shredded wheat	58	Grapefruit	23
Doughnut	76	Sweet potato	54	Yogurt (w/ fruit)	30
Honey	73	Bran muffin	60	All-Bran	42
Jelly beans	80	Oatmeal	61	Whole wheat	37
Potatoes	83	Wheat crackers	67	Spaghetti	41
Rice (instant)	91	Cookies	60	Beans	48
Rice cakes	82	Orange juice	57	Lentils	28
Cracker (soda/water)	76	Soft drinks	68	Milk (skim)	32
Glucose	100	Sucrose	65	Fructose	23

a slow insulin response and have a relatively low GI. Finally, foods containing some protein and fat along with carbohydrates come in lower on the scale.

This last piece of information is useful if you don't have the gumption to memorize and use this index. Consuming some protein and fat during each of your carbohydrate feedings serves to moderate the overall glycemic response of the meal. So for a long day at the crags, select a sports drink that contains some protein and pack mainly balanced-type energy bars (those containing nearly equal amounts of calories from protein, carbohydrate, and fat).

The one good time to consume high-GI foods such as juice, soda pop, and most sports drinks (like Gatorade) is at the end of your workout or day of climbing. Intense exercise primes the muscles to immediately reload energy reserves in the form of glycogen. High blood sugar and the insulin spike help drive this repletion process. The optimal window for these high-GI foods is the first two hours following exercise. After that, favor low- to medium-index foods for slow, steady refueling. See chapter 12 for more information on this and other recovery strategies.

DAILY REQUIREMENTS

Carbohydrates should account for nearly two-thirds of your daily calorie intake. This means that roughly two-thirds of your plate should be covered with pasta, rice, potatoes, and vegetables, with the other third comprising lean, protein-rich foods. Be sure to apply the same rules when snacking. Try to pair up carbos such as a bagel or fruit with some protein like skim milk, yogurt, or a small amount of peanut butter. The protein helps slow down the digestion of carbohydrates and results in longer-lasting energy.

You can also calculate your approximate need for carbohydrates according to your body weight. Training for two hours per day, you would need roughly seven grams of carbohydrate per kilogram of body weight. For example, if you weigh seventy-two kilograms (160 pounds), the requirement would be for

Table 11.3 Estimated Nutrient and Calorie Needs

Climber	Macronutrient	Grams Needed	Calories	Total
Male (160 lbs./72kg), active day	carbohydrate	520g	2,080	
	protein	115g	460	3,170
	fat	70g	630	
Male (160 lbs./72kg), rest day	carbohydrate	360g	1,140	
	protein	85g	340	2,230
	fat	50g	450	
Female (110 lbs./50kg), active day	carbohydrate	350g	1,400	
	protein	80g	320	2,170
	fat	50g	450	
Female (110 lbs./50kg), rest day	carbohydrate	250g	1,000	
	protein	60g	240	1,582
	fat	38g	342	

approximately 500 grams of carbohydrates; at four calories per gram of carbohydrate, this would equal 2,000 calories. Engaging in a full day of strenuous climbing, however—compared with two hours of training—may demand as much as ten to fourteen grams per kilogram of body weight.

Water

Water may be the most important nutrient to get right when you are climbing, yet I sense that many climbers are chronically dehydrated. Dr. Kristine Clark, director of sports nutrition at Penn State's Center for Sports Medicine, says that "even a 1 to 2 percent drop in water will cause problems in performance." The earliest symptoms of mild dehydration are a loss of concentration and enhanced fatigue. Clark adds that "a 3 percent drop in water level can create headaches, cramping, dizziness." Furthermore, a recent study found that dehydration leading to just a 1.5 percent drop in body weight resulted in a statistically significant drop in maximum strength (Schoffstall 2001).

In a sport as stressful as climbing, dehydration also increases your chance of a joint or tendon injury. Consider that proper hydration facilitates transport of nutrients to the cells, helps protect tissues from injury, and maintains joint lubrication. Therefore, for the purpose of injury prevention, maintaining proper hydration as you train or climb is as important as a proper warm-up.

RECOMMENDATIONS FOR PREVENTING DEHYDRATION

As a rule of thumb, it's a good idea to prehydrate ("camel up," as it's called) before you go to the gym or head out climbing by drinking two cups (about sixteen ounces) of water. Follow this with a minimum of an eight-ounce serving every hour or two throughout the day. This would total one to two quarts of water consumed over an eight-hour period on the rocks. This is a bare-minimum amount—what you might drink, say, on a cold day when you perspire very little. Climbing on a humid, eighty-degree day, however, would roughly double this requirement. That means carrying three to four quarts of water with you for a hot eight-hour day of climbing. Of course, I doubt you know of very many, if any, climbers who carry this amount of liquid to the crags—thus the mass of climbers are unknowingly detracting from their climbing ability and increasing injury risk due to mild dehydration.

Optimal Macronutrient Ratio

As you may have gleaned from the previous sections, the optimal macronutrient ratio for a climber depends on the type of climbing activity. High-intensity, stop-and-go climbing like bouldering or cragging is best fueled with a 65:15:20 ratio of carbohydrate, protein, and fat, respectively. The long, slow distance training and climbing of an alpine climber demands a higher total calorie count per day than the typical rock climber, and this need would be more easily met with a higher-fat diet (though adequate carbohydrates are still necessary). Consequently, a macronutrient ratio of 55:15:30 would be more suitable for the alpine climber. See table 11.3 for sample calorie counts for a typical male and female rock climber, but realize that you personally could have significantly different requirements.

Diet and Nutritional Tips

1. Strive for a 65:15:20 caloric ratio of carbohydrate, protein, and fat in your overall daily diet.
2. Consume 1.2 to 1.5 grams of protein per kilogram of body weight per day to facilitate maximum recovery and muscular regeneration.
3. Limit fat consumption to mono- and polyunsaturated fats from vegetable and fish oils. Avoid saturated and trans fats, fried foods, and prepackaged snack products.
4. Consume several small carbohydrate snacks throughout the day to provide sustained energy, positive mood, and clear thinking. Favor low- to mid-GI foods.
5. Drink an eight-ounce serving of water every hour or two throughout the day—and twice this amount on hot days.

Micronutrients and Sports Supplements

The subject of micronutrients and sports supplements is so broad that it's impossible to discuss in a comprehensive manner in an instructional text like this. Still, the use of vitamin supplements and functional foods is so common in sports that the subject is worthy of at least a primer.

Sales of vitamin and sports supplements is a multibillion-dollar industry that bombards us with multilateral, never-ending advertising. Some of the weight-loss and strength-gain claims are truly remarkable, but very few of these claims are backed by reliable scientific studies. Many products are promoted with strong anecdotal claims and well-paid pitchmen, but very few actually do what the advertisers claim.

It's my belief that up to 90 percent of the sports supplements on the market are nothing other than modern-day snake oil, yet a serious athlete looking to maximize performance must be careful not to throw the baby out with the bathwater. On the pages that follow, we'll sort out the handful of products that could potentially enhance your training response and climbing performance.

Micronutrients

Vitamins and minerals are the essential dietary micronutrients. Although the body needs only very small amounts of these nutrients (compared with the macronutrients), they do play a vital role in almost every bodily function—from muscular growth and energy metabolism to neural conduction and memory. Consequently, your health and athletic performance can suffer in a number of ways if you are not consuming enough of these micronutrients.

Studies have shown that as much as two-thirds of self-selected diets contain less than the recommended daily allowances (RDA) of certain vital vitamins and minerals. Furthermore, despite being updated in recent years, RDAs are still believed by many experts to represent low-end requirements for a serious athlete. Therefore, taking a daily multivitamin would be prudent for any serious athlete. It's a remarkably cheap nutritional investment—a generic multivitamin, purchased at CVS or Walgreens, costs less than $15 for a three-month supply.

Magnesium and zinc are two important minerals shown to be consumed in less than recommended amounts by a majority of the population. Although both are included in most daily multivitamin brands, they aren't well absorbed, and a deficiency in these minerals could mean you're getting shortchanged on training response. Several recent studies have shown a statistically significant increase in muscular strength in a group of athletes taking supplemental magnesium and zinc (in the form of a patented supplement known as ZMA) versus a control group of athletes taking a placebo (Brilla 1998). Clearly, any climber engaging in serious strength training could benefit from taking ZMA or by consuming foods rich in magnesium (spinach, nuts, beans and lentils, whole grains, and low-fat dairy) and zinc (seafood, beef, cashews, pork, and chicken).

Calcium and iron are two other minerals that some climbers may be lacking. Vegetarians often fall short on iron consumption, and some women may not get enough iron and calcium in their diets. A multivitamin is the best way to obtain extra iron, especially since its absorption is enhanced in the presence of vitamin C (also in a multivitamin). Females wanting to get extra calcium in their diets could take a calcium supplement (Tums are cheap and taste good!) or simply drink a few glasses of skim milk each day.

Sports Supplements

The most effective way to increase climbing performance is through a long-term, dedicated effort to improve your technique, mental control, and upper-body strength. Unless you are working to dial in each of these areas, the few sports supplements that do work are probably a waste of money. If you are actively honing your technical skills and training to increase your physical and mental fitness, however, you may be able to further improve your performance through the use of a handful of ergogenic (performance-enhancing) supplements.

PROTEIN POWDERS

As discussed earlier, athletes have a greater daily protein requirement than sedentary people, since strenuous exercise results in a higher protein turnover. While mega amounts are not necessary (as some supplement companies and fitness magazines suggest), a 160-pound climber does need to consume between 86 and 108 grams of protein per day. This modest amount can be met through a well-rounded diet; it may be tough to consume adequate protein, however, if you do not eat meat such as chicken, fish, and lean red meats. There is also the limiting factor relating to the biological value of the protein source consumed. Not all protein sources are equal when it comes to providing your body with the necessary building blocks.

Consequently, scientists have developed a number of ways to measure the quality of protein sources. The biological value (BV) is one of the most commonly used; it's based on how much of the protein consumed is actually absorbed and utilized by the body. The higher the BV, the greater the amount of protein that is actually available for use by the body to strengthen muscles and connective tissues, and to support enzyme formation, among other things.

When the BV scale was originally developed, the egg was considered the perfect protein source (remember Rocky?) and sat alone atop the chart with a value of one hundred. Since then new technologies have enabled the creation of super-proteins that are equally valuable to the body but without the fat found in many high-protein foods. Whey

Table 11.4 Biological Values of Protein Sources

Food	BV
Whey	104
Whole egg	100
Milk	91
Egg white	88
Fish	83
Beef	80
Chicken	79
Soy	74
Beans	49
Peanuts	43

Not all protein sources are equal when it comes to providing your body with the necessary building blocks. Select mostly high-BV foods from the top half of the list.

is the current superstar of proteins—its BV is 104, meaning that it provides even better nitrogen retention than eggs. Therefore, whey protein could be viewed as superior to the lower-BV foods such as fish, beef, chicken, or soy in helping meet the protein needs of an athlete.

While whey protein costs approximately $0.60 to $0.90 per twenty-gram serving, the investment is a good one considering its ease of use and high BV. Many brands are available from health food stores, supplement catalogs, and online merchants, so shop around for the best deal—look specifically for a blend of "whey isolate and whey concentrate," which is the highest quality and mixes easily in milk, juice, or water. Such liquid protein is ideal first thing in the morning, and it can increase your rate of recovery when consumed immediately following your workout or a day of climbing (more on this in chapter 12).

One of the highest-quality and most affordable protein sources is skim milk (see table 11.4). Since each glass contains ten grams of protein, consuming a quart of milk per day would provide forty grams toward your total protein requirement. As someone who only occasionally eats meat, I have relied on skim milk as my primary source of protein for the last thirty-five years (since I first read that John Gill slammed back milk protein after climbing). In drinking about two gallons of milk per week for more than thirty-six years, I've somehow consumed nearly 4,000 gallons of skim milk since I started climbing. All I can say is, "Got milk?"

Even those who are lactose-intolerant can consume milk without any nasty side effects by purchasing acidophilus milk. Regardless, be sure to always select 1 percent or skim milk (best), since whole milk contains a significant amount of saturated fat.

SPORTS DRINKS

Since the invention of Gatorade in the early 1970s, sports drinks have grown into a massive industry. It's now hard to find a serious athlete who does not consume sports drinks to help replenish energy. Dozens of different sports drinks are available in bottled form, including Gatorade and Powerade, the two most popular drinks on the market right now. Many others are sold in a bulk powdered form ideal for mixing up at home before a workout or day at the crags.

As you might expect, not all sports drinks are the same. Some are merely glorified sugar water, while others include electrolytes or any number of vitamins, minerals, herbs, or other nutrients said to increase athletic performance. Clearly, many of the claims are unsubstantiated—and at up to three bucks a bottle, some are just a big rip-off.

The active ingredients in these products fall into two main categories: electrolytes and fuel replacements (although some drinks like Red Bull are laced with caffeine, herbs, and vitamins, too). A simple understanding of both will help you understand how these drinks might be of benefit to you.

Electrolytes such as potassium, magnesium, calcium, sodium, and chloride are critical for

Snack and rehydrate every hour or two. You'll climb better all day long and top out on long routes with energy to spare!

concentration, energy production, nerve transmission, and muscle contraction. Fortunately, electrolyte loss during exercise is quite slow, so even a full day of climbing won't cause significant depletion. A reasonable diet and multivitamin provide you with all the electrolytes you need for ordinary training or a day of climbing. Still, a sports drink with electrolytes may be beneficial if your food supply will be limited for a few days, as in big-wall or alpine climbing.

Fuel sources in the sports drinks are mainly carbohydrates, including glucose, sucrose, fructose, maltodextrin, and lactates. Glucose and sucrose (table sugar) are the fuel sources in the original sports drink Gatorade and have since been adopted by many other companies. Ironically, some athletes now shun drinks with large amounts of glucose and sucrose to avoid a blood sugar spike. Unless you are engaged in an activity that continues steadily for a couple of hours (such as long-distance biking, running, or hiking), this quick increase in blood sugar may be followed by an energy crash as insulin kicks in to reduce the elevated blood sugar level. In a stop-and-go sport like climbing, this pullback on blood sugar can leave you feeling more "flat" and lethargic than before you consumed the drink!

Consequently, you should avoid any drink whose first ingredient (after water) is glucose or high-fructose corn syrup—both are signs that the drink has a high glycemic index and will release sugar rapidly into the blood. Instead, shop around for powdered sports drink mixes that list fructose (not the same as high-fructose corn syrup) or a protein source such as whey as the first or second ingredient. These have a lower glycemic index and hence provide a slower, more sustained release of carbohydrate ideal for climbers. Accelerade by Pacific Health Labs or PowerBar's Performance Recovery are two good choices.

Carbohydrate (glycogen) depletion in the muscles and liver is a primary cause of fatigue when performing long-duration activities of more than ninety minutes. The traditional use of sports drinks is for situations when additional fuel is needed for prolonged activity lasting more than ninety minutes. Therefore, consuming a fructose-based or protein-containing sports drink during the course of a day at the crags will help maintain energy levels throughout the day, though consuming some food would be beneficial as well. Conversely, an hour or two of bouldering or a short gym workout will not benefit from the added fuel of a sports drink.

While a slow-release, fructose-based or protein-containing sports drink is ideal for when you are climbing, it might be better to consume a high-GI drink upon completion of your workout or day of climbing. Numerous studies have shown that elevating blood sugar as soon as possible after exercise provides the substrate for synthesis of muscle glycogen (Robergs 1991). This is especially important if you plan to climb the very next day—replenishing glycogen stores takes up to twenty-four hours, so you need to get the process started immediately and at high speed (see chapter 12 for more recovery tips).

ENERGY BARS

Energy bars have been a dietary mainstay of many climbers since PowerBar hit the scene back in the late 1980s. Originally intended for endurance athletes like bikers and runners, many of the energy bars are designed to deliver a rapid release of sugar into the bloodstream. Therefore, many energy bars possess a high glycemic index (greater than seventy); these are easily identified by their first ingredient, high-fructose corn syrup. Climbers in search of sustained energy are better off sticking to foods with a GI of less than seventy, since they provide more sustained energy and less of an insulin response.

The numerous balanced-style bars that have entered the market in recent years typically possess a glycemic index in the forty-to-sixty range (my favorites are Balance Bar and PowerBar Protein Plus). The higher amount of protein and fat contained in these bars helps slow the release of sugar into the bloodstream. The balanced 40:30:30 macronutrient ratio also helps conserve glycogen and may even help spare muscle protein from being used for energy during a long day of climbing. Consequently, consuming a couple of Protein Plus PowerBars (Fig Newtons are also good) and drinking lots of water may be the single best combination to maintain energy, spare muscle protein, and prevent dehydration.

CREATINE

There are dozens of sports supplements that claim to increase strength/power and to help build muscle. While most are, in fact, worthless, creatine has been shown to produce increases in muscular strength in dozens of well-executed studies. Based on this, creatine must be a good supplement for climbers. Right? Not so fast, my highball-sending, redpoint-crushing friend!

Let's look at the facts. First, creatine is by far the most effective, legal sports supplement on the market. Not only has it been shown to enhance explosive strength in numerous well-controlled studies (Toler 1997 and Kreider 1998), but when consumed in large doses the user actually increases lean mass (large, harder muscles). Consequently, creatine has become the biggest selling sports supplement in the country, and it's widely used by football and baseball players, weight lifters, bodybuilders, MMAers, CrossFitters, sprinters, and millions of fitness buffs.

Creatine is a compound that's natural to our body and, as you learned in chapter 5, creatine phosphate it is used in the muscles to help create ATP (the energy source for brief, explosive movements) as part of the anaerobic alactic energy pathway. Creatine is present in animal foods such as red meat; however, the amount consumed in a normal diet is quite small (typically just a gram or two per day). Studies have shown that taking twenty grams per day of supplemental creatine for five or six days will enhance performance in short-duration, high-intensity exercise such as sprinting or weight lifting. This "creatine loading" protocol is the method used by most athletes in search of greater strength/power and gains in lean body mass. (Long-term use of the creatine loading protocol may be stressful on the kidneys, so it would be wise to cycle on and off creatine if you are consuming "loading" amounts.)

Two side effects of creatine loading are weight gain and "cell volumizing." Both these effects occur because creatine associates with water as it is stored in the muscles (95 percent of the creatine is stored inside muscle cells, and so intracellular water almost certainly increases). Over the six-day loading phase, more and more creatine is stored, and an increasing amount of water is drawn into the muscle cell—this gives muscles a fuller, "pumped" feel and look, just what bodybuilders and fitness buffs want. This loading process, therefore, typically results in a water weight gain of two or three pounds (or more). This is a good thing for athletes in sports where increased lean body mass and speed (inertia) can be used to your advantage (e.g., football, swinging a bat, or swinging your fist). However, in a sport that requires a high strength-to-weight ratio, it can have a negative impact on performance.

Some climbers have argued that stronger muscles (due to creatine loading) can easily lift the extra weight gained. The problem, however, is that creatine loads in all muscles of the body, not just the "climbing" muscles. Furthermore, creatine will load proportionally more in the largest muscles of the body—the legs!—not exactly the place smart climbers would want to increase muscle mass. Therefore, I'm sure you'll agree that the creatine loading protocol would likely be counterproductive for a serious climber.

If you are still not convinced, let's consider the cell volumizing effect of heavy creatine use. Bodybuilders love the fact that their muscles pump up more easily when they are loaded with creatine (and water). I quickly noticed this same effect when experimenting with creatine when it first appeared on the market in 1993. It seemed strange at the time, but I pumped out more quickly when I was "on" creatine, despite the fact that I felt like I had a little more zip in my muscles. What I theorize is that the cell volumizing effect may lead to faster occlusion of important capillary blood flow within the muscles during strenuous exercises, thus causing a severe pump and rapid muscle failure when the energy pathway shifts away from anaerobic alactic (after ten to fifteen seconds). So while creatine use may have a positive effect on brief powerful climbs lasting less than fifteen seconds, the "pump effect" may very well hamper climbing performance on longer boulder problems and difficult roped ascents.

All this said, I do believe that well-timed, small doses of creatine can help climbers (especially boulderers) slightly increase their anaerobic power and recover a bit more quickly. The protocol I've developed and used for several years now is to add just two to five grams of creatine to a quart of sports drink that I sip throughout my workout (or climbing day). This provides just a few grams more than a normal "dietary dose" of creatine—enough to hasten recovery of maximal power between exercises and boulder problems, yet likely without the undesirable side effects of "loading."

The Truth About Creatine for Climbers

Small-dose creatine usage (two to five grams per day) may yield a slight increase in power and a small edge in recovery between strenuous exercises, boulder problems, and routes, without any significant undesirable side effects.

The high-dose "creatine loading" protocol (ten to twenty grams consumed daily) is likely counterproductive for climbers, due to weight gain (commonly two to four pounds) and increased muscle "pump" during long boulder problems or routes.

A small percentage of individuals are creatine "nonresponders," meaning that creatine consumption results in no observable positive or negative effects (possibly because they have an unusually low percentage of fast-twitch muscle fibers).

Creatine usage can cause cramping, particularly in the foot and leg muscles, in some individuals. Long-term creatine use may be harmful to the kidneys.

Creatine is not a banned substance, nor is it on the World Anti-Doping Agency (WADA) list of prohibited substances.

CAFFEINE

If you are a coffee aficionado like me, then you'll surely enjoy this section. Your addiction—er, culinary ritual—may actually give you an extra edge both in training and climbing!

Moderate caffeine consumption can energize your training and, perhaps, enhance performance slightly. Here, Matilda Söderlund is amped to be training at Café Kraft! HANNES HUCH

Caffeine (the active ingredient in coffee) is the number one ergogenic aid of the common man and athletes alike. It's caffeine's well-documented effects on the central nervous system that help you wake up in the morning, gather your focus at school or work, and become a bit more powerful at the gym. Remarkably, caffeine has also been shown to have numerous positive impacts on health—most notable is its protective effect when it comes to neurodegenerative diseases (Parkinson's and Alzheimer's) and cancer (bladder, pancreatic, breast, ovarian, colon, and colorectal).

If you consume a daily coffee, espresso, tea, or another caffeine-laced drink like Red Bull or Mountain Dew, then you know firsthand the stimulant effects of caffeine. But there are several other ways that caffeine might help you train and climb harder, as well as a few undesirable side effects that you need to be aware of. Let's sort things out.

Here are the most notable performance-enhancing effects of caffeine, as summarized in an excellent meta-analysis research paper by Bülent Sökmen, et al. (2008).

- Improved concentration, alertness, and mood, especially in sleep-deprived athletes.
- Enhanced reaction time and improved accuracy in skilled movements.
- Lowered peripheral pain perception and rating of perceived exertion.
- Increased work output and time to exhaustion during aerobic-powered endurance exercise (e.g., endurance routes and multipitch climbs).
- Increased power output and isokinetic strength in maximum-strength and power events lasting less than ten seconds (e.g., short, maximal boulder problem, campus training, one-arm pull-ups).

Table 11.5 Caffeine Content of Common Energy Drinks

Product	Serving Size	Caffeine (mg)
Cola (Coke, Pepsi, Ale 8-1)	12 oz.	approx. 35
Tea	8 oz.	25–50
Mountain Dew	12 oz.	54
Red Bull	8.5 oz.	80
Monster Energy Drink	16 oz.	160
Rockstar Energy Drink	16 oz.	160
Coffee "weak" (McDonalds)	16 oz.	160
5-Hour Energy Drink	2 oz.	200
Anhydrous caffeine (No-Doze, Vivarin)	1 tablet	200
Coffee "strong" (Starbucks, Caribou)	16 oz.	300

Considering these cognitive and physiological effects, it's not surprising that so many climbers consume caffeine, not only in the morning but also upon arriving at the gym or crag. Still, you must be careful not to develop a more-is-better mind-set when it comes to quaffing your favorite caffeinated drink—there are some potential negative impacts to consider.

- High doses can make you jittery and nervous—not ideal for a delicate face climb (requiring fine motor control) or before competition.
- High doses may impart a generalized ill feeling due to gastrointestinal distress, headache, and perhaps even heart palpitations.
- Given caffeine's half-life of four to six hours, consumption in the afternoon or evening may lead to insomnia or a restless night's sleep.
- High doses of caffeine have been shown to lower blood pH (more acidic), and therefore it may negatively impact high-intensity exercise performance relying on the glycolytic energy system (e.g., short, pumpy sport routes).

Vitamin and Sports Supplement Tips

1. Take a daily multivitamin each morning with breakfast.
2. Consider consuming extra protein (especially if you eat little meat or dairy products) by drinking a whey protein shake each morning and evening.
3. When climbing, snack on fruits, balanced-style energy bars, sports drinks (choose those possessing some fructose and/or protein), and other lower-GI foods. Consider adding two to five grams of creatine (never more) to your bottle of sports drink to further enhance recovery.
4. Small, well-timed doses of caffeine and creatine may provide an edge in both training and climbing.
5. Avoid mass-marketed sports supplements, especially those with the wildest claims—most are frauds.

So how much caffeine should you consume to gain a performance edge? Ultimately that depends on your tolerance to this drug, which is a function of the amount you habitually consume daily. Across the research literature, subjects consumed between 3 and 13 milligrams of caffeine per kilogram of body weight; however, low to moderate dosing of 3 to 9 milligrams per kilogram seems optimal (most upsides with fewest negative side effects). For the average-size climber, this equates to consuming somewhere between 200 and 600 milligrams of caffeine—use the low end of this range if you are caffeine "naïve" and upper-range dosing if you are a regular, heavy consumer. See table 11.5 for approximate caffeine content in common beverages.

The bottom line: Caffeine use can potentially enhance your training and climbing performance, but caffeine "overdose" will likely hurt your performance. The key is to experiment with and understand caffeine's unique effects on you. Ideally, you'll learn to manipulate your caffeine dosage to get the best performance-enhancing effect via moderate dosing—that is, decrease daily dosing in the days leading up to a critical climb or competition, then return to your "normal" moderate dose on the day of the event. This is a superior approach to simply doubling your caffeine dose on the performance day, thus risking the negative side effects listed above.

SPORTS SUPPLEMENTS THAT DON'T WORK

The list of sports supplements that don't work is too long to detail here. I will, however, name a couple of the most popular, most hyped supplements that have little or no reliable research to back up the big claims.

First and foremost is anything marketed as a "testosterone booster." They don't work—period. Fortunately, you can naturally increase your testosterone levels by eating a protein-rich diet, exercising intensely, shunning alcohol and sweets, and getting enough sleep. Next on the list of "bogus supplements" are nitric oxide boosters, most of which yield no effect at all; the exceptions are citrulline malate and beet root concentrate, both of which may support nitric oxide production and produce a slight beneficial vasodilation effect.

Let me cut to the chase: Pretty much everything touted as a "performance enhancer" or "miracle cure" is likely nothing more than expensive snake oil. Certainly there are performance-enhancing drugs that could help you train harder and perform better, but why would you want to go down that path? Outside of caffeine and creatine—by far the two most effective sports supplements—any substance that truly aids performance in a significant way is either illegal or on the WADA prohibition list.

Matty Hong on the first ascent of La Cucaracha (5.14c), Rifle, Coloardo.
MATTY HONG COLLECTION

CHAPTER TWELVE

Accelerating Recovery

What sets great climbers apart from others is not their physical prowess (amazing as it may be) but their brains. Peak performers (of all kinds) think and act in unique ways.

If you are serious about climbing performance, then you must be serious about accelerating recovery. Knowing how to limit fatigue and speed recovery is as important as knowing how to perform a drop-knee, lock a finger jam, or float a deadpoint. The bottom line: If you are not playing a proactive role in the recovery process, then you are definitely not training optimally or climbing up to your capability.

We all know, firsthand, that physical fatigue is a primary limiting factor whether pulling down at the crags or training in the gym. Therefore, it stands to reason that being able to accelerate recovery means you will get more back during a mid-climb shakeout and while resting between climbs and days of climbing. As a result, you will perform better on the rocks today, tomorrow, and on all your future outings. Similarly, more rapid recovery between training sessions can translate into more long-term strength gains, since you can work out more often while still getting adequate rest and without risk of overtraining.

While many of today's enthusiastic climbers are keen on staying current on the latest climbing and training techniques, surprisingly few individuals are aware of the numerous strategies for accelerating recovery. Recovery from exercise has been the subject of dozens of recent research studies, and any serious climber would be wise to heed the findings of these sports scientists. On the pages that follow, I will present the leading-edge recovery strategies used in these studies, as well as provide instruction on specific techniques that will help you slow fatigue and speed recovery while on the rock.

Clearly, recovery ability is a function of several factors, including age, sex, and level of conditioning. Regardless of these factors, however, I guarantee that you can recover more quickly by playing a proactive role in the recovery process—instead of just letting it happen, as many climbers do. By placing the same importance on optimal recovery as you do on training optimally, you will enhance your training response as well as your overall climbing performance!

The Basics of Fatigue and Recovery

Proactively managing fatigue and taking the steps to accelerate recovery require an understanding of the basic physiological processes involved in energy production, fatigue, and recovery. Chapter 5 presented a detailed study of energy systems and fatigue, but let's recap the key points before getting into specific recovery techniques.

Causes of Fatigue

Several factors contribute to the fatigue you experience while training or climbing. These factors include the depletion of muscle fuels, the accumulation of metabolic by-products, low blood glucose, muscular cramps and microtraumas, and, finally, central fatigue.

DEPLETION OF ATP-CP

Adenosine triphosphate (ATP) and creatine phosphate (CP) are energy-rich phosphate compounds stored within the muscle cells in small amounts. Brief, maximum-intensity activities (such as a short, vicious boulder problem, a one-arm pull-up, or a 100-meter sprint) are fueled by ATP and CP; the supply of these fuels, however, limits this action to between five and twelve seconds.

This constraint on power output explains why it's next to impossible to perform double dyno campus training for more than about ten to twelve seconds, or why you have less than about ten seconds to pull a maximal move (for you) on a route before your muscles give out. Continued exercise beyond this time threshold is only possible by lowering the intensity of the activity so that the glycolytic energy system can handle the energy production.

Fortunately, ATP and CP are continually synthesized within the muscles, and ATP-CP stores become fully replenished in just three to five minutes of complete rest (Bloomfield 1994).

ACCUMULATION OF METABOLIC BY-PRODUCTS

Sustained high-intensity activity lasting between twelve seconds and two minutes is fueled primary by the anaerobic metabolism of glycogen fuel (see table 5.3). Unfortunately, metabolic by-products of this energy production—chiefly, hydrogen ions (H+)—result in muscular discomfort and, eventually, muscular failure. How long you can exercise during periods of rising intracellular acidosis (and hypoxia) depends on your intra- and extracellular buffering capacity and the broader capability of your body to metabolize the numerous by-products of anaerobic glycolysis.

Strength/power-endurance training will increase your tolerance to acidosis as well as improve cellular and systemic buffering of H+. Furthermore, anything you do to enhance blood flow through the working muscles will help disperse excess lactate to lesser-stressed muscles, where it's consumed for aerobic energy production, and your liver, where it's converted back to glucose. Sustained high-intensity exercise (with no rest), however, will cause acidosis and lactate levels to skyrocket above tolerable levels, and, hence, muscular failure will occur in one to two minutes (sooner if you're truly climbing near your limit). This explains why the "pump clock" runs out in less than two minutes on sustained, near-maximum (for you) crux sequences.

During rest periods, the clearance time of H+, lactate, and other metabolic by-products can be anywhere from ten to sixty minutes, depending on the initial level of the H+ and lactate accumulation and whether the rest is active or passive (more on this later).

DEPLETION OF GLYCOGEN

Steady, long-term exercise typically depletes glycogen stores in ninety minutes to two hours. Running out of glycogen causes the infamous hitting-the-wall phenomenon in marathon running, and it is a contributing factor to your inability to climb hard toward the end of a long day on the rock.

Fortunately, climbing is a stop-and-go activity, so a full two-hour supply of glycogen can be stretched out to last nearly all day. You can also spare your glycogen supplies through regular consumption of additional fuel (sports drinks and foodstuffs) throughout the day. Research implies that carbohydrate feeding during exercise can help extend your glycogen supply by 25 to 50 percent (Coyle 1984).

Your starting level of glycogen is also a crucial factor in determining how long and hard you will be able to climb. If you are climbing for a second or third straight day, you will likely have less than the full ninety-minute to two-hour supply of glycogen. This is because complete replenishment of glycogen stores takes twenty-four hours—a good dinner and a full night's sleep are not enough to restock the supply completely. When climbing on successive days, it's therefore vital to consume more calories throughout the day (to spare glycogen)—and even so, you may hit the wall a bit sooner on day two than you did on day one.

LOW BLOOD GLUCOSE

Blood glucose (sugar) is but one of the possible fuel sources for working muscles, but it's the only fuel source available to the brain and nervous system. As glycogen supplies dwindle during long-duration activity, the working muscles become increasingly reliant on blood glucose for fuel. As a result, blood glucose levels drop and increasing levels of exhaustion and mental fatigue set in.

As mentioned above, ingestion of carbohydrates will help delay this fatigue by helping to maintain an adequate level of blood glucose.

MUSCLE CRAMPS AND MICROTRAUMAS

Muscle cramps and microtraumas can contribute to the sense of muscular fatigue, though in somewhat different time frames. Muscle cramps typically occur near the end of an exhausting period of muscle action—for instance, when some of the muscles in your back or arms lock up after a long, strenuous section of jamming or upon reaching complete exhaustion in the midst of a long sport climb. In such an instance, twenty to thirty minutes of rest, gentle stretching, and massage, as well as consuming some fluids, will help alleviate the cramping and restore normal muscular function.

Microtraumas are a primary cause of the all-too-common delayed-onset muscle soreness (DOMS). This muscle soreness, which becomes evident from twenty-four to forty-eight hours after strenuous exercise, is a result of microscopic muscle tissue tears and the accompanying tightness and swelling (and, no, this day-after muscle soreness is not caused by "lactic acid," per the common myth). Strength will be diminished for as long as pain persists, possibly as long as two to five days.

CENTRAL FATIGUE

Unlike muscular (peripheral) fatigue, central fatigue is brain-based—think of this as the brain's self-protective central governor limiting the amount of stress (and damage) you can levy on yourself. This so-called central fatigue is realized through a reduction in neural drive (recruitment), impaired coordination, decreased concentration and focus, and diminishing ability to execute difficult motor skills or maximal movement. Repeated high-intensity movements such as lunging and campus training are the hardest on the central nervous system. However, excessive amounts of any specific training stimulus—fingerboard, Hypergravity Isolation Training, campus training, and such, or performing the same type of bouldering movement over and over, can also produce central fatigue. Central fatigue is often most noticeable after back-to-back-to-back days of hard bouldering or projecting; a generalized sense of malaise and the inability to summon peak strength and power, even after days of rest, is the hallmark of central fatigue.

Unfortunately, severe central fatigue can take longer to recover from than that due to any of the other causes. Consider that recovery of a nerve cell takes up to seven times longer than a muscle cell (Bompa 1983). Of course, this level of fatigue may never be experienced by the typical recreational climber, whereas elite climbers, who push the envelope both in the gym and on the rock, are likely to experience central fatigue. If you still feel physically "off" even after a few successive rest days, you may be experiencing central fatigue. It may take another two to ten days away from training and climbing to recuperate completely.

Three Recovery Periods

Recovery is not linear, but instead exponential (see figure 12.1). For example, recovery from an exhaustive crux sequence, climb, workout, or day of climbing will initially be rapid, with about 70 percent of complete recovery taking place in the first

Figure 12.1 Recovery Curve

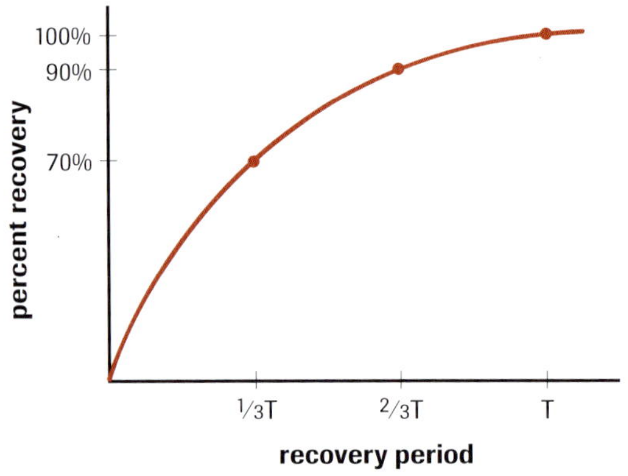

Recovery to 90 percent of baseline levels occurs in about two-thirds of the time needed for complete recovery.

one-third of the recovery period (Bompa 1983). Recovery improves to 90 percent after two-thirds of the time needed for complete recovery.

Knowing that recovery is an exponential process is powerful information that can be applied to the three crucial recovery periods that I've defined as recharge, refuel, and rebuild.

RECHARGE (IMMEDIATE/SHORT-TERM RECOVERY)

This first recovery period takes place from ten seconds to sixty minutes following the completion of muscular action. The recharge period includes the ten-second shakeout you take in the midst of a crux sequence, as well as the mid-climb rest you milk for five, ten, or even twenty minutes, if possible.

The two metabolic processes at work during this recovery period are resynthesis of ATP-CP and the removal of H+, lactate, and other metabolic by-products from the working muscles. As stated earlier, ATP-CP resynthesis takes less than five minutes, and complete H+ and lactate removal occurs in less than sixty minutes. As depicted in figure 12.1, however, recovery to 90 percent of baseline levels occurs in about two-thirds of the time needed for complete recovery. Therefore, you can assume that the majority of ATP-CP resynthesis has occurred in just over three minutes and that blood pH has returned to near-normal levels (90 percent of H+ removed) in about forty minutes. Strategies to further hasten recovery during the recharge period will be detailed later in this chapter.

REFUEL (MEDIUM-TERM RECOVERY)

The refuel recovery period occurs from sixty minutes to twenty-four hours following cessation of exercise. Therefore, this phase of recovery takes place during the two-hour break between climbs that you might take during the hottest part of the day (or while belaying your partner on their project) and, of course, during the overnight period following a training or climbing day.

With ATP-CP resynthesis and H+ removal completed in the first sixty minutes, the refuel stage is defined by the replenishment of blood glucose and glycogen stores (in muscles and the liver), and some minor repair of tissue microtraumas. Since refueling is the hallmark of this period, consuming a large amount of the right type of carbohydrates is necessary to facilitate the process.

Numerous strategies for enhancing this replenishment process will be described later in the chapter, but—as mentioned earlier—you can assume that about 90 percent of this refueling has taken place in about sixteen hours (two-thirds of the total recovery period). Thus the typical twelve-hour break between consecutive days of climbing will result only in approximately 80 percent replenishment of glycogen stores (assuming you begin refueling immediately upon finishing up the first day on the rocks).

Rebuild (Long-Term Recovery)

Muscle growth and neuromuscular adaptation typically take place from one to four days following strenuous exercise. The degree of delayed-onset muscle soreness experienced is proportionate to the amount of microscopic damage inflicted on muscle fibers during exercise. Minor DOMS may subside in forty-eight hours, while severe soreness signals a greater degree of damage that may take four or more days to rebuild.

You can now see that a single rest day is enough to allow the muscles to recharge and refuel, yet complete supercompensation—that is, rebuilding the muscle to a stronger level than before the exercise stimulus—requires additional rest for the neuromuscular system to recuperate. Therefore, while you may be able to perform at a reasonably high level after just one day of rest, truncating the rebuilding process negates the supercompensation period (see chapter 5) and will inhibit gains in strength. In the long term, chronic under-resting can result in decreased performance, injury, and even risk of illness.

Whether you are training indoors or climbing a personal-best route outside, the ability to accelerate recovery is tantamount to elevating your absolute level of performance. In the gym faster recovery between exercises or climbs translates to higher-intensity stimuli or faster learning, respectively. On the rock hastened recovery at a marginal rest may make the difference between a brilliant on-sight or hardest-ever flash and dangling on the rope in frustration.

On the pages that follow, you will learn fourteen powerful techniques for accelerating recovery and thus improving the quality of your training and climbing. But knowing is not enough—you must apply these strategies with the same dedication and resolve as when pursuing your endeavors in the gym or at the crag.

Accelerating Short-Term or Intraclimb Recovery

Your capacity to perform difficult moves or exercises repeatedly, with only short rest breaks, is directly proportionate to your recovery ability in the short term. Described above as the recharge period, only certain recovery mechanisms come into play during the first ten seconds to sixty minutes following strenuous activity. As detailed in chapter 5, short-term recovery is driven by the aerobic energy system—therefore, your potential to recover quickly (in minutes rather than hours) is a direct function of your generalized aerobic fitness level. Anyway, your goal during this mid-climb or between-climb recovery period is to act in ways that will expedite the recharge process. This is done by minimizing the magnitude of fatigue (in the first place), engaging in steady, deep breathing, enhancing forearm recovery with the G-Tox (described below) and active rest, and engaging in pre-exercise hydration.

Limit Fatigue by Climbing More Efficiently

Let's start off with the most simple, yet powerful, method to enhance short-term recovery—limit the magnitude of fatigue, as much as possible, through economy of movement and optimal climbing technique. Obviously, you will use less ATP- CP and glycogen, as well as produce fewer metabolic by-products if you can lower the intensity of muscular contraction and the total time under load. In this way you immediately reduce the magnitude of the fatigue you must recover from, and you will return to baseline strength more quickly.

It's in this area that the average climber can realize a windfall of unknown capability. The fact is, most climbers move too slowly, possess less-than-ideal technique, and stop to place gear or think when they should be pushing on to the next rest. While lack of experience and technical ability are the real limiting factors here, slow climbing and hesitation will lead you to believe that a lack of strength is the primary problem.

If any of this sounds familiar, then some dedicated technique-training practice will go a long way toward elevating your game (see chapter 4). By learning to move swiftly and accurately through hard moves, and by relaxing your grip and lowering tension in the antagonist muscles, you will use less glycogen on difficult sequences and reduce muscular acidosis and hypoxia. In this way you lower the magnitude of the fatigue you must recover from at a mid-climb rest position, and you will return to baseline strength more quickly between attempts or sends.

Enhance Forearm Recovery with the G-Tox

The dangling-arm shakeout is the technique traditionally used to aid recovery in the commonly fatigued forearm muscles. A few seconds or, hopefully, a few minutes of shaking out provides some recovery, but often not enough. The effects of a full-on pump can take frustratingly long to subside, and when hanging out at a marginal rest, it's possible to expend as much energy hanging on with one arm as is being recouped in the other. Such a zero-net gain in recovery does nothing to enhance performance—in such a situation you would likely have fared better by blowing off the so-called rest and climbing onward.

Research has shown the G-Tox technique to be effective in speeding forearm recovery at marginal rest positions.
ILLUSTRATION BY MIKE TEA

Luckily there is the G-Tox, a shakeout technique that I developed to accelerate recovery of finger strength while hanging out at a mid-climb rest. For more than twenty years, I have been promoting the benefits of alternating the position of your resting arm between the normal dangling position and an above-your-head raised-hand position. This simple practice provides a noticeable increase in recovery rate—an effect pronounced enough to be confirmed in a 2003 university research project by Luke Roberts. I named this recovery technique the G-Tox, because it uses gravity (as an ally, for once) to help detoxify the fatigued muscle and speed recovery.

The discomfort and pump that develop in your forearms while climbing is largely the result of increasing intracellular acidosis and hypoxia in the working muscles. Contractions of as little as 20 percent of maximum intensity begin to hamper capillary blood flow, and at 50 percent of maximum contraction blood flow is largely occluded. When the contraction ends, blood flow resumes (reperfusion) at an accelerated rate to re-oxygenate the tissue and remove metabolic by-products. This reactive hyperemic response is what you recognize as "the pump."

The pump effect is then amplified by the dangling-arm position (the traditional shakeout technique), because the rate of blood flow into the muscles may slightly exceed the rate of venous return ("old blood" exiting the muscle). This traffic jam of sorts perpetuates the pump and slows recovery, yet many climbers continue to dangle their arms and complain about how sickening a pump they have.

The G-Tox technique puts gravity to work by aiding venous return of blood toward the heart. By helping get blood out of the arm more quickly, this practice enhances the removal of H^+ and other by-products and therefore returns you to a homeostatic baseline more quickly. The effects of this technique are unmistakable—you will literally see the pump drain from the elevated arm due to the interesting fact that arterial flow into the arm is less affected by gravity than is venous return flow.

So why not just use the raised-arm position for the full duration of the rest instead of using the alternating technique as described above? Since the raised-arm position requires some muscular contraction in the upper arm, shoulder, and chest, these muscles would fatigue and possibly hamper climbing performance if you held the raised-arm position for a long time. Consequently, the best protocol for recovery is alternating between the two arm positions—raised-arm and dangling-arm—every five to ten seconds. Do so and you will definitely feel the difference the G-Tox makes!

Engage in Active Rest

Along with the G-Tox, active rest is another underused yet highly effective strategy for accelerating recovery. While the G-Tox shines in its effectiveness to enhance recovery at a mid-climb shakeout, use of active rest between climbs is an equally effective strategy for increasing the rate of H+ and lactate removal from the working muscles and bloodstream.

Several recent studies, including one excellent study on climbers (Watts 2000), have shown that active rest significantly reduces blood lactate compared with the more common practice of passive rest. In the Watts study, fifteen advanced climbers attempted to redpoint a twenty-meter, 5.12b gym route, with eight of them engaging in active rest (recumbent cycling) and the others assigned to passive rest immediately following completion of the route. Periodic measurements of blood lactate revealed that the active-rest group returned to preclimb levels within twenty minutes, while the passive group took thirty minutes to return to baseline levels. Therefore, low-intensity active rest accelerated the clearing of lactate from the blood by almost 35 percent.

Applying this research finding at the crag is simple. Upon completing a pumpy route or redpoint attempt, instead of sitting down and resting passively (or worse yet, having a smoke), grab your water bottle and go for a casual twenty-minute hike. This will help accelerate the removal of H+ and lactate, as well as provide a mental break from the action. Both these factors will enhance your performance on the next route!

Another study compared recovery after maximum exercise in four groups: passive rest, active rest, massage, and combined massage and active rest (Monedero 2000). After fifteen minutes of rest, blood lactate removal was greatest in the group performing combined active rest and massage. Therefore, you may be able to further improve the Watts strategy of active rest by performing some self-massage on your most fatigued muscles (usually the forearms, upper arms, and shoulders).

A more recent study has shown that shorter periods of active recovery provide similarly positive effects on lowering blood lactate concentrations compared with equal periods of passive rest. The study tested ten climbers engaging in five, two-minute climbing trials, followed by two minutes of either active or passive recovery. The active-recovery group started the next trial with lower arterial lactate concentration than the passive-recovery group, and they recorded lower perceived exertion scores at the end of each climb (Draper 2006). The bottom line on this study is that in bouldering, it's better to walk around between ascents or attempts and sustain a higher heart rate to speed recovery.

Prehydrate Within Two Hours of Exercise

Muscles are more than 70 percent water, and it plays a vital role in cellular function and the transport of nutrients and metabolic waste. If you are dehydrated, it will hurt your performance and slow recovery. Therefore, it's prudent to prehydrate by consuming up to a quart of water in the hours preceding a workout or climbing. Continue sipping

Tips to Accelerate Short-Term Recovery

1. Strive to limit fatigue in the first place by climbing with maximum economy, optimal technique, and brilliant strategy!
2. Accelerate recovery at mid-climb shakeouts by using the G-Tox recovery technique.
3. Engage in active recovery between climbs by walking around and performing light stretching and massage. Research has shown that this accelerates recovery by up to 35 percent compared with just sitting around between ascents or attempts.
4. Do not smoke! Smoking decreases circulation and slows recovery. Worse yet, smoking inhibits the production of collagen and thus slows healing of tendons and ligaments.
5. Camel up by drinking a quart of water in the hours preceding a workout or day of climbing. Continue drinking water as you climb at a rate of eight ounces every hour or two.
6. Add moderate amounts of generalized aerobic exercise to your training-for-climbing program. A stronger cardiovascular system will provide faster recovery both at mid-climb rests and between boulder problems and routes.

water throughout the duration of activity at a minimum rate of eight ounces every hour or two (twice this if it's hot).

Accelerating Medium-Term or Intraday Recovery

Intraday recovery is the medium-term recuperation that occurs throughout the day and up to twenty-four hours following exercise. What you do (or don't do) during this recovery period plays a direct role in how much energy you will have during the latter part of a long day of climbing; it's also the primary factor in how much recovery you can acquire in a single night of rest. Of course, this is of big-time importance if you are in the midst of a long, all-day route or when you plan to climb two days in a row.

Earlier I referred to this medium-term recovery phase as the refuel period, since restoring a normal blood glucose level and replenishing glycogen is the basis for most recovery gained from sixty minutes to twenty-four hours following exercise. Consequently, consuming the right carbohydrates at the right time is the single most vital action to accelerate recovery. Still, stretching, massage, foam rolling, and the use of relaxation exercises will also increase your rate of recuperation. Let's delve deeper into each of these areas.

Refuel Early and Often

The single biggest error in recovery strategy by most climbers is delayed consumption of calories during and after a day of climbing. The natural tendency is to become so engaged in the activity of climbing that you forget to eat and drink. This is compounded by the fact that strenuous exercise naturally suppresses hunger.

REFUELING WHILE YOU CLIMB

Earlier it was explained that consuming calories throughout the day helps maintain blood glucose and thus helps slow the use of your limited supply of glycogen. Toward this end, you should take in your first dose of calories between one to two hours after beginning your climb. If you are cragging, this might mean consuming a piece of fruit, a Protein Plus PowerBar, or eight ounces of sports drink after completing the first strenuous climb of the day. Continue eating a small serving of food every two hours throughout the day. In the case of all-day climbing, this means a total of four snacks—for example, two pieces of fruit and two energy bars.

Quality efforts—and project sends!—come when you take a proactive role in the recovery process. Make each attempt count, by beginning with fresh muscles and a focused mind ready to try hard!
BRUCE WILSON

This may seem like an awful lot of food, and it is if you are only climbing for half a day or going bouldering (halve these amounts in those situations). To keep climbing hard throughout the day and to speed recovery for a second day of climbing, however, you should consume a minimum of 600 to 800 calories during the course of the day.

Selecting the right kinds of food at the right time is a matter of using the glycemic index (GI). As introduced in chapter 11, high-GI foods elicit a rapid rise (then drop) in blood sugar, while medium- and low-GI foods release fuel into the bloodstream more slowly (see table 11.2). In a stop-and-go sport like climbing, steady blood sugar is vital for maintaining steady concentration and steady energy. Therefore, consume only low- and medium-GI foods while you are still engaged in physical activity. Upon completing your day on the rocks or reaching the end of your workout, however, it's best to consume higher-GI foods and beverages. This latter distinction is powerful—there is a growing body of research indicating that what you eat in the first thirty minutes after exercise is the single largest determining factor in how fast you recover.

KICK-STARTING GLYCOGEN REPLENISHMENT AFTER CLIMBING OR TRAINING

As incredible as it may seem, recent research has shown that waiting two hours after exercise to consume carbohydrates will reduce your glycogen replenishment by 50 percent compared with eating immediately upon cessation of the activity (Burke 1999). Therefore, when planning to climb a second day, you significantly handicap tomorrow's performance by delaying refueling. Similarly, delayed refueling after training slows the recovery and rebuilding processes and, possibly, delays complete recovery by as much as a full day.

Let's take a closer look at the best refueling strategies in the hours following climbing or a vigorous workout.

First thirty minutes after climbing: Ingestion of high-GI foods immediately after exercise substantially increases the rate of muscle glycogen replacement (Richter 1984). More recent studies have shown that glycogen resynthesis may take place another 40 percent faster if protein and carbohydrate are consumed together, due to a greater insulin response (Niles 1997). Consequently, the best protocol for accelerating glycogen replenishment appears to be a 4:1 ratio of carbohydrate to protein consumption (Burke 1999).

Since solid foods enter the bloodstream more slowly than liquids, it's best to drink this carbohydrate–protein blend post-exercise. For example, a 160-pound climber would want to consume approximately one hundred grams of carbohydrate and twenty-five grams of protein. Drinking a pint of Gatorade, juice, or another glucose- or high-fructose-corn-syrup-based sports drink would provide about fifty grams of high-GI carbohydrate, while consuming a high-protein energy bar or a whey protein shake would provide around twenty grams of protein. Another highly practical option is to drink a 4:1 (carbohydrate-to-protein ratio) sports drink such as Accelerade or a pint of chocolate skim milk. Yes, chocolate skim milk is a most excellent post-exercise recovery drink, considering that it contains over fifty grams of carbohydrate and seventeen grams of high-quality protein.

Two hours after climbing: Assuming you consumed the initial feeding of carbohydrates and protein within the thirty-minute time frame, you can wait until about two hours post-activity to eat a complete meal. Ideally, the meal will include foods providing a macronutrient ratio of about 65:15:20 (calories from carbohydrate, protein, and fat, respectively), as explained in chapter 11. Such a meal might include a moderate serving of pasta, a piece of lean meat, and a large salad or some vegetables. Whereas high-GI foods are best eaten immediately after exercise, medium- and low-GI foods are more advantageous in the two to twenty-four hours after exercise. They will provide a slower, longer-lasting trickle of glucose into the bloodstream that will support steady glycogen resynthesis.

Before going to sleep: A small meal of carbohydrate and protein within thirty minutes of going to sleep will further support glycogen resynthesis and tissue remodeling overnight. Skim milk may be the perfect before-bedtime food—it possesses low-GI carbohydrate, high-quality protein, and the amino acid tryptophan, a precursor to serotonin, which slows down brain activity. Drink a tall glass of skim milk (consider mixing in some whey protein powder) or have some skim milk on a small bowl of whole-grain cereal before bedtime. It'll do your body good!

Stretch and Massage the Hardest-Working Muscles

Earlier, you learned about an impressive research study showing that combining active rest and massage accelerates recovery by enhancing the removal of metabolic by-products from the working muscles. Deep-fiber-spreading sports massage is also an effective practice to enhance medium- and long-term recovery.

HOW IT WORKS

Traditional massage has long been used to increase blood flow and oxygen transport in the muscles. The benefits of this superficial "rubbing" are brief, however, and have little residual effect on performance.

Sports massage utilizes a deep-fiber-spreading technique that produces hyperemia (vasodilation) through the full depth of the muscle. Furthermore, the state of hyperemia lasts long after the procedure has ended, so the enhanced blood flow can accelerate recovery and aid healing after strenuous exercise.

Sports massage also helps reduce the number of small and often unfelt spasms that regularly occur in the muscles. These spasms may go unchallenged by conventional stretching and warm-up exercises and, left unchecked, can rob you of coordination and induce mechanical resistance and premature fatigue.

HOW TO DO IT

There are several strokes you may want to learn, but the most effective is called cross-fiber friction. This stroke is best executed with a braced finger (see photo). The motion is a simple push in followed by a short push back and forth across the muscle fiber. Keep the stroke short and rhythmic; only gradually increase the pressure to penetrate deeper into the muscle.

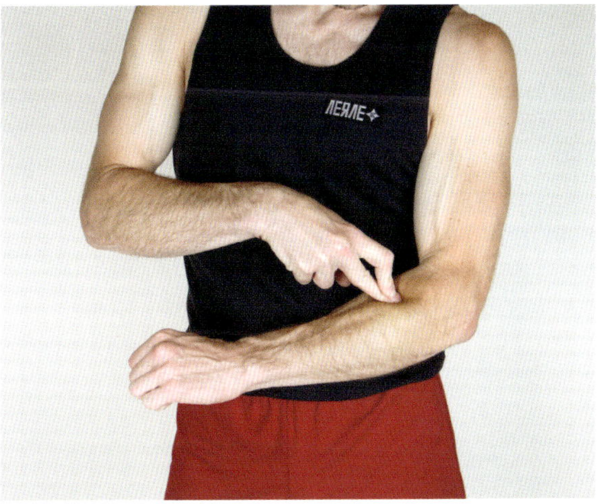

Cross-fiber friction (with braced finger) self-massage is an excellent way to increase blood flow and warm up the forearm muscles prior to training. Armaid's Rubbit (see page 122) is a wonderful invention, as it provides additional leverage for attacking trigger points in the forearms.

Although sports massage can be used on all muscles, focus your efforts on the upper body and, in particular, the finger flexors and extensors, the pronator teres and brachioradialis (upper forearm muscles), the biceps and triceps (muscles of the upper arm), and the large muscles of the shoulders and back. Incorporate five to ten minutes of massage into your regular warm-up routine. This, along with the warm-up activities and stretches detailed in chapter 6, will better prepare you for an excellent workout or day on the rocks.

SPORTS MASSAGE TO ACCELERATE RECOVERY

Your body has inherent mechanical weaknesses where sport-specific movements can trigger stress overload. In climbing, the muscles most overloaded are the forearms, upper arms, and back. These muscles are the first to tire, and they are typically the slowest to recover. Fortunately, you can modulate fatigue and hasten recovery through application of sports massage to the specific stress points—often called *trigger points*—inherent to climbing movements.

Use of sports massage and trigger point therapy will help relieve these stress points and speed recovery. You can best address these trigger points with what is called the direct-pressure stroke. Apply firm, constant, straight-in pressure with a braced finger, an Armaid device, a wooden Bodo or shepherd's crook, or a friend's elbow, and hold for fifteen to thirty seconds. Direct pressure is especially useful when applied to the trigger points near the base of the muscles. This will help relieve any known or unknown spasms, increase local circulation, and aid healing. (Be sure never to apply sports massage tactics to tendons, joints, or injured tissues, however.) Conclude your massage with some foam rolling and mild stretching.

Use Relaxation Techniques

Chapter 3 described an excellent relaxation technique called the Progressive Relaxation Sequence.

Tips to Accelerate Medium-Term Recovery

1. Refuel early and often. Consume a piece of fruit, a balanced-style energy bar, or eight ounces of sports drink every hour or two throughout the day of climbing. Favor low- to medium-GI foods and drinks.
2. At the end of a workout or day of climbing, kick-start recovery by consuming a high-GI sports drink or a 4:1 ratio carbohydrate-to-protein sports drink within the first thirty minutes of cessation of strenuous activity. Chocolate skim milk is an excellent choice!
3. Within two hours of concluding your workout or climbing, consume a meal comprising approximately a 65:15:20 percent breakdown of carbohydrate, protein, and fat, respectively.
4. Avoid consumption of alcoholic beverages, since alcohol has been shown to slow supercompensation, reduce beneficial growth hormone response, and possibly even slow protein synthesis.
5. Stretch, massage, and use a heating pad or whirlpool to increase blood flow to sore, tired muscles. Use cross-fiber friction massage, foam rolling, and direct pressure to relieve trigger point pain and spasms.
6. Engage in progressive relaxation (see chapter 3) to further relax muscles and quiet the mind during midday breaks from climbing and before going to sleep.

Though commonly used before going to sleep, progressive relaxation is also highly effective for relaxing the muscles and quieting the mind during a midday break from climbing. When resting between climbs or taking a break before returning to work on a project, find a quiet spot, lie down, and spend ten to twenty minutes performing progressive relaxation. Upon completing this process, sit up for a few minutes and enjoy the day before proceeding to the next climb.

Make a midday relaxation break a regular part of your climbing ritual and you'll find yourself climbing better, with less fatigue, late into the day.

Accelerating Long-Term or Interday Recovery

The interday recovery period involves the long-term recuperation from a severe workout or a couple of hard days of climbing. Depending on the intensity and volume of the activity, full recovery could take anywhere from one to four days.

When you wake up in the morning with sore muscles (delayed-onset muscle soreness), it's a sign that you incurred microtraumas and that a recovery period of at least another twenty-four hours is needed. Of course, you have two choices in this situation. The first is to go climbing (or work out) for a second straight day, despite the soreness, realizing that your performance will be less than ideal and your risk of injury may be increased. Or you could take a day or two off and allow your neuromuscular system to recuperate to a level of capability higher than before the workout.

Certainly, there are times when you will select the first option of climbing a second day straight, but there should be an equal number of instances when you decide that "less will be more." Weekend climbing trips are the classic situation in which you'd want to climb two days in a row, regardless of sore muscles. Given proper nutrition, a good warm-up, and a prudent approach to pushing yourself on the second day, you can usually get away with climbing sore.

Choosing to take a day or two of rest, however, is clearly the intelligent decision when climbing indoors or during an off-season training cycle. Hopefully, you gleaned from chapter 5 that proper rest is as important as training stimulus in becoming a stronger climber, and that under-resting is a primary cause of injury. Enthusiastic indoor and sport climbers are most commonly guilty of under-resting, but regardless of your climbing preference, it's important that you distinguish yourself from the mass of climbers who overtrain. If you find yourself drawn to overtraining with the crowd, remember that in order to outperform the masses, you must act in ways that they do not!

Eat Frequent, Small Meals

Instead of eating the typical three meals per day, you can accelerate recovery by consuming six smaller meals or snacks spaced evenly throughout the day. Avoid high-GI foods; they are less effective for recovery after the first two hours post-exercise. Instead select low- and medium-GI foods for all your meals, and drink at least two quarts of water throughout the day.

At least three of your meals should contain a significant portion of protein. For instance, breakfast could include a couple of eggs, skim milk, or whey protein; lunch might include some low-fat yogurt, skim milk, or a can of tuna; and for dinner it might be good to eat a piece of lean red meat, chicken, or fish. Each of these meals should also include some carbohydrate, and at all costs avoid fat-laden fried foods and any snack foods containing hydrogenated oils. Strive for a macronutrient profile of roughly 65:15:20 (carbohydrate:protein:fat) for each major meal.

While the other three feedings need be only a couple hundred calories, they are vital for maintaining steady blood glucose and continuing the recovery processes throughout the day. Low- and medium-GI foods are the best choice, with a piece of fruit or a balanced-type energy bar being ideal selections.

Take a Multivitamin

In today's world of highly processed foods, it's often difficult to consume enough of the vitamins and minerals that athletes need by simply eating a well-rounded diet. Consider taking a daily multivitamin as a must; additional magnesium is beneficial in a number of ways and may even help your muscles relax and return to normal function.

Stretch, Foam Roll, and Massage Sore Muscles

Gentle stretching, foam rolling, and sports massage are widely accepted as effective means to lengthen the muscles and enhance recovery following strenuous exercise. Professional athletes have full-time trainers who help with post-exercise stretching and rest-day massage (must be nice!). Though I won't pay for you to add a masseur to your climbing-support staff, I do suggest that you stretch and foam roll for at least ten to twenty minutes per day. Follow the stretching and foam rolling procedures outlined in chapter 6 and, of course, the primer on sports massage provided earlier in this chapter.

Get Plenty of Sleep

Here's an important recovery technique that this full-time working, four-day-a-week-training, weekend-climbing, book-writing, forty-year veteran of the rocks wishes he could get more of! Although most neuromuscular regeneration occurs during sleep, I always fall back on the fact that nothing is produced or achieved during sleep. But I digress.

Seriously, sleep is vital for any climber serious about training and passionate about maximizing ability. The bare minimum amount of sleep per night is six to seven hours, though eight to ten hours is ideal following an extremely strenuous workout or exhaustive day of climbing. No doubt, it's a busy world—and sleep may seem like the only activity that's expendable. If you closely evaluate a typical day, however, you will likely be able to identify some low-value activities like surfing the Net, watching TV, and certain social events that can be reduced or eliminated to allow for more sleep. It

Long-Term Recovery Tips

1. Eat small, frequent meals—consume six smaller meals and snacks comprising low- to mid-GI foods and protein sources.
2. Drink eight ounces of water every one to two hours to rehydrate and flush toxins from your body.
3. Take a daily multivitamin; supplemental magnesium is also highly recommended.
4. Avoid excessive consumption of alcoholic beverages, since these provide little quality nutrition, enhance dehydration, and in high doses suppress growth hormone response and protein synthesis following exercise.
5. Engage in daily stretching, foam rolling, massage, and active-recovery activities such as hiking, biking, and easy running.
6. Apply a heating pad to sore muscles, twice daily for ten to fifteen minutes, to increase blood flow and accelerate recovery and healing. Note that you should never place a heating pad on a swollen or acutely injured body part.
7. Get at least six to seven hours of sleep per night, eight to ten hours (or more) after mega-long day climbs or multiday big-wall or alpine ascents.
8. Strive for a calm, relaxed, easygoing disposition every day—this will help lower cortisol levels and foster more rapid recovery.

can take great discipline to give up some of these activities—visualize your climbing goals!—but the long-term payoffs will dwarf the hollow pleasure of these low-value pastimes.

Engage in Light Activities

Earlier you learned of a couple of great research studies that showed the value of active rest in accelerating recovery from strenuous exercise. In the context of long-term recovery, active rest is also beneficial because it enhances circulation of nutrients to the damaged muscles and produces a general loosening effect on stiff muscles.

The best active-rest activities for climbers are hiking, jogging, light mountain biking, and even some limited less-than-vertical or big-hold climbing (ARC training protocol). Still, it's crucial that each of these activities be performed at a low enough intensity that you don't get heavily winded or pumped and break only a light sweat. Limit yourself to thirty to sixty minutes of active-recovery exercise, and remain disciplined in not letting the activity escalate into anything more than active rest.

Possess a Positive, Calm Personality Each and Every Day

This last recovery tip is subtle yet very powerful. Possessing a positive, relaxed, and easygoing attitude not only puts you in a better performance state, but it also has been proven to increase recovery and maybe even encourage muscular growth.

Strenuous exercise and stressful situations cause a drugstore's worth of chemicals and hormones to be released into the bloodstream. Some of these hormones have long-term positive effects, such as growth hormone, which is anabolic. The fight-or-flight hormones like epinephrine and cortisol, however, can have a long-term negative effect when released chronically. In particular, cortisol has been shown to be catabolic, meaning that it results in breakdown of muscle.

In light of the above factors, elite athletes have long been interested in enhancing the release of growth hormone and preventing high levels of cortisol. This is the very reason some athletes take anabolic steroids.

Fortunately, you can modulate levels of growth hormone and cortisol with proper training, quality nutrition, and adequate rest, as well as through adjustments in your lifestyle. For instance, individuals with Type A, aggressive behavior naturally exhibit higher levels of cortisol (Williams 1982) and reduced levels of growth hormone. It's also been shown, however, that behavior modification and reduction of the stressors in life can reverse this effect and provide more beneficial training (Dinan 1994). Therefore, possessing a relaxed approach to climbing and a humorous attitude about life in general will play an underlying but beneficial role by enhancing the quality of your training adaptations, accelerating recovery, and boosting climbing performance.

It's important to recognize that training and recovery are opposite sides of the same coin. You must place equal importance on doing both optimally and to the best of your ability. Clearly, it requires a shift in perspective to actually plan and engage in the process of recovery in the same way you plan and engage in the process of training. But in doing so, you will distinguish yourself from the masses by producing uncommonly good results, and by avoiding downtime due to injury and illness.

Inge Perkins on Bobcat Logic (12b/c), Wild Iris, Wyoming.
SAVANNAH CUMMINS

CHAPTER THIRTEEN

Injury Treatment and Prevention

Remember that in training, as in life, everything has a cost—but not everything has a benefit.

This last chapter might not be necessary if this were a book on training for bowling or training for badminton. Despite what we tell our moms, however, climbing is a sport with an unusually high incidence of injury. Several studies report that up to three-quarters of all recreational and elite climbers have suffered a climbing injury. Fortunately, only a small number of injuries are severe traumas produced by falls—the majority are overuse and minor acute injuries that most commonly occur in the fingers, elbows, and shoulders. These insidious "nuisance injuries," while far from life threatening, can become chronic and debilitating, and they are extremely frustrating for an otherwise healthy individual passionate about climbing.

The goal of this chapter is to increase your awareness of the causes and symptoms of the most common overuse injuries. Early identification is the best way to mitigate an overuse injury, whereas ignoring the early pangs and hoping that it will go away is almost always a recipe for a chronic injury that could sideline you for months. Ultimately, learning to recognize at-risk situations both when you're training and when you're climbing, and embracing a prudent approach to these activities that errs on the side of caution, is the best medicine for preventing injury.

Over the last decade numerous relevant studies have been presented by British, French, German, and American researchers, among others, and several excellent articles were published in climbing magazines by physicians experienced in treating injured climbers. Based on this growing body of knowledge, I will present a primer on the most prevalent injuries and basic treatment protocol for minor strains. Still, I urge you to seek professional treatment of any injury that's more than "minor," as well as any injury that remains symptomatic for more than a few weeks. Countless climbers have fallen into the trap of self-treatment and trying to "climb through" an injury—these approaches often make matters worse and can lead to unnecessarily long-term downtime. The bottom line: View this chapter as simply a coach's advice rather than a dissertation written by a medical expert (which I'm not!).

Overview of Climbing Injuries

A wide variety of injuries can result from climbing and sport-specific training activities, and a survey of literature yields a broad range of pathologies from tendinitis to broken bones. While fall-related trauma is always a concern when recreating in the vertical extreme, this overview of climbing injuries focuses on the acute and chronic overuse injuries that typically result from the process of climbing and training.

For the most comprehensive and expert coverage of climbing injuries, I strongly recommend you read the excellent book *One Move Too Many* by Drs. Volker Schöffl and Thomas Hochholzer. Volker and Thomas are not only climbers of more than three decades, but they are researchers and surgeons that treat climbers on a daily basis, and they are also two of the world's leading authorities on the subject. Another excellent book, written from the perspective of a physical therapist, is Dr. Lisa Erikson's *Climbing Injuries Solved*—this text is loaded with dozens of effective methods of self-treatment. Both of these books are available at www.Training4Climbing.com.

Types of Injuries

Over the past twenty years, there's been a growing body of research analyzing types of injuries, the common causes, and risks involved in climbing. The latest data reveal that most overuse injuries occur in the upper extremities, while most acute trauma involves fall-related injuries to the lower extremities (Schöffl 2012).

A breakdown of overuse injuries confirms what experienced climbers have known anecdotally for years: The fingers, shoulders, hands, and elbows are the most common sites of non-fall-related injuries (see figure 13.1). A recent four-year German study (Schöffl 2015) of 836 patients with a total of 911 independent climbing injuries revealed that more than half (52 percent) involved the fingers. The second most common injury site was the shoulder (17 percent). It should be noted that most of the climbers included in these studies specialized in bolt-protected climbing, bouldering, and gym climbing (although some were also traditional-style climbers), and so the data primarily reflects the injury trends in what you might generally classify as "modern sport climbing."

Figure 13.1 Sites of Nonfall Injuries

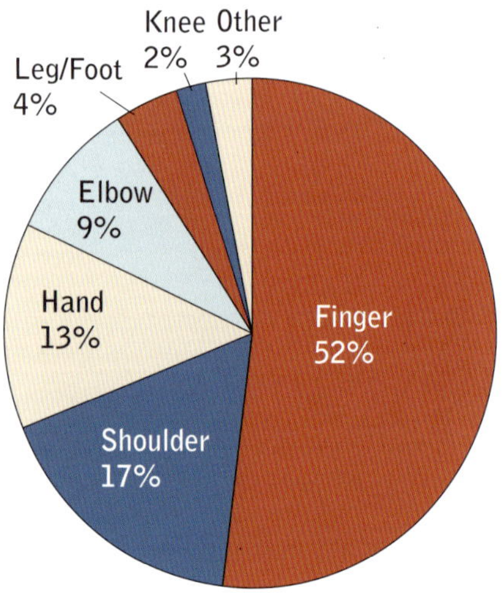

Interestingly, the injury data has changed significantly since Schöffl's previous study conducted a decade earlier. Most notable is the increase in shoulder injuries, which has increased from the sixth most common injury site (5 percent of cases) to second place (17 percent) in the latest analysis. One theory for the escalation of shoulder injuries is the recent proliferation—and inappropriate use—of campus training boards. One positive trend, however, is a slight decrease in elbow injuries (dropping from 13 percent to 9 percent of cases).

Contributing Factors

An almost unanimous conclusion of the many injury studies is that occurrence of overuse injuries is directly proportionate to climbing ability and the perceived importance of climbing to the individual. Other cofactors include use of indoor climbing walls and use of campus boards and fingerboards in training for climbing.

A British study (Doran 2000) found a dramatic increase in injury rates among 5.11 climbers versus 5.10 climbers (see figure 13.2). At the 5.12 level, nearly 88 percent of climbers surveyed had experienced overuse injuries in the prior two years. By comparison, only 20 percent of individuals climbing at levels below 5.9 incurred overuse injuries, the lowest relative frequency of all categories.

At least two studies show a statistically significant relationship between perceived importance of climbing and incidence of injury. Doran (2000) says, "The frequency of injury occurrence was significantly higher in those who perceived climbing to be very important to those who rated it as not so important." An important corollary to this

Figure 13.2 Overuse Injuries

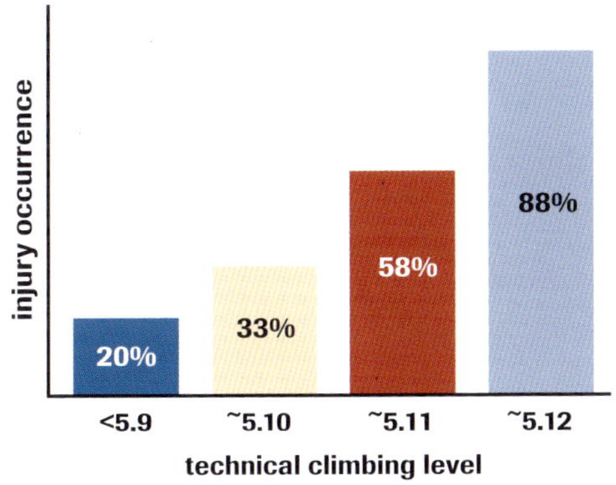

Occurrence of overuse injuries is directly proportionate to climbing ability.

relationship is that enthusiastic climbers are more likely to return to climbing before full rehabilitation has occurred, thus leading to a pattern of recurrence.

Another British study of 295 climbers at a recent World Cup event found that those most at risk for overuse injuries were climbers with "the most ability and dedication to climbing." The analysis showed a linear relation between lead-climbing grade and overuse injuries (Wright 2001). A number of other variables have been identified as cofactors in contributing to overuse injuries, including climbing preference and training practices.

Consensus among experts in the field is that incidence of overuse injuries has increased since the advent of indoor walls and sport-climbing tactics. An article in *Sports Medicine* proposes that the preponderance of overhanging terrain at indoor climbing facilities is a contributing factor to the increase in upper-body injuries (Rooks 1997). Indoor walls do enable year-round climbing and make it oh-so-easy to test your absolute limit, thanks to toprope belays and well-bolted leads. Clearly, this is an environment that can lend itself to overtraining and a general lack of rest time away from the stresses and strains of climbing. I know of a few individuals who climbed indoors five or six days per week—and nearly all, sooner or later, suffered some kind of finger, elbow, or shoulder injury.

Training practices have also been implicated as a contributing factor in overuse injuries of climbers at all ability levels. Doran (2000) reported that most of the climbers in his study performed some form of supplementary training; in particular, fingerboards and dynamic double-handed campus training were popular among the injured climbers. The obvious implication is that these high-stress, ultra-specific forms of training may be injurious or at least exacerbate low-grade preexisting injuries. These conclusions all make good sense, and therefore underscore the importance of a prudent, mature approach to climbing-specific training that knows when to say enough and errs on the side of over-resting rather than overtraining.

A statistical analysis of Schöffl's latest data (2015) shows that more experienced, older climbers had significantly more overuse injuries than acute injuries. Two other novel findings of the Schöffl study: A4 pulley injuries are now more common than those to the A2 pulley, and the incidence of growth plate factures in youth climbers has increased an alarming 600 percent in the decade since his previous study (more on this in a bit).

Common Injuries and Treatment

Based on the research outlined above, we know that the majority of climbers will someday experience some form of overuse or acute injury. Furthermore, it's well documented that the five most common sites of injury are the fingers, shoulders, hands, elbows, and knees. In this section we'll take a closer look at each of these problem spots. Hopefully, this information will empower you to recognize symptoms early on and thus modify your activity or seek medical attention before the injury becomes more severe or chronic. One caveat that all climbers must heed: It's essential to seek medical attention for any condition that gets worse even after withdrawal from climbing and training—this could indicate an infection, tumor, or other disease that needs immediate medical attention.

Finger Injuries

Considering the incredible mechanical loading we place on our fingers when climbing, it's no surprise that they are the most common site of injury. At the early (mild) stage, these pesky finger injuries are easy for a passionate climber to ignore or deny—I've heard this behavior rationalized by the belief that it's okay to climb with one injured finger, since there are nine healthy fingers to carry the load! Of course the truth is that continuing to climb on an injured finger may increase the severity of the injury, and ultimately double or triple (or more) the downtime needed to recover.

Understanding the most common injuries requires some knowledge of hand anatomy (see figure 13.3). To begin with, there are no muscles in the fingers. Flexion of the fingers and wrist is produced by the muscles of the forearm that originate from the medial (inside) elbow and terminate via long tendons that attach to the middle phalanx (MP) and distal phalanx (DP) of each finger. The flexor digitorum superficialis (FDS) muscle inserts into the palm side of the MP and produces flexion of the proximal interphalangeal (PIP) joint. The long tendon of the flexor digitorum profundus (FDP) muscle passes through a split in the FDS and then inserts on the palm side of the DP.

The FDP controls flexion of the distal interphalangeal joint (DIP).

Both flexor tendons (FDS and FDP) pass through a tunnel-like, synovia-lined tendon sheath that provides nourishment and lubrication. The flexor tendon and sheath are held close to the bone by five annular pulleys (A1, A2, and so forth) and three (sometimes four) cruciform pulleys that prevent tendon "bowstringing" during flexion. Biomechanical studies have shown that the A2 and A4 pulleys are the most important (Lin 1989). As a conceptual model, visualize the whole system of the

Figure 13.3 Finger Anatomy

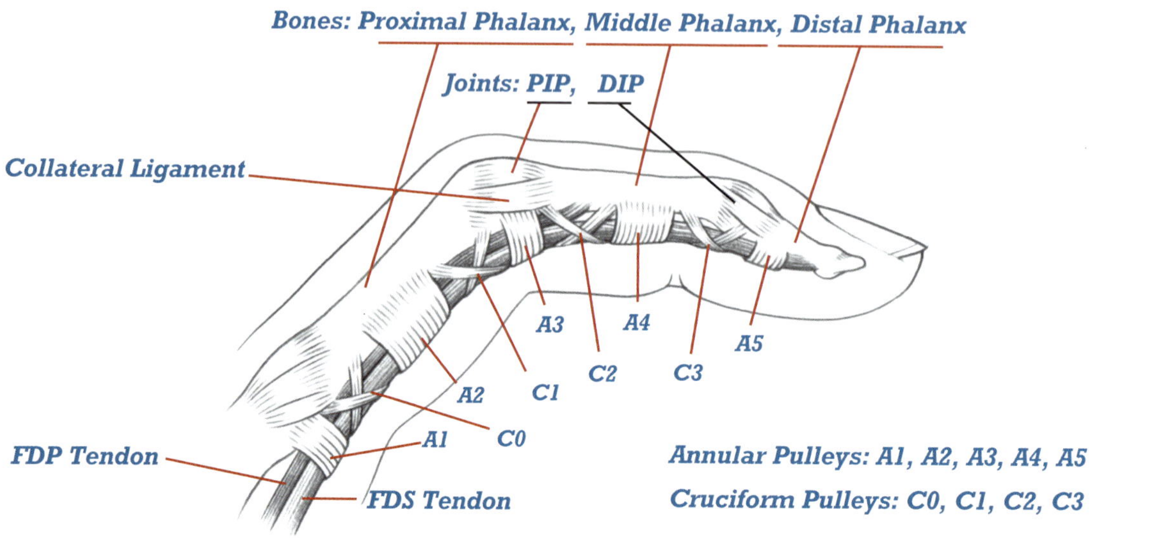

Figure 13.4 Annular Pulley Injuries Anatomy

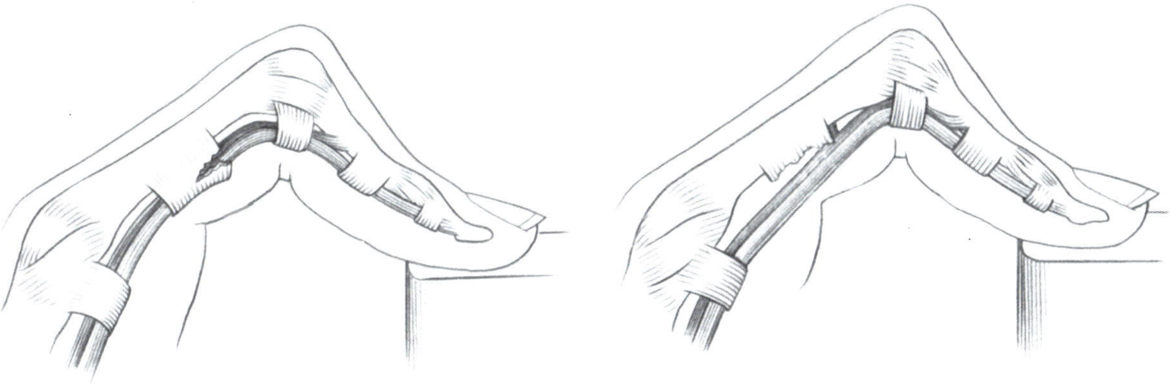

A2 pulley injury: partial tear (left) versus complete tear (right).

flexor tendon, sheath, and annular pulley as functioning like a brake cable on a bike.

TENDON PULLEY INJURIES

The most common finger injuries experienced by climbers involve partial tears or complete ruptures of one or more of the flexor tendon annular pulleys (see table 13.1). In many cases, only a partial tear of a single pulley occurs; in more serious incidences, however, one or more pulleys may rupture entirely, resulting in palpable or visible bowstringing, respectively. The extent of the pulley injury can often be determined via ultrasound, although additional magnetic resonance imaging may be necessary to diagnose some cases.

Historically, the A2 pulley is the most commonly injured of the five annular pulleys; however, a recent study of 140 pulley injuries has found a shift toward the A4 pulley being the most frequently injury (Schöffl 2015). Injuries to the A2 and A4 pulleys can range from microscopic to partial tears and, in the worst case, a complete rupture (see figure 13.4). Small partial tears are generally insidious because they develop over the course of a few climbs, a few days of climbing, or even gradually during the course of a climbing season. Overdependence on use of the crimp grip, with its near-90-degree flexion of the PIP joint, may increase the risk of this injury. Crimping produces a tremendous force load on the annular pulleys, and it's therefore considered a more stressful grip than the open hand.

Less frequent are acute ruptures that result during a maximum move on a tiny crimp hold or one-finger pocket. Some climbers report feeling or hearing a pop—a likely sign of a significant partial tear or complete rupture—though other injuries could also produce this effect.

Depending on the severity of an A2 pulley injury, pain and swelling at the base of the finger can range from slight to so debilitating that you can't perform everyday tasks like picking up a jug of milk. Swelling may limit the range of motion during flexion, and bowstringing may be felt or seen (Marco 1998) if one or two additional pulleys (usually A3 and A4) are ruptured, respectively. Slight tears may be asymptomatic when the finger is at rest, but become painful during isometric contraction (as in gripping a hold) or when pressing on the base of the finger near the top of the palm.

Treatment of a pulley injury must begin with complete cessation of climbing and discontinuation

Table 13.1 Ten Most Frequent Finger Injuries

Pulley injury	30%
Capsulitis	18%
Tenosynovitis	17%
Flexor tendon strain	8%
Strained joint capsule	5%
Flexor tendon ganglion	4%
Collateral ligament injury	4%
Epiphyseal (growth plate) fracture	3%
Lumbrical shift syndrome	3%
Osteoarthritis	3%

of any other activity that requires forceful flexion of the injured finger. Doing anything that causes pain will slow healing of the injured tissue and may make the injury worse. Therefore, the prudent response to developing finger pain is to cease climbing immediately so as to prevent further damage—a low-grade tweak may heal in a matter of weeks. By contrast, ignoring the onset of finger pain and trying to "climb through the injury" all but guarantees a worse tear and a much longer withdrawal from climbing.

The goal during the first few days following injury is to control inflammation (if present) with ice and non-steroidal anti-inflammatory (NSAID) medicines like ibuprofen or Naprosyn. Cease use of NSAIDs within three to five days (or less), since long-term use has been shown to impede the healing process and may even weaken tendons (see the "Vitamin I" sidebar in this chapter). "Buddy taping" (to an adjacent finger) or splinting of the injured finger can be beneficial during the first few days following injury, especially if you find it hard to limit use of your injured finger. Once swelling subsides, you want to begin daily finger flexing against a foam block, large sponges, or a ball of putty—such movement is therapeutic and essential to successful tendon remodeling.

Depending on the severity of the tear, pain typically subsides in two to ten weeks. Becoming pain-free, however, is not the go-ahead to resume

Treating an A2 Pulley Injury

1. Immediately cease climbing and any other activity that requires forceful flexion of the injured finger. Consult a doctor if there is noticeable bowstringing on the flexor tendon.
2. Use ice and NSAID medications only if the injury produces palpable or visible swelling. Cease use of ice and NSAIDs as soon as swelling diminishes. Smokers should consider breaking the habit, since smoking has been shown to slow healing of tendons and ligaments.
3. Immobilize with a splint or buddy taping for a few days up to a week or two, if daily activities cause acute pain.
4. As pain decreases—and only when all swelling is gone—begin light daily finger activity including finger flexions; squeezing putty, foam blocks, or a rubber doughnut; mild stretching; and massage. This light exercise is important to accelerate and ensure proper healing.
5. Use a heating pad for ten to fifteen minutes, three times a day, to increase blood flow and accelerate healing. Alternating heat and cold (ice bath) may further enhance beneficial circulation.
6. Use the therapy described in steps 4 and 5 for at least two to four weeks before beginning a gradual return to climbing. Use prophylactic taping ("H method" is best) every time you climb, and spend the first week or two climbing relatively easy routes with big holds and good footholds.
7. Return to maximal climbing if easy climbing yields no pain. Continue taping for at least six months, since complete tendon remodeling can take many months. Climb smart!

climbing! This is where many climbers go wrong—they return to climbing too soon and reinjure the partially healed tissue. As a general rule, wait an additional two weeks beyond becoming pain-free, then slowly return to easy climbing. In the case of a modest pulley injury, this may mean a total of about forty-five days of climbing downtime.

A French study of twelve elite climbers with A2 pulley injuries found that eight subjects were able to successfully return to climbing after forty-five days of rest (Moutet 1993). More severe pulley tears, however, may require as much as two or three months of rest before you can progressively return to climbing. Regardless of the degree of injury and length of withdrawal from climbing, use of prophylactic taping is essential during a return to climbing. Dr. Schöffl recommends taping the injured finger for up to six months. Three different taping techniques are shown in the "Prophylactic Taping Methods" sidebar.

In the case of a complete rupture or multi-pulley injury, surgical reconstruction is often necessary. Hand surgeons have long performed reconstruction of annular pulleys in nonclimbing cases where a deep laceration had damaged the flexor tendon and tendon pulleys. Free tendon grafts are the most common method of pulley reconstruction (Seiler 2000). The grafts are most often harvested from the dorsal wrist extensor retinaculum or the palmaris longus, and loops of the tendon are sewn in place of the damaged pulley (Moutet 2003; Seiler 1995; Lister 1979). It has been shown that reconstruction with three loops can withstand as much force load to failure as a normal annular pulley (Lin 1989).

An Austrian study reveals that annular pulley reconstruction has produced good functional and subjective results in climbers after eighteen to forty-three months of recovery time (Gabl 1998). German physician Volker Schöffl is a leading expert on climbing injuries, and he's had great success with pulley plastic surgery. As a general guideline Schöffl recommends a conservative nonsurgical approach to treating single-pulley injuries, whereas he recommends surgical repair when two or more pulleys are ruptured.

FLEXOR TENDINITIS, TENOSYNOVITIS, AND TENDON RUPTURE AND AVULSION

Several other injuries can produce pain and diminished function in ways similar to an injured annular pulley. (As stated earlier, diagnosis can be difficult—see a physician to be completely sure what you are dealing with.) Tendinitis can develop in the FDS or FDP tendon as a result of repetitive stress. In this case, pain may be limited to the palm side of the finger or extend into the palm or forearm. Extended rest is the primary treatment, followed by a gradual return to climbing a few weeks after cessation of pain (as described for tendon pulley injuries).

Interestingly, most cases diagnosed as "flexor tendinitis" actually involve tendinitis of the flexor tendon sheath and not necessarily the tendon itself. Therefore, the more correct diagnosis would be tenosynovitis or tendovaginitis. Regardless of what you call it, this overuse injury can evolve into a vicious cycle as inflammation of the tendon sheath impairs flexor tendon function, thus leading to increasing pain and inflammation. A constant dull ache with each finger movement and pain that radiates down the tendon is the hallmark symptom. Withdrawal from climbing is essential—follow the A2 pulley treatment protocol on page 284.

In rare cases a flexor tendon may rupture or avulse (pull out at the point of insertion). Jebson (1997) states that an FDS tendon rupture may occur with the crimp grip, while an FDP tendon rupture is more likely with an open-hand pocket grip. Either rupture or avulsion would occur acutely with immediate onset of pain. Jebson states that symptoms include pain at the FDS or FDP tendon insertion, finger swelling, and an absence of active flexion of the PIP joint (FDS rupture) or DIP joint (FDP rupture). Surgical reattachment may be required.

Prophylactic Taping Methods

Reinforcing flexor tendon pulleys with athletic tape is a common practice—but is this practice really effective? Several physicians and researchers are on record as stating that firm circumferential taping is beneficial. Rohrbough (2000) notes that "tape is a tremendous help, giving support to a weak or healing pulley, helping to hold the tendon against the bone." Swiss researcher Schweizer (2000) measured force on tendon pulleys with and without taping and determined that tape applied just below the PIP joint absorbed about 12 percent of the total force. Doctors Jebson (1997), Hochholzer (2003), and Schöffl (2015) all advise use of protective taping for two to six months upon returning to climbing after an annular pulley injury.

Given these endorsements, I hope climbers and coaches will acknowledge that finger taping is a somewhat effective—though far from absolute—prophylactic measure. Here are three valid methods of taping, including the lesser-known "H method"; this taping technique was shown to be the most effective at holding the flexor tendon closer to the bone (Schöffl 2007). Use the strongest, stickiest tape you can find—German Leukotape is the best (one application may last all day), while many cheaper American tapes quickly stretch, loosen, and lose effectiveness (thus frequent retaping is necessary).

A2 Ring Method

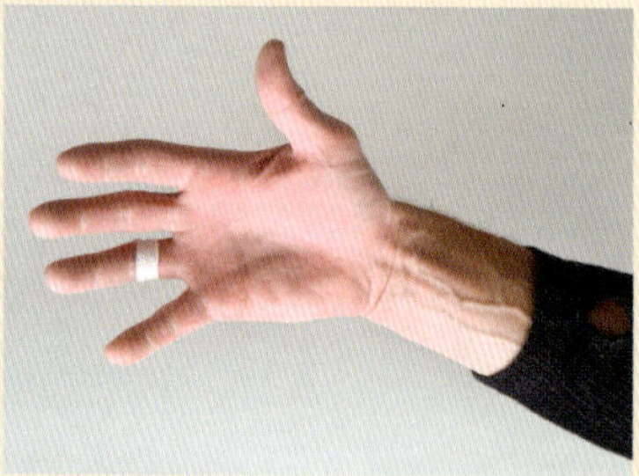

The A2 ring method (as used in the Swiss study mentioned earlier) involves firm circumferential taping at the distal end of the proximal phalanx—that is, just above the A2 pulley and immediately below the PIP joint. Use a narrow strip of tape, approximately 0.4 inch (10mm) wide, and wrap as tightly and as close to the PIP joint as possible without restricting blood flow. This may take a bit of experimentation, but remember that loose finger taping serves no function other than protecting the skin. Remove and reapply fresh tape every few hours to maintain the necessary tightness throughout a full day of climbing.

Figure-8 Method

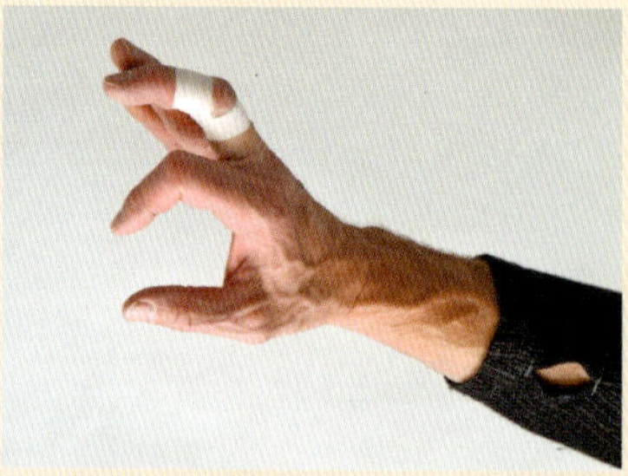

The Figure-8 method may provide additional tendon support to the A3, A4, and cruciform pulleys, and it's very effective at preventing skin wear (and pain) when you're climbing on sharp pockets or rough indoor holds. Tear a long strip of tape, approximately 16 inches (40cm) in length by 0.75 inch (18mm) wide. With a slight bend in the finger, begin with two turns of tape over the proximal phalanx (on top of the A2 pulley), and then cross under the PIP joint and take two turns around the middle phalanx. Cross back under the PIP joint and conclude with another turn or two around the base of the finger.

H method

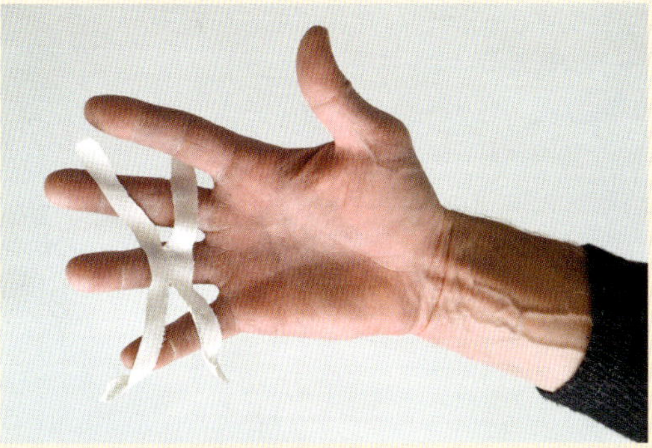

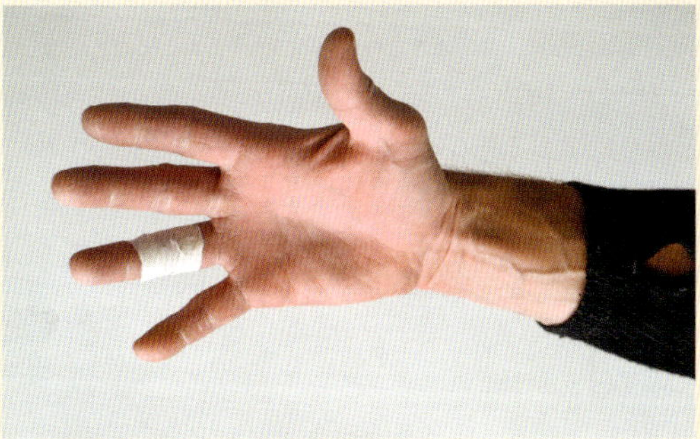

Here's a relatively new method of taping the annular pulleys, and it's been shown to be the most effective method in terms of decreasing the tendon-to-bone distance of a bowstringing pulley. Begin with a 4-inch-long (10cm) piece of 1- or 1.5-inch (25mm) width tape. Use a rip or cut the tape longways from each end so that there's just a 0.5-inch (12mm) "bridge" in the middle, forming the center of the "H." Position this bridge over the palm side of the PIP joint, then wrap the free ends of the tape around the finger just above and below the PIP joint. Remove and reapply fresh tape every few hours to maintain the necessary tightness throughout a full day of climbing.

You may be surprised to learn that flexor tendon ruptures, avulsions, and to a lesser extent annular pulley injuries occur occasionally among football players. These acute injuries, commonly called "jersey finger," occur when a tackler with an outstretched arm catches a finger on the jersey of the ball carrier sprinting past him. It is interesting to observe that many linemen and linebackers use prophylactic taping to support the flexor tendon and the A2 and A4 pulleys—it would seem that professional football players have also concluded that prophylactic taping works!

CAPSULITIS AND SPRAINED JOINT CAPSULE

Capsulitis most often presents as visible swelling and a reduced range of motion in the middle (PIP) joint of the finger. Though not debilitating, a long season of climbing—especially hard climbing with habitual use of the crimp grip—often leads to swelling of the PIP joint and, most bothersome, the sensation of achy, stiff fingers upon waking in the morning. These symptoms develop from cartilage stress and an increase in synovial fluid that, again, is usually the result of persistent, forceful loading of a sharply flexed PIP joint (as in crimping).

A reduction in climbing frequency, along with a conscious shift to using the open-hand grip, should prevent worsening of the condition. Use ice to address the swelling in acute cases, whereas low-grade chronic capsulitis may improve somewhat with finger flexing exercises, mild stretching, and application of heat. Ultimately, it may take complete withdrawal from climbing for the joint to fully heal.

Finger jamming (in cracks) and dynamic pocket pulling on just one or two fingers can sprain the joint capsule, thus producing similar symptoms to capsulitis. A joint strain, however, typically causes more acute pain that may make further climbing unpleasant and difficult. Buddy taping or splinting can be helpful during the early stages of healing. Prudence dictates withdrawal from climbing and a few weeks of movement therapy before a gradual return to the rock.

COLLATERAL LIGAMENT INJURIES

Ligaments connect bone to bone across a joint, providing stability (see figure 13.3). Collateral ligament sprains and avulsions at the PIP joint are known to occur in climbers, particularly as a result of a powerful lunge or awkward torque off a "fixed" finger (as in a jam or tight pocket). A ligament sprain manifests with mild to moderate pain and swelling around the PIP joint, but with no loss of stability (Jebson 1997). A rupture or avulsion will produce significant pain and swelling as well as loss of stability, medially or laterally.

Treatment of incomplete collateral ligament injuries typically involves splinting the PIP joint for ten to fourteen days, after which buddy taping can be used and range-of-motion exercises started (Bach 1999). Climbing can gradually be reintroduced despite persistent low-grade pain and swelling, which may take months to resolve (Jebson 1997).

Complete collateral ligament injuries at the PIP joint are usually treated operatively. If the collateral ligament is completely avulsed from the bone, nonoperative treatment may result in chronic swelling and long-term instability (Bach 1999). Surgical repair can improve this, and full function is often restored in approximately three months.

GROWTH PLATE INJURY IN JUNIOR CLIMBERS

Junior climbers make up one of the fastest-growing demographics, with thousands of young climbers now entering competitions and beginning structured training programs. Correlating to the rising popularity of junior competitions and the intensive training used by many participants is an increase in non-traumatic growth plate fractures, known as epiphyseal fractures. The common symptoms are slow onset of pain and swelling of the middle finger joint, and in some cases the inability to crimp grip on holds. The condition is easily diagnosed via X-ray.

A 2005 German study (Hochholzer 2005) evaluated twenty-four junior climbers with non-traumatic epiphyseal fractures. Interestingly, only one of the injured climbers was a girl—so boys seem to be at greater risk—and all were between the ages of thirteen and sixteen. A recent follow-up analysis (Schöffl 2015) found an alarming 600 percent increase in these growth plate fractures among youth climbers! Inappropriate training activities (e.g., intensive fingerboard and campus training), a singular focus on hard bouldering, and simply climbing too much (more than three or four days per week) are all contributing factors.

Injury to growth plates can cause permanent damage, so a temporary withdrawal from climbing is essential for adolescents experiencing finger joint pain. Parents and coaches must enforce a rest period of at least a few months or more away from climbing until the youth climber is asymptomatic. In terms of prevention, parents and coaches should limit climbing activity to three days per week during the adolescent growth spurt (most GP fractures occur between ages thirteen and fifteen), and disallow use of advanced training exercises such as campus training, hypergravity training, and intensive fingerboard training until at least age sixteen or the end of puberty (achievement of maximum adult height). See page 244 for more on this important topic.

Other Finger and Hand Injuries

A wide variety of other finger and hand injuries are possible in a sport that requires fingers to crimp, pinch, and jam under high passive and dynamic force loads. No doubt you will experience your share of household injuries like torn tips, palm flappers, or back-of-hand gobies. There are a few more subtle injuries that can affect climbers, however, including carpal tunnel syndrome and osteoarthritis.

CARPAL TUNNEL SYNDROME

Carpal tunnel syndrome (CTS) is a condition in which a nerve passing through the wrist, with the flexor tendons, is exposed chronically to too much pressure. This syndrome affects a small number of climbers, but its occurrence does not appear to be disproportionately common in climbers (Robinson 1993). Therefore, it's difficult to conclude whether a climber with this syndrome incurred it from the repetitive gripping of rock holds or from some other source. Regardless, the symptoms include numbness, burning, and tingling of the fingers; these symptoms may become worse at night or during activity or elevation (Lewis 1993). Treatment involves cessation or lowering intensity of climbing, anti-inflammatory medicines, and splinting of the wrist in a neutral position at night for three to six weeks. Surgical decompression of the carpal tunnel may be required if this conservative treatment fails and symptoms are severe enough to be disabling.

ARTHRITIS

For years I have heard speculation that active "rock climbers will someday become severe arthritis sufferers." Fortunately, anecdotal evidence of many twenty- and thirty-year veterans, as well as recent studies of longtime climbers, indicates that these predictions are not quite panning out. In one study, radiographs of the hands of veteran elite climbers were compared with an age-matched control group. An increased rate of osteoarthritis for several joints was found in the climber group, though no significant difference in the overall prevalence of osteoarthritis was found between the two groups (Rohrbough 1998). A more recent study compared recreational climbers to non-climbers by measuring bone strength and dimensions and occurrence of osteoarthritis. The study concluded that climbers are not at an increased risk for developing debilitating osteoarthritis; it also discovered that climbers' finger and hand bones are wider (indicating that additional bone is deposited subperiosteally) and stronger (Sylvester 2006). These studies are really good news for those of us entering middle age with many years of climbing under our belts!

Still, it's possible that individuals who predominantly use the crimp grip may experience some swelling and arthritis in the PIP and DIP joints. As shown in figure 13.4, use of the crimp grip produces hyperextension of the DIP joint under large passive force, while the PIP joint is sharply flexed under great force. Therefore, both the DIP and PIP joints are possible sites for capsulitis and arthritis (Robinson 1993).

If you are an aging climber who experiences some swelling, pain, or stiffness of the DIP and PIP joints, you will find some relief through use of nonsteroidal anti-inflammatory medications. A growing body of research also points to a supplement called glucosamine sulfate as a possible treatment for mild osteoarthritis. Daily supplementation of 1,500 milligrams of glucosamine sulfate has been shown to reduce pain and stiffness, and—more important—to slow the degradation of affected joints (Reginster 2001). Acquiring these benefits requires a long-term commitment to taking glucosamine sulfate, because the effects are cumulative, not immediate as in taking anti-inflammatory medicines. But the promise of slowing or halting joint degradation is a huge benefit for individuals—climbers and non-climbers—over forty years of age who take glucosamine sulfate daily.

Many supplement manufacturers are now adding two other compounds, chondroitin and MSM, to their glucosamine sulfate supplements. Chondroitin is believed to produce benefits similar to glucosamine sulfate, and one study showed positive results in patients with joint problems from four to eight weeks of taking both supplements together (McAlindon 2000). However, a more recent meta-analysis of the best-designed studies showed no positive effects in taking chondroitin alone (Juni 2007). MSM shows more promise based on a recent pilot study. Participants who received three grams of MSM, twice per day, for twelve weeks experienced a significant reduction in pain and improved physical function compared with a placebo group

"Vitamin I" Use: The Good, the Bad, and the Alternatives

Pain is a common companion of climbers. For some it's the benign pain of muscular soreness after a hard day of climbing or a severe workout. Many others, however, unfortunately experience the pain of acute or overuse injury. Given the ubiquity of injured and sore climbers, use of NSAID medications to treat inflammation and mask pain is widespread. In fact, some climbers joking refer to ibuprofen as "vitamin I," since they take it as if it were a daily vitamin.

Daily use of NSAIDs, such as ibuprofen (Advil and Motrin), naproxen (Aleve and Naprosyn), and aspirin, does have its drawbacks, including risk of ulceration of the stomach, impaired kidney function, and anti-blood-clotting effects. Furthermore, regular NSAID use may actually slow muscle cell regeneration and hamper healing of muscles, ligaments, tendons, and cartilage (Almekinders 1999, 2003). In aggregate, these risks and side effects make a compelling case against regular NSAID use—and, the latter study may perhaps help explain why so many ibuprofen-using climbers experience tendon injuries.

So what are the alternatives for treating the pain and inflammation of an acute injury, delayed-onset muscle soreness (DOMS) after climbing or training, and the persistent pangs of an overuse injury? Let's first examine the immediate response to acute injury, which is best treated with the RICE method (rest, ice, compression, and elevation). Icing the injured area for twenty minutes, three to six times a day, is highly effective for controlling swelling and reducing pain in the hours following acute injury. Continued use of RICE beyond the first few days following injury, however, will inhibit the healing process. (Get professional medical care if you have any sense that your injury might be serious or if it does not begin to improve given several days of rest.)

What about the most common cause of pain among climbers—delayed-onset muscle soreness? Some climbers use topical rubs containing methyl salicylate, menthol, camphor, or various herbs such as arnica for spot treatment. While the stimulation of massage and the warming or numbing effect of some preparations may reduce the sensation of pain, there is little evidence that these concoctions promote healing beyond the effect of massage itself. It seems that any measure or activity that increases circulation will promote healing; thus engaging in low-intensity general exercise, foam rolling, or use of a whirlpool or heating pad are effective treatments for DOMS.

Finally, there are those frustrating, slow-to-heal overuse injuries such as annular pulley strain, elbow tendinosis, shoulder impingement, and such. As outlined in this chapter, rest and rehabilitative exercise are the primary methods of treatment. NSAID use should be avoided in the long term, since these anti-inflammatory agents may slow healing and reduce tendon strength (as does smoking). Conversely, regular massage, heat therapy, and gentle stretching will encourage blood flow to the injured tissues and thus seem to be the best method to encourage healing once acute pain and inflammation have subsided.

Perhaps the best non-NSAID alternatives are the omega-3 essential fatty acids found in fish. You may be familiar with omega-3 EFA for its well-promoted preventive effects on coronary artery disease. Interestingly, daily consumption of fish, or fish oil supplements, also has been shown effective for treating musculoskeletal injuries and discogenic diseases (Maroon 2006). The effective dose to be heart-healthy is just one gram of omega-3 EFA per day; however, an everyday dose of two to four grams (more than you could likely consume from eating fish) is needed to provide the natural anti-inflammatory effects that would benefit climbers.

(Kim 2006). In summary, all relevant studies showed these compounds to be safe and with almost no side effects; however, only glucosamine sulfate and MSM, taken in long-term daily doses of 1.5 to 3.0 grams each, produced statistically significant beneficial results.

Elbow Tendinopathy

Pain near the bony medial (inside) or lateral (outside) epicondyles of the elbow is a common ailment among serious climbers. In most cases the onset of pain is gradual: A schedule of frequent climbing produces microscopic injury that fails to repair before the tendon is subjected to additional strain. A tendinosis cycle develops and amplifies as breakdown exceeds repair and the microtraumas accumulate over many weeks and months. In the early stage of tendinosis, pain is dull and may be felt only after a day of climbing; however, pain experienced in the course of everyday activities such as opening a door or washing your hair is a sign of more advanced tendinosis. The hallmark of tendinosis is its gradual onset and lack of visible swelling.

A similar yet less common and often misdiagnosed injury is tendinitis. The suffix itis means "inflammation," and the term tendinitis should be reserved for acute tendon injury accompanied by inflammation and palpable swelling. In climbing, tendinitis occurs most often near the medial epicondyle as the tendon is injured during a maximal one-arm pull on a small hold or in performing advanced training exercises without adequate warm-up or training experience.

A third, more subtle class of tendon injury is tenosynovitis (also known as paratenonitis and tenovaginitis), an inflammation and degeneration of the outer layers of the tendon and the synovia-lined tendon sheath. Tenosynovitis can develop in the tendons of the arms and fingers and in concert with either tendinosis or tendinitis.

Regardless of which tendon ailment you possess, the one commonality is the extremely slow rate of healing. While muscles possess abundant blood flow and a relatively rapid rate of healing, blood flow to the ropelike collagenous tendons is poor, and laying down new collagen may take a hundred days or more (Khan 1999). Exacerbating these slow-healing injuries is the tendency of enthusiastic climbers to rush back into training and climbing prematurely. Worse yet, researchers have discovered that an enduring tendinosis cycle often leads to collagen repair with an abnormal structure and composition, thus making the repaired tendon less able to withstand tensile stress and more vulnerable to further injury. Following acute injury, the strength of a repaired tendon can remain as much as 30 percent lower than normal for months or even years (Leadbetter 1992; Liu 1995).

In severe, chronic cases of elbow tendinitis or tendinosis, surgery may offer the only lasting remedy. The most popular procedure is to simply excise the diseased tissue from the tendon, then reattach healthy tendon to the bone. Eighty-five to 90 percent of patients recuperate in three months, 10 to 12 percent have improvement but some pain during exercise, and only 2 to 3 percent have no improvement (Auerback 2000).

Following is a closer look at the two most common elbow injuries and their treatments.

MEDIAL EPICONDYLITIS AND TENDINOSIS

Pain near the medial epicondyle is commonly called golfer's elbow or climber's elbow. Pain develops in the tendons connecting the pronator teres muscle and/or the finger flexor muscles to the knobby, medial epicondyle of the inside elbow.

In many cases medial tendinosis is caused by muscular imbalances of the forearm and an accumulation of microtraumas to the tendons that result from climbing too often, finger training too hard, and, most important, resting too little. Consider that all the muscles that produce finger flexion are anchored to the medial epicondyle. Furthermore, the muscles that produce hand pronation (that turn the palm outward to face the rock) originate from the medial epicondyle. This subtle fact plays a key role in causing this injury: Biceps contraction produces supination (turning of the palm upward), but in gripping the rock you generally need to maintain a pronated, palms-out position. This battle between the supinating action of the biceps pulling and the necessity to maintain a pronated hand position (to maintain grip with the rock) strains the typically undertrained teres pronator muscle and its attachment at the medial epicondyle.

Given the above factors, it's easy to see why the tendons attaching to the medial epicondyle are subjected to sustained stress and, inevitably, develop microtraumas. Just as muscular microtraumas are repaired to new levels of capability, tendons increase in strength and can withstand higher stress loads given adequate rest. Unfortunately, the repair and strengthening process occurs more slowly in tendons than in muscles. Eventually the muscles are able to create more force than the tendons can adapt to—the result is injury.

Tendinosis will reveal itself gradually through increasing incidence of painful twinges or soreness during or after climbing. Tendinitis, however, is evidenced by acute onset of pain in the midst of a single hard move, and is usually followed by inflammation and palpable swelling. Even in these cases, however, cumulative microtrauma may be involved in making the tissue vulnerable to acute trauma.

As in treating other injuries, you can more easily manage tendinopathy (any tendon injury) and speed your return to climbing by early recognition of the symptoms and proactive treatment. The mature and prudent approach of attending to the injury early on versus trying to "climbing through it" could mean the difference between six weeks and six months (or more) of climbing downtime.

Treatment of tendinosis and tendinitis has two phases: Phase I involves steps to relieve pain and reduce inflammation (in the case of tendinitis); Phase II is engaging in rehabilitative and stretching exercises to promote correct alignment of collagen tissue and prevent recurrence.

Phase I demands withdrawal from climbing (and all sport-specific training) and commencement of pain-reducing and anti-inflammatory measures. Icing the elbow for twenty minutes, three to six times a day, and use of NSAIDs will help reduce inflammation and pain following injury; cease use within a few days to a week. A cortisone injection may be helpful in chronic or severe cases, though this practice is somewhat controversial among physicians and, in fact, may be detrimental to the healing process (Nirschl 1996). Depending on the severity of the injury, successful completion of Phase I could require anywhere from two weeks to two months.

The goal of Phase II is to retrain and rehabilitate the injured tissues through use of mild stretching and strength-training exercises. Since forearm-muscle imbalance plays a primary role in many elbow injuries, it's vital to perform exercises that strengthen the weaker aspects of the forearm—hand pronation for medial tendinosis and hand/wrist extension for lateral tendinosis.

Although some dull pain is likely during this rehab phase, avoid any exercise or activity that causes sharper pain or lingering (or worsening pain) after a workout. Pull-ups, fingerboarding, and campus training are often problematic and should only be done in small doses, if at all, until the condition has resolved.

Always perform some general warm-up activity and consider warming the elbow directly with a heating pad before beginning the stretching and strengthening exercises. Stretch twice daily the forearm flexor, extensor, and pronator muscles as described in chapter 6. Once the stretching exercises have successfully restored normal range of motion with no pain, you can introduce strength training with the forearm pronator exercise shown on page 136. It's important to progress slowly with training exercises and to cut back at the first sign of pain. Begin with just a couple of pounds of resistance and gradually increase the weight over the course of a few weeks. Use the stretching exercises daily, but do the weight-training exercises only three days per week.

After three to four weeks of pain-free training, begin a gradual return to climbing. Start with low-angle and easy vertical routes, and take a month or two to return to your original level of climbing. Continue with the stretching and strength-training exercises indefinitely—as long as you are a climber, you must engage in these preventive measures. Failed rehabilitation and relapse into chronic pain may eventually lead to a need for surgical intervention.

Finally, let's take a look at the use of counterforce bracing, or circumferential taping of the upper forearm, as a curative (or preventive) measure for elbow tendinosis. A counterforce brace designed specifically for elbow tendinosis can provide some comfort by dispersing forces away from the underlying tissues (Nirschl 1996). These braces are not a substitute for proper rehabilitation, however; they instead act only to help prevent recurrence after full rehabilitation.

LATERAL TENDINOSIS

Lateral tendinosis, commonly called tennis elbow or lateral epicondylitis, is an irritation of the tendons that attach the finger/wrist extensor muscles to the lateral epicondyle on the outside of the elbow. The finger extensor muscles are antagonists to the finger flexor muscles used so prominently in gripping the rock, and therefore the extensors are often disproportionately weak compared with the flexors. Furthermore, grip strength is greatest when your hand is in the extended position—this explains why your arm "chicken wings" away from the rock when you struggle to grip small crimp holds. It's the extensor muscles that help facilitate this chicken-wing position; thus constant straining to grip small crimp holds can lead to tendon injury where the extensor muscles attach to the lateral epicondyle. (Note that reducing your use of the crimp grip will lower your risk of tendinosis.)

Onset of pain is typically gradual and will first appear after a hard day of climbing. Without rest and treatment, the condition will progressively worsen to the point that climbing becomes prohibitively painful and even everyday tasks are hampered. Since such a severe case often requires a six-month (or longer) rehabilitation period away from climbing, it's paramount that you take the necessary steps to mitigate this injury early on.

The treatment protocol for lateral tendinosis is similar to that described above for medial tendinopathy. Time away from climbing is mandatory—very few people successfully climb through elbow tendinosis of either kind. Frequent icing and limited use of anti-inflammatory medication is helpful during the initial period of pain, but these treatments should not be used to allow continuation of climbing. As pain and swelling subside, daily use of the stretching exercises is absolutely necessary as the first step in the rehabilitation process. Gradually introduce reverse wrist curls and reverse arm curls (page 134) to strengthen the finger/wrist extensor muscles; add weight incrementally over the course of a few weeks. Use a heating pad for a few minutes before stretching—daily use of a heating pad may also speed rate of healing. In mild cases of tendinosis, you may be able to complete the rehabilitation process and begin a slow return to climbing in six to eight weeks. A counterforce brace worn just below the elbow may be beneficial upon beginning a slow return to climbing.

Long term, it's essential that all climbers take a proactive approach to preventing elbow tendinosis. As detailed in chapter 6, I feel that all climbers should engage in daily forearm stretching and twice weekly antagonist muscle training of the wrist extensor muscles. Furthermore, post-climbing and rest day tissue management, via self-massage or an Armaid (see chapter 6 As Essential as Your Climbing

Treating Elbow Tendinosis

1. Cease climbing and climbing-specific training.
2. Apply ice to the injured area and take NSAID medications only if the injury produces palpable swelling (most elbow tendinopathy does not) or persistent pain. Cease use of ice and NSAIDs as soon as swelling and pain diminish—further use may slow healing.
3. Never use NSAIDs to mask pain in order to continue climbing while injured. Regular use of NSAIDS (and smoking) may actually weaken tendons!
4. If no swelling is present, begin mild stretching, light massage, and use of a heating pad (ten to fifteen minutes) three times per day. Most important is twice-daily use of the forearm stretches shown in chapter 6.
5. Use an Armaid daily to improve forearm muscle tissue quality (never use on tendons).
6. If no swelling is present and if pain is minor, engage in rehabilitative exercises on an every-other-day basis. Perform some warm-up activities such as arm circles, finger flexions, massage, or use of a heating pad. Use reverse wrist curls and reverse arm curls for lateral tendinosis and forearm pronators for medial tendinosis.
7. Cautiously return to climbing when your elbow is pain-free and no sooner than after two to four weeks of strength-training exercise. Begin with easy, foot-oriented climbing for the first few weeks, and limit use of the crimp grip. Cease climbing if you experience pain while climbing and immediately return to step 2.
8. Commit to long-term training of the forearm pronator and extensor muscles, and enjoy daily stretching and Armaid use for as long as you are an active climber.

Shoes—Armaid!), will help release spasms and adhesions, lengthen the muscle, and increase circulation. Do all the above, and you'll climb stronger and vastly reduce your risk of elbow injury.

Shoulder Injuries

The shoulder joint takes lot of punishment from climbing, especially in those obsessed with V-hard bouldering, roped climbing on steep terrain, and intensive climbing-specific training. As shown in figure 13.1, shoulder injuries are the second most common climbing injury (Schöffl 2015). A variety of injuries can occur, ranging from impingement or tendinitis to a partial dislocation, rotator cuff, or SLAP tear. Given the complexity of the shoulder joint, however, a diagnosis can be difficult; expert consultation or an MRI will likely be required to detect small tears of the rotator cuff and other subtle injuries.

In comparing recent injury statistics with data from a decade earlier, the frequency of shoulder injury has increased significantly. As revealed in table 13.2, the SLAP tear is now the number one shoulder disorder among climbers, and I'm alarmed by the number of climbers needing to go under the knife for a SLAP or rotator cuff repair. No doubt today's super-steep sport climbs, jumpy/lunging boulder problems, and the popularization of campus training have all contributed to this increase. Each of these activities places great strain on the shoulder joint, which, without sufficient development of the stabilizing muscles, will become unstable, causing impingement, tendinitis, or worse.

In chapter 6 I detailed the importance of training both the large and small muscles that contribute to proper shoulder function and stability—use the exercises and stretches religiously and you'll vastly lower your injury risk. While any moderate to severe injury of the shoulder should be examined by a physician, many minor shoulder problems can be effectively treated with these shoulder exercises and stretches.

Here is a brief exposé on the most common shoulder injuries—consult Dr. Schöffl's *One Move Too Many* for in-depth, expert coverage that has no peer.

Table 13.2 Distribution of Diagnoses in Shoulder Injuries

SLAP tear	33%
Impingement	26%
Shoulder sprain	11%
Dislocation	10%
Supraspinatus tendonitis	5%
Instability	5%
Tendinosis of long biceps tendon	3%
Rupture of long biceps tendon	3%
Rotator cuff tear	3%

IMPINGEMENT SYNDROME, BURSITIS, AND TENDINITIS

These conditions are closely related, and they are a common source of shoulder pain among athletes in sports that demand consistent, forceful overhead arm movements. Without sufficient strength in the rotator cuff muscles and large shoulder muscles, the head of the humerus (upper arm bone) will elevate. Tight biceps and pectoralis muscles compound the problem by inwardly rotating the shoulders. Finally, weak rhomboid and trapezius muscles fail to place the scapula in the proper position for overhead arm moves. All combined, these physical handicaps are at the root of most shoulder problems.

Pain and inflammation often develop under the acromion, the bony top portion of the shoulder where the shoulder blade and collarbone meet, as a result of tendinitis and swelling of the bursa (a fluid-filled sac that provides cushion between the bone and surrounding tissues). Onset of pain is gradual over weeks and months, and may eventually lead to pain in the upper arm and difficulty sleeping on the arm or shoulder.

Diagnosis begins with a physical examination, including movement and strength testing to evaluate pain and weakness throughout the range of motion. X-rays and an MRI may be performed to rule out other causes of shoulder pain, such as arthritis, bone disease, and tears in the rotator cuff. Impingement syndrome may be confirmed if injection of a small amount of anesthetic under the acromion relieves pain.

Treatment of these conditions begins with steps to reduce pain and inflammation: icing for twenty minutes, three to six times per day; limited use of NSAIDS (such as ibuprofen and Naprosyn); and cessation of climbing and overhead hand movements. As pain subsides, gentle stretching and strengthening exercises can be introduced gradually—these rehabilitative exercises are essential to lower the risk of injury relapse upon returning to climbing (see the Training Rotator Cuff and Scapular Stability exercises in chapter 6). In minor cases followed up by dedicated rehabilitation, a return to climbing may be possible in one to two months. More serious cases may require six months or more away from climbing, and perhaps even steroid injections or surgery.

SHOULDER INSTABILITY

Shoulder instability is a condition that's become increasingly common among high-end climbers with a taste for overhanging routes, as well as individuals who engage in excessive fingerboard training with poor technique (relaxed, shrugged shoulders). The condition develops gradually from long-term, repeated exposure to straight-arm hangs, Gaston moves, and severe lock-offs, as well as from overzealous stretching, or climbing on overhanging routes day after day or on hard boulder problems without adequate rest and training of the stabilizing antagonist muscles.

No matter the mechanism, constant stretching of the ligaments and a growing imbalance of the muscles that surround and stabilize the shoulder joint can lead to instability and risk of injury. In most cases the ball portion of the shoulder joint is levered forward during extreme movements with the elbow located behind the plane of the body. Furthermore, the force of the levering motion on the shoulder joint increases when the arm is extended with the elbow pointing outward (and extending behind the plane of the body), as in grabbing a high Gaston hold, chicken winging on a small crimp hold, or making a long reach on overhanging rock.

Fresh shoulder injuries should be treated with the two-phase process of resting until pain diminishes and then use of rehabilitative exercises to strengthen the rotator cuff muscle group. Climbing activity must be markedly reduced or eliminated while you engage in the rehabilitative process, and you should also avoid any overhead motion or other activity that causes pain in the shoulder. Anti-inflammatory medicine and ice applied twice daily are useful in reducing initial pain and swelling.

The common course of therapy begins with gentle stretching and strengthening of the shoulder, but with no exercises above the level of the shoulder. Perform the exercises described in the "Training Scapular Stability" section of chapter 6 on an every-other-day basis, and increase the weight used in small increments over several weeks. Similarly, you should use some of the basic antagonist exercises (also in chapter 6) that strengthen the larger pushing muscles. Decrease resistance on or eliminate completely any exercise that is too painful. Of course, rehabilitation is best guided by a professional physical therapist, and you may need anywhere from two to six months before you can reintroduce climbing activities.

Unfortunately, a significant number of people with shoulder injuries ultimately require a surgical solution. The procedure may include removal of damaged tissue, repair of minor rotator cuff tears, or surgical tightening of affected ligaments and tendons. Surgery will be followed with long-term physical therapy; given a successful outcome, climbing activity may resume in six to twelve months.

SLAP TEAR

A SLAP tear is one of the most severe—and unfortunately most common—injuries experienced by modern sport climbers and boulderers. SLAP is an acronym for "superior labral tear from anterior to posterior," and it's an injury that almost always requires surgery. Symptoms include aching pain after a strenuous workout or day of climbing, a "catching" feeling in the shoulder while climbing, shoulder pain while sleeping, and a decrease in arm and grip strength. An MRI will be needed to confirm the diagnosis, however.

By now I'm sure you can guess the cause of a SLAP tear—out-of-control dynamic arm moves, campus training with straight-arm grabs (or any similar move while climbing on steep terrain), and power training or near-limit steep climbing while in a high state of fatigue. This is another injury that, as described above, results from the inability to properly stabilize the humeral head and scapula during forceful overhead moves.

Treatment usually begins with arthroscopic surgery to repair the tear and address other associated injuries such as a rotator cuff tear. A long, gradually progressive rehabilitation follows, beginning with a few weeks of range of motion exercise and, after about two months, a slow introduction of strengthening exercises. A return to full activity takes six months or more—as a rule, an extremely fit climber with a lower-grade SLAP tear will be the quickest to return to rigorous climbing.

Knee Injuries

Injury to the knee is a relatively new phenomenon in climbing that correlates directly to the proliferation of indoor and sport climbing. New climbing techniques like the drop-knee weren't popularized until the 1990s, but this is now a staple move of the steep indoor and outdoor climbs that are so prominent today. Repeated use of the drop-knee, especially under high force load, can tear the specialized cartilage in the knee called the meniscus (Stelzle 2000), as can high-stepping in a full-hip-turnout position. A meniscus tear—or, worse, a tear of a knee ligament—can also occur during a forceful, uneven landing when jumping off a boulder problem.

MENISCUS TEAR

Meniscus is a tough, fibrous type of cartilage that sits between the ends of the femur and tibia (see figure 13.5). The menisci serve primarily as shock absorbers between the ends of the bones to protect the articulating surfaces (McFarland 2000). There are two separate C-shaped meniscal cartilages in the knee, one on the inner half of the knee (the medial meniscus) and the other on the outer half (the lateral meniscus). A partial or total tear of a meniscus can occur during forced rotation of the knee while the foot remains in a fixed position. In climbing, these tears most often occur in severe drop-knee positions, which produce internal rotation of the knee under pressure.

A small meniscus tear can develop gradually from repeated use of these climbing moves, or a tear may occur suddenly. Some tears involve only a small portion of the meniscus, while others produce a bucket handle, or complete separation of a piece of cartilage. Symptoms can range from mild pain and no visible swelling to severe pain and swelling and reduced mobility (McFarland 2000). Many meniscal tears cause popping, clicking, and locking of the knee in certain positions.

Not all meniscus tears cause big problems. A minor tear in the thick outer portion of the meniscus may be able to repair itself given fairly good blood supply. Also, use of the supplement glucosamine sulfate is believed by some to support the formation of new cartilage and may enhance the healing process—this is controversial, however. In minor cases, symptoms will disappear on their own; persistent pain that affects daily activities or produces significant pain in certain climbing positions may require surgery, however.

Figure 13.5 Meniscus Tear

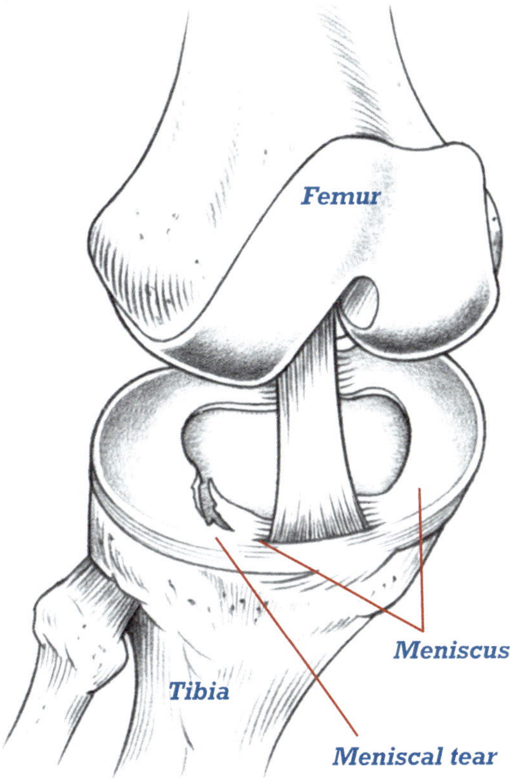

The meniscus can tear when the knee is forced to rotate while the foot remains in a fixed position. A severe drop-knee move or a twisting jump off a boulder problem can cause this injury.

Arthroscopic surgery is very successful in relieving pain and restoring full function to the injured knee. The goal of arthroscopic surgery is to preserve as much of the meniscus as possible so as to decrease the chance of future arthritis (McFarland 2000). Tears on the outer margin of the meniscus are more amenable to repair, since they have greater blood flow compared with the thin, inner margin of the meniscus. Tears in the thin portion of the meniscus are typically excised; entirely detached pieces of cartilage are removed.

Recovery from arthroscopic surgery is rapid. The procedure is generally performed as outpatient surgery, followed by three to seven days of rest, ice packs, and elevating the limb. Crutches are often used during the first postoperative week, though weight can be placed on the injured leg as can be tolerated. Most patients return to work in less than a week, and other normal activities can be added during the second and third week after surgery.

Physical therapy may be beneficial but is not required for fit individuals who can begin a gradual return to physical activity after two or three weeks. A full return to training activities and climbing typically takes two to three months.

Youth Climbing Injuries (and Prevention)

Climbing is a wonderful brain-, body-, and character-building sport for kids, but it's also a sport that presents a very real risk of injury. Fortunately, professional instruction/coaching can largely eliminate the risk of serious injuries due to falls or human error. Still, there's the hidden, more subtle risk of various overuse injuries, which is the focus of this section.

The most common non-impact injuries among teenage climbers are overuse injuries to tendons, joints, and bones of the fingers, including stress fractures and damage to the growth plates. Any youth climber, regardless of age, experiencing chronic pain in the fingers (or elsewhere) should cease climbing for a few weeks and consult a doctor if the pain continues. As a hard-and-fast rule, climbing and climbing-specific training must be limited to an aggregate of four days per week. The guidance of an adult climber or professional coach is extremely beneficial both in helping structure workouts and in monitoring rest and nutritional habits. Let's delve deeper into the subject, including important strategies for preventing overuse injuries in youth climbers.

Injuries to the Growth Plates of the Fingers

The most disturbing injury trend among youth climbers is the increase in fractures to the epiphyseal (growth) plates of the fingers. Though most often observed in the hardest-training, hardest-climbing youths, all youth climbers should be monitored for the onset of joint pain in the fingers. Growth plate injury often develops over time, first revealing as minor joint swelling and pain (commonly in the middle and/or ring fingers) while crimping and, if not treated with rest, progressing to acute pain, increased swelling, reduced range of motion, and, in the worst cases, disfigurement that can become permanent.

Adolescent climbers are most at risk for growth plate fractures during their growth spurt years (ages eleven to fourteen in girls, and twelve to sixteen in boys), although they can occur up to the age of eighteen, prior to complete fusing of the growth plates. European research and anecdotal evidence here in the United States reveal that campus training is a leading cause of growth plate injuries. However, epiphyseal fractures can also develop in youths who engage in frequent intensive bouldering—the kind involving copious dynamic movements and repeated extreme crimping moves.

Regardless of how the injury develops, complete withdrawal from climbing is essential until pain and swelling subside (typically two to six months). Resumption of climbing should be gradual, with a primary focus on large-hold bouldering and moderate roped climbing, rather than a quick return to the same program that produced the injury in the first place. Recurrence of finger pain and swelling will require a longer break from climbing—perhaps a full year. Consulting a doctor would be likewise prudent.

Preventing Growth Plate Fractures and Other Injuries

First and foremost, climbers ages eleven through sixteen should do absolutely no double-dyno campus training. A small amount (a few sets, once or twice per week) of controlled hand-over-hand campus laddering on large holds may be permitted by climbers strong and mature enough to do it with smooth, low-impact movements. Also of high importance, during all practice climbing, is a conscious favoring of the open-hand grip over the crimp grip on all but the smallest holds (which require use of the crimp grip). Finally, youth climbers should do little, if any, hypergravity training—that is, climbing or hangboard training with weight added to the body in the form of a weight vest or belt. Some weighted pull-ups on a bar or bucket hold is okay for older, stronger youths.

Given the immense popularity of bouldering today, many youth climbers come to prefer it over roped climbing. Unfortunately, year-round specialization in bouldering places them in a high-risk group for growth plate fractures as well as other maladies such as finger-tendon injury, elbow tendinosis, and shoulder injury. A far better approach is for a coach to direct a near-equal focus on roped climbing and bouldering. Roped routes generally have less severe cruxes and fewer dynamic moves, and instead test a climber's endurance, serial movement skills, and mental abilities. By alternating between roped climbing and bouldering every few weeks or months, injury risk is reduced, while at the same time climbing skills are expanded thanks to the exposure to a wider range of climbing situations. In terms of climbing frequency, three or four days per week is ideal—anything more vastly increases injury risk, especially in hard-climbing youths.

In chapter 6 I covered the importance of warm-up exercises and stretching, antagonist-muscle training, and end-of-session or nighttime flexibility training. Disciplined follow-through in all these areas will both reduce youth climbers' injury risk and enhance on-the-rock performance.

Proper nutrition and adequate sleep are the other side of the training-for-climbing coin. Calorie restriction is inappropriate in almost all situations for adolescents, although some restriction in the consumption of unhealthy junk and fast foods can be beneficial and is certainly wise. Youth athletes should be encouraged to eat "three squares" a day, including lots of fruits, vegetables, lean meats, and low-fat dairy products. Healthy snacks, such as energy bars, bagels, and even low-fat chocolate milk, are excellent as between-meal and climb-time snacks. In terms of sleep, nine to ten hours per night is best, with eight hours being the bare minimum.

In closing, perhaps the best way to prevent the various injuries mentioned above, including mental burnout, is for youth climbers to participate in activities and sports outside the climbing world. While an overbearing coach or parent may preach otherwise, young climbers absolutely can come to perform at a national- or even world-class level while at the same time participating in other extra-curricular activities and sports.

With proper planning, guidance, and encouragement, youths can become excellent in several life areas and enjoy the rich experiences available in both the horizontal and the vertical world. Need proof? Consider superstar Sasha DiGuilian, who in high school ran cross country and track, climbed a few evenings per week at the gym, and aced her classes at school—and, oh yeah, upon completing high school she become one of the first women to climb 5.14c/d! Similarly, my sons, Cameron (fifteen) and Jonathan (thirteen), have both climbed multiple 5.14a/8b+ routes, despite having an annual four-month off-season from climbing so as to play American football each autumn.

Ultimately, it's through a balanced, non-full-time approach to climbing that today's youths are most likely to remain healthy, happy, and on a steady, sustainable track to becoming accomplished climbers for life!

Ten Tips for Reducing Your Injury Risk

This chapter began by quoting studies that place your odds—as an avid rock climber—of getting injured as at least three to one. As a coach of more than thirty years, it's my observation that if a person climbs passionately for many years with the intention of pushing their limits, the likelihood of suffering some kind of acute or overuse injury is close to 100 percent. Therefore, it seems appropriate that we conclude this tome with some advice for lowering those odds!

Following are ten tips for lowering your risk of getting injured. Employ them all in your training and climbing, and you'll significantly reduce your chances of suffering an overuse or acute injury.

1. Focus on technique training over strength training.

Many overuse injuries result from too much strength and power training too early in an individual's climbing career. As advised throughout this book, it's fundamental to develop a high level of technical competence before jumping full-bore into climbing-specific training. Not only does good technique help reduce stress on your fingers and shoulders, but it also helps maximize economy of movement and thus increases apparent strength on the rock.

No climber—beginner or elite—is exempt from the specter of injury. Beginner and intermediate climbers are at risk because tendons strengthen at a much slower rate than muscles (among other reasons). The number of climbers who become injured during their first year or two in the sport—as they quickly progress from, say, 5.6 to 5.12 (or higher)—is alarming. Obviously, it's important to avoid the added stress of using highly specific training tools, such as a fingerboard or campus board, during the first year or two in the sport.

Elite climbers, chasing their genetic potential, will need to engage in both a higher frequency and intensity of physical training. Still, the mental and technical aspects can't be ignored, and so it's good for these elites to engage in a balanced program with nearly equal amounts of training and climbing. Most important, experienced climbers must heed the proprioceptive "warnings" of impending injury—those subtle pangs (from fingers, shoulders, knees, or elsewhere) that caution you of a potentially injurious situation.

2. Perform a progressive warm-up before every training and climbing session.

Anyone with experience in traditional sports knows firsthand the importance of a proper warm-up and cool-down. Unfortunately, I have observed more than a few climbers who just tie in and start climbing without any preparatory warm-up activity, dynamic stretching, or submaximum climbing.

All that's needed for a good warm-up is to elevate your heart rate (and break a light sweat) by way of five to ten minutes of jogging, hiking, rowing, or cycling; gym climbers can also do a few sets of jumping jacks or burpees. Next, do a few of the mobility exercises and stretches detailed in chapter 6—most important are the finger, arm, and shoulder warm-ups, although doing some core and lower-body stretching is also beneficial. Begin your climbing with a few moderate boulder problems (or routes) and progress to problems/routes near your limit over the course of thirty minutes to an hour.

A brief cool-down is also beneficial, since it will loosen up tight muscle groups and enhance the recovery process. If possible, engage in five to fifteen minutes of light aerobic activity and perform a few minutes of stretching and/or foam rolling. These cool-down activities will enhance blood flow and help disperse metabolic by-products from the most fatigued muscles—the payoff is lowered injury risk and hastened recovery!

3. Regularly train the antagonist and stabilizing muscle groups.

Training the antagonist muscles is one of the most overlooked—and vital—parts of training for climbing. Muscle imbalances in the forearms, shoulders, and torso are primary factors in many of the injuries covered in this chapter. If you are serious about climbing hard for many years to come, then you must commit to training the antagonist muscles twice per week. Priority one is training scapular stability and the rotator cuff (to protect your shoulders) as well as the extensor muscles of the forearm (to protect your wrists and elbows).

The time and equipment involved is minimal. Most of the antagonist-muscle exercises described in chapter 6 can be performed at home with nothing more than a few pairs of dumbbells and a TRX trainer. As for the time commitment, it's only twenty to forty minutes, twice per week. No excuses, friends—just do it!

4. Stretch and foam roll daily to enhance recovery and improve mobility.

My foam Rumble Roller may be the most-used piece of training equipment I own, and that's saying a lot given my equipment-packed home gym! A daily ritual of foam rolling and stretching will not only become one of the more pleasurable parts of your day, but it will also go a long way to helping you move better, climb harder, and reduce risk of injury.

Begin by foam rolling the large muscles of your legs and back. Locate tight spots, knots, and spasms, and then dwell on these trigger points for a minute or two until you feel the tension diminish. You can similarly address the tight/sore spots in the climbing muscles of the forearm and upper arm with an Armaid or Rubbit (a must-have for every serious climber). Conclude with some gentle stretching of the muscles, especially the hamstrings, hip flexors, lower and upper back muscles, and arms and forearms. I highly recommend doing all of the above for ten to twenty minutes before bedtime.

5. Climb with self-awareness and caution through potentially injurious-feeling moves.

With increasing climbing experience comes a growing sixth sense of potentially injurious climbing moves. This important type of self-awareness is critical for advanced climbers pushing their limits in the gym and at the crags, as there will inevitably be moves encountered that present a real injury threat (e.g., a shoulder-wrenching or finger-tweaking move).

The goal is to consciously evaluate the situation—is what you are feeling "good pain" (muscle pump and acute fatigue) or "bad pain" (a tendon or joint being stressed to its limit)—and then make a snap decision as to whether or not to proceed with the move. In recognizing that you are entering a perilous situation (say, a one-finger pocket pull with poor feet) and in sensing that you are near injury on a move, you are empowered to either disengage from the move or cautiously navigate through the sequence.

Interestingly, it's not uncommon to escape injury on the first attempt or pass through a dicey, painful move, only to get injured when attempting (or repeatedly rehearsing) the painful move again, as in working a limited boulder problem or project route. It's in these situations that the smart, mature climber recognizes the risk and decides to move on to another climb. Surely no boulder problem or route is worth getting injured over.

6. Avoid passive hanging on straight arms, especially a single, fully extended arm.

One of the fastest ways to wreck your shoulders is to do frequent hanging on a straight arm (or arms) and catching lunge moves without the scapular stabilizer and rotator cuff muscles engaged. Listed below are several common situations, both in training and climbing, that you must be aware of as potentially damaging to your shoulders. If anything on this list sounds familiar, Coach Hörst kindly insists that you must stop!

Here are five common straight-arm situations to avoid:

- Dropping all the way into a straight-arm position (with relaxed shoulders) when doing pull-ups.
- Doing fingerboard training with fully straight arms and shrugging shoulders.
- Hanging on a straight arm with a completely lax shoulder and disengaged scapular stabilizers while at a rest position on an overhanging climb.
- Catching a lunge with a fully extended arm and shoulder.
- Any campus training move, especially drop downs and long upward grabs, that forceful engages a straight arm and extended shoulder.

In previous chapters you learned the importance of keeping your scapular stabilizer and rotator cuff muscles turned on in all upper-body training and advanced climbing movements. By training this supporting crew of muscles and avoiding passive straight-arm hanging positions, you will vastly lower your risk of a shoulder injury.

7. Don't climb to complete exhaustion.

There is nothing I enjoy more than occasionally maximizing a day of climbing fun by pulling down hard routes right into the evening twilight. As a regular practice, however, doing a high volume of hard climbing—and in particular pushing yourself to the limit late in the day—increases injury risk. This chapter covered a range of overuse injuries that are largely caused by accumulated stress beyond what the body is capable of handling—these injuries gradually develop as a result of both too many climbing/training sessions in a week and too many excessively long days of climbing.

Knowing when to say "when"—in training or climbing—is one of the subtle climbing skills that you can't learn from a book or video. Such wisdom comes from experience and, sadly, as a result of getting injured by overdoing it in some way. Understandably, ultra-passionate climbers often train and climb excessively in a desire to maximize improvement (and enjoyment). Beyond a point, of course, more is not better! The chapters on physical training stressed the distinction of quality of training over quantity of training—this concept should be applied when pushing your limits on the rocks as well.

One rule of thumb you might adopt is to end your climbing day early (with a little gas left in the tank) when you're planning to climb again the very next day. In this way you will limit the day's accumulated stress (and jump-start your recovery) and avoid the end-of-day injury trap when mental and physical fatigue can compromise your technique and movement patterns. Conversely, when sandwiching a single day of climbing between two rest days, you can feel better about packing in as many climbs as possible into a wonderful marathon day on the rocks!

8. Don't climb and train (specifically) more than a total of four days per week.

In the long run, it often turns out that climbing and training (specifically) more than a total of four days per week is counterproductive. Climbing is obviously a stressful activity that focuses high loads on the relatively small muscle groups and tendons of the fingers, arms, and shoulders. While you may feel that you can safely climb hard more than four days per week, the accumulated strain will—more likely than not—eventually lead to overtraining syndrome and/or injury.

Here are a few guidelines for planning your training and climbing. First, if you climb hard for a total of four per days a week (combined indoor and outdoor), you should do no other climbing-specific training (save a casual ARC training session) on the three remaining days of the week. Keep in mind that even with three days of rest out of seven, your body will struggle to repair microtraumas in the most stressed tendons and muscles. You can, however, do some generalized training (e.g., aerobic conditioning, antagonist and stabilizer exercises, yoga and other mobility movements, etc.) on your three climbing rest days per week. Most important: Immediately reduce your climbing days to three (or even two) at the first sign of finger, tendon, or joint pain.

9. Use periodization or autoregulation to vary your training schedule.

Many sports scientists consider periodization to be the gold standard for medium-term planning of an optimally effective strength-training program. As described in chapter 5, periodization involves a premeditated variation in workout focus, intensity, and volume, which in the long run produces a maximum training response. Periodization and autoregulation may also reduce the risk of overuse injury, since the training focus and intensity change every workout or every few weeks at the most.

While beginners will see steady improvements simply climbing a few days per week, intermediate and advanced climbers—who climb and train with greater intensity—must introduce some variation into their program. Chapter 10 presented a few sample periodization schedules. By following one of these programs, you'll benefit from the variation in training stimulus, which fundamentally changes the target and nature of the stress imposed on your body. Furthermore, these periodized schedules all include an extended rest period (a few days to a week) that offers precious catch-up time for recovery deficits and healing time for any localized pain or systemic fatigue.

Finally, there's autoregulation—a self-directed ad lib–like approach to varying workout intensity based on an aggregate of subjective feelings of fatigue and objective biofeedback early in the workout. Successful autoregulation requires an accurate, intuitive sense of what's optimal given your current state, as well as a more-than-basic knowledge of exercise physiology. Knowing what training stimulus is appropriate—and beneficial—on a given day is at the heart of the matter. The bottom line: The goal of autoregulation is to consciously select and engage only in exercises that will target a muscle group or movement in an optimal way. Likewise, you must willfully avoid exercises that will stress not-yet-recovered muscle groups (from the previous workout).

10. Make getting proper rest and nutrition top priorities.

Getting proper rest and nutrition seems like a no-brainer for a serious athlete, yet I'm often surprised by the bad dietary and sleep habits I observe among serious climbers. Chapter 11 on "Performance Nutrition" and chapter 12 on "Accelerating Recovery" provide many useful strategies to employ as you increase the priority placed on these subjects. If you use most of these strategies, most of the time, I am confident that you will outperform the masses and reduce your risk of overuse injuries.

Certainly an occasional late night out or free day of "anything-goes" eating won't hurt; in fact, rewarding yourself in this way is totally appropriate after sending a major project or completing a competitive season! Still, consistent lack of sleep and poor nutrition will slow recovery between workouts and days of climbing—it will also increase vulnerability to injury. Taking control of your diet and sleep habits is most important during periods of high-volume, high-intensity training and in the days leading up to a big climb or competition. Ultimately, strive to make your modifications in these areas permanent lifestyle changes.

Ronni Dixon crushing Low Tide (V6), Joe's Valley, Utah. ANDREW CHAO

Afterword

The power of climbing is awesome. The simple act of moving over stone can change your day, and it can change your life. Climbing takes you to places you have never been before—breathtaking vistas that few humans ever see, and deep into the very core of your being. In this way climbing helps us discover who we are and gives us the gift of insight into our true potential and what really is possible in our lives. Many "flatlanders" never gain this insight, and, worse yet, far too many people around the world will never have the opportunity to experience the wonder of climbing (or any other pleasure-seeking activity) because they spend each day of their life just trying to get by. From this perspective I trust you will agree that in simply being able to go climbing and pursue self-actualization, we are better off than the majority of people on this planet. Regardless of your current disposition, vow to live each day with an attitude of gratitude. Look for ways to brighten the day of everyone you meet, and consider contributing some time or money to aid those who are less fortunate. I invite you to check out some of my favorite charities listed below. Share some of your climbing power with the world!

- Paradoxsports.org
- EscalandoFronteras.org
- SharmaFund.org
- MakeAWish.org
- WoundedWarriorProject.org
- RedCross.org
- WorldVision.org

Appendix A

Muscular Anatomy

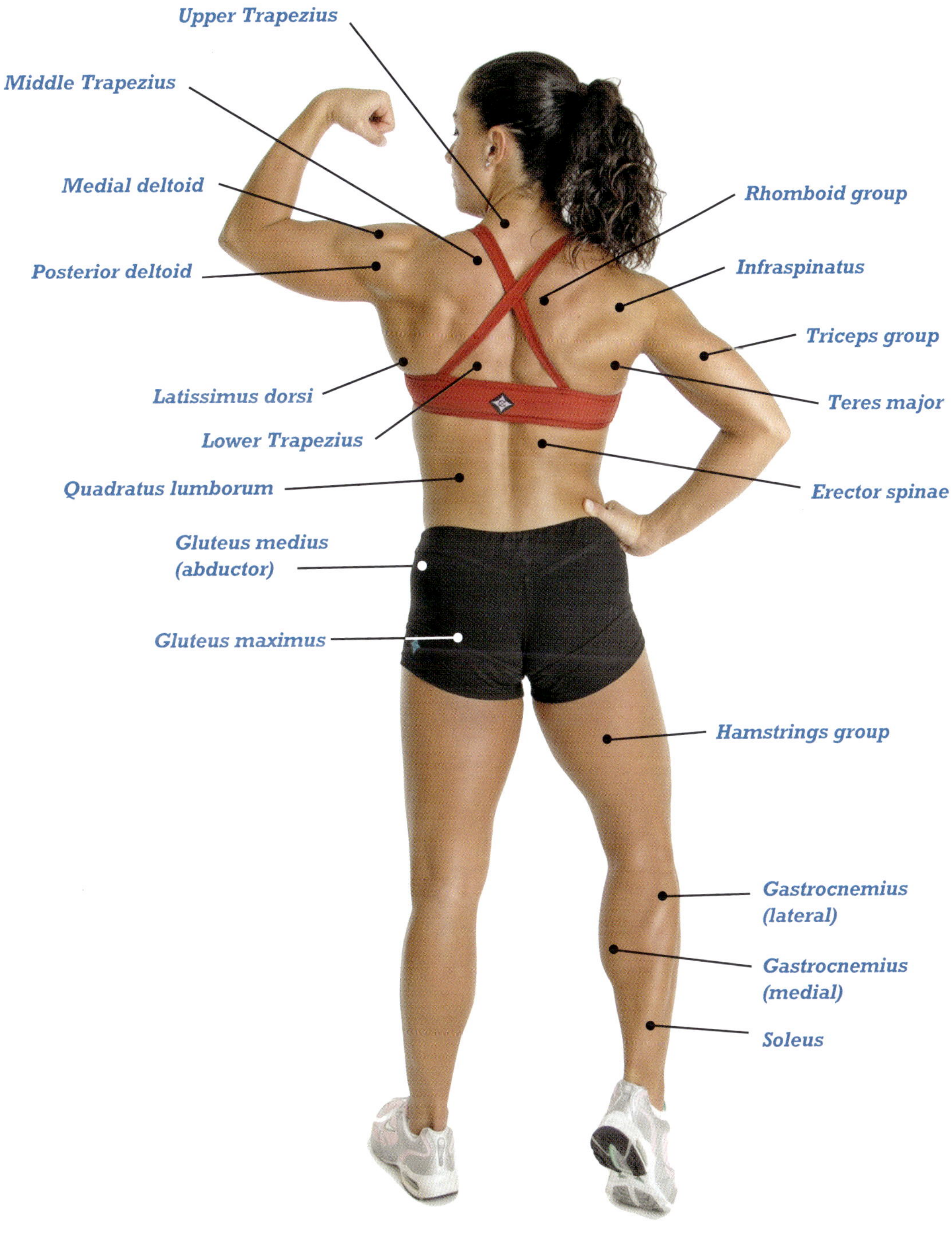
Upper Trapezius
Middle Trapezius
Medial deltoid
Posterior deltoid
Rhomboid group
Infraspinatus
Triceps group
Latissimus dorsi
Teres major
Lower Trapezius
Quadratus lumborum
Erector spinae
Gluteus medius (abductor)
Gluteus maximus
Hamstrings group
Gastrocnemius (lateral)
Gastrocnemius (medial)
Soleus

Appendix B

Training Charts

Use the two blank training charts on the following pages to track your training progress. The "Training and Climbing Macrocycle" will enable you to set annual training objectives and seasonal climbing goals as well as record your actual progress. You can use the chart to plan your training for the four seasons, target specific types of training, track the number of days you train, and record your achievements throughout the year.

Use the "Energy–Emotion Levels" chart to track your physical energy and emotional mind-set hour by hour throughout the day. You can use this chart to observe patterns, identify negative triggers, modify your emotional state, and better manage your energy and emotions for optimal performance.

Training and Climbing Macrocycle

Name/Year	Training Objectives and Seasonal Climbing Goals																																																		
Month	**Jan**					**Feb**				**Mar**				**Apr**					**May**				**Jun**				**Jul**					**Aug**				**Sep**				**Oct**					**Nov**				**Dec**			
Week	1	2	3	4	5	6	7	8	9	10	11	12	13	14	15	16	17	18	19	20	21	22	23	24	25	26	27	28	29	30	31	32	33	34	35	36	37	38	39	40	41	42	43	44	45	46	47	48	49	50	51	52
Training Focus: Stamina/skill																																																				
Training Focus: Max. strength and power																																																				
Training Focus: Anaerobic endurance																																																				
Training Focus: Taper/Rest																																																				
Total number of days per week of climbing and climbing-specific training: 7																																																				
6																																																				
5																																																				
4																																																				
3																																																				
2																																																				
1																																																				
Benchmark achievements and notes																																																				

Energy–Emotion Levels

Name: ______________________ Date: ______________

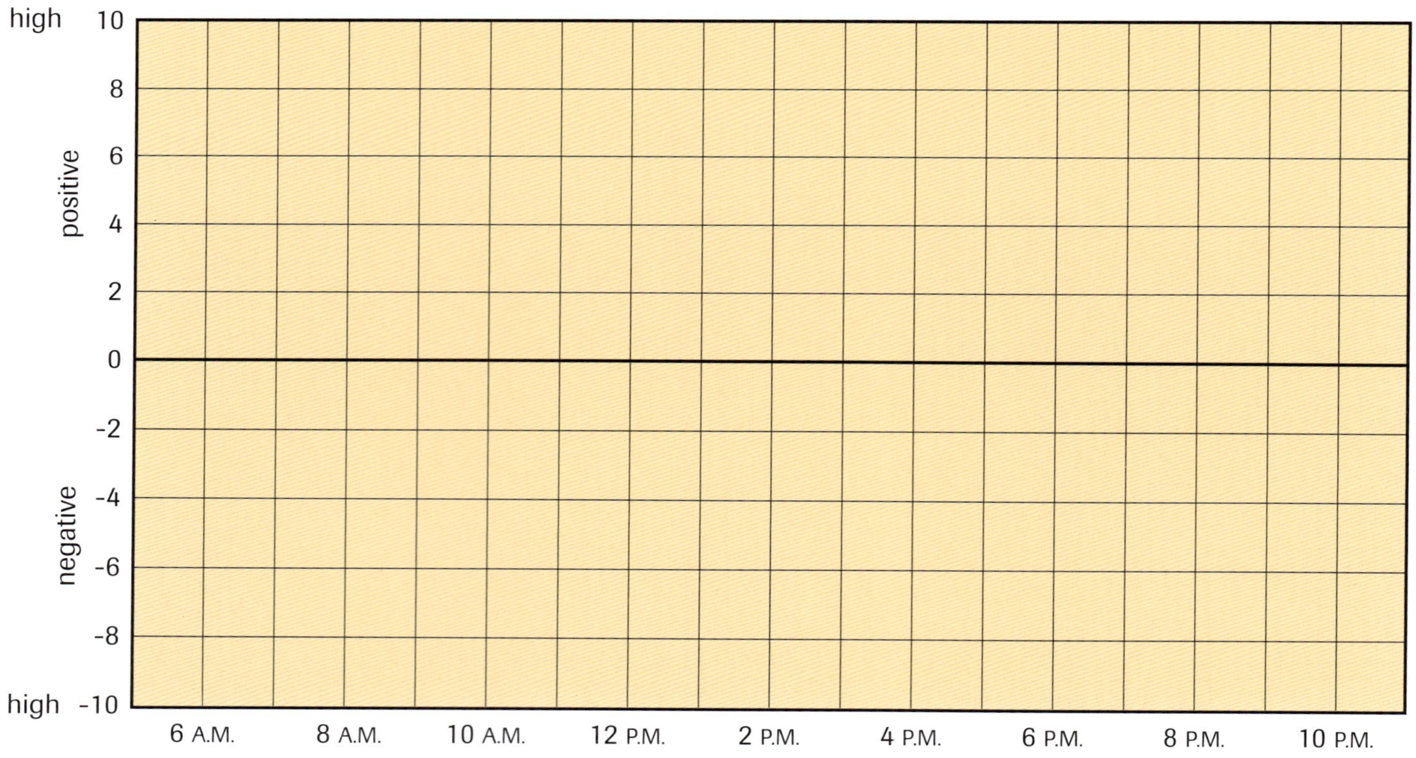

Appendix C

Self-Assessment Test Comments and Training Tips

The Self-Assessment Test in chapter 2 covers physical strength, mental focus, and techniques and tactics. Taking the test should help you to gauge your overall strengths and weaknesses and pinpoint some specific areas for improvement. If you gave yourself a score of 3 or lower on any of the questions, you've identified weak spots that should be targeted for training. Here is a brief comment on each of these common problems as well as some specific tips for improving your climbing performance. For more in-depth information on any of these topics, see the chapters referenced below.

1. If your footwork deteriorates during the hardest part of the climb, you might be focusing on the lack of good handholds instead of zeroing in on crucial footholds (often the key to unlocking hard sequences).

   TIP: When the going gets tough, focus on your feet! (See chapter 3.)

2. If your forearms balloon and your grip begins to fail, you are probably overgripping the holds and/or climbing too slowly.

   TIP: On near-vertical walls, relax your grip and place maximum weight over your feet. When the wall angle is overhanging, the number one rule is to climb fast from one rest to the next. (See chapter 4.)

3. If you have difficulty stepping onto critical footholds during hard sequences, lack of flexibility or weak hip flexor muscles is the likely problem.

   TIP: Begin daily stretching for a minimum of ten minutes and practice high steps in a gym setting. (See chapter 6.)

4. If you find you get anxious and tight as you head into crux sequences, normalizing your breathing is the key to reducing tension and anxiety.

   TIP: Before starting up a climb, close your eyes and take five slow, deep breaths (each breath should take at least ten seconds). Try to maintain steady breathing as you climb. Take three more slow, deep breaths at each rest position and before you begin the crux sequence. (See chapter 3.)

5. If your biceps pump out before your forearms, it usually means you're hanging out with bent arms. Straight-arm positions are fundamental to good climbing technique.

   TIP: Whenever possible, hang "by the bone" and not with flexed arm muscles. Straight-arm positions are especially important when placing gear, shaking out, or pausing to decipher the next sequence (see chapter 4).

6. Do you have difficulty hanging on to small, necessary holds? Although poor body positioning can make small holds even harder to use, it's likely that your contact strength (grip) needs work.

   TIP: Spend more time training on steep walls and gym cave areas, and go bouldering more often. Some weighted fingerboard training is essential for intermediate and advanced climbers. (See chapter 8.)

7. If you fail on sequences you know by heart, you might be making the common mistake of trying or inventing new sequences during a redpoint attempt.

TIP: When you find a sequence that works, it's usually best to stick with it. Counter any mid-climb thoughts of trying a new sequence with the definitive belief that you already know (and can do) the best sequence.

8. If you stall at the start of crux sequences, you might be suffering from paralysis by analysis.

   TIP: When faced with a crux sequence, visualize two possible sequences, and then immediately try the one that looks more promising. Once you commit to a sequence, go for it! Only one thing should be on your mind—getting to the next good hold (or rest) as fast as possible.

9. Do you climb three or four days in a row? Unless you are one of those genetically gifted extreme outliers, climbing or training on three or four consecutive days is a practice that will lead to overtraining, injury, and a drop in performance.

   TIP: In this case, less is more. Switch to a two-day-on, one-day-off (or one-day-on, one-day-off) schedule and you will be training smarter and climbing harder!

10. Sewing-machine leg is common in the tight, anxious climber.

    TIP: Lengthen your warm-up and begin working on some of the relaxation exercises described in this text. (See chapter 3.)

11. If you pump out on overhanging climbs, you should be aware that the pump clock starts running when you leave the ground. You might not be too weak to climb the route—just too slow!

    TIP: Practice climbing more quickly on known (wired) routes and when redpointing. Foster a watchful eye that's on the lookout for creative rests that might stop the clock for a few moments. (See chapters 3 and 4.)

12. Do you get out of breath when you climb? Rapid breathing while climbing results from excess tension, irregular breathing, or poor aerobic fitness.

    TIP: Concentrate on maintaining relaxed, normal breathing while you climb. Also consider engaging in some aerobic training (preferably running) three to four days per week. Build up to a maximum of four, twenty-minute runs per week. (See chapter 7.)

13. If you begin thinking about how you might fail on a route before you even start, you should know that belief gives birth to reality. If the thought of failing crosses your mind, you likely will.

    TIP: Before you start up a climb, always visualize yourself successfully climbing the route from bottom to top. (See chapter 3.)

14. Do you miss hidden holds on routes? Tunnel vision is a common cause of failure, especially during on-sight climbing.

    TIP: Scope the route from a few different vantage points before leaving the ground. As you climb, keep an open mind for hidden holds—the key hold always seems to take a little extra effort to locate. If a route feels really hard for its grade, chances are there's a good handhold or foothold escaping your view. (See chapters 3 and 4.)

15. If you have difficulty hanging on to small holds or pockets, keep in mind that open-hand grip strength is crucial. Expert climbers favor it, while beginner climbers avoid it.

    TIP: While training and bouldering, force yourself to use the open-hand grip at least 50 percent of the time. Most intermediate and advanced climbers can significantly improve open-hand grip strength via weighted fingerboard hangs and campus training. (See chapter 8.)

16. It's common to grab onto gear rather than risk a fall trying a hard move. Assuming the potential fall is safe, always go for the move instead of grabbing gear or hanging on the rope. The bad habit of grabbing gear is easy to develop and very hard to break. Plus, you'll never learn where your true limit is if you give up in this way.

    TIP: Counter any thought of grabbing gear with the belief that there is absolutely a good hold just a few moves above you (there probably is!).

17. If much of your body weight is hanging on your arms, you might not be placing your weight (center of mass) over your feet.

    TIP: Invest more time practicing technique and body positioning. Focus on keeping your crotch and hips in near the wall (except on slabs) and experiment with moves where you turn one hip or the other to the wall. Some flexibility training may be beneficial, too (see chapter 4).

18. Intense soreness after only one day of cragging means that your training volume and intensity are not congruent with your outdoor climbing goals.

    TIP: Step up your indoor training and always try for two solid training days during the workweek.

19. Do you have difficulty visualizing yourself successfully climbing the route? All peak performers acknowledge the importance of visualization.

    TIP: Get into the habit of climbing each route in your mind's eye at least twice before giving it a real go. (See chapter 3.)

20. If you think you cannot reach key holds on difficult routes, you should be aware that this is the oldest excuse in this sport. Funny thing is, some great short climbers never use this excuse! The reason—there is almost always a technical solution or intermediate hold to be discovered that will solve apparent reach problems.

    TIP: Try a move five, ten, or even twenty different ways and you'll almost always find one that works!

21. If your feet cut loose and swing out on overhanging routes and roofs, it's possible that poor footwork and body positioning are responsible. More often, however, it results from weak core muscles (torso).

    TIP: Perform the core-muscle exercises, described in chapter 7, at least thrice weekly. Also, spend more time in a bouldering cave working on your steep-wall footwork and body position.

22. If you get distracted by activity on the ground, remember that while climbing your focus must be locked onto the moves at hand, not directed downward. If less than 95 percent of your focus/attention is targeted on the climb, you don't have much chance of success.

    TIP: Clear your mind of what's happening on the ground. If you need confirmation that your belayer is paying attention, a simple "watch me" will do, then refocus on the move at hand. (See chapter 3.)

23. It's common for beginning climbers to have difficulty reading sequences. Reading sequences comes from experience—each time you go climbing is money in the bank!

    TIP: Climb up to four days a week to increase your rate of deposit. Always try to figure sequences from the ground and minimize use of beta (a real handicap to learning) except when climbing for performance.

24. Do you experience a deep flash pump on the first climb of the day? A flash pump results when you push your muscles too hard, too soon.

TIP: Lengthen your warm-up period, add more stretching and some sports massage, and always do a few increasingly difficult routes before attempting your project.

25. If you have more difficulty climbing when people are watching, remember that the pressure of needing to perform is entirely self-imposed. Therefore, it can be turned off as easily as you turn it on.

TIP: Commit to climb for yourself—for the challenge, adventure, and fun of it (all the reasons you got into climbing in the first place). Forget about the rest of the world, engage the process of climbing, and let the outcome take care of itself. (See chapter 3.)

26. If your feet unexpectedly pop off footholds, take heart that this is a common problem, even among some advanced climbers.

TIP: Refocus your attention on your feet for a few weeks. Evaluate whether you carefully place your feet on the best part of a hold or simply drop them onto the biggest-looking part. Also, do you hold your foot position stationary as you stand up or does your shoe move on the hold? These are things you need to practice in a nonperformance setting. (See chapter 4.)

27. Do you experience frequent elbow pain? There are two types of elbow tendinosis common to climbers. If you climb enough years, chances are you'll someday experience some elbow pain. Take heed!

TIP: Reverse wrist curls and forearm rotation exercises as well as regular forearm stretching and self-massage (or Armaid use) will help prevent these problems. Perform three sets of reverse wrist curls (twenty-five reps with a five- to fifteen-pound dumbbell) and two sets of forearm pronators, three days per week, year-round. Stretch both sides of your forearms each day. (See chapter 6.)

28. If you have trouble pushing yourself to the limit on a safe lead climb, your problem is more likely mental than physical. Keep in mind that mental fortitude is as important as brawn.

TIP: On safe routes consciously push yourself into the mental discomfort zone. At first this will feel like bitter medicine, but in time it will redefine your mental limits. (See chapter 3.)

29. If you have difficulty finding mid-route rest positions, you are missing one of the keys to sending routes near your limit.

TIP: Creative practice (in a nonperformance setting) at finding funky rest positions, modeling the rest positions of other climbers, and climbing experience at a wide range of crags will, in time, make finding "thank God" rests instinctual!

30. If your first attempt on a hard route is usually better than your second or third attempts that day, lack of muscular endurance and stamina are likely a contributing factor.

TIP: Climbing laps on training routes, doing twice-weekly threshold intervals, and generalized aerobic training will yield significant improve over the course of a few months. (See chapters 8 and 9.)

Glossary

The following is a compilation of some of the technical terms and climbing jargon used throughout this book.

active recovery—The restoration of homeostasis following vigorous exercise that involves continued light-intensity movement; facilitates faster recovery by enhancing lactate removal from the blood.

acute—Having rapid onset and severe symptoms.

adaptive response—Physiological changes in structure or function particularly related to response to a training overload.

adipose tissue—Body fat.

aerobic energy system—ATP production via oxidation of glycogen, fats, and, occasionally, proteins.

agonist—A muscle directly engaged in a muscular contraction.

anaerobic glycolysis—ATP production in the muscles involving the breakdown of glycogen in the absence of oxygen; metabolic by-products, including chiefly hydrogen ions, result in rapid fatigue and cessation of physical activity.

antagonist—A muscle providing an opposing force to the primary muscles of action (agonist).

ape index—Fingertip-to-fingertip distance (across your chest with arms out to each side) minus your height; a positive ape index is associated with above-average reach for a given height.

arousal—An internal state of alertness or excitement.

artery—A vessel that carries oxygenated blood away from the heart to the tissues of the body.

arthritis—A disease that causes inflammation, swelling, and pain in the joints.

ATP—Adenosine triphosphate; a high-energy molecule that is stored in the muscles in very small amounts; it's the body's ultimate fuel source.

atrophy—Gradual shrinking and deconditioning of muscle tissue from disuse.

backstepping—Outside edging on a foothold that is behind you while climbing a move with your side to the wall.

barndoor—Sideways swinging or uncontrolled turning of the body resulting from poor balance or body positioning.

basal metabolic rate—The minimum level of energy required to sustain the body's vital functions.

beta—Any prior information about a route, including sequence, rests, gear, clips, and so on.

biological value (BV)—A method for evaluating protein sources; a high BV protein source has a high percentage of nutrients actually absorbed from the human intestine as opposed to excreted.

blocked practice—A practice routine in which a specific task is practiced repeatedly, as in working a crux move or sequence.

campus (or campusing)—Climbing an overhanging section of rock or artificial wall with no feet, usually in a dynamic left-hand, right-hand, left-hand (and so forth) sequence.

campus training—A climbing-specific form of plyometric exercise, developed by Wolfgang Güllich at the Campus Center, a weight-lifting facility at the University of Nürnberg, Germany.

capillary—The tiny blood vessels that receive blood flow from the arteries, interchange substances between the blood and the tissues, and return the blood to the veins.

capillary density—The number of capillaries per unit area of muscle tissue. Capillary density increases, mainly in slow-twitch fibers, in response to aerobic training.

catabolic—A breaking-down process in the body, as in muscle breakdown during intense exercise.

center of mass—The theoretical point on which the total effect of gravity acts on the body.

chronic—Continuing over time.

concentric contraction—Any movement involving a shortening of muscle fibers while developing tension, as in the biceps muscle during a pull-up.

contact strength—Initial grip strength upon touching a handhold; directly related to the rate of force development in the finger flexor muscles.

cortisol—A hormone, released in response to emotional or exercise stress, that promotes fat utilization, inhibits inflammatory response, and facilitates breakdown of muscle proteins for energy.

cortisone—A synthetic form of cortisol used (injected) as an anti-inflammatory.

creatine phosphate (CP)—A high-energy phosphate compound stored in skeletal muscle and used to supply energy for brief, high-intensity muscle action.

crimp grip—The most natural (and stressful) way to grip a rock hold, characterized by hyperextension of the first joint in the fingers and nearly full flexion of the second joint.

crux—The hardest move, or sequence of moves, on a route.

deadpoint—The high position in a dynamic movement where, for a moment, all motion stops.

detraining—Reversal of positive adaptations to chronic exercise upon cessation of an exercise program.

drop-knee—An exaggerated backstep, commonly used on overhanging rock, where the inside knee is dropped toward the ground, resulting in a stable chimney-like position.

dynamic move—An explosive leap for a hold otherwise out of reach.

dyno—Short for "dynamic."

eccentric contraction—A muscle action in which the muscle resists as it is forced to lengthen, as in the biceps during the lowering phase of a pull-up.

electrolyte—A substance that, in solution, is capable of conducting electricity. Certain electrolytes are essential to the electrochemical functioning of the body.

endurance—The ability to perform physical work for an extended period of time. Cardiovascular endurance is directly related to VO_2 max, whereas muscular endurance is influenced by circulation and available oxygen and energy substrate.

enzyme—A protein molecule that aids chemical reactions.

epicondylitis—Inflammation of the tendon origins of the forearm flexors (medial) or extensors (lateral) near the elbow.

ergogenic—Performance enhancing.

estrogen—The sex hormone that predominates in females, but also has some functions in males.

extension—A movement that moves the two ends of a jointed body part away from each other, as in straightening the arm.

fast-twitch fibers—The muscle fiber type that contracts quickly and is used mostly during intense, powerful movements.

flagging—A climbing technique in which one foot is crossed behind the other to avoid barn-dooring and to improve balance.

flash—To climb a route on the first try without ever having touched it, but with the aid of beta.

flash pump—A metaboreflex characterized by a rapid, often vicious, muscular pump resulting from strenuous training or climbing without first performing a proper, gradual warm-up.

flexion—A movement that brings the ends of a body part closer together, as in bending the arm.

G-Tox—A technique that uses gravity to help speed recovery from a forearm pump. It involves alternating, every five to ten seconds, the position of the resting arm between the normal hanging-at-your-side position and a raised-hand position above your shoulder.

glycemic index (GI)—A scale that classifies how the ingestion of various foods affects blood sugar levels in comparison with the ingestion of straight glucose.

glycogen—Compound chains of glucose stored in the muscle and liver for use during aerobic or anaerobic exercise.

Golgi tendon organ—Sensory receptors located between the muscle and its tendon that are sensitive to the stretch of the muscle tendon produced during muscular contraction.

gripped—Extremely scared.

hangdogging—Climbing a route, usually bolt-to-bolt, with the aid of a rope to hang and rest while practicing the sequence.

heel hook—Use of the heel on a hold, usually near chest level, to aid in pulling and balance.

homeostasis—The body's tendency to maintain a steady state despite external changes.

honed—In extremely good physical shape; with low body fat.

hormone—A chemical secreted into the bloodstream to regulate the function of a certain organ.

hyperemia—Increased blood flow in the working muscles during exercise or as a result of deep sports massage.

Hypergravity Isolation Training (HIT)—A highly refined and specific method of training maximum finger strength and upper-body power by climbing on identical finger holds (isolation) with greater than body weight (hypergravity). Also known as Hörst Isolation Training.

hypertrophy—Enlargement in size (e.g., muscular hypertrophy).

insertion—The point of attachment of a muscle to a distal or relatively more movable bone.

insulin—A hormone that decreases the blood glucose level by driving glucose from the blood into muscle and fat cells.

interval training—A method of anaerobic endurance training that involves brief periods of intense training interspaced with periods of rest or low-intensity training.

isometric—A muscular contraction resulting in no shortening movement of the muscle.

kinesthetic—The sense derived from muscular contractions and limb movements. See proprioception.

killer—Extraordinarily good, as in a killer route.

lean body weight—The weight of the body, less the weight of its fat.

ligament—Fibrous tissue that connects bone to bone, or bone to cartilage, to hold together and support the joints.

lunge—An out-of-control dynamic move; an explosive jump for a far-off hold.

macronutrients—Basic nutrients needed for energy, cell growth, and organ function (carbohydrates, fat, and protein).

maximum strength—The peak force of a muscular contraction, irrespective of the time element. Also known as "limit strength."

micronutrients—Noncaloric nutrients needed in very small amounts, such as vitamins and minerals.

modeling—A learning technique where an individual watches, then attempts, a skill as performed properly by another person.

motor learning—A set of internal processes associated with practice or experience leading to a relatively permanent gain in performance capability.

motor program—Motor programs are the way in which the brain controls movements. Motor programs become more hardwired and lasting via deliberate practice.

motor skill—A skill where the primary determinant of success is the movement component itself.

motor unit—A motor neuron, together with a group of muscle cells, stimulated in an all-or-nothing response.

NSAID—Non-steroidal anti-inflammatory drugs, usually available over the counter, that reduce pain, fever, and inflammation.

on-sight—When a route is climbed on the first try and with absolutely no prior information of any kind.

open-hand grip—The less-stressful finger grip involving only slight flexion of the finger joints.

osteoarthritis—A joint disease of older persons in which cartilage in the joints wears down and there is bone growth at the edges of the joint.

overload—Subjecting a part of the body to greater efforts (intensity or volume) than it is accustomed to in order to elicit a training response.

overtraining—Constant severe training that does not provide adequate time for recovery; symptoms include increased frequency of injury, decreased performance, irritability, and apathy.

overuse—Excessive repeated exertion or shock that results in injuries such as inflammation of the muscles and tendons.

plyometric—An exercise that suddenly preloads and forces the stretching of a muscle an instant prior to its concentric contraction, as in dynamic up-and-down campus training. Also known as reactive or shock training.

power—A measure of both force and speed (speed = distance x time) of a muscular contraction through a given range of motion. Power is the explosive aspect of strength.

pronation—The inward turning of a body part, as in turning the forearm inward and the palm facedown.

proprioception—Sensory information from within the body arising from the sensory receptors found in muscles, tendons, joints, and the inner ear that detect the motion or position of the limbs and body.

proprioceptors—Sensory receptors found in muscles, tendons, joints, and the inner ear that detect the motion or position of the limbs and body, thus providing kinesthetic awareness.

psyched—Raring to go or very happy.

pumped—When the muscles become engorged with blood due to extended physical exertion.

random practice—A practice sequence in which tasks from several classes are experienced in random order over consecutive trials.

reactive training—A power-building exercise that couples, in rapid succession, a forceful eccentric contraction with an explosive concentric contraction.

recommended dietary allowances (RDA)—Quantities of specific vitamins, minerals, and other nutrients needed daily that have been judged adequate for maintenance of good nutrition. Developed by the Food and Nutrition Board of the National Academy of Science.

recruitment—The systematic increase in the number of active motor units called upon during muscular contraction.

redpoint—Lead climbing a route bottom-to-top in one push.

schema—A set of rules, usually developed and applied unconsciously by the motor system in the brain and spinal cord, relating how to move and adjust muscle forces, body positions, and so forth, given the parameters at hand, such as steepness of the rock, friction qualities, holds being used, and type of terrain.

send—short for "ascend," as in *I'm going to send that climb* . . . or, past tense, *I sent my project!*

sharp end—The lead climber's end of the rope.

skill—The capability to bring about an end result with maximum certainty, minimum energy, and minimum time.

slow-twitch fibers—The muscle fiber type that contracts slowly and is used most in moderate-intensity endurance activities such as easy to moderate climbing or running.

sport climbing—Usually refers to any indoor or outdoor climbing on bolt-protected routes.

spotter—A person designated to slow the fall of a boulderer, with the main goal of keeping the boulderer's head from hitting the ground.

stabilizer muscle—A muscle that is stimulated to help anchor or stabilize the position of a bone.

strength—The amount of muscle force that can be exerted; speed and distance are not factors of strength.

supination—Rotation of the forearm outward and palm-upward.

synovial fluid—A viscid fluid secreted by the membrane lining joints, tendon sheaths, and bursae to lubricate and cushion them during movement.

tendinitis—An acute disorder involving the inflammation of a tendon and synovial membrane at a joint.

tendinopathy—A general term that just refers to tendon injury, without specifying a particular type of injury such as tendinitis (inflammation) or tendinosis (failed healing).

tendinosis—Chronic tendon pain due to an accumulation of microscopic injuries that don't heal properly; the main problem, then, is failed healing, not inflammation.

tendon—A white fibrous cord of dense connective tissue that attaches muscle to bone.

trad—Short for a traditional climb (or climber) that requires natural protection placements.

training effect—A basic principle of exercise science that states that adaptation occurs from an exercise only in those parts or systems of the body that are stressed by the exercise.

transfer of learning—The gain or loss in proficiency on one task as a result of practice or experience on another task.

trigger point—A long-lasting muscle spasm or contracture often associated with local muscular fatigue or injury.

tweak—To injure, as in a tweaked finger tendon.

variable practice—Practice in which many variations on a class of actions are performed; opposite of blocked practice.

vein—A vessel that returns blood from the various parts of the body to the heart.

visualization—Controlled and directed imagery that can be used for awareness building, monitoring and self-regulation, healing, and, most important, as mental programming for good performances.

VO_2 max—Maximal oxygen uptake, as in the measurement of maximum aerobic power.

wired—Known well, as in a wired route.

working—Practicing the moves on a difficult route via toprope or hangdogging.

Twelve-year-old Jonathan Hörst sending Cow Reggae (5.13b), Wild Iris, Wyoming.
SAVANNAH CUMMINS

Suggested Reading

Ament, Pat. *Master of Rock*. Mechanicsburg, PA: Stackpole Books, 1977, 1998.

Anderson, Mark and Mike. *The Rock Climber's Training Manual*. Boulder, CO: Fixed Piton Publishing, 2014.

Armstrong, Lawrence E. *Performing in Extreme Environments*. Champaign, IL: Human Kinetics, 2000.

Bechtel, Steve. *Strength: Foundational Training for Rock Climbers*. Lander, WY: Elemental, 2014.

Benardot, Dan. *Advanced Sports Nutrition*. Champaign, IL: Human Kinetics, 2006.

Csikszentmihalyi, Mihaly. *Flow: The Psychology of Optimal Experience*. New York: Harper Perennial, 1990.

Erikson, Lisa. *Climbing Injuries Solved*. 2014.

Gnade, Lisa, and Petro, Steve. *Crack Climbing!* Guilford, CT: Globe Pequot/FalconGuides, 2009.

Hörst, Eric J. *Maximum Climbing: Mental Training for Peak Performance and Optimal Experience*. Guilford, CT: Globe Pequot/FalconGuides, 2010.

———. *How to Climb 5.12*. Guilford, CT: Globe Pequot/FalconGuides, 2003.

———. *The Rock Climber's Exercise Guide*. Guilford, CT: Globe Pequot/FalconGuides, 2016.

Ilgner, Arno. *Espresso Lessons*. La Verge, TN: Desiderata Institute, 2010.

Long, John. *How to Rock Climb!* Guilford, CT: Globe Pequot/FalconGuides, 1993.

MacLeod, Dave. *9 out of 10 Climbers Make the Same Mistakes*. Scotland: Rare Breed Productions, 2010.

Matros, Patrick, Korb, Dicki, and Huch, Hannes. *Gimme Kraft*. Nuremburg, Germany: Café Kraft GmbH, 2013.

Schmidt, R. A., and Wrisberg, C. A. *Motor Learning and Performance: A Problem-Based Learning Approach*. Champaign, IL: Human Kinetics, 2004.

Schöffl, Volker, and Hochholzer, Thomas. *One Move Too Many*. Ebenhausen, Germany: Lochner-Verlag, 2016.

Stricker, Lauri. *Pilates for the Outdoor Athlete*. Conifer, CO: Fulcrum, 2007.

References

Chapter 1

Barss, Stephanie J. (1997). "Physiological attributes of recreational rock climbers." A master's thesis presented to the faculty of Western Washington University.

Bloomfield, J., Ackland, T. R., and Elliot, B. C. (1994). *Applied Anatomy and Biomechanics in Sport.* Carlton, Victoria, Australia: Blackwell Scientific Publications.

Ericsson, K. A., Krampe, R. T., and Tech-Rsmer, C. (1993). "The role of deliberate practice in the acquisition of expert performance." *Psych Rev* 100(3): 363–406.

Fox, P. W., Hershberger, S. L., and Bouchard, T. J. (1996). "Genetic and environmental contributions to the acquisition of a motor skill." *Nature* 384: 356–58.

Mermier, C. M., Janot, J. M., Parker, D. L., and Swan, J. G. (2000). "Physiological and anthropometric determinants of sport climbing performance." *Brit J Sports Med* 34(5) (Oct): 359–65.

Seiler, S. (2000) "Limits to performance." *Sportscience* 4(2).

Watts, P. B., Martin, D. T., and Durtschi, S. (1993) "Anthropometric profiles of elite male and female competitive sport rock climbers." *J Sports Sci* 11(2) (Apr): 113–17.

Chapter 3

Feltz, D., and Landers, D. (1983). "The effects of mental practice on motor skill learning and performance." *Sport Psych* 5.

Garfield, C. (1984) *Peak Performance.* New York: Warner Books.

Knudson, D.V., and Morrison, C. S. (1997). *Qualitative Analysis of Human Movement.* Champaign, IL: Human Kinetics.

Kubistant, T. (1986). *Performing Your Best.* Champaign, IL: Leisure Press.

Levinson, W. (1994). *The Way of Strategy.* Milwaukee: ASQC Quality Press.

Chapter 4

Schmidt, R. A. (1991) *Motor Learning and Performance: From Principles to Practice.* Champaign, IL: Human Kinetics.

Schmidt, R. A., Wrisberg, C. A. (2004) *Motor Learning and Performance: A Problem-Based Learning Approach.* Champaign, IL: Human Kinetics.

Chapter 5

Bloomfield, J., Ackland, T. R., and Elliot, B. C. (1994). *Applied Anatomy and Biomechanics in Sport.* Carlton, Victoria, Australia: Blackwell Scientific Publications.

Bloomfield, J., Fricker, P., and Fitch, K. (1992). *Textbook of Science and Medicine in Sport.* Carlton, Victoria, Australia: Blackwell Scientific Publications.

Booth, F. W. (1977). "Effects of endurance exercise on cytochrome c turnover in skeletal muscle." *Annals NY Acad Sci* 301: 431–39.

Chu, Donald A. (1996). *Explosive Power and Strength.* Champaign, IL.: Human Kinetics.

España-Romero V., et al. (2009). "Climbing time to exhaustion is a determinant of climbing performance in high-level sport climbers." *Eur J Appl Physiol* 107(5): 517–25.

Fryer, Simon, et al. (2015). "Oxygen recovery kinetics in the forearm flexors of multiple ability groups of rock climbers." *J Strength Cond Res* 29(6) 1633–39.

Grant S., et al. (2003). "Climbing-specific finger endurance: A comparative study of intermediate rock climbers, rowers and aerobically trained individuals." *J Sports Sci* 21(8):621–30.

Köstermeyer, G. (2000). "Strength endurance training for elite rock climbers." High Performance seminar for British Mountaineering Council, Plas y Brenin (Wales, UK).

Maurizio, Fanchini. (2013). "Differences in climbing-specific strength between boulder and lead rock climbers." *J Strength Cond Res* 27(2): 310–14.

O'Shea, K., and O'Shea, J. (1989). "Functional isometric weight training: Its effect on dynamic and static strength." *J Appl Sport Sci Res* 3:30–33.

Schöffl, Volker, et al. (2006). "Development of a Performance Diagnosis of the Anaerobic Strength Endurance of the Forearm Flexor Muscles in Sport Climbing." *Int J Sports Med.*

Terjung, R. L. (1979). "The turnover of cytochrome c in different skeletal-muscle fiber types of the rat." *Biochem J* 178: 569–74.

Tidow, G. (1990). "Aspects of strength training in athletes." *New Studies in Athletics* 1.

Watts, P. B., Martin, D. T., and Durtschi, S. (1993) "Anthropometric profiles of elite male and female competitive sport rock climbers." *J Sports Sci* 11(2) (Apr): 113–17.

Watts, P., Newbury, V., and Sulentic, J. (1996). "Acute changes in handgrip strength, endurance, and blood lactate with sustained sport rock climbing." *J Sports Med Physical Fitness* (Dec).

Chapter 6

Shrier, I. (1999). "Stretching before exercise does not reduce the risk of local muscle injury: A critical review of the clinical and basic science literature." *Clinical J Sport Med* 9: 221–27.

———. (2000). "Stretching before exercise: An evidence based approach." *Brit J Sports Med* 34(10): 324–25.

Chapter 7

King, J., et al. (2001). "A comparison of high intensity vs. low intensity exercise on body composition in overweight women." American College of Sports Medicine Annual Meeting.

Watts, P. B., Martin, D. T., and Durtschi, S. (1993). "Anthropometric profiles of elite male and female competitive sport rock climbers." *J Sports Sci* 11(2) (Apr): 113–17.

Wilmore, J. (1983). "Body composition in sport and exercise: Directions for future research." *Med Sci Sports Exercise* 15.

Chapter 8

Adams, K., O'Shea, J., O'Shea, K., and Climstein, M. (1992). "The effect of six weeks of squat, plyometric, and squat-plyometric training on power production." *Appl Sport Sci Res* 6.

Lopez-Rivera, Eva, and Gonzalez-Badillo, J. (2012). "The effects of two maximum grip strength training methods using the same effort duration and different edge depth on grip endurance in elite climbers." *Sports Technology*, DOI: 10.1080.

Vigouroux, L., et al. (2006). "Estimation of finger muscle tendon tensions and pulley forces during specific sport-climbing grip techniques." *J Biomech* 39, 2583–92.

Chapter 10

Bloomfield, J., Ackland, T. R., and Elliot, B. C. (1994). *Applied Anatomy and Biomechanics in Sport.* Carlton, Victoria, Australia: Blackwell Scientific Publications.

Bosquet, L. (2007). "Effects of tapering on performance: A meta-analysis." *Med Sci Sports Exercise* 39(8) (Aug): 1358–65.

Davis, B., Elford, J., and Jamieson, K. (1991). "Variation in performance in simple muscle tests at different phases of the menstrual cycle." *J Sports Med Physical Fitness* 31.

Wilmore, J. (1974). "Alterations in strength, body composition and anthropometric measurements consequent to a ten-week weight training program." *Med Sci Sports* 5.

Chapter 11

Brilla, L. R., and Conte, V. (1998). "A novel zinc and magnesium formulation (ZMA) increases anabolic hormones and strength in athletes." *Sports Med Training Rehab J* (Nov).

Kreider R. B., et al. (1998). "Effects of creatine supplementation on body composition, strength, and sprint performance." *Med Sci Sports Exercise.*

Robergs, R. A. (1991). "Nutrition and exercise determinants of post-exercise glycogen synthesis." *Int J Sport Nutrition.*

Schoffstall, J., et al. (2001). "Effects of dehydration and rehydration on the one-rep maximum bench press of weight-trained males." *J Strength Cond Res* 15.

Sökmen, Bülent, et al. (2008). "Caffeine Use in Sports: Considerations for the Athlete." *The Journel of Strength and Conditioning Research.*

Toler SM. (1997). "Creatine is an ergogenic for anaerobic exercise." *Nutr Rev.*

Chapter 12

Bloomfield, J., Ackland, T. R., and Elliot, B. C. (1994). *Applied Anatomy and Biomechanics in Sport.* Carlton, Victoria, Australia: Blackwell Scientific Publications.

Bompa, Tudor O. (1983). *Theory and Methodology of Training.* Dubuque, IA: Kendall-Hunt Publishing Co.

Burke, Edmund R. (1999). *Optimal Muscle Recovery.* Garden City Park, NY: Avery Publishing Group.

Coyle, E. F., and Coggan, A. R. (1984). "Effectiveness of carbohydrate feeding in delaying fatigue during prolonged exercise." *Sports Med* 5.

Dinan, T. G., et al. (1994). "Lowering cortisol enhances growth hormone response in healthy individuals." *Acta Physiol Scand* 151(3) (Jul).

Draper, Nick, et al. (2006). "Effects of active recovery on lactate concentration, heart rate and RPE in climbing." *J Sports Sci Med* 5: 97–105.

Monedero, J., and Donne, B. (2000). "Effect of recovery interventions on lactate removal and subsequent performance." *Int J Sports Med* (Nov).

Niles, T. S., et al. (1997). "The effects of carbohydrate-protein drink on muscle glycogen resynthesis after endurance exercise." *Med Sci Sports Exercise* 29 Suppl 5.

Richter, E. A., et al. (1984). "Enhanced muscle glycogen metabolism after exercise." *Amer J Physiol* 246.

Watts, P. B., Daggett, M., Gallagher, P., and Wilkens, B. (2000). "Metabolic response during sport rock climbing and the effects of active versus passive recovery." *Int J Sports Med* (Apr).

Williams, R. B., et al. (1982). "Type A behavior and elevated physiological and neuroendocrine responses to cognitive tasks." *Science* 29 (Oct): 218.

Chapter 13

Almekinders, L. (1999). "Anti-inflammatory treatment of muscular injuries in sport." *Sports Med* 28: 383–88.

———. (2003). "An in vitro investigation into the effects of repetitive motion and nonsteroidal anti-inflammatory medication on human tendon fibroblasts." *Am J Sports Med* 23: 119–23.

Auerback, David, M. (2000). *Tennis Elbow/Lateral Epicondylitis.* Southern California Orthopedic Institute. www.scoi.com.

Bach, Allan W. (1999). "Finger joint injuries in active patients." *Physician Sportsmedicine* 27(3).

Doran, D. A., and Reay, M. (2000). "Injuries and associated training and performance characteristics in recreational rock climbers." In *The Science of Rock Climbing and Mountaineering.* Champaign, IL: Human Kinetics Publishing.

Gabl, M., Rangger, C., Lutz, M., Fink, C., Rudisch, A., and Pechlaner, S. (1998). "Disruption of the finger flexor pulley system in elite rock climbers." *Am J Sports Med* 26(5) (Sep–Oct).

Hochholzer, T., Schöffl, V. R., and Lightner, S. (2003). *One Move Too Many*. Ebenhausen, Germany: Lochner-Verlag.

Hochholzer, T., and Schoffl, V. R. (2005). "Epiphyseal fractures of the finger middle joints in young sport climbers." *Wilderness Environ Med* 16(3) (fall): 139–42.

Jebson, Peter, Steyers, J. L., and Curtis, M. (1997). "Hand injuries in rock climbing: Reaching the right treatment." *Physician Sportsmedicine* 25(5).

Juni, P. (2007). "Meta-analysis: Chondroitin for osteoarthritis of the knee or hip." *Ann Intern Med* 146(8): 580–90.

Khan, K. M. (1999). "Histopathology of common tendinopathies. Update and implications for clinical management." *Sports Med* 27(6) (June): 393–408.

Kim, L. S. (2006). "Efficacy of methylsulfonylmethane (MSM) in osteoarthritis pain of the knee: A pilot clinical trial." *Osteoarthritis Cartilage* 14(3): 286–94.

Leadbetter, W. B. (1992). "Cell matrix response in tendon injury." *Clin Sports Med* 2(3): 533–77.

Lewis, R. A., Shea, O. F., and Shea, K. G. (1993). "Acute carpal tunnel syndrome: Wrist stress during a major climb." *Physician Sportsmedicine* 21(7).

Lin, G. T., et al. (1989). "Biomechanical analysis of flexor pulley reconstruction." *J Hand Surg Brit* 14.

Lister, G. D. (1979). "Reconstruction of pulleys employing extensor retinaculum." *J Hand Surg Am.*

Liu, S. H. (1995). "Collagen in tendon, ligament, and bone healing." *Clin Orth Related Res* 318: 265–78.

Marco, R. A., Sharkey, N. A., Smith, T. S., and Zissimos, A. G. (1998). "Pathomechanics of closed rupture of the flexor tendon pulleys in rock climbers." *J Bone Joint Surg Am* 80(7) (Jul).

Maroon, J. C. (2006). "Omega-3 fatty acids (fish oil) as an anti-inflammatory: An alternative to nonsteroidal anti-inflammatory drugs for discogenic pain." *Surg Neurol* 65(4) (Apr): 325.

McAlindon, T., et al. (2000). "Glucosamine and chondroitin for treatment of osteoarthritis." *JAMA* 283: 1469–75.

McFarland, Edward G., et al. (2000). "Patient Guide to Knee Arthroscopy." Johns Hopkins Department of Orthopaedic Surgery. www.hopkinsmedicine.org.

Moutet, F., Guinard, D., Gerard, P., and Mugnier, C. (1993). "Subcutaneous rupture of long finger flexor pulleys in rock climbers." *Ann Chir Main Memb Super* 12(3).

Moutet, F. (2003). "Flexor tendon pulley system: Anatomy, pathology, treatment." *Chirurgie de la Main* 22(1).

Nirschl, Robert P., and Kraushaar, Barry S. (1996). "Assessment and treatment guidelines for elbow injuries." *Physician Sportsmedicine* 25(4).

Reginster, J. Y., et al. (2001). "Long-term effects of glucosamine sulfate on osteoarthritis progression: A randomized, placebo-controlled clinical trial." *Lancet* 357(9252) (Jan 27).

Robinson, Mark. (1988). "Fingers: Get a grip on injury prevention and treatment." *Climbing* (Aug).

———. (1993). "Snap, crackle, pop: Climbing injuries to fingers and forearms." *Climbing* (Jun–Jul).

———. (1993). "The elbow: Understanding a common sore subject." *Climbing* (Apr).

Rohrbough, Joel. (2000). "'Pop' goes your climbing season." *Climbing* (Nov).

Rooks, M. D. (1997). "Rock climbing injuries." *Sports Med* 23.

Schöffl, Volker, et al. (2007). "Physiological responses to rock climbing in young climbers." *Br J Sports Med* 41(12) (Dec): 852–61.

Schöffl, Volker, et al. (2012). "The epidemiology of injury in mountaineering, rock and ice climbing." *Med Sport Sci* 58: 17–43.

Schöffl, Volker, et al. (2015). "Injury Trends in Rock Climbers: Evaluation of a case series of 911 injuries between 2009 and 2012." *Wilderness Environ Med* 26, 62–67.

Schweizer, A. (2000). "Biomechanical effectiveness of taping the A2 pulley in rock climbers." *J Hand Surg* 25: 102–7.

Seiler, J. G., and Leversedge, F. J. (2000). "Digital flexor sheath: Repair and reconstruction of the annular pulleys and membranous sheath." *J S Orth Assn* 9(2).

Seiler, J. G., et al. (1995). "The flexor digitorum longus: An anatomic and microscopic study for use as a tendon graft." *J Hand Surg Am* 20.

Stelzle, F. D., Gaulrapp, H., and Pforringer, W. (2000). "Injuries and overuse syndromes due to rock climbing on artificial walls." *Sportverletz Sportschaden* 14(4) (Dec).

Sylvester, A. D., Christensen, A. M., and Kramer, P. A. (2006). "Factors influencing osteological changes in the hands and fingers of rock climbers." *J Anatomy* 209(5).

Wright, D. M., Royle, T. J., and Marshall, T. (2001). "Indoor rock climbing: Who gets injured?" *Brit J Sports Med* 35(3) (Jun).

Index

Italicized page numbers indicate photographs.
Figures and tables are indicated with "f" and "t" respectively, following the page number.

About the Author

HÖRST COLLECTION

Eric J. Hörst (pronounced "Hurst") is an internationally renowned author, researcher, climbing coach, and accomplished climber of forty years.

A student and teacher of climbing performance, Eric has coached hundreds of climbers, and his training books and concepts have spread to climbers in more than fifty countries. He is widely recognized for his innovative training techniques and equipment, and he has been a training products design consultant and Training Center editor for Nicros, Inc. since 1994. Eric is author of eight books (with many foreign translations) with worldwide sales of over 300,000 copies. In addition to his best-selling *Training for Climbing*, now in its third edition, Eric's other popular texts include *Maximum Climbing, The Rock Climber's Exercise Guide, How to Climb 5.12*, and the gym climbing book *Learning to Climb Indoors.*

Eric has written more than one hundred magazine articles and appeared on numerous TV broadcasts, and his techniques and photos have appeared in many publications including *Rock & Ice, Climbing, Outside, DeadPoint, Men's Health, Fortune, Men's Journal, Muscle Media, Muscle & Fitness, Paddler, Urban Climber, Parents, Wall Street Journal, Experience Life, Outdoor 4X,* and *National Geographic Adventure*, as well as European magazines such as *Desnivel, Alpen, Climax,* and *Climber*. He has co-authored one research paper ("Behavior Analysis and Sport Climbing," *Journal of Behavioral Health and Medicine*, 2010, with Dr. Richard Fleming). Eric is a member of the International Rock Climbing Research Association (IRCRA) and the National Strength and Conditioning Association (NSCA).

A self-professed "climber for life," Eric remains active at the cliffs, traveling widely with his wife, Lisa, and sons, Cameron and Jonathan (both of whom climbed 5.14a/8b+ at age eleven). Driven by his passion for adventure and challenge, he has established over 400 first ascents, primarily on his home cliffs in the eastern United States. Still pushing his personal climbing limits at age fifty-two, Eric's focus is now on R & D of new training techniques, traveling and sharing his knowledge with new climbers, and coaching the next generation of elite climbers.

Other Books by Eric J. Hörst

Maximum Climbing (FalconGuides, 2010) presents a climber's guide to the software of the brain, based on the premise that you climb with your mind—your hands and feet are simply extensions of your thoughts and will. Becoming a master climber, then, requires that you first become a master of your mind. In this breakthrough book, Eric Hörst brings unprecedented clarity to the many cognitive and neurophysical aspects of climbing and dovetails this information into a complete mental-training program.

How to Climb 5.12 (FalconGuides, 2011) is a performance guidebook to attaining the most rapid gains in climbing ability possible, and it's written specifically for intermediate climbers looking to break through to the higher grades. It provides streamlined instruction on vital topics such as accelerating learning of skills, training your mind and body, and becoming an effective on-sight and redpoint climber.

Learning to Climb Indoors (FalconGuides, 2012) is the most complete book available on indoor climbing. Topics covered include beginning and advanced climbing techniques, tactics, strategy, basic gear, safety techniques, self-assessment, and a primer on mental training and physical conditioning. This guide includes everything you need to know from day one as a climber through your first year or two in the sport.

PROTECTING CLIMBING ACCESS SINCE 1991
ACCESS FUND
JOIN US
WWW.ACCESSFUND.ORG
Jonathan Siegrist, Third Millenium (14a), the Monastery, CO. Photo by: Keith Ladzinski